ANTHONY TROLLOPE: THE ARTIST IN HIDING

ANTHONY TROLLOPE
The Artist in Hiding

R. C. TERRY

ROWMAN AND LITTLEFIELD
Totowa, New Jersey

FIRST PUBLISHED IN THE UNITED STATES 1977
BY ROWMAN AND LITTLEFIELD, TOTOWA, N.J.

Library of Congress Cataloging in Publication Data

Terry, Reginald Charles, 1932–
    Anthony Trollope: the artist in hiding.

    Bibliography: p.
    1.   Trollope, Anthony, 1815–1882—Criticism and
interpretation.
PR5687.T4   823'.8   77–8957
ISBN 0–87471–875–9

Printed in Great Britain

To my Mother and Father

Contents

List of Plates

Acknowledgements

In writing this book I am indebted to the University of Victoria, British Columbia, for leave in the early stages of my research, and to the Canada Council for generous financial support.

I am grateful to Professor Kathleen Tillotson for her guidance in my initial studies on Trollope and for her encouragement at various stages during the writing. I wish to thank the staff of several libraries: the British Library, the Bodleian, the Senate House Library of the University of London, the libraries of Bedford College and of the Universities of Exeter and Victoria. Thanks are also due to Lady Faber for the loan of the photograph of Harting Grange, and to Hertford-shire Library Service–Cheshunt Library for the photograph of Waltham House.

I also wish to thank Mrs Beth Clarke, Mrs Alice Lee and Mrs Joan Whitfield for typing and secretarial help.

Finally, to my wife, Judith, I owe a special debt for invaluable practical help in discussing the novels with me and giving meticulous attention to my writing.

R.C.T.

December 1976

I find myself asking myself that terrible question of *cui bono* every morning. I am struggling to make a good book, but I feel that it will not be good.

Trollope to George Eliot and G. H. Lewes, Melbourne, 27 February 1872

I did think much of Messrs. Longman's name, but I liked it best at the bottom of a cheque.

Trollope, *An Autobiography*, ch. vi

Though he wrote his share of rubbish, Trollope at his best was an artist pretending to be just a hunting-man earning enough to keep four horses. But secretly he was hunting for fame, not foxes, and now he has it.

J. B. Priestley, *Victoria's Heyday*

1 The Equal Mind

MICHAEL SADLEIR: Trollope's quality remains intangible, baffles resolution . . . It seems hardly fitting that a being, who in himself was so definite and so solid, who – like a solitary tower upon a hill – was visible for miles around in the wide landscape of Victorian England, should as a literary phenomenon be so difficult to seize and to describe; it is almost irritating that books in themselves so lustily prosaic should be so hard of definition.
C. P. SNOW: Trollope wrote so much and, of all writers, he is the one least adapted for most kinds of academic approach. How do you start to dig into him? And with what books?[1]

Over forty years separate these comments, which share a common bewilderment about the nature of Trollope's character and achievement. In fact every critic I have come across points to the difficulty of defining Trollope – though some maintain he is hardly worth the trouble – with the result that today Trollopes seem to stretch out in the glass of literary fashion to the crack of doom. There is Trollope of Barsetshire, whom everyone knows; Trollope the Social Historian; Trollope the Entertainer, who wrote novels as a hen lays eggs; the 'dark' Trollope of Professor A. O. J. Cockshut; Trollope the Psychologist; Trollope the Moralist. It would be presumptuous, I feel, to add a 'new' Trollope, and so in this study I am concerned rather with a consolidated Trollope: a reassessment of this tantalising character and the disarmingly placid world of his novels.

The strangeness of Trollope's case becomes apparent immediately one begins to compare his literary fortunes with those of his contemporaries. There is no complete edition of his work. His first novel has been out of print since 1906. What major English novelist has had such a singular fate? The texts of nearly all his novels have received negligible attention and only thirty-three manuscripts of his forty-seven novels are now in existence.[2] It was only in 1972 that a forgotten early work, *The New Zealander*, found its way into print. Much of his journalism remains uncollected. And when we consider his stature it is clear that we speak of Trollope without that confidence or consensus of judgement with which we approach other Victorians. We accept without question the supremacy of George Eliot's intellectual subtlety, Dickens' comic invention, Thackeray's satire of manners; but Trollope? He holds his place in the literary pantheon on slightly insecure, ambiguous terms. Either we defend him timidly, as Paul Elmer More noted at the time of the Trollope revival in the twenties, or we patronise him as an entertainer. Clearly he does not belong with Collins, Reade, Kingsley or Disraeli, yet he is a not altogether welcome guest at the high table of the Victorian novel; an odd fish, Pamela Hansford Johnson has called him, who does not fit most of our criteria, yet whose work we cannot help but admire.[3]

The most significant study of Trollope in recent years, Ruth ap Roberts' *Trollope, Artist and Moralist*, makes the point that our difficulty arises from the inadequacy of our literary criteria to deal with such a novelist. I am inclined to doubt this. There are some authors difficult to accommodate – Peacock, for instance, or Samuel Butler – not so far outside the convention as to dictate their own standards for judgement, as Sterne does, but sufficiently beyond the normal framework to embarrass the critic relying on his academic case histories and methodology of plot, character and point of view. Trollope is not in the least like that. Who could be more in the tradition of Fielding and Scott: loose-running plots with interlocking lines of action, sometimes merely a peg of a story on which to attach a panorama of society, the anthill uncovered and characters scurrying about their business? For this type of novel a perfectly adequate critical vocabulary has developed.

Trollope stayed close to tradition; we have only to read his common-places about fiction to realise how close. Well-read in the history of the novel, he absorbed Scott, Edgeworth, Austen, began writing, and remained close to the taste of the age, changing as it changed, until movements he did not like or understand, eventually to shape into the naturalism and aestheticism of Zola, Moore, Gissing, left him behind. Even so he kept up very well. The transition from social panorama to more intense studies of individual psychology in his later period represent very clearly this response to taste. To recognise this is largely to meet the two major points of attack on Trollope: his triviality (failure to go beneath the surfaces of life) and escapism (bed-book stuff).

Trollope has always been a difficult writer to pin down, for all his 'rational, pleasant and straightforward' approach to life – to quote his own words in *John Caldigate*.[4] Critics have tended to respond to him with a mixture of enjoyment and derision, not knowing how to praise him or put him down (in all senses of the phrase), recoiling from his terrible fertility and falling for his immense readability. Saintsbury is a good example of the way Trollope baffled enquiry, his weighty words belying their indecisiveness: 'qualms may sometimes arise as to whether genius is justly denied to him'.[5] A generation earlier Henry James, whose antennae for literary merit were impeccably attuned, had divined beneath the placid surface of Trollope's comfortable world the same troubled motions that guided his own pen, and he paid just and magnanimous tribute at Trollope's death: 'Trollope will remain one of the most trustworthy, though not one of the most eloquent, of the writers who have helped the heart of man to know itself'.[6] James' essay remains also one of the most trustworthy impressions of the varied, equivocal and contrary subtleties of Trollope's fiction.

His fellow writers have on the whole been kind to him. Besides James, George Eliot, Shaw and Tolstoi acknowledged that Trollope had in one way or another exercised a helpful influence on their work. And even the next generation, reputedly so hostile to him, produced some complimentary, though grudging appreciations, from Stevenson, Gissing and Swinburne.[7] It is when we come to the critics that the Trollope problem becomes acute. Even the best admit he is something of a mystery: there is something about him, Donald Smalley wrote, that continues to elude precise definition.[8] And some years ago Bradford Booth remarked on the chaos of criticism surrounding the fiction. Improvements have certainly occurred: you have only to compare such trite essays as 'Mr. Trollope's Young Ladies', in an early issue of *Nineteenth Century Fiction*, with Pamela Hansford Johnson's 'Trollope's Young Women', to see that Trollope the Novelist is beginning to come into his own, but there is still a great deal of spade-work to be done.[9] For this reason the study of Trollope offers a tremendous attraction: he is yet to be explained. There is no critical base, it seems, for Trollope, no ground rules, and as he once more flies like an ungainly bird over the horizon, the critical sport appears to take a pot-shot or two.

Consider, for example, Laurence Lerner's 'Trollope the Entertainer', in which the thesis is advanced that 'his books are not the products of a real creative act'.[10] To see Trollope as a purveyor of anodyne romance and to dismiss his heroines as vapid shadows of a rose-water school of fiction suggests a mandarin stance, deriving from post-Jamesian criticism based on criteria of ideas, form and high seriousness. But it is sinful, Anthony Burgess has observed, to take the novel too seriously.[11] On the other hand such criticism suggests also some of the obloquy caused by the squibs Trollope left behind in the *Autobiography*, not to mention an extremely partial view of the Trollopian heroine. Take another example, Richard Crossman on Trollope's politics: Trollope knew Westminster, Mr Crossman alleged, from 'two months of bored inattention in the Press Gallery', concluding that he

had no political vision and what he chose to call his political philosophy was reactionary claptrap with unpleasant undertones of xenophobia and anti-semitism.[12]

These examples are worth mentioning because they show what diverse responses Trollope arouses in the intelligent reader. One can understand that opinions should differ as to the relative merits, say, of *Phineas Finn* and *The Eustace Diamonds*, but it is surprising that they differ so extremely, and so often with such ill temper.

Similarly diverse opinions surround Trollope's style, where the secret of his perennial appeal is surely at its most potent. Is he without style, wit, trenchancy, fire, or poetic feeling, as Raymond Mortimer suggests, or can we agree with the late Geoffrey Tillotson, who found a near Augustan clarity and grace in his expression, 'a kind of felicity' as another critic put it? [13]

Around these variations of view the problem of Anthony Trollope has grown. It is easy to see why, for the sheer bulk of his *œuvre* faces the critic with considerable difficulties of study and organisation, since it comprises forty-seven novels, five travel books, four collections of short stories, eight other non-fiction works, an autobiography, a play, several lectures and a wide miscellany of journalism. It is not unusual, therefore (and this is one cause of the confusion), for a critic to venture into firm statements based on the most accessible of the novels, only to discover later that the reverse is true – or at least that the original statement must be considerably modified. The amount of the fiction is only equalled by the variety of points of view.

Trollope is always the middle-of-the-roader and the casuist, not only in moral problems, as Mrs ap Roberts has shown, but in love, politics, and every other branch of human activity as well. Although his prejudices are also very apparent, towards nonconformist piety, for example, Civil Service examinations, or Women's Liberation, they are surprisingly few for such a positive and disputatious individual. In fiction, if not in life, he showed an unfailing capacity to let the other fellow speak, to be wary of absolutes, to consider individual cases on their merits, to accept the relativity of moral action, to be mindful of the gaps between ideal and reality, a man's good intentions and his unconscious wishes. All of which led him towards a workable, middle truth, a taste for compromise, 'the equal mind' as it is expressed in *Orley Farm*,[14] which at once make him very English and very difficult for the critic to pin down.

The two comments I quoted earlier illustrate how easy it is for Trollope's ambiguity to confound criticism. On the evidence of Lopez in *The Prime Minister* and one or two other foreigners it is unwise to accuse Trollope of xenophobia and anti-semitism, for there are a number of shabby gentlemen crooks in the novels, like the Hon. Undecimus Scott and Nathaniel Sowerby, indubitably Anglo-Saxon. And what about the good-natured Jews in *Nina Balatka*? 'I have invariably found Jews to be more liberal than other men', Trollope claimed.[15] Similarly, for Mr Lerner to dismiss the Trollopian female as a romantic stereotype is to miss an extraordinary range of characters. This kind of charge is frequently levied, quite without foundation; there are the shy and bashful heroines, of course, but others have the energy and charm we associate with the Shakespearean heroine. Not for nothing did Trollope refer to Lily Dale in his *Autobiography* as a female prig.

The only safe resort for the critic is to follow the labyrinthine path of the whole of Trollope's output and come to terms with a fiction of manifold ambiguities that has the true flavour of human experience. Trollope has an acute sense of the world being various and wonderful in its everyday ordinariness, and his achievement is to lift the veil of familiarity which obscures the beauty of commonplace things. Trollope's people are those who

> Maintain themselves by the common routine,
> Learn to avoid excessive expectation[16]

No Heathcliff or Cathy Earnshaw comes from his pen. Yet tucked away in the corners of his fiction are transcendent moments, poignant insights, quite staggering bits of human folly and determination: during the remorseless progress of time (of which series novels like the Pallisers make us very aware) there is an awakening to love or responsibility, the exhilaration of success or the sickness of failure, the bitter knowledge of error and opportunities not realised, the agonies of indecision. Trollope is true to these and the normal tempo of life: longer-drawn-out experiences, such as the temperamental differences which can change marriage into silent, rancorous bondage. Such things become his monuments and give him the right to be called the laureate of the commonplace. And for this charting of the average human experience Trollope developed an appropriate style, a flat (but not dull), meandering, tussocky prose, which rolls before the eyes like the haunting landscape of the fens. The coloration is subfusc but beautifully apt and eloquent.

By far the most popular critical method of approaching Trollope's work has been through its detailed rendering of the English middle class in the full bloom of Victorianism. He came to prominence when photography was becoming popular, and only late in his career was the term 'photographic' applied disparagingly to his work. He was one of those novelists who seem without effort to have caught the 'hum of implication' which constitutes the character of an age, and critics have often spoken of his capacity to pick up signals and bounce them back to his generation. He does not need to keep a scrapbook like Reade, or get up his material from Blue Books like Disraeli, but seems to absorb climates of opinion, news of the day, the latest fad and fashion, through the pores. At its height his fame rested securely on the vivid actuality of his prose which delighted middle-class readers who demanded truth to life. Consider the tiny gems of social observation that leap from every page: the abhorred fashion of the chignon; the ritual of morning call and *carte de visite*; the questionable practice of cigar-smoking in the presence of ladies; the etiquette of a flirtation during croquet; and all the complicated rites of social strategy that are part of every Trollope novel. No historian emulating Macaulay, wrote R. H. Hutton, his most discerning contemporary critic, would begin to discribe English society of the period without a familiar knowledge of Trollope's work.[17]

A journalistic flair for assimilating seemingly inconsequential detail and soaking up atmosphere is even more noticeable in his travel books, which come to life through fragments of human trivia rather than sociological insights. We may dismiss Trollope's portentous comments on race relations in the West Indies, or the rights and wrongs of the American senatorial system, but we sit up and take notice when he describes ill-mannered shoving to get a seat on a bus, or the evils of American central heating. It was Meredith's friend, Sir William Hardman (the model for Blackburn Tuckham in *Beauchamp's Career*), who decided that the best part of *North America* was Trollope's dismay at seeing babies fed on pickles.[18] The same feeling for the odd human detail is part of the magic of the novels too. And the stuff of journalism, the current affairs, the gossip at the club, enrich the texture of everything he wrote. The Phineas novels are a quarry of topics of the day : the scandal of potted meats supplied under contract to the army; the proposed Canadian railroad; pollution of the Thames; the garrotting scare of the early sixties; and the large issues of tenant right in Ireland and extension of the franchise.

To be a Trollopian is to succumb to that comfortable, well-ordered world among the sheltered wives and daughters of the well-to-do in which *Burke's Landed Gentry* is revered almost as much as the Bible; to move from cathedral town to country seat, from fox-hunt to gentlemen's club; to mix with fashionable society in Grosvenor Square or Mayfair and listen to the urbane conversation of Bar, Church, Politics or Commerce; or to venture among that vast upward-moving, anonymous bourgeoisie spreading into new suburbs beyond the metropolis. This external world, densely peopled, correct at every point and projected with compassionate irony and love, is obviously a focal point of attention and responses to it are varied. Historians like Asa Briggs and Kitson Clark have made legitimate use of Trollope's 'feel' of the period, but literary judgements on the same basis have tended to reduce Trollope to the level of a fat and amiable beach photographer snapping the holiday scene. Such a view pandered to sentimental recollections of the Victorian heyday so prevalent in the Trollope revivals during both World Wars, and encouraged map-making in Barsetshire, the short-lived Trollope society in America, and etiolated descendants of the Barsetshire worthies in the work of Angela Thirkell. Certainly there are strong reasons for reading Trollope in this way, and his appeal to the general public has been primarily one of nostalgia, an appeal beautifully expressed in the tribute of Monsignor Knox.[19] But it is a pity so to limit his value, or to place this aspect of his fiction first among his merits, as his latest biographer has.[20]

To read Trollope as escapism is to enjoy him at a minimal level, but it is, in fact, only the lower end of the same scale by which he is commonly measured as social historian. 'To read Trollope', the American bibliophile A. E. Newton claimed, 'is to take a course in modern English history – social history to be sure, but just as important as political and much more interesting',[21] indicating that for him what really mattered was Trollope's grasp of the dynamics of his society, the whole complex, interdependent structure, as well as man's role in it; the individual seeking fulfilment in work and social relationships; the strategies effected through money and marriage, played out against the drama of a culture under stress, as the industrial, urban order gradually superseded the traditional rural pattern. Whether Trollope's novels in fact reflect much of this wider cultural crisis is open to question in this book, which makes fewer claims for Trollope as social thinker than is currently fashionable. To my mind it is possible to assume that Trollope is more *engagé* than he really is as one means of raising his status: one example is the current view of *The Way We Live Now* as a highly subversive statement about money values in his society to which Trollope had at last woken up; whereas in fact it is simply more unified than earlier satires on business ethics such as *The Three Clerks* or *The Bertrams*. A reading of *Barchester Towers* by Ulrich Knoepflmacher in *Laughter and Despair* (1972) makes a case for it as a kind of eighteenth-century satire involving the opposition of town and country values. This is not altogether inaccurate, but it makes heavy weather of such a bright little jewel in the Barset crown. What is *Barchester Towers* after all but a comedy of humours, a play in which the oaks of Barchester are shaken for a while by an Italian zephyr? Nor are those who disturb the peace symbolic of new ideas, despite Slope's sneers at Mr. Harding (Slope himself is more probably a study in Trollope's favourite theme of man's limitless self-delusion). They are merely an exotic alien, a scold, a coward and a parasite. We must not forget that Barchester itself *is* a very worldly world even while it remains a backwater.

The major limitation, then, of the sociological standpoint, is that it prevents us from recognising Trollope's concern with the deep and un-changing elements of human behaviour: what constitutes, in fact, the inner world of his novels, and is produced by imaginative vision rather than transcribed from external evidence. A social historian may mine the novels productively, but he will miss the rich vein of the real

Trollope glimpsed by Rebecca West: 'His novels are for the most part pure fantasy'.[22] The symbolic vein, for instance, though rare in him, does occasionally find expression, notably in the much neglected *The Bertrams*. Newman came across the novel in 1862 and found the first volume 'tragic, instructive, humiliating—' and with 'a touch of scepticism which I have never seen in him before'.[23] *The Bertrams* deliberately employs fantasy to show a crisis in the hero's development. George Bertram, one of those young men poised equivocally between idealism and self-interest, journeys to the Holy Land, trying to make up his mind whether to become clergyman or lawyer. Irony is strong as his father scoffs at his ideals, and holy relics convey the opposite of a spiritual reality. On the Mount of Olives George decides on the church, but this moment of decision is threatened when he meets the wayward heroine, Caroline Waddington. Twice he sees beautiful women, as though they are visions, physical distractions from his spiritual quest. The first is at the Tabernacle, acquitting herself of her sins in a proud and joyous manner, the second more plainly foreshadowing the disruptive force Caroline is to be. Newman clearly had a sense of the book's oddity, and the reader who ventures outside the familiar surroundings of Barsetshire will find other novels with a similar exoticism like *The Macdermots of Ballycloran*, *The Claverings*, *Kept in the Dark* and *The Landleaguers*, evidence of an imaginative range that often goes unrecognised.

A. O. J. Cockshut, in *Anthony Trollope: A Critical Study*, contributed towards a fuller understanding of Trollope's art in a more eclectic survey of his novels, and although I think he exaggerates the novelist's progress towards pessimism (a kind of parallel growth to the 'dark' Dickens) it has resulted in more serious investigation and debate over the range of Trollope's work. This in its turn has led to large claims for Trollope's psychological awareness and the extent to which he probed the reaches of sin and sorrow. He was no Dostoievski. It is unreasonable, for example, to see such a slight work as *Cousin Henry* in relation to Kafka, or to claim a relationship between the little boy, Florian Jones, in *The Landleaguers*, and Henry James's *enfants diaboliques* in *The Turn of the Screw*.[24] Such interpretation goes thoroughly against the grain of Trollope's mind. There is also the temptation, in a search for profundity, to remove Trollope from the climate of his age and interpret him in terms of modern *Angst*, whereas Trollope's world is abundantly secure, sunny and stable. The road to Hiram's Hospital is a long way from Beckett's no-man's land. Helen Darbishire was nearer the truth when she drew attention to fixed and enduring elements in Trollope's scene: 'a world of which the very essence is stability, a peaceful acceptance of fixed standards'.[25]

Leslie Stephen made a similar observation: Trollope's society, he said, was 'entirely unconscious of any approaching convulsions'.[26] The substance of the comment is true: the society he chose to write about was largely cocooned in its way of life, confirmed in the values it spread to the new, mercantile *bourgeoisie*, strong in its comfortable Anglicanism, generally complacent about government – since it supplied the members of the ruling oligarchy – and largely unmoved by the social problems of the mushrooming towns. Only in Trollope's first novel is there the social conscience and radical awareness we find in Dickens, enough reason for considering with hesitation a 'dark' Trollope of growing pessimism and greater social awareness in later years.

So while many of his novels (*The Bertrams, The Three Clerks, Orley Farm, The Eustace Diamonds* come readily to mind) make use of the changing character of travel, commerce, science, faith and social progress, they merely reflect rather than scrutinise or question. There is no blowing off steam as in Dickens; no troubled sense of Arnold's iron time of doubts, distractions, fears; no really profound expression of the duality of conscience and conquest at the core of Victorian life; none of the incipient schizophrenia between town and country we find in Jaggers and Wemmick of *Great Expectations*, although I see traces of it in *The Eustace Diamonds*. Trollope is the novelist of acquiescence and compromise, Dickens of protest and aspiration. In *Orley Farm* the express trains race up and down the country, but the social order of Noningsby and the Cleeve remains largely unchanged. In *The Way We Live Now* Roger Carbury's estate stands apart and aloof from the new barbarism.

In this respect Trollope's is an unchanging world, for Barchester sleeps on, to a great extent a fairyland in which aliens and disturbers of the peace are routed: the Bishop's clammy-handed chaplain is defeated and Adolphus Crosbie, the man of fashion, receives a punch on the nose. Yet Trollope is too much the realist to avoid the issues altogether. Nearly all his books involve at some point the confrontation of cultural movements roughly in balance: the traditional, paternalistic, agrarian pattern and the new, urban-centred, forward-looking and reforming spirit. He knows that the old must give way (it had done so before the end of his life), he recognises the historical imperative, supports progress and reform intellectually, but in his heart he is with the squires and landed families, the Luftons, the de Guests, even the useless Duke of Omnium. Indeed this essentially nostalgic attachment to the traditional order guaranteed his popularity with an audience of already 'displaced' persons, chained to the ritual of job, career, and advancement up the professional ladder, beginning to experience the pressures of the bureaucratic machine, the split between work and home (so potent in Dickens), the accelerated communication by express train and telegraph – all the incipient strains of modern civilisation. Writing of the new suburbs of Bayswater and Enfield, as well as for them, Trollope in a sense gave voice to the pressing desire of every Englishman to be a squire: a dream, one may say, with even more appeal today to the commuters of Gerrards Cross and Brighton.

Much of the drama in his stories arises from the interaction of two cultural movements struggling for supremacy. The railway has reached Barchester, bringing retired brewers and tallow chandlers to houses in the close once leased to prebendaries. The situation gives ample scope for irony; the jaded aristocracy of the land seek refuge in revivals of medieval chivalry, and it is Mr Slope who enters as the champion of new men, new blood, new ideas. In *The Warden* the confrontation between radical dynamism and conservative reaction provides a classic study of this uniquely Trollopian subject.

Many other novels display the Victorian cultural dilemma: in *Orley Farm* and *The Way We Live Now* it dominates the action. In both it is interesting to note that the traditions of the fixed world of landed gentry and those close to the earth are seen as reservoirs of moral action and the guarantee of civilisation. It is a solution no less valid than Dickens' to his painful social concerns: the man with both a heart and a pot of gold as *deus ex machina*. But where Dickens speaks out boldly, condemning the wrongs that society has created, Trollope is silent; where Dickens is radical, crusading, intense, Trollope is conservative, serene, down-to-earth. His natural affinity for the ruling class which he had dedicated himself to joining from an early age, his wariness of zeal, his sentimental conservatism, an unfailing scepticism which led him to look all round the subject, and not least a limitation he set himself as a commercial writer, all combined to make him in certain ways evade the important issues. To this extent he is one of the great 'imperfect story-tellers', as Charles Morgan described him.[27]

He chose to compromise in ways that no one can say were altogether admirable. He set very clear limits to his work, which indicate at best a certain bluntness of sensitivity. He would work so hard, go so far, and then he would stop. There is no doubt Trollope was largely content to satisfy public taste and to be, in Saintsbury's words, an *amuseur*, although it is fortunate that his terrible competence and two hundred and fifty words every quarter of an hour by his watch did not deny him some intimations of immortality: Crawley at the Palace; Melmotte's downfall; Mrs Proudie's death. On the other hand he made frequent triumphs of compromise, deploying that characteristic of Englishness Walter Bagehot spoke of as the genius of English politics in all branches of human affairs. Compromise serves the conventional moral shields of Victorian life: Truth, Duty, Love and Courage, which Tennyson advanced against the perils of the age. Trollope's novels in fact express the moral sentiments of the *Idylls*, and much of their romance is in Browning's C Major of this life – the dominant chord of useful living. Compromise for Trollope is bringing practical wisdom (a phrase he used of Montaigne) to bear on life, and exercising voluntary controls on the appetites and desires common to mankind.

To speak of compromise as a governing principle of Trollope's fiction is to refute the idea of a descent into pessimism. For the cast of Trollope's mind remained much the same throughout his life : optimistic, acquiescent, equable. By the time he began writing novels he had none of the grand illusions that once broken can leave a man cynical; he had instead a clear idea of the limited possibilities of happiness, and this was enough to make life worth living. It was his genius to extol the happiness of everyday existence in which the worth of the individual was gauged by the extent of his honesty and love.

Thus the ruling principle of this book is one which takes into account the overall consistency and continuity of Trollope's work, recognising a unity of intention and achievement from first to last of staggering dimension. Inevitably, the vast amount of his fiction prevents treatment of the individual novel as an entity, although in several cases I have tried within a scheme of vital thematic concerns – love, marriage, social issues, public life – to discuss sections of major novels as fully as possible, so as to bring out Trollope's artistic accomplishment. The ardent Trollopian would wish perhaps to have a chronologically detailed account to do justice to this protean author; but that would need a very long book indeed. I have used the Barsetshire novels without, I hope, giving them undue prominence. They have held the stage for a long time and do not reveal all Trollope's skills. Within the framework of this study the theme of consistency recognises that *The Way We Live Now* is substantially of the same kind as *The Three Clerks*, only more unified in its presentation. The principle of continuity, likewise, reveals that at both ends of his career Trollope could be satirical and savage or cheerful and optimistic. *The Bertrams*, for example, written in 1868, is full of painful events, unhappy love affairs, a suicide, an unattractive hero, and a relentless view of age – as sour a book as any he wrote. *Ayala's Angel*, on the other hand, published in 1881, one year before his death, is one of his happiest novels. Consistency applies very much to the level of workmanship, to Trollope's scant regard for the 'purity' of the novel : just as he is quite willing to interpolate an essay on the Civil Service in *The Three Clerks* (1858), he will digress on Gladstone's Irish policy in *The Landleaguers* (1883).[28] Pot-boilers he wrote both early and late, operating his literary mill with the thriftiness and zeal of a successful factory owner. He wasted nothing. Like Disraeli's Millbank he consumed his factory's smoke in short tales and miscellaneous journalism.

Early writers on Trollope, especially his first biographer, T. H. S.

Escott, were fond of saying that he offered a mirror to his age in which his readers saw themselves flatteringly reflected.[29] This is true, but allows Trollope only surfaces, no depth. His general sympathy with his age and with the public he served made him a peerless witness of the social scene, but at the same time, as the true descendant of Jane Austen, his preoccupation with place, behaviour and conduct leads him to interpret the subtleties of human relationships. However much is overlaid by the concessions he was willing to make – however much the artist is thus in hiding – it is this instinct and ability to go beneath the surface and, at his best, mine what is ageless and mysterious in human affairs that is Trollope's title to genius. The flux and ambiguity Trollope explores in his inimitably generous and gentle fashion are themselves often hidden in the general landscape and the unremarkably even style of narrative; perhaps one reason why Henry James hesitated in his verdict in *Partial Portraits* or why Saintsbury's judgement was so querulous. Much of Trollope, as James said, has 'no great spectacular interest'.[30] Just so. And this is peculiarly his hold on posterity. The habitual temper of his work is that of moderation, compromise and middle truth. In the spirit of such criteria this book has been written.

2 The Man and the Mask

Thackeray forbade an autobiography, Trollope left us one – and a mystery. To be without it is unthinkable, for it sets out with such grace the facts we need to know: the misery of his schooldays at Harrow, a gentleman's son, out-at-elbows and sneered at by boys no better born than he; the years of service in the Post Office, travelling all over Ireland and Southern England; the slow rise to fame and fortune as the creator of Barsetshire. All is meticulously set down: the word-counting and the stop-watch precision of his writing, hunts, visits, travels, whist at the club, and good health into the bargain. It is the archetypal Victorian success story; self-help and virtue rewarded by a happy home and a comfortable balance in the bank – a David Copperfield come to judgement.

And yet we put down the book with our curiosity unsatisfied, realising that where we most want enlightenment Trollope has slipped out of sight. We still know so little about the way he thought, still less of his inner life. What of those feckless years in London which sat so heavily on his conscience? How did his relationship with his mother and father colour his adult life? Although it is not in Trollope's nature to dissimulate, he turns aside from matters of a personal nature: 'My marriage was like the marriages of other people, and of no special interest to any one except my wife and me'.[1] Yet it emphatically is, since the pangs and adjustments, the rows and the failures of married life are central to his fiction. Trollope steadfastly refuses to divulge his thoughts on matters of supreme importance to the biographer; indeed, he maintains that it is impossible in a neat and ironical disclaimer at the end of the book: 'It will not, I trust, be supposed by any reader that I have intended in this so-called autobiography to give a record of my inner life. No man ever did so truly—and no man ever will' (ch. xx). He wraps the *Autobiography* round him like a cloak, for all his candour and honesty. In many ways his finest work, certainly his most studied, and one of the masterpieces of English autobiography, it has proved a mixed blessing to Trollope's reputation.

One has the impression that Trollope, fully aware of how little he is revealing in those carefully chosen phrases and exquisite cadences, is enjoying something of a joke on posterity: 'I do not think it probable that my name will remain among those who in the next century will be known as the writers of English prose fiction; . . . Now I stretch out my hand and from the further shore I bid adieu to all who have cared to read any among the many words that I have written' (ch. xx). The shadowy figure stealing across the water salutes with a slightly mocking wave of the hand.

At any rate the character of Anthony Trollope has preserved its enigmatic quality down the years. There have been four biographies since his death in 1882, the foremost being Michael Sadleir's *Trollope: A Commentary* (1927), which with his *Trollope: A Bibliography* (1928) launched the revival of interest between the wars. After the Second World War two studies appeared, so dissimilar that it seemed scarcely possible they were about the same subject. In one, *The Trollopes, The Chronicle of a Writing Family* (1946), by Lucy Poate and Richard Poate Stebbins, Trollope emerged as an embittered egoist, rancorous towards his parents (his mother in particular), envious of other writers and cynical about his career and public. Here was a clear example of how Trollope's reticence could frustrate biography; there being no skeletons in the Waltham cupboards some had to be invented. Redressing the balance in *Anthony Trollope, Aspects of His Life and Work* (1957), a great Trollopian, the late Bradford Booth, described him as the 'apotheosis of normality', and dwelt on his acquiescent humanism.[2] Trollope's most recent biographer, James Pope Hennessy, acknowledged a debt to a breezy memoir by T. H. S. Escott, *Anthony Trollope, his Work, Associates and Originals* (1913), but seemed to have been more influenced by the Stebbinses in so far as he failed to bring out the zest and wholesome vigour of Trollope's life, expressed by the dominant concerns of his fiction with romantic love, marriage and family life.

Trollope is, I have said, a difficult subject. Like the *Autobiography*, his correspondence keeps personal disclosure to a minimum. 'Virtually a log-book of the busiest man of Victorian letters', much of it concerned with Post Office business and his writing, it is the correspondence of a man in a perpetual hurry.[3] But being unpremeditated and off-the-cuff it can be combed for the human detail we require; there remains much for investigation once a fully detailed collected letters is available.[4] The unself-conscious quality of the writing brings us once more to the question of Trollope's modesty: he obviously had no thought of his letters being published. He kept none addressed to him, and detested having occasionally to send out photographs to his correspondents. 'He was a man not apt to betray the secrets of his inner life', as he says of Judge Bramber in *John Caldigate* (ch. liv).

As a result many people were shocked by the depths of suffering he confessed in the early chapters of the *Autobiography*. Sir William

Gregory, who had occupied the next desk at Harrow, found his own conscience jolted by reminders of sorrow Trollope had not referred to over later years of their acquaintance.[5] An intensely private man, he shrank from personal advertisement, and unlike Dickens, who increasingly needed close contact with his public (embarking on his readings partly to satisfy this need), Trollope kept out of the public eye. A sense of what became a gentleman obviously influenced his attitude towards any invasions of personal privacy, but Trollope was also reticent by nature. The cardinal error of biography is to interpret this as lack of feeling, and to depict him as cold and passionless, mechanically grinding out novels to the steady ticking of the stop-watch, with little time or inclination for his own domestic circle. In fact the evidence points strongly the other way: to an emotional – even romantic – attitude to life, which he found it necessary to curb and control. Inheriting his father's temper and his mother's volatility, Trollope continually put the brake on feelings (not always to the advantage of his novels), checking an open and vulnerable spirit, which in the formative years learned all too quickly what sensitivity receives in hurts and blows. He acquired reserve and caution by hard experience, but they were continually breached in adult life by strong emotional responses. This led to the inconsistency which puzzled some of his contemporaries: the contrast between the loud man and the quiet novels. He was frank, open, honest, but he was also guarded. He had many friends but confided in few. Reticence, which masked his emotionalism and hid the secrets of his overburdened childhood, became an important principle of life, as well as an integral part of his creativity. He felt that to lack reserve was to lack propriety, hence his response to the first volume of Forster's *Life of Dickens*, in a letter to George Eliot and Lewes:

> Dickens was no hero; he was a powerful, clever, humorous, and, in many respects, wise man; – very ignorant, and thick-skinned, who had taught himself to be his own God, and to believe himself to be a sufficient God for all who came near him; – not a hero at all. Forster tells of him things which should disgrace him, – as the picture he drew of his own father, & the hard things he intended to have published of his own mother. (490, p. 291)

It is interesting to find Trollope expressing himself so forcibly on this matter. As he grew older Trollope seems to have become steadily more convinced of the need to separate public and private life, possibly to safeguard, rather in the manner of the Victorian poets, the integrity of his own voice.

Yet for all his shyness Trollope enjoyed society. Lacking the austerity of Thackeray's manner he was an eminently clubbable man, belonging to at least three London clubs: the Garrick, the Athenaeum and the Cosmopolitan. From the time of his success, clubland became an important part of his life and of his fiction, for it was one of the outward tokens he continually sought of having escaped the shame and loneliness of youth and childhood.⁶ The Garrick 'was the first assemblage of men at which I felt myself to be popular'.⁷

In his later days Trollope became as much a lion as Browning. He had always been drawn to the society of the rich and the well-born, and by the seventies knew nearly everyone of note in the professional spheres, a good many influential members of the upper middle class, and a useful portion of the aristocracy. All these brought him gossip and opinion as well as traits of character and behaviour which could be adapted for immediate use, as his flexible plotting allowed, or stored away for the future. Trollope did not copy from life (which makes the hunt for real identities for his characters singularly unprofitable), but made composite pictures with traits from this person and that. He said once of a story: 'I have written to that crack-brained lady about Lady Anna. My story was pure fiction. I never made use of stories from private life. But I think she is mad.'⁸ His mother once resolved the question of whether she copied real people or not by saying that she made a regular practice of pulping her acquaintances before serving them up – so that it was impossible to see the pig in the sausage. *Romans à clef* are far removed from Trollope's mode.

Similarly, his setting is an ideally rendered place appropriate to the mood and unity of his story. A few weeks before Trollope's death, when the historian E. A. Freeman took him on a ramble in the West Country, argument ensued as to the source of Barchester:

> He allowed Barset to be Somerset, though certainly Gatherum Castle has been brought to us from some other land. But he denied that Barchester was Wells. Barchester was Winchester, where he was at school, and the notion of Hiram's Hospital was taken from Saint Cross.

Freeman, as cantankerous as the novelist, pressed his argument, suggesting that perhaps other places besides Wells had been in Trollope's mind, especially as the towers were more conspicuous at Wells than at Winchester. And did not the idea of the hospital come from the foundation for woolcombers at Wells?

> But no; Barset was Somerset, but Barchester was Winchester not Wells. He had not even taken any ideas from Wells; he had never heard of the Wells woolcombers.⁹

Naturally enough, the amount of physical detail in Trollope's fiction and critical bias towards his social-historical accuracy has made it

difficult for us to see him as he truly is: a thoroughly imaginative writer, with what Gordon Ray called a gargantuan obsession with
his created world – a world in which inner significances are the
vital issue rather than externals of historical or sociological importance.[10]

Despite his reserve, or to compensate for it, Trollope in society was
loud, communicative and overbearing. Yet on the whole he was well-
liked, being, according to one witness, the most popular man in London
society for a while.[11] Certainly among the many recollections of him
between the mid-sixties and his death, hostile accounts are very few
indeed. Among young writers he was thought to be a sympathetic and
genial adviser.[12]

But what was he like? So many brief recollections exist that we can
make a composite character sketch. As the shyest men are sometimes
drawn into the theatre Anthony Trollope had a tendency to seek the
limelight, dominating any company by his vitality, loud laughter and
natural good humour. His physical presence was impressive: a heavy
build and upright carriage made him appear taller than his five feet
ten inches. Browning had the look of a rich banker; Trollope was of
rougher clay, his clothing less well preserved, his large domed head
fringed with unruly hair, and around his ruddy, healthy-looking face
a thick hedge of mottled white and reddish beard, more like a gentleman
farmer who had 'spent all his life in the country, growing turnips and
preserving game'.[13] Being very short-sighted he wore tiny gold-rimmed
glasses, and would come up close with an intimidating intensity of
expression in his black eyes, more daunting from vertical furrows in
his forehead. It was the face of an irate Santa Claus, full of thunderous
potential. He once said of his own photograph:

It looks uncommon feirce [sic] as that of a dog about to bite; but that
I fear is the nature of the animal portrayed.[14]

The most striking feature of the man was the animation, which started
from him like an electrical charge around the halo of white hair and
beard. He glowed, Julian Hawthorne said, a conversational stove, and
gesticulated wildly with his cane, to the danger of those in the immediate vicinity.[15] Seeing him with his brother in Florence, Kate Field
noted that Thomas Adolphus was calm, magisterial – half Socrates and
half Galileo – while Anthony was full of almost boyish enthusiasm
and impulsive argument.[16] Undoubtedly he had a magnetic personality.
A typical social call would begin with a thunderous knock on the
door and his resonant voice demanding who was at home. Then,
entering the house like a frantic windmill, sometimes observed by
small children peering though banisters from the upper landing, he
would take his stance, back to the fire, hands clasped behind him and

feet somewhat apart.[17] He had a trick of holding his thumb erect while smoking, his cigar between the first and second fingers, his pockets sticking out of his trousers, his coat straining over his small but comfortable corporation.[18] When he came into a room it grew smaller. Eleanor Smyth recalled that as a child she shrank from that stentorian voice:

> Indeed, he reminded us of Dickens's Mr. Boythorn, minus the canary, and gave us the impression that the one slightly-built chair on which he rashly seated himself during a great part of the interview, must infallibly end in collapse, and sooner rather than later.[19]

The severe expression of his contracted brows and peering vanished when he spoke, in a rumbling port-winey way, giving his whole attention to the subject in hand. His conversation was rather disjointed, being punctuated with roars of simulated wrath or laughter, although one witness declared that unless he was with intimate friends he laughed very little. He was not a wit, but had a knack of making things more amusing than they really were, and he would hold on to a point like a terrier. What he lacked in intellectual vigour he made up for in pertinacity and lung power.

Among men of intellect he probably did himself some injustice by his bluster. James Russell Lowell described a conversation between Oliver Wendell Holmes and Trollope as a battle of roaring repartee, with Emerson and Lowell crouched down out of range enjoying their quiet talk while the salvoes crashed overhead.[20] Russell's dinner with Huxley and Knatchbull Hugessen was marred one evening in 1867 by the sound of Trollope drowning out Huxley, who was certainly more worth hearing.[21] And there is an amusing account by Mark Twain of Trollope in 1873, as host to himself, Thomas Hughes, the American humorist, Joaquin Miller, and the Honourable Frederick Leveson Gower, the brother of Lord Granville. Twain described himself on this occasion as an obliterated guest, noting with sharp republican eyes that Trollope was but vaguely aware that any other person was present excepting him of the noble blood. Reverence towards the acting deity from all present made Mark Twain feel he was at a religious service.

> [Miller] and Trollope talked all the time and both at the same time, Trollope pouring forth a smooth and limpid and sparkling stream of faultless English, and Joaquin discharging into it his muddy and tumultuous mountain torrent, and – well, there was never anything just like it except the whirlpool rapids under Niagara Falls.[22]

At least the occasion was a greater success than Trollope's visit to John Stuart Mill, whom he much admired. As usual Trollope was awkward and out of place with a man so much his superior in intellect, and roared louder than ever. It was a relief, noted Frederic Harrison drily, to get the bull safely away from the china shop.[23]

Perhaps because of these deficiencies, Trollope in fiction makes a virtue of out inarticulateness, showing indulgence towards men of few words like Johnny Eames and Will Belton. At its worst his distrust of intelligence comes out in men who strike first and ask questions afterwards, like Lord Chiltern, whose absurd duel with Finn at Blankenberg reflects a profound sense of honour Trollope rather admires. Trollope is often simplistic about the man of action, extolling the foolhardy courage of a Major Caneback as one of the nobler manly qualities. The combination of brute strength and gentleness of disposition in Stubbs of *Ayala's Angel* is a tiresome convention he too often accepts, although it has a certain relevance to his own character. Eloquence and intellectual power, on the other hand, is frequently equated with smartness and trickery, in characters such as Crosbie, Lopez and Undy Scott.

In conversation Trollope had a Johnsonian relish for tossing and goring, and his emotion was apt to get the better of him. It was only his manner, Yates observed, but it was 'a demd uncomfortable madhouse sort of manner' all the same.[24] Once, at a meeting of Post Office surveyors, Trollope leapt to his feet to interrupt a speaker, saying 'I entirely disagree with you. What is it you said?'[25] Meetings of the Royal Literary Fund, on which he sat with Browning, Locker-Lampson, and Sir Frederick Pollock, were frequently contentious but good-humoured, as Trollope argued with everyone in sight. G. A. Sala's recollection of the first Cornhill dinner Trollope attended is of his being well to the fore, contradicting everybody, and *afterwards saying kind things to everybody* [my italics].[26] Trollope's combative talk was merely the consequence of his ebullient personality and had the saving grace of goodwill. In his clumsy, impetuous way Trollope often gave offence – Froude speaks slightingly of old Trollope banging about the world – and was sometimes judged insensitive because of it. He rushed around with the energy of an English sheepdog anxious to please, and often his excitability got the better of him.

An amusing instance of this is Frederic Harrison's anecdote of his behaviour at one of George Eliot's gatherings in St John's Wood. Trollope told his usual tale about going to work like a cobbler, writing two hundred and fifty words every quarter of an hour for three hours every day, allowing half an hour for rereading the previous day's output. Eliot positively quivered with horror – there were days when she could not write a line. 'Yes,' said Trollope, 'with imaginative work like yours that is quite natural; but with my mechanical stuff it's a sheer matter of industry. It's not the head that does it – it's the cobbler's wax on the seat and the sticking to my chair!' He accompanied the

B

answer 'with an inelegant vigour of gesture that sent a thrill of horror through the polite circle there assembled'.[27]

His tempestuous manner was both admired and feared. The Reverend A. K. H. Boyd observed Trollope closely on a visit in 1868 to Strath-tyrum, John Blackwood's estate. Boyd, filled with enthusiasm for the author of *The Last Chronicle of Barset,* had a great shock. The novelist was singularly unkempt, and his clothes were wrinkled and ill-made. Instead of the melodious accents he had expected, he heard repeated swearing. Indeed, said Boyd, he was the only man I had heard swear in decent society for uncounted years. On the golf-course he was a sight to behold:

> It is a silent game, by long tradition: but Trollope's voice was heard all over the Links. One day, having made a somewhat worse stroke than usual, he fainted with grief, and fell down upon the green. He had not adverted to the fact that he had a golf-ball in his pocket: and falling upon that ball, he started up with a yell of agony, quite unfeigned.[28]

One cannot get away from the feeling that Trollope took a mischievous delight in confounding the expectations of the earnest clergyman.

Mrs Gerald Blackwood Porter, who knew him a great deal better than Boyd, saw Trollope's visit to Strathtyrum in an altogether different light:

> The echo of Mr. Trollope's laugh seems to come back to me as I strive to recall his genial presence, . . . the walks, the games of golf he insisted on playing on the Ladies' Links, pretending to be faint when he made a bad shot, his immense weight causing a sort of earthquake when he fell on the sandy ground; his riding off with my mother for a scamper on the sands, his host and Mrs. Trollope watching them set out from the doorsteps.[29]

If his temper was aroused Trollope had the demeanour of a wild boar. His visits to the offices of Chapman & Hall, a staff member recalled, had struck terror in him as a boy. Trollope would sometimes arrive in his pink coat with a sheaf of proofs in his pocket, bang on the table with his hunting crop and swear like a sergeant-major because there was no one in authority to receive his hectic instructions. He demoralised the staff, Arthur Waugh noted, 'among whom he splashed around like a Triton in a shoal of minnows'.[30] To subordinates in the Post Office he was a martinet, and even at Rowland Hill, his chief, he would bluster and roar.[31] The granddaughter of James Ward, the artist, visiting Lord Lytton in the sixties, caught this intriguing glimpse of Trollope at his most pugnacious:

One day we were driving through Lord Cowper's fine estate of
Panshanger, when we saw to our intense amusement Anthony
Trollope about to have a fight with a broad-shouldered rubicund
tradesman. Anthony had divested himself of his coat and was shaking
his fists in his opponent's face, as he danced around him. Though we
never heard which gladiator won, the betting was all on Anthony,
who had gained a reputation for never risking defeat when he made
a challenge.[32]

This gives a just idea of how Trollope struck most of his friends and
contemporaries: a rumbustious, domineering, extrovert and assertive
good fellow, in many ways a familiar Victorian John Bull.[33] The ideal
beefeater, Sir Leslie Stephen called him.[34] To Wilkie Collins he seemed
'an incarnate gale of wind. He blew off my hat; he turned my umbrella
inside out.'[35] Lowell recorded his impression of 'a big, red-faced, rather
underbred Englishman of the bald-with-spectacles type. A good roaring
positive fellow who deafened me (sitting on his right) till I thought of
Dante's Cerberus.'[36] But in nearly every reminiscence, there is a sense
that first impressions of ferocity gave way to appreciation of his
kindness and good nature. 'He struck me as outwardly a curmudgeon,
inwardly the soul of good fellowship', said Walter Sichel,[37] and G. A.
Sala recalled that he 'had nothing of the bear but his skin'.[38] James
Payn left this comment:

> Trollope was the least literary man of letters I ever met; indeed, had
> I not known him for the large-hearted and natural man he was, I
> should have suspected him of some affectation in this respect . . .
> His manners were rough and, so to speak, tumultuous, but he had a
> tender heart and a strong sense of duty.[39]

Beyond doubt to come to him from his books was something of a shock.
For many there was a puzzling disparity between the man and his
work. As W. P. Frith put it: 'The books, full of gentleness, grace and
refinement; the writer of them, bluff, loud, stormy, and contentious.'[40]
'Some of Trollope's acquaintances', said Frederick Locker-Lampson, 'used
to wonder how so commonplace a person could have written such excellent novels.'[41] Julian Hawthorne summed up the general bewilderment: 'Beyond a doubt, Anthony Trollope is something of a paradox.'[42]

MUD AND SOLITUDE AND POVERTY

Trollope's life falls into five phases: his childhood and Harrow schooldays; his adolescence and entry into the Post Office service; his life in
Ireland and beginnings as a writer; his prosperity in the 1860s and
1870s; and the final years to his death on 6 December 1882.

Anthony was the son of Thomas Anthony Trollope and Frances (née Milton), the daughter of a Hampshire clergyman, who is remembered as a prolific authoress, notably of *Domestic Manners of the Americans* (1832) and *The Life and Adventures of Michael Armstrong, the Factory Boy* (1840).[43] Her husband, a failed lawyer who turned to farming and business with equal lack of success, ended his days in stupefying obsession, rather like Eliot's Mr Casaubon, with a voluminous book of arcane ecclesiastical history.

Frances bore seven children between 1810 and 1818, only three of whom reached adulthood, and one of these, Cecilia, died at thirty-three. Anthony, the fifth child, was born in 1815. The eldest son, and first-born, Thomas Adolphus (1810–92), also became a novelist as well as art critic and connoisseur. His elegant house in Florence, the Vilino Trollope, was for many years a centre of Italian and English society.

The Trollopes could claim lineage to medieval times. Anthony's strong dynastic sense comes through many of his novels, not so much as respect for rank *per se*, but for an ancient name; a good line from yeoman stock means far more than a mushroom peerage. The highest distinction belongs to the man whose ancestors came over with the Conqueror. There was even a story that a Trollope in the days of the Plantagenet kings had slain three wolves at a stroke and earned the name 'Trois loups', a story Anthony unwisely told at school in an uneasy bid for friendship, only to be ragged unmercifully for swanking. Another story that went the rounds was far more popular: that young Trollope's father was an outlaw. 'It is the nature of boys to be cruel,' Trollope observes.[44] But the Trollopes were undoubtedly gentry. In the novelist's background were a baronet, a bishop and an admiral. Thomas Anthony's own father was the Rector of Cottered, Hertfordshire, and the sixth son of Sir Thomas Trollope of Casewick, Lincolnshire. What delight Anthony would have known could he have foreseen that the title would eventually come down to the descendants of his second son, Frederick Anthony, who settled in Australia as a sheep-farmer in 1869.

Not only was there ancestry but also the prospect of wealth, when in 1809 the twenty-nine-year-old daughter of William Milton, Vicar of Heckfield, Hampshire, married her reserved and grave-faced Thomas Anthony, barrister of Lincoln's Inn. Her husband's expectations centred on the son of an uncle by marriage, a rich gentleman of Dutch descent by the name of Adolphus Meetkerke, who owned Julians, a large estate in Hertfordshire.

Until 1816 the Trollope family lived at 16 Keppel Street, London, only a few houses away from Fanny's adored brother, Henry Milton. Although they were not well off they lived comfortably; the father, on the strength of his expectations and position as a gentleman, liked to keep up appearances. His novelist son was to express in later years better than anyone the humorous and pitiful aspects of fading gentility and impoverished rank. But in keeping with their status the Trollopes, largely one suspects through Fanny's good sense and management, lived well enough. A liveried footman proclaimed to all the world that the establishment was *comme il faut*.[45] Bloomsbury was still a fashionable area at this period, inhabited chiefly by professional men, mostly lawyers, and a few artists. Constable had enjoyed living in Keppel Street between 1817 and 1822, in a small house 'like bottled wasps upon a southern wall'.[46] In Red Lion Square were the Merivales, who became friends. Herman Merivale, like Thomas Anthony, was struggling to make headway as a barrister. Charles Merivale, his son, later Dean of Ely, recalled that from Bloomsbury one could get into the country in a few minutes.[47] Close at hand were the Long Fields, notorious for duels and vagabondage, which are mentioned by Thackeray in *Henry Esmond* and *The Virginians*. It was not until the third and fourth decades of the century that Bloomsbury began to decline, and its environs became useful to Trollope as an index of the fortunes of some of his characters. Harry Clavering blushes to tell Julia Brabazon he has lodgings in Bloomsbury Square, 'as he named so unfashionable a locality'.[48] Lady Anna lives for a while in Keppel Street, which 'cannot be called fashionable' (this is in the 1830s) 'and Russell Square is not much affected by the nobility',[49] the centre of fashion having by then moved further westward. Trollope's use of London streets and squares to define and place his characters is faultless. A cottage in Park Lane seems perfect for Madame Max Goesler, as the Edgware Road is apt for Mr Emilius, a popular preacher who induced Lady Eustace to marry him. Cecil Street has the proper theatrical overtones for Rachel O'Mahony's lodgings (*The Landleaguers*) and Grosvenor Place has all the grandeur one would expect for Augustus Melmotte.

In the year after Anthony's birth his father left Keppel Street on the pretext of failing health and leased four hundred acres in Harrow from Lord Northwick, intending to farm – doubtless in readiness for his long-awaited role as gentleman of means. Somewhat precipitately anticipating his inheritance from Uncle Meetkerke, he had a large house built which he named 'Julians'. 'It was', wrote Anthony, 'the grave of all my father's hopes, ambition, and prosperity.'[50] Whilst farming, for which he had no training or aptitude, Thomas Anthony maintained his tottering legal practice, alienating clients and colleagues alike by his tactless, quarrelsome manner. The *Autobiography* recalls those dreary chambers in Lincoln's Inn, in which a forlorn pupil had committed suicide, and where one sad vacation Anthony amused himself by reading a bi-columned Shakespeare because there was nothing else to do.

After the move to Harrow, Thomas Anthony's life ran down in a series of tragic absurdities. He quarrelled with Meetkerke, who married a young girl and produced his own heirs, an ironical turn of events not unlike the plot of one of his son's novels. The blow made a congenitally unhappy man even more gloomy, and as events were to turn out father and son were thrown into more uncomfortable proximity. Anthony's two elder brothers were day boarders at Harrow and missed some of the discomforts Anthony endured. Henry was his father's favourite, while Thomas Adolphus had been from the Keppel Street days closest to his mother, who came to see in him qualities of sociability and resilience that her husband lacked. After Henry's death in 1834 Frances leaned even more heavily on Thomas Adolphus, and she eventually chose to settle with him and his family in Florence from 1844 until her death in 1863. Certainly from the biographies of the Trollopes many references to Tom and his affairs indicate that he was the centre of attention, and imply a certain disregard for Anthony. At the time of Henry's death Frances wrote immediately to Tom; Anthony would receive his letter in a day or two. On another occasion he was mentioned in a kind of conscience-stricken afterthought: 'My poor dear Anthony will have outgrown our recollection!'[51]

For all that his brother always remained Anthony's close friend, despite what we read in the *Autobiography* of the Winchester thrashings Tom gave the wretched new boy. Recording a bout of single-stick with his younger brother in his diary for 1832 Tom noted: 'Anthony is far my superior in quickness and adroitness, and perhaps in bearing pain too'; unquestionably *les mots justes*.[52] Anthony sent a photograph to a relation in June 1864 with the wry comment: 'Here you have my brother and self. You will perceive that my brother is pitching into me. He always did'.[53] As youths they spent much time together, no doubt discussing their hapless father, about whom the whole family revolved in awe and dislike. Once they did a fourteen-mile walk to Vauxhall, and it was Anthony, clumsy and awkward as he was, who danced all night. Ties strengthened as they grew older, and although Anthony was oddly out of place among the marble pillars and armour of the Vilino Trollope, they confided in each other about their work (Tom provided the plot of *Dr. Thorne*) and their families. Always fond of young people Anthony had especial affection for Tom's daughter 'Bice', Beatrice (1853–81), who lived with the family at Waltham House for a time after the death of her mother in 1865. Bice remained fond of her Uncle Anthony, and in later years would visit the family at Montagu Square, where her singing delighted him. That Anthony was very much family-oriented is quite clear from the interest he took in his own relations and the affection of the young for him. During his life he 'adopted' for various periods (apart from Bice) his sister Cecilia's daughter,[54] another child niece whose name has not survived, and in 1863 Florence Bland, a niece on his wife's side who became his amanuensis.

There is little to suggest that Trollope felt aggrieved or embittered towards his parents, despite his mother's spasmodic and rather absent-minded affection. He paid her worthy tribute in the *Autobiography* and, as far as my reading of the novels tells, firmly resisted the temptation to punish or judge her for real or imagined failings of maternal duty. If he felt the hurt of her frequent absences, he was infinitely more aware of her gifts, which had plainly been passed on to himself: her courage, humour and capacity for hard work.

As to his father, there was inevitably more to be reconciled and more to be worked out, but he bore no ill-will and judged him compassionately in the *Autobiography*.

I sometimes look back meditating for hours together, on his adverse fate. He was a man, finely educated, of great parts, with immense capacity for work, physically strong very much beyond the average of men, addicted to no vices, carried off by no pleasures, affectionate by nature, most anxious for the welfare of his children, born to fair fortunes, who, when he started in the world, may be said to have had everything at his feet. But everything went wrong with him. The touch of his hand seemed to create failure . . . We were all estranged from him, and yet I believe that he would have given his heart's blood for any of us. His life as I knew it was one long tragedy. (ch. ii)

Here Trollope tells us of one of the germs of his inspiration, his curiosity as to man's nature and destiny which was to underlie the commonplaceness of his fiction. Josiah Crawley, in his false pride, self-pity, rancour towards those who wished him well, his quaint approach to his children's lessons, must come near Trollope's memory of his own father, who had a great talent for making everyone around him miserable. Trollope never ceased to marvel at his own escape to a life of normality. For his fiction, the intelligence acquired in that close unremitting study of his father resulted not only in dark, obsessional figures like Kennedy, Trevelyan and the great Crawley, destroyed by a combination of fate and the working of their own natures, but in the engagement of the novelist at levels of ambiguity which go into the making of literature.

Trollope was exceedingly miserable during childhood. For three years from the age of seven he underwent daily purgatory at Harrow School, where the other pupils looked down on him because of his disreputable appearance and ungainliness. Then he spent two years at a private school where he was always in disgrace. At twelve, in accordance with his father's wishes, he was transferred to Winchester in a year of memorable disaster, 1827. This was the year the furies descended upon the house of Trollope. The unlucky Thomas Anthony had already learned that arrangements over his marriage settlement and the deeds of the Keppel Street House had been so mismanaged that financial ruin was inevitable. His farming venture had brought only mounting debt. So 'Julians' had to be abandoned and the family moved to 'Julians Hill', later immortalised as 'Orley Farm'. It is significant that Trollope re-capitulated his childhood wretchedness when he was writing in the *Autobiography* about his stresses of the early sixties:

> In my boyhood, when I would be crawling up to school with dirty boots and trousers through the muddy lanes, I was always telling myself that the misery of the hour was not the worst of it, but that the mud and solitude and poverty of the time would ensure me mud and solitude and poverty through my life. Those lads about me would go into Parliament, or become rectors and deans, or squires of parishes, or advocates thundering at the Bar. They would not live with me now, – but neither should I be able to live with them in after years. Nevertheless I have lived with them. (ch. ix)

Then came the crowning absurdity in the family history. To recoup their fortunes, Fanny Trollope, egged on by her desperate husband, set out for Cincinnati to sell trinkets – pincushions, pepper-boxes and pocket-knives, Trollope wryly recalled – in a bazaar conceived in the grandest manner, 'a large Graeco-Moresco-Gothic-Chinese looking build-ing . . . the effect of which is eminently grotesque'. Harriet Martineau described it as 'the great deformity of the city', and it came to be known as Trollope's Folly.[55] To forward this preposterous enterprise Thomas Anthony and his eldest son followed Fanny to Ohio, leaving Anthony to endure the rigours of Winchester quite alone. It was at this stage in his school career that his loneliness became almost in-supportable:

> I had no friend to whom I could pour out my sorrows. I was big, and awkward, and ugly, and I have no doubt, skulked about in a most unattractive manner. Of course I was ill-dressed and dirty. But, ah ! how well I remember all the agonies of my young heart; how I considered whether I could not find my way up to the top of that college tower, and from thence put an end to everything?

But still worse was to come: another move downhill to Harrow Weald, to a tumble-down farm that merged into cowshed and dunghill, and as an extra turn of the screw a return to Harrow School even more obviously the poor boy. Trollope was now fifteen, with other problems of adolescence to cope with. He faced a daily walk of twelve miles through muddy lanes to be either ostracised or humiliated. For once recollection stirs up some bitterness: 'What right had a wretched farmer's boy, reeking from a dunghill, to sit next to the sons of peers, – or much worse still, next to the sons of big tradesmen who had made their ten-thousand a-year?'[56]

What are we to deduce from the facts of his childhood as Trollope gives them? From a modern standpoint it was certainly harsh, but in the light of so many accounts of Victorian childhoods by no means unusual, and better than some. Tom Hughes struck a familiar chord with his account of life at Rugby, and the memories of F. C. Burnand at Eton and Charles Merivale at Harrow show how widespread were the inhumanities and injustice of the public school system at the time. Indeed, Merivale had experiences remarkably close to Trollope's, and confessed in his own *Autobiography* 'the sense of social inferiority which was impressed upon me at Harrow was not only extremely distressing at the time, but left, I think, a certain self-distrust and shame-facedness which have often stood me in very bad stead in later life'.[57] Even allowing for Charles Merivale's acidulated tongue and the possible influence of Trollope's *Autobiography*, such confessions at least indicate that Trollope's indignities were shared by others. The question is whether he exaggerated them.

Escott tended to think so, mentioning the diary which Trollope had kept since the age of twelve: a 'friendless little chap's exaggerations of his woes', while R. P. Stebbins, ever watchful for anachronisms, tried to prove that not only did the young boy hold his own against bullies, but in the end did rather well at Harrow.[58] Certainly there are grounds for suggesting that Trollope magnified the physical horrors of his early life. On the other hand, it is equally evident that like Dickens he was intensely affected by his childhood. Whatever the actual facts of the case, he *felt* ashamed, neglected, unwanted, unloved. His suffering apparently centred on two sources, one of which is clearly acknowledged: his consciousness that he was a gentleman's son unjustly rejected by his peers. The second, not mentioned directly, is the isolation and loneliness within the family circle. These are the factors which drove the boy into a private world of make-believe and private story-telling and indirectly produced a novelist. The agonies he experienced alone also bred in him his sturdy independence, his craving for friendship, his preoccupation with wealth, status and security. They created in him a sense of inferiority and insecurity which he covered up with pugnacity. By middle age the extrovert personality fitted him well, and in the successful years we have the intriguing and on the whole attractive combination that observers in such numbers have witnessed. The vital point in Trollope's experience (although it is commonplace among Victorian biographies) is that will, courage, optimism prevailed. He bore no serious scars; he seems to have triumphed over sorrows and defeat with a remarkable degree of wisdom and equanimity; he settled no scores (even if any existed) with his parents in his fiction. Dickens was scarcely as magnanimous.

After about eighteen months of the Harrow Weald existence Mrs Trollope reappeared and, largely on the proceeds of *Domestic Manners*, established the family once more in Julians Hill. Although her withered husband took to his bed more and more often to seek respite from migraine attacks, Fanny rallied everyone, as she had done at Keppel Street and Julians. She had always believed in the family, despite her globe-trotting and restlessness, writing once to Thomas Adolphus: 'But remember dear Tom, that, in a family like ours, *everything* gained by one is felt personally and individually by all'.[59] Once more there was music in the house, and thanks to Fanny's sociability a wide circle of acquaintance with eminent men in politics and literature.

Frances Trollope retained her energy into old age. Meeting her mother-in-law soon after marriage Rose Trollope was surprised to find her 'always the life and soul of the party' even in her sixty-fourth year.[60] Her son made much in the *Autobiography* of her incapacity for sustained thought and surrender to emotion, and was aware, I think, of this propensity in himself and better able to control it. But his tribute to her is handsomely done: 'Of the mixture of joviality and industry which formed her character, it is almost impossible to speak with exaggeration' (ch. ii).

In Anthony's late adolescence, his mother's endurance was put to its hardest test. The proceeds of her book on America soon dwindled and another crisis developed. Her husband prostrated by migraine and calomel, Frances Trollope decided in April 1834 to move the family to Bruges. They escaped as the bailiffs descended on Julians Hill, an incident which provided Mrs Trollope with one of the strongest scenes of *Michael Armstrong*. Fanny organised everyone with impulsive muddleheaded goodwill. By some eccentric manœuvre Anthony was to be commissioned in an Austrian cavalry regiment and put to learn French and German as an usher in a school at Brussels. Blackness closed in with the inevitability of a Greek tragedy. Just before Christmas 1834 Henry died of consumption, soon followed by his father. Fanny returned the rest of the family to England, only to lose her youngest child, Emily, aged seventeen, also to consumption.

In the autumn of 1834, at the age of nineteen, Anthony Trollope found himself in dreary London lodgings, working without spirit or purpose for the General Post Office at St Martin's le Grand. Of the next seven years we know very little indeed. It was a time of even more intense loneliness and uncertainty, made worse by the late-developing conflicts of adolescence, some of which he hints at in

Chapter iii of the *Autobiography*. Snatches of experience in novels like *The Three Clerks*, *The Small House at Allington*, *Phineas Finn* and *Ralph the Heir* are all we have to fill the gap. The Roden-Crocker scenes in *Marion Fay* perhaps recall his London office life, with its camaraderie and mild debaucheries, late nights at cards, lamb-chops and beer : the lurid temptations of the metropolis. Who can doubt, however, that behind this picture of Harry Clavering is the lonely fellow by turns brutish and lazy, bewildered and self-accusing, fuming over his lack of purpose?

> Has it ever been the lot of any unmarried male reader of these pages to pass three or four days in London without anything to do, – to have to get through them by himself – and to have that burden on his shoulder with the additional burden of some terrible, wearying misery, away from which there seems to be no road, and out of which there is apparently no escape? (ch. xxvi)

Insecurity is even more real in the person of Charley Tudor, whose scrapes in *The Three Clerks* closely resemble the few facts Trollope divulges in the third chapter of his *Autobiography*. Charley is a member of the Internal Navigation office, a branch of the Civil Service, occupying dingy offices saturated with fog, along whose corridors bargees come and go in hobnailed boots leaving behind a smell of tobacco. The clerks or 'navvies' are the *hoi polloi* of the Civil Service thoughtless, rollicking young men, who 'dive at midnight hours into Shades, and know all the back parlours of all the public-houses in the neighbourhood of the Strand' (ch. ii). Charley is idle and improvident, gets into debt, flirts and comes perilously near marrying a barmaid. In the narrative one notices the intensity of Charley's self-disgust, which is not unlike Trollope's excessive condemnation of his own past in the *Autobiography* : 'I was entirely without control, – without the influences of any decent household around me' (ch. iii). In fact, as Escott and others noted, the situation was not so desperate; family friends were at hand, but Trollope seems to have indulged his hopelessness with a kind of wilful pleasure, another manifestation of adolescence. 'Could there be any escape from such dirt? I would ask myself; and I always answered that there was no escape' (ch. iii). For a time he was involved with a moneylender, a circumstance which he twice put to fictional use, in *The Three Clerks* and in Phineas Finn's predicament with Mr Clarkson, who dogs him at Westminster with his humbly mocking 'Do be punctual'.

The memories of an actual flirtation that almost led to disaster contributed to Trollope's perennial interest in romantic entanglements, broken promises or inveigled proposals. His preoccupation with this aspect of romance, a staple of Victorian fiction it is true, no doubt reflects to some extent anxious moments his own adolescent affairs gave him, possibly guilt in a nature intensely honourable and scrupulous. His fictional young men are clumsy, naïve, inarticulate, but fundamentally high-principled – thrown off balance temporarily, but with a reservoir of gentleness and good-nature. Perhaps Will Belton comes nearest to Trollope at this time in his life, and his qualities recur in many characters, from Johnny Eames to Tom Tringle – 'one of those overgrown lads who come late to their manhood'.[61]

Trapped in gloomy lodgings in Northumberland Street (the home of the Meager family and Mr Emilius when Bonteen was murdered in *Phineas Redux*), Trollope saw his life continuing the pattern of his childhood, confirming his sense of worthlessness: 'in truth I was wretched, – sometimes almost unto death, and have often cursed the hour in which I was born. There had clung to me a feeling that I had been looked upon always as an evil, an encumbrance, a useless thing, – as a creature of whom those connected with him had to be ashamed'.[62] This is probably why, from a kind of stubborn pride, he refused to seek help and companionship from relatives such as the uncle in Fulham Road mentioned in the *Autobiography*. He speaks of fending off creditors, sponging off equally poor cronies, getting his mother to pay some of his debts, and of twice being apprehended by sheriff's officers. Even the view from his room was of Marylebone Workhouse. It is hardly surprising that in his fiction he tended to see his characters' happiness as much dependent on money and security as true love.

In his lodgings he began to read French and Latin authors as well as English and to make sporadic attempts at writing. In a letter to the publisher Richard Bentley in May 1835, dealing with some of his mother's affairs, he diffidently mentions 'lucubrations of my own' which he hoped might find favour.[63] Clearly the Trollope spirit was not altogether crushed.

After nearly seven years in London during which he suffered a severe, almost fatal illness, about which we know nothing, a vacancy for a surveyor's clerk arose in Ireland, and Trollope at once volunteered: 'This was the first good fortune of my life.'[64]

20 HORSE POWER OF VIVACITY

The significance of Trollope's life in Ireland and its fictional consequences are so great as to call for a separate chapter. It is only necessary to record here that within a year of his arrival in August 1841 he was engaged to Rose Heseltine, the daughter of a Rotherham bank manager, whom he married in June 1844. His first son, Henry Merivale, named after his great friend, was born in 1846, and his second son,

Frederick James Anthony, in 1847, the year he published his first novel, *The Macdermots of Ballycloran*. Marriage and family life were his salvation, and his literary career, though as yet without promise, was begun. Likewise his professional status in the Post Office was miraculously altered; he was soon promoted to Deputy Postal Surveyor and, in 1845, Surveyor. His whole life had been transformed within a few years; even his character had suddenly seemed to burst from the husk.

No one had divined the latent powers, the kindly and upright nature of the man up to now, but increasingly in the late forties and fifties Trollope showed himself a man of mettle. His brother Tom was amazed at Anthony's poise, authority and well-being, and wrote in his own autobiography that from a bad office clerk continually in hot water he had become 'one of the most efficient and valuable officers in the Post Office'.[65] Trollope's move into entirely different surroundings provided the impetus to escape the limitations of his upbringing, in small ways at first, by assuming authority in his work, by riding reasonably well, above all by being acceptable to his Irish hosts. By September 1852 he was writing joyfully to his mother:

> I can't fancy any one being much happier than I am, or having less in the world to complain of. It often strikes me how wonderfully well I have fallen on my feet. (32, p. 16)

Reading his letters of the fifties, glowing with energy and high spirits, we can savour the transformation. 'I seem to be living away at a perpetual gallop' he wrote to Tom in March 1852 (31, p. 15). In the late summer of that year he was working in South Wales while Rose and the children swam at Llanstephan. The rest of the decade he consolidated his position in the Post Office. Already by November 1851 he had recommended the use of pillar letter boxes to his superiors at St Martin's le Grand. In November 1852 he applied unsuccessfully to the Earl of Hardwicke, then Postmaster General, for the post of Superintendent of Mail Coaches. He looked eagerly for promotion, having proved himself thorough, dedicated and efficient, travelling, inspecting and organising postal routes across Ireland and Southern England, concluding a postal treaty with the Egyptian Government in March 1858, and making a special mission to the West Indies in November of that year. Some of the time he was sightseeing or knocking about Paris and Rome with Tom, and always pursuing the hard, steady stint of daily writing that eventually led to success.

The ten-year period of the fifties saw his translation from utter obscurity as a writer to the peak of celebrity, his greatest success coming between 1858–59 and 1870. The sixties was a decade of ferocious activity in which he had twenty novels either appearing, published, or ready for publication, a total of twenty-seven works in all, not to mention sundry journalism. His correspondence reflects fanatical absorption in his work. Every aspirant to literary fame writing to him henceforth (and there were many) is told plainly: Work, work, work! Trollope is 'a man leaning on his pen with delight'[66] and spreading his literary interests widely. He helped found the *Fortnightly Review* (1865), and became associated closely with the *Pall Mall Gazette* in the same year. In 1866 he began a *History of English Prose Fiction* which he reluctantly abandoned. In 1867 he undertook the editing of James Virtue's new publication, *St. Paul's Magazine*, and in the same year resigned from the Post Office, disappointed at not getting the vacant office of Under-Secretary after his brother-in-law had moved into the Secretaryship vacated by Trollope's old enemy, Sir Rowland Hill. Simultaneously he was being lured into politics, and offered himself unsuccessfully as Liberal candidate for Beverley in the General Election of 1868. Also in the decade he visited the United States twice on important postal missions, the second visit combining negotiations on a copyright agreement. It was a time of industry and authority, doubly interesting to the biographer because certain cracks in the writer's world were just beginning to reveal themselves.

The successful period begins with Trollope's *annus mirabilis*, 1860, which saw his collaboration with Thackeray in the *Cornhill* and the popular appeal of *Framley Parsonage*. The sixties also begin with the well-known tribute by Nathaniel Hawthorne in a letter to the publisher James T. Fields, quoted with such pride in the *Autobiography* (ch. viii). In 1861 he was elected to the Garrick Club, and in 1864 to the Athenaeum. Upon Thackeray's death in 1863 he took his place as Chairman of the Garrick Club Committee, and then in 1864 came the final accolade of literary celebrity, the portrait in oils by Samuel Laurence. He occupied himself henceforth with affairs of the Royal Literary Fund, of which he was treasurer for many years, and lectured often on civil service and literary affairs,[67] at least once, in 1864, combining a lecture in Bury with getting up at 6 a.m. to hunt thirty miles away.

His busy social round, particularly club life, was doubtless valuable quarry to the novelist. In addition to membership of three clubs he had connections with the Alpine and the Arts, where he discussed the issues that are the general currency of debate in his political novels, and found raw material for his gallery of characters, from old-style Tory landowners to shady hangers-on like Count Pateroff. His friends were talented men at the pinnacle of their professions: Lord James of Hereford, Sir William Gregory, Sir Henry Taylor, and Sir Richard Quain, who had a large, fashionable medical practice in London.[68] Sir William Frederick Pollock, the Queen's Remembrancer, a man of liberal culture and rare social charm, was Trollope's neighbour in Montagu Square, as was Lady Wood, whose novel *Sorrow on the Sea* Trollope vigorously defended from charges of immorality.[69] Among artists Trollope was especially close to Millais and Frith. With nearly everyone in the world of publishing, journalism and authorship he enjoyed cordial relations, a fact worth remembering in a man with such a reputation for pugnacity.

Increasingly drawn into the political arena during the sixties, Trollope made his own 'leap in the dark' – his candidacy at Beverley. It was a great blow when he failed to get elected. Standing for Parliament was in many ways the ultimate ambition to bury the past and guarantee his social status. He remembered from his early days in London an uncle's mockery when he proposed for himself a future parliamentary career; another ghost had to be exorcised. Dickens, drily surprised, found Anthony's ambition 'inscrutable', but wrote to Tom Trollope: 'Still it is the ambition of many men; and the honester the man who entertains it, the better for the rest of us, I suppose.'[70] Escott took the strange view that Trollope's ambitions had little to do with being useful. One need only observe Trollope's frequent reference to the role of the member of parliament, the satire directed against men of Freddy Gower's indolence, such as Laurence Fitzgibbon, and his praise of work-horses like Barrington Erle, Phineas Finn, and Plantaganet Palliser, to see how Trollope valued parliamentary life. It was the natural step from the lesser public service in which he had distinguished himself:

> It is the highest and most legitimate pride of an Englishman to have the letters M.P. written after his name. No selection from the alphabet, no doctorship, no fellowship, be it of ever so learned or royal a society, no knightship, – not though it be of the Garter, – confers so fair an honour.[71]

If he was a man who wanted public esteem, he was also one who craved to serve society. Writing to Sir Arthur Helps in January 1869, he rather wistfully compared his own role with that of the distinguished clerk of the privy council:

> With me, it often comes to me as a matter, I will not say of self-reproach but of regret, that I can express what I wish to express only by the mouths of people who are created – not that they may express themselves, but that they may amuse. You have gained your laurels after a more manly fashion.[72]

This is a consistent reaction to his parliamentary failure. After Beverley he relied on Palliser and the rest as safety-valves to deliver up his soul. The Palliser novels gave him proxy membership of the House of

Commons, enabling him 'to have that fling at the political doings of the day which every man likes to take, if not in one fashion then in another'.[73]

From the date of the Beverley fiasco the tide for Trollope begins slowly to ebb; his letters reveal more melancholy, and although he is still only in his fifties he begins to feel old. The routine of work is scarcely slackened, but he struggles with mental fatigue, and welcomes the diversions of amateur scholarship such as his little book on Caesar (1870) and his study of Cicero (1880). Moments of despair are interspersed with his usual paeans to work; the exhilaration of writing remains uppermost, but is sustained with greater will. *Labor ipse voluptas*, however, remained his watchword. Amidst the editorial duties, which troubled him as they had Thackeray, he saw his brother's books through the printers and engaged in a massive task of reading, both for his contemplated history and his political novels. He also buckled to that bane of the successful writer, reading his friends' manuscripts. Of Kate Field's bad poems he wrote tenderly : 'Ah me, it gives me much pain to write this . . . I too have written verses, and have been told that they were nought.' He was to find Kate, after longer acquaintance, made of sterner stuff, and he greeted her later efforts with more frankness : 'In spite of Dogberry, the thing is to be done by cudgelling.'[74] The basis of his advice to the neophyte always boiled down to the need for constant and concentrated effort, which in later years was accompanied by solemn warnings as to the precariousness of his profession. The best account of his attitude to writing is in a letter to Catherine Gould, which draws on the analogy about shoemaking well over a year before its famous mention in the presence of Lowell, Emerson and Holmes. It makes the point more succinctly than the well known passage in the *Autobiography* (ch. vii), in which Trollope trails his coat with scornful remarks about inspiration that his immediate posterity took so amiss.

Trollope's literary fortunes began slowly to decline from the end of 1866, when he threw in his lot with James Virtue, a sound printer but inexperienced publisher. He also encountered greater difficulty negotiating with publishers, a tell-tale sign of gradually decreasing sales. After the peak sums obtained for *Phineas Finn* and *He Knew He Was Right*, of £3200 in 1867 and 1868 respectively, he encountered an inevitable diminution in prices. Great novels were still to come, but Trollope was not quite the draw he had been up to the publication of *The Last Chronicle of Barset* (1866/67). One sign of change was the proposal that publication of *The Vicar of Bullhampton* (1868) should be deferred to give pride of place to a novel of Victor Hugo's, commissioned concurrently for *Once a Week* edited by E. S. Dallas. To make matters worse the ramifications of a dubious publishing arrangement caused the book to appear in the now unfashionable monthly instalments, and as a result it failed to reach a large public.

Editing *St. Paul's Magazine* proved a further strain and disappointment and he resigned in June 1870. To a man entirely committed to literature for his income, and with deep-seated anxieties about money from childhood, the strain of hard bargaining with publishers added to the burden of creation. To undermine his confidence still further, a modest venture into scholarly fields, a translation of the *Commentaries of Caesar* (1870) undertaken for his friend, William Lucas Collins, was slighted by the very people Trollope had wanted to impress, the academics, among whom Trollope was conscious of being an outsider. Herman Merivale recalled the response of his uncle, the Dean of Ely, when Trollope proudly sent him a copy: 'Thank you for your Comic History of *Caesar*.' Trollope commented wryly 'I don't suppose he intended to run a dagger into me.'[75]

The early seventies was also a period of severance and leave-takings within the family. Trollope's younger son, Frederick, had decided by the spring of 1869 to settle permanently in Australia to farm. Now in 1871 Trollope sold his house at Waltham and took Rose on an extended visit to Fred. Throughout the next few years his letters reflect growing restlessness, his fiction more emphasis on psychological problems. Of Trollope, as of many Victorians, it may be said that the older he became the harder he worked, but the stresses are now more apparent. From Australia, in February 1872, he writes to the Leweses: 'I am beginning to find myself too old to be 18 months away from home. Not that I am fatigued bodily – but mentally I cannot be at ease with all the new people and new things' (490, pp. 290–1). Writing outside the demands of his daily quota of copy becomes an increasing burden. As he explained to a correspondent: 'When I have done my daily work, . . . I have always a certain number of letters to write, which are de rigueur. Then I am tired of my pen, – often indeed sick of it; and cannot get myself to write more.' Finally with devastating gaiety: 'In all your letters there is ever so much that I should like to answer, – only there would be no end' (624, p. 355; 634, p. 359).

Although he relaxed his rigorous schedule of rising at 5.30 a.m., Trollope maintained his output of fiction, leaving at his death, besides the unfinished *Landleaguers*, the manuscripts of *An Old Man's Love* (published 1883) and the *Autobiography* (also published 1883). Writing was still a passion and a drug. 'My only doubt as to finding a heaven for myself at last,' he once wrote to Alfred Austin, 'arises from the fear that the disembodied and beautified spirits will not want novels' (484, pp. 285–6). It struck him also that to be deprived of hunting would be equally disappointing, and dreamed of an elysium where hunting lasted twelve months of the year. Increasingly he dreaded having to give it up, writing to George Smith from Melbourne in May, 1872 : 'I have been journeying about from Colony to Colony till I am heartily homesick. I seem to regret greatly last years [*sic*] hunting, – feeling that there can be but few more years of hunting left to me & that I should lose none of it' (494, pp. 292–3). He continued living, as he said in praise of Sir Walter Scott, at '20 horse power of vivacity' (*Letters*, 593, p. 342), hunting until 1878, and undertaking many social engagements. His travels in the latter years included voyages to Australia (1871–2, 1875) and an exhausting trip to Africa (1877–8), which was immediately followed by a short cruise to Iceland. Even in the last year of his life research for *The Landleaguers* took him twice to Ireland with a short Italian holiday between. His celebrity was marked by honours such as the 84th dinner of the Royal Literary Fund at the Freemasons' Hall on 28 May 1873. He was frequently invited to lecture or to distribute prizes at gatherings of working men. With W. P. Frith in November 1876 he spoke at a London prizegiving. 'Trollope made a good speech,' Frith noted, 'and I made a bad one.'[76] Also in that year he served on the Royal Copyright Commission. In December he was on the platform with Gladstone, Lord Shaftesbury, Evelyn Ashley and the Duke of Westminster, speaking on the Eastern Question. Thomas Hardy was present and recorded this typically Trollopian scene :

> Trollope outran the five or seven minutes allowed for each speech, and the Duke, who was chairman, after various soundings of the bell, and other hints that he must stop, tugged at Trollope's coat-tails in desperation. Trollope turned round, exclaiming parenthetically, "Please leave my coat alone," and went on speaking.[77]

The last phase of his life was shadowed, but by no means darkened, by the waning of his career as new tastes sprang up which he no longer had the energy to satisfy. 'The world has had enough of everything,' he wrote wearily to Rose on the way to Ceylon in the spring of 1875, 'and there is nothing left but rechauffes' (585, p. 337). He quarrelled for a second time with the contumacious Charles Reade, who had borrowed the plot of *Ralph the Heir* for a play. He was troubled by the family complaint of deafness, and other minor painful discomforts – hernia, writer's cramp, touches of gout, and fatigue. He wrote to Henry : 'Nothing really frightens me but the idea of enforced idleness. As long as I can write books, even though they be not published, I think that I can be happy' (804, p. 446). Like Tennyson's Ulysses, feeling how dull it was to pause, he could find no peace. The Phoenix Park murders in May 1882 took hold of his imagination, suggesting that something near the end might yet be done, and with his usual doggedness he set himself to the task. The seizure which struck him down on the evening of 3 November 1882 is said to have resulted from two manifestations of his temperament. During the afternoon he had exchanged angry words with a strolling German band playing under his hotel window. In the evening, surrounded by friends at the home of his well-loved brother-in-law, Sir John Tilley, he was exuberantly part of the family circle, roaring with laughter at the group's reading aloud of F. Anstey's highly popular novel, *Vice Versa*. After his stroke he lingered until 6 December, paralysed, then rallying slightly, but all that time almost bereft of speech. The most recent account, by C. P. Snow, reveals how much Trollope brooded on death in his later years, yet his appetite for work remained and his resilient spirit kept its hold on life.[78] To the very end he preserves that enigmatic balancing of qualities which constitute the elusive character of his art.

Reasons for the contrast between Trollope in public and in private are not difficult to fathom. They are to be found in the legacy of his parents' incompatible natures and his childhood. Early blows to his self-esteem spurred his ambition, driving him to excel in one field after another: public service, writing, politics, editing, amateur scholarship, even in hunting and whist. I am convinced that his anonymous publication of *Linda Tressel* and *Nina Balatka* constituted a self-imposed qualifying examination to prove his abilities yet again to his own satisfaction. But in such circumstances the victim never passes his own tests. And this one came amid other assaults on his self-confidence: the realisation that his history of the novel would have to be abandoned, his discomforts as an editor, his failure at Beverley.

If we sense contradiction in Trollope at times, it stems from a paradox common enough in human nature. The ego that survives early difficulties emerges stronger and more demanding: hence the ambition, the self-assertion, the will to succeed. But the instinct for self-protection develops strongly at the same time, and so in situations where the ego might be vulnerable one finds excessive self-depreciation. Thus in Trollope there is a discrepancy between his professed merchandising of novels and his references to the gentleman in Paternoster Row who spawned three novels a year; between his desire to vindicate his calling by writing a history of fiction, and his deliberate flourishing of the commercial motive. The central contradiction is between the labour and discipline he urges so often to everyone who asks his advice about writing, and the careless way he refers to his own work. The paradox of Trollope was neatly explored by Elizabeth Bowen, who conjured up Trollope's genial spirit in a charming play for radio. Diffidence was uppermost in the portrayal. Were there two Trollopes? she asked: the anxious outcast, and the successful man of the world, and was the first, perhaps, never quite absorbed in the second?[79]

Ambivalence of feeling about himself and his fiction throughout the *Autobiography* led to a frankness that cut through the mystique of authorship, and it also gave him protection among his great contemporaries. It suited him to be accompanist rather than soloist, in which role he offered George Eliot some advice on improving her public relations in this typical piece of practical criticism of *Romola* in a letter of June 1862 :

> Do not fire too much over the heads of your readers. You have to write to tens of thousands, & not to single thousands. I say this, not because I would you alter ought [*sic*] of your purpose. That were not worth your while, even though the great numbers were to find your words too hard. But because you may make your full purpose compatible with their taste. (176, pp. 115–16)

What a strange bond that is, on reflection, between the sensitive, analytical George Eliot and the robust, hearty Anthony Trollope. Yet they were great friends. She claimed that but for *The Way We Live Now* she would never have had the courage to forge ahead with *Middlemarch*. He thought highly of her work, finding her sometimes too abtruse but like an egg always full of meat. His note to Charles Lee Lewes after her death was touchingly brief : 'I did love her dearly. That I admired her was a matter of course. But my affection for her was thorough and the wound, though not such as yours or poor Cross's, is severe' (805, pp. 446–7).

Yet their dissimilarity as artists is easily apparent, and a measure of Trollope's lesser rank. Where Eliot yielded little to public taste Trollope deliberately compromised, setting conscious limitations to the time he would work, the kind of article he would manufacture. His devotion to the theme of romantic love (which he depicts with greater skill than any of his contemporaries) was in part an intelligent response to what the public most wanted. By the same token, avoiding the darker elements of life was partially governed by sense of the public which Dickens, the greater artist, rose above. John Forster praised Yates' first novel to Dickens as being quite as good as the work of Mr Anthony Trollope; 'That is not very high praise', said Dickens, and sat down to his lunch.[80] There is also something of a contradiction between Trollope's literary calling and his other avocations. Henry James observed with some amusement that Trollope contrived to arrange his exceedingly demanding writing schedule in accordance with the hunting season. These are all factors of the Trollope problem which become more comprehensible in the light of his self-doubt; it becomes easier to condone his obstreperous manner before George Eliot's guests, or his mischievous debunking of inspiration in the *Autobiography*, the writing of which itself seems to contradict his persistent undervaluing of his work.

The *Autobiography* was begun in the upheaval following Trollope's resignation from the Post Office in September 1867, and the failure of his political hopes the next year. The poor reception of *The Prime Minister* (1876), together with disappointment over his *Commentaries of Caesar*, renewed unpleasantness with Charles Reade, and memories awakened by visiting his son in Australia, must have provoked fresh anxieties about himself. And in this climate of setback and emotional disturbance Trollope felt the need to exorcise the past once and for all by setting down an account of his life, to repair defences he had carefully built up through the years and to reassure himself once more that he had succeeded. So he wrote his memoirs, as men do write such things, to leave a record of his achievements to posterity; but in a far more important sense the book was meant for himself, to justify the way he had chosen to live and assert some purpose for a future clouded with uncertainty.

PATERFAMILIAS

One key to the dramatic change in Trollope's life, from failure and misery to success and happiness, is his wife Rose, about whom we know so little. It is in the sphere of his marriage and family, where we most need enlightenment, that we are balked by his reticence. Yet herein lies the most significant element of Trollope's life story and the major inspiration of his fiction.

Julian Hawthorne, who met the Trollopes in the mid-seventies, noted they were an affectionate couple and even claimed that 'his wife was his books'.[81] Anthony and Rose were undoubtedly devoted, although we have only the merest hints about their private life, chiefly from the letters, particularly those written towards the end of his life. Tender, solicitous, chaffing, reminiscent, they are a perfect expression of his dependence and fondness. He is in Ireland collecting material for *The Landleaguers*, and writes wistfully home: 'How is the garden, and the cocks and hens, especially the asparagus bed' (887, p. 482). He gossips about long-forgotten haunts and people they had once known; grumbles about his asthma, the food, and the tiring round of engagements; speculates about her summer trip to Herne Bay and Gladstone's Irish policy. Once he advises her not to stay a Sunday in London, for it would 'kill you with dullness' (898, p. 490). On another occasion he teases her with a joke from the early days of their marriage: 'I will give up being Surveyors clerk as you don't seem to like it, but in that case must take to being guide at Killarney' (888, p. 483). A few minor points of evidence as to their compatibility can be gleaned from other scraps of information. Rose treasured thirty letters from eminent men praising her husband's work, which she kept in a small red leather portfolio. In the fourth copy of his lecture 'On English Prose Fiction' is the inscription 'Rose Trollope from her obedient slave/The Lecturer'.

Throughout their lives Rose took an active part in his work, discussing his stories, copying manuscripts, proof-reading, while managing his household with tireless efficiency. Of all the reticences of Trollope's autobiography, his meagre account of Rose is the most tantalising, for she is surely the source of much of his inspired rendering of womankind. It is unlikely that we shall learn more about her; she too, like the artist, will remain in hiding, a figure of some ambiguity. To a great extent she must have willingly submerged her own personality to accord with the Victorian ideal of domesticity preserved in this passage of *The Landleaguers*:

> In temper she was perfect; in unselfishness she was excellent. In all those ways of giving aid, which some women possess and some not at all, – but which, when possessed, go far to make the comfort of a house, – she was supreme. If a bedroom were untidy, her eye saw it at once. If a thing had to be done at the stroke of noon, she would remember that other things could not be done at the same time. If a man liked his eggs half-boiled, she would bear it in her mind for ever. She would know the proper day for making this marmalade and that preserve; and she would never lose her good looks for a moment when she was doing these things. With her little dusting-brush at her girdle, no eyes that knew anything, would ever take her for aught but a lady. (III, ch. xl)

On the other hand it is probable that the dusting-brush was sometimes raised in anger. There are enough women of spirit in the fiction to suggest Rose had her rebellious moments and the occasional aside in a letter which indicates she was far from the weak lily of popular convention. In a letter on the occasion of his brother becoming a father, as well as indications that the jovial bearishness Anthony assumed in public spilled over into relations with his children, there is a remark about wives that one cannot but apply to Rose:

> I am glad you are to have a child. One wants some one to exercise unlimited authority over, as one gets old and cross . . . One's wife may be too much for one, and is not always a safe recipient for one's wrath. But one's children can be blown up to any amount without damage, – at any rate, for a considerable number of years. (33, p. 17)

It is extremely satisfying to imagine Rose doing the blowing up now and then, and quite in order for the supreme Victorian chronicler of normal marriage, which as in all times embraces antagonisms, adjustments and a good deal of self-sacrifice. There is no reason to suppose that Trollope did not remain as in love as he was when he wrote to Lewes in April 1861 (perhaps a little tactlessly in view of his friend's domestic situation at the time):

> I have daily to wonder at the continued run of domestic & worldly happiness which has been granted me; – to wonder at it as well as to be thankful for it . . . no pain or misery has as yet come to me since the day I married; & if any man should speak well of the married state, I should do so. (138, p. 88)

Rose was undoubtedly lively and made the most of her appearance. She got on well with people. Her mother-in-law (not the easiest of old ladies to deal with) was obviously fond, and made her a gift of a brooch given her by Princess Metternich. This treasured possession, a cherub with iridescent wings drawing a pearly nautilus shell chariot on a black ground, came eventually into the ownership of her granddaughter, Muriel Rose, whose short account of the family adds a few more details to what we know of Rose.[82] Apparently she loved travel almost as much as Anthony, and often accompanied him on his more ambitious expeditions, taking along portmanteaux of fashionable clothes. On their trips to Europe she could walk through miles of galleries and piazzas without tiring.

Rose had conventionally feminine artistic interests. A letter of 1851 records Anthony's delight at the prospect of seeing her embroidered screen win a bronze prize in the Great Exhibition. In view of what has already been said about Trollope's family pride, it is interesting that the screen had a central panel with a knight bearing the Trollope crest. She was interested in the garden and flowers and managed efficiently her pigs and poultry. A letter of 1880, when the family moved to Harting Grange, near Petersfield, Hampshire, shows Trollope vigorously at work on the new garden:

> We have got a little cottage here, just big enough (or nearly so) to hold my books, with five acres and a cow and a dog and a cock and a hen. I have got seventeen years' lease, and therefore I hope to lay my bones here. Nevertheless I am as busy as would be one thirty years younger, in cutting out dead boughs, and putting up a paling here and a little gate there. We go to church and mean to be very good, and have maids to wait on us. (807, p. 447)

What Trollope fails to tell us, and what biography has not sufficiently stressed, is his intense attachment to hearth and home. All the Trollopes had a gift for home-making: Tom and Theodosia were devoted, and one must not forget that even Julians, and before it Keppel Street, had been a scene of festive family occasions; even the staid, melancholy barrister, Thomas Anthony, would promote amateur dramatics and charades. The sanctity of the domestic routine became a cardinal rule for Anthony. In this respect he typifies one of the strengths of the Victorian way of life. Trollope does allow us a glimpse in the *Autobiography* of his pleasure in Waltham, but it is tantalisingly brief: 'A house in which I could entertain a few friends modestly, where we grew our own cabbages and strawberries, made our own butter, and killed our own pigs' (ch. ix). Others have spoken warmly of the house Trollope lived in for his twelve most successful years. Thackeray's daughter, Anne, later Lady Ritchie, stayed there in the winter of 1865, and left this charming recollection:

> It was a sweet old prim chill house wrapped in snow . . . I can also remember in the bitter cold dark morning hearing Mr. Trollope called at 4 o'clock. He told me he gave his man half a crown every time he (Mr. Trollope) didn't get up! 'The labourer is worthy of his hire,' said Mr. Trollope in his deep, cheerful lispy voice.[83]

A year later Sir Frederick Pollock was a guest, and described it more fully:

> an old-fashioned red-brick house of about Wm the Third's time, with a good staircase and some large rooms in it, and standing in equally old-fashioned grounds . . . There was a *corps de logis* and two wings, one of which held the stables in which Trollope's hunters were lodged, and the other was converted into an office for the Post Office clerks who were under him in his work of superintending the cross-post arrangements of the eastern counties.[84]

The home where all's accustomed, ceremonious meant much to Trollope and in his fiction often represents order and stability in an uncertain world.

When he gave up Waltham House in 1871 he moved into the heart of London, to 39 Montagu Square, where he had friends such as the Pollocks and Lady Wood. His town house was again elegantly furnished and given homely comforts by Rose, while Trollope himself took pleasure in having his vast collection of books arranged and catalogued in the library, which filled an extension of the house and where it was his practice to write. The books were in open cases and dusted twice a year against the London soot. It is remarkable that Trollope managed prodigious amounts of reading in his strenuously busy life. The research, for example, which went towards his classical books takes them far beyond the 'harmless fads' his latest biographer terms them.

Trollope was a doting father, particularly towards his elder son, Harry, who drew closer to him in his declining years. Biography can make no greater error than to suppose Trollope was cold or aloof. When his children were small he seems to have shown few elements of the Podsnap or Pontifex, and much patience and understanding towards other members of his family, willingly looking after his nieces from time to time, particularly Florence Bland, who came to live at Waltham Cross in 1863 as a little girl and became an invaluable secretary. Doubtless the domestic circle revolved around the ever busy and at times crotchety novelist, but such evidence as we have points to a happy household rather like Judge Staveley's in Noningsby in *Orley Farm*. The patriarchal rule was benevolent. As Mrs Porter, Blackwood's daughter, told Muriel in 1926: 'You can have no idea of the hold your grandfather had on those who knew him. To know him was to love him.'[85]

Unlike Dickens, who was disappointed in his sons, Trollope took much pride in their careers and refrained from driving them, the temptation of most great men. Of his younger son, Frederick, whose emigration to Australia at eighteen cost his parents some heartache, he wrote in January 1875: 'If he dont succeed in the long run I can no longer believe in honesty, industry and conduct' (568, p. 330). He provided £4000 for Fred's sheep farm, and twice visited him for long periods. He showed the same generosity to his elder son, Harry, assisting him to a partnership in Chapman & Hall with £10,000 at the end of 1869. If Harry disappointed him by staying with Chapman less than four years, he quickly reconciled himself, showing keen interest in his son's subsequent journalistic ventures, and a touching pride when Harry was elected to the Athenaeum in February 1882.

Emphasis on a 'dark' Trollope has produced a tendency to think of him as more disenchanted in the last decade of his life than he really was. A man driven by such external goals as money, fame, ambition, without the sustaining resources of wife and family, might easily have become cynical and misanthropic. Trollope was never so. We can discount his confession to Millais of 'some weakness of temperament that makes me, without intelligible cause, such a pessimist at heart',[86] as a piece of characteristic self-recrimination for falling short of a standard of manliness which he had set for himself: the kind of exaggeration of his shortcomings we find in allusions to his youthful escapades in London. Trollope had a favourite expression to describe a character's fortune: 'his lines had lain in pleasant places'. This he would have applied to his own life. If his diminished hold on the public disappointed him, he bore it philosophically, as he did giving up hunting in 1878. His letter to William Blackwood on this subject is nobly done: 'The abnegations forced upon us by life should be accepted frankly. I have not therefore waited to draw the cup to the last drop' (685, p. 390).

The depressions and irascibility of his last years were the result of diminishing strength and physical ailments mortifying to a man of his active nature. Having driven himself hard all his life he aged prematurely, and by his early fifties looked like an old gentleman, though hale and hearty. It was a role, too, he enjoyed playing, particularly among the young: Uncle Tony to his niece 'Bice', and to Kate Field the protective, avuncular man of the world. Consistent in his writing, he was consistent in this aspect of his personality, and remained a cheery old white-headed gentleman to the end. Coming to fiction in middle age, he wrote with a good deal of a lifetime's wisdom behind him, from a standpoint of serenity and balance, yet also with much humour and compassion, sympathetic to the youthful point of view but stressing the tribute due to the paterfamilias, sober, industrious, judicious, deserving of respect and obedience. Old age *can* be stupid, intransigent, mistaken in Trollope, but youth's follies are usually more ridiculous. The natural order of family life is implicit throughout: sons shall honour their parents.

His later books, such as *The Duke's Children*, *Mr. Scarborough's Family*, and *An Old Man's Love*, published posthumously in 1883, turned more significantly to clashes between youth and age, and the pathos of the old person's grip on life. *The Fixed Period*, that strange fantasy, loosely a science fiction novel, predicts euthanasia at sixty-seven (ironically the age when he died), and in typical fashion contrasts the theory embraced by the leading citizens of Britannula with the individual's real confrontation of a time limit on his own life. The story seems, however, to have had special significance to its author. When a close friend asked him if he had written it as a joke, he stopped suddenly, grasped him energetically and exclaimed: 'It's all true – I *mean* every word of it.'[87] It is not likely that Trollope was uttering a death-wish in *The Fixed Period*; rather, he was expressing the very common fear among elderly people of being unable to fend for themselves. As it turned out he did have to endure the incapacity he most dreaded, but only for five weeks before he died.

Unlike his father Trollope was not a despondent man, and he lived out his life in comparative calm and contentment. There is no doubt that he literally worked himself to death, but that does not invite us to see analogies with Dickens' suicidal compulsion to read the death of Nancy. From the time of his initial success in his post office career, Trollope seems to have been devoted to work. 'Enjoying myself!' he wrote to the Leweses in May 1865, 'revising a post office with 300 men, the work and wages of all of whom are to be fixed on one's own responsibility!' (264, p. 166). During one of their frequent partings, he counselled Rose in February 1858: 'Do not be dismal if you can help it – I feel a little that way inclined, but hard work will I know keep it off' (60, p. 40). And in 1873 we find him writing to an Australian friend, George William Rusden: 'There is nothing like an *opus magnum* for thorough enjoyment of life' (511, p. 303). This is so typical of Victorian attitudes, and so consistently part of Trollope's life that it cannot be thought of as in any way peculiar. Dickens found routine stimulating in a similar way and was prone to call his children's attention to his unremitting labours with self-righteous regularity.

So, ailments and irritations apart, Trollope continued to live with zest. Some five years before he died he wrote to Alfred Austin:

> I observe when people of my age are spoken of, they are described as effete and moribund, just burning down the last half inch of the candle in the socket. I feel as though I should still like to make a 'flare up' with my half inch. In spirit I could trundle a hoop about the streets, and could fall in love with a young woman just as readily as ever; as she doesn't want me, I don't – but I could. (911, pp. 495–6)

Such high spirits are typical of the man who was yet to write so ebullient a tale as *Ayala's Angel*.

Who can doubt the autobiographical element in this idea of romance at sea in *John Caldigate*? : 'You may flirt and dance at sixty; and if you are awkward in the turn of a valse, you may put it down to the motion of the ship' (ch. v). Energetic to the end, Trollope continued to leap from cabs and leave his compartment while the train was still moving into the station. His life did not wind down in disappointment and despair, but snapped while the spring was at full stretch and another novel churned in his mind. Nor are his novels noticeably darker in the later years: as Gordon Ray observed, even *Mr. Scarborough's Family* is a cheerful book.[88]

The meaning of the *Autobiography* is as clear as the philosophy behind the novels, that the battle is won by courage, integrity, honour, labour and love. Trollope's life story is that of a man who has come through: as Giles Hoggett counsels Mr Crawley in *The Last Chronicle*, 'It's dogged as does it'. And so in many ways he is the apotheosis of the Victorian ethic of self-help. His dominant characteristics were his good nature, and joy in the common experiences of living, which he transmits in equally simple terms in his fiction. Consider this response to George Smith, who had sent him a present after the success of *Framley Parsonage* in its early numbers for the *Cornhill*:

> Yesterday as I was sitting with my wife over the 'damp' number of the last, – rather next – Cornhill, a large parcel arrived from the railway. One attains by experience an intuitive perception whether or no a parcel is or is not agreeable; whether it should be opened on one's study table, or sent down to the butlers pantry. This parcel I myself opened at the moment, & took from it fold after fold of

packing paper – varying from the strongest brown to a delicate tissue
of silver shade – till I reached, – a travelling bag.

'I never ordered it' said I angrily.

'It's a present,' said my wife.

'Gammon – It's a commission to take to Florence for some dandy
and I'll be – '

For a moment I fancy she imagined it was intended for her, but
we came at once on a brandy flask & a case of razors, and that illusion was dispelled.

'It's the lady who said she wrote your book intending to make
you some amends,' she suggested.

And so we went on but never got near the truth.

No one is more accessible to a present than I am. I gloat over it
like a child, and comfort myself in school hours by thinking how
nice it will be to go back to it in play time. In that respect I have
by no means outgrown my round jacket, & boy's appurtenances
(109, pp. 70–1)

This is an interesting letter, for apart from a rare glimpse of Trollope
and his wife together, it shows how close his childhood experiences
always were. There is pathos beneath this expression of gratitude too,
and here we have the true voice of feeling which is distilled in everything Trollope wrote.

Yet he is, more than Dickens, free from sentimentality. There is a
power of perspective, an edge of commonsense on the writing that
prevents his social comedy becoming flaccid and trivial, and gives it at
times almost Jamesian objectivity. Within a framework of ordinary
events told in an ordinary way, he becomes capable of subtle analysis
of motive and human character. Such powers were the development of
his struggle against odds that had seemed insuperable in childhood. In
consequence he looked upon his eventual good fortune almost with dis-
belief, certainly without smugness or self-satisfaction. His life did in
fact resemble one of the romances he made up in his head while trudg-
ing along the lanes of Harrow Weald, and it accounts for the unfailing
optimism of his fiction, his great love, as the *Saturday Review* put it
of 'whatsoever things are lovely and of good report'.[89] Yet his candour,
common sense and honesty are geared to authentic experience, not
escapism for juvenile minds. In a magnificent closing passage of the
Autobiography the legacy of experience, reflection and human understanding has its finest expression :

If the rustle of a woman's petticoat has ever stirred my blood; if a cup
of wine has been a joy to me; if I have thought tobacco at midnight
in pleasant company to be one of the elements of an earthly paradise;
if now and again I have somewhat recklessly fluttered a £5 note over

a card-table; – of what matter is that to any reader? I have betrayed no woman. Wine has brought me to no sorrow. It has been the companionship of smoking that I have loved, rather than the habit. I have never desired to win money, and I have lost none. To enjoy the excitement of pleasure, but to be free from its vices and ill effects, – to have the sweet, and leave the bitter untasted, – that has been my study. The preachers tell us that this is impossible. It seems to me that hitherto I have succeeded fairly well. I will not say that I have never scorched a finger, – but I carry no ugly wounds. (ch. xx)

Such a confession seems to go to the heart of Trollope's character; one can only echo Sir Walter Raleigh: 'I wish there were a Trollope movement, it would be so healthy.'[90]

3 Apollo of the Circulating Library

It is to be feared that Trollope's books are dead.

Herbert Paul, *The Nineteenth*
Century, May 1897

I have suggested that Trollope's career and character prove more complex than at first appear, and were partly responsible for the failure of a later generation to arrive at a wholly satisfying account of the man. This is particularly true of his reputation and views on writing, where once more myth and misunderstanding have obscured his achievement.

On the face of it there is little room for misinterpretation. The facts of his career, set out by Michael Sadleir and others, may be encompassed quite briefly. Trollope reached a pinnacle of fame with the valedictory Barsetshire novel published in 1867. After losing ground slightly, he recovered his public with *The Eustace Diamonds* in 1872. But, too obviously a star of an earlier epoch, as Sadleir said, he failed to win the restless younger generation of the seventies, and antagonised with *The Way We Live Now* (1875) those older readers still loyal to him.[1] *The Prime Minister* (1876) encountered such criticism (that of the *Spectator* being particularly painful) that Trollope wondered if he should not give up novels altogether.[2] But he did in fact produce, with still dwindling success, fifteen more, and a volume of short stories, a study of Cicero, two travel books, a monograph on Thackeray, and his *Autobiography*. Certainly he had to accept lower prices and less distinguished imprints, but was his decline in public esteem as sudden and drastic as Sadleir suggested, or as long-lasting as the headnote to this chapter implies?

Trollope's downfall has been much exaggerated, and it may be useful to review some of the facts, concentrating on Sadleir's monumental study on which so much subsequent research has been based, for it is largely from the pen of this ardent Trollopian that the unfortunate legend of Trollope's oblivion in the early part of this century has come. When he came to write his *Trollope: A Commentary* (1927),

Sadleir saw himself leading a crusade to re-establish the forgotten novelist with Thackeray, George Eliot and Dickens, adopting in the book what Paul Elmer More blamed as an unnecessarily apologetic tone.[3] More was right. Much was explained about the artist's background and his life, but modest claims were advanced for the books themselves, and Sadleir obviously saw himself as a lonely pioneer for a writer with fairly dubious claims on posterity. Perhaps, too, in an understandable spirit of pride in his own role as an explorer of dangerous literary territory, he made more than he need have done of the alleged disappearance of the novelist. It was not just that Trollope had suffered the inevitable fate of any writer who enjoys fame over many years – a gradual decline, followed by a period of hostility from a new generation – but that by some weird destiny Trollope's reputation was snuffed out overnight with his death. Then came the *Autobiography*, with its damning revelations of his work methods which condemned him to oblivion.

Upon this reading of Trollope's fate Sadleir continued to descant even as late as 1952, when he authorised reissue of the introduction (written in 1923) to the World's Classics edition of the *Autobiography*. Although modern scholars have begun to disprove the attacks on Trollope which were most certainly reactions against the revelations in the *Autobiography*, no one has yet demolished the half-truths surrounding the novelist's reputation which his first biographer perpetuated.

It is difficult to reassess the account of a man's fame once it has got into the history books. Trollope has been particularly unfortunate, in comparison with Dickens or other major nineteenth-century writers, in the accretion of legend after his death. To begin with we must consider the scale of Trollope's immense popular success in his lifetime, next try to get at some reliable information to measure Trollope's fall from popularity and assess the eye-witness accounts on which Sadleir based his conclusions. This will inevitably mean a probing of Sadleir's critical approach which I do without intending to derogate from his magnificent study.

Trollope died a happy, fulfilled and prosperous man. The result of his labours (to *John Caldigate* published in 1879), he regarded as 'comfortable, but not splendid',[4] a mock-modest estimate of no mean fortune for a writer in his day: a sum of £70,000 (with more novels to come), which in our terms represents well over half a million pounds. Fine books were still to be written, and one has only to study reviews of several of these late works, *Ayala's Angel* and *Mr. Scarborough's Family*, for example, to realise that Trollope was still a force to be reckoned with. *The Landleaguers*, also, though unfinished at his death, was received with some warmth, and, as my later discussion of this

little-known book shows, is not insignificant. He undoubtedly maintained a strong hold on his public up to his death, as he undoubtedly
displayed a rare consistency of achievement throughout his career.

So, in speaking of Trollope's decline we must begin to think first of
his extraordinary eminence and popularity. All the obituaries testify
to this. Richard Littledale in the *Academy*, a journal not in the least
sympathetic to middlebrow fiction, called him the most representative
figure of contemporary literature, and one who had achieved the almost
rarer distinction of having become an object of personal goodwill to his
uncounted readers. No one, said Viscount Bryce in the *Nation*, was
so representative of English fiction both by his books and by his personality. The *Month*, reviewing Trollope's *Autobiography*, noted that
scarcely and English novelist during his lifetime had been more
deservedly popular.⁵ It is sometimes forgotten that the creator of Mrs
Proudie succeeded to Dickens' place in public regard and for many came
to represent, more than the creator of Pickwick, the strength, sanity
and worthiness of the British way of life. As gentleman, public figure
and unquestionably self-made man Trollope embodied much that was
central, admirable and thoroughly English.

The *Times* obituary (probably by Mrs Humphry Ward), which
Sadleir thought grudging, was perceptive, praising his remarkable consistency of attainment: 'the wonderful uniformity of quality in each
of his novels', his versatility and range: 'He has enriched our English
fiction with characters destined to survive.'⁶ As a sampling shows, the
tributes were neither eulogy nor half-hearted respect; they ring with
personal sadness and sincerity:

> An instinctive revelation of life which delighted the most fastidious
> critic ... [*Saturday Review*] ... probably no English writer of his day
> has amused Englishmen so much as Mr. Trollope, or has given them
> that amusement from sources so completely free from either morbid
> weaknesses or mischevious and dangerous taints [*Spectator*] ... more
> innocent amusement and entertainment than any other writer of
> this generation [*Dublin Review*] ... wholesome and innocent mental
> pleasure [*Graphic*]. .... his worst work is better than a great many
> people's best [*Macmillan's Magazine*]. .... at his best in kindly
> ridicule of the approved superficialities of life [*Athenaeum*] ...
> capable, indefatigable, and conscientious [*Edinburgh Review*]. ... no
> man ever took more pains to show the way in which the mind
> justified to itself a certain course of action [*Good Words*]. .... he
> was all things, in thought and deed, the high-minded English gentle-
> man he delighted to portray [*Blackwood's Magazine*]. .... he had
> secured a respectable position in the rich English literature of our
> century [*Nation*] ...⁷

Particularly fine tributes were left by Walter Herries Pollock in *Harper's New Monthly Magazine*; R. H. Hutton in the *Spectator*; Alfred Austin, 'Last Reminiscences of Anthony Trollope'; Cuthbert Bede, 'Some Recollections of Mr. Anthony Trollope'; Viscount Bryce in the *Nation*; Henry James in the *Century*; and in the *Saturday Review*.[8] Only this latter seemed to Michael Sadleir to give sufficient estimate of Trollope's achievement. But in fact the obituaries, and more sober assessments of Trollope's contribution to literature in the few years after publication of the *Autobiography*, gave him just approval, sometimes claiming that in certain respects he surpassed Dickens and George Eliot.

Sadleir's *Commentary* made too little of this commendation for the man and his work, while it exaggerated antagonism towards him during the last decade of his career. Over-reacting with the same uncomprehending distaste which had greeted the work of Zola, Crane and Moore, he exalted Trollope against the nineties, which he described as

> an age of intellectual snobbery and economic restlessness . . . which found beauty in abnormality, which despised contentment and quiet friendliness, which – because subversiveness was due to be the *chic* – throve on disgruntlement and judged complacency the deadliest sin.

Where this is not patent nonsense (and Sadleir toned down his hostile references to the Edwardians in the later edition of his *Commentary*), it is certainly not much of a factor in Trollope's decline, and it does invite us to give Sadleir's case closer scrutiny, especially as he goes on to argue that the *Autobiography* brought a sudden end to Trollope's popularity:

> Then it was that affectionate depreciation became malevolent hostility; then did the tempest of reaction against his work and against all the principles and opinions it represented break angrily and overwhelm him.[9]

Nothing so cataclysmic occurred. In the natural course of events changes in taste brought a diminution in sales, as it does to any writer in the generation after his death, and Trollope's identification with the Victorian heyday made him an obvious target, but it is important to take into account much favourable comment and evidence of a still wide audience. It must also be remembered that for a writer of Trollope's immense public in the sixties and seventies a considerable loss of readers would still have left a very sizeable following.

What were the sources on which Sadleir based his gloomy findings? The *Saturday Review* of 20 October 1883, welcoming the *Autobiography* (as did most of the journals), reckoned that its timely appearance would do much to clear the air and remove some of the atmosphere of discredit caused by certain unwise books of late. These books, known to Sadleir, included sketches by forgotten literary hangers-on like J. Hain Friswell and J. C. Heywood.[10] Sadleir took them too seriously, anxious for his subject's reputation and understandably sensitive to adverse criticism in a period when Victorian writers were generally unappreciated. To take up the cudgels for so central a writer of his time inevitably fostered a degree of paranoia.

But it remains a weakness in Sadleir's case that he set any store by nonentities and hacks for his account of Trollope's decline. J. Hain Friswell – 'Frizzle' among his associates – was a gossip and a dabbler in literary life, whose entrée to London society was gained in 1861 by *Footsteps to Fame: A Book to open Other Books*, one of the many self-improvement manuals that followed in the wake of Samuel Smiles *Self-Help* (1859). An ardent social worker, particularly for the Ragged Schools, he also wrote novels, magazine articles and edited the *Censor*. Friswell included Trollope in *Modern Men of Letters Honestly Criticised* (1870), a work of Pecksniffian proportions as its title suggests, the honesty of which, in a pen-portrait of G. A. Sala, landed him in the courts. His comment on Trollope is the invention of a nobody, malicious probably because he had been snubbed.

Sadleir also cites Edmund Yates among those failing to give Trollope due appreciation. One would hardly expect it to be otherwise, since they were implacable enemies. Sadleir's over-reaction to Sir Leslie Ward's 'Spy' cartoon in Vanity Fair further illustrates how evidence can be wrongly weighted. Ward had persuaded James Virtue, the publisher, to let him meet Trollope on neutral ground so that he might study the great man. This was what cut Trollope to the quick when the cartoon appeared, for it seemed a flagrant breach of gentlemanly conduct. He had indeed been spied upon, and wrote an excoriating letter to Virtue, who in turn gave the artist a blowing-up. But the picture – a wild-maned, pot-bellied Victorian squire in baggy pants, gesticulating on the hearth-rug – was neither unjust nor really malicious. Ward could not understand what all the fuss was about and plumed himself on the caricature and text, 'for I had not praised the books with faint dams', he wrote in his memoirs.[11] In the climate of jaded Victorianism, the cartoonists were in their element, but in the case of a public figure lampooned and parodied as Trollope was in the last decade of his career, it is rather a question of his popularity than the reverse.[12]

Sadleir also absorbed greater authorities, such as Lewis Melville and Herbert Paul, whose verdict prefaces this chapter. In 1897 Paul noted that twenty years previously half the novels on a railway station bookstall would have borne Trollope's name: 'Now his books are never seen there, and seldom seen anywhere else'.[13] All the same there were many, like Frederic Harrison, still enjoying Trollope, even though the *Autobiography* had been long out of print. William Tinsley, the publisher, agreed with Paul: 'No one reads or thinks about Mr. Trollope's novels now' (in 1900), and Sadleir quoted him in his introduction to the World's Classics edition of the *Autobiography* in 1923. It was Tinsley who encouraged the story that 'as soon as death stopped his prolific pen, the author and the books died almost at the same time', revealing a tone of condescension that verges on dislike.[14] A more responsible critic, Lewis Melville, claimed in 1906 that Trollope had suffered the worst possible fate for an artist: he had not been abused after his death, he had been ignored.[15] Sadleir certainly knew this essay and indeed quoted Melville's phrase 'a chronicler of small-beer', as a convenient catch-all for the turn-of-the-century attitude to Trollope, ascribing it to Richard Garnett, although it does not appear in Garnett's portrait of the author for the *Dictionary of National Biography*.

In fact the period of neglect lasted at most some dozen years between the eighties and the turn of the century. While Melville and Paul were lamenting Trollope's oblivion, the first Trollope revival was well under way. In 1899 the New Century Library issued the Barsetshire novels, and in 1902 John Lane embarked on their useful 'New Pocket Library' series, which had reached ten volumes by 1907. Lane's eight-volume Barset edition followed in 1928. Blackie & Son published *Barchester Towers* and *Framley Parsonage* between 1903 and 1904. G. Bell & Sons and Everyman's Library were also producing the Barsetshire novels between 1906 and 1908. In America a thirty-volume edition of Trollope was put out by Gebbie of Philadelphia, with a biographical introduction by Harry Thurston Peck (1900). Dodd, Mead and Co. of New York were busy with reissues from 1892, and produced their 'Manor House Series' of the novels in thirteen volumes during the first decade of the twentieth century.

Trollope was even less neglected in the United States than in England, perhaps because Americans continued to be fascinated by his world of dukes and encumbered estates. At any rate there were many Trollopians at work in this period: William Dean Howells in *Harper's Bazaar* and Amelia Edwards in the *Contemporary Review*, Peck in the *Bookman*, New York, and Smalley in *McClure's Magazine*. In the *Atlantic Monthly* of March 1902 Gamaliel Bradford Junior welcomed the Trollope revival, while in the same journal a year later Edward Fuller said that 'once again . . . his name creates a stir of interest'. One article in the *Dial*, Chicago, was called 'The Recoming of Anthony Trollope'.[16] Had he been long away? In England, from Mrs Oliphant's 'Success in Fiction' of 1889 and Frederic Harrison's eloquent plea for the novelist in May 1895, there had been steady reminders by notable critics such as G. S. Street, Leslie Stephen, Viscount Bryce and Stephen Gwynn. F. G. Bettany's 'In Praise of Anthony Trollope' in the *Fortnightly Review* (1905) was followed by T. H. S. Escott's 'Anthony Trollope: An Appreciation and Reminiscence', in which he welcomed Trollope's 'present revival'. This article and an essay in the *Quarterly Review* became the basis of the first biography of the novelist published in 1913.[17] It is quite clear from reprints and articles that the early years of the century saw Trollope's reputation rising rapidly. On 9 September 1909, *The Times Literary Supplement* devoted its entire front page to the novelist. Trollope was back in vogue.

TRADE SECRETS

'To be unknown to Mudie is to be unknown to fame', said the magisterial *Times* on 23 May 1859. This remained broadly true for another twenty-five years in which the great circulating library, founded by Charles Edward Mudie in 1842, continued to dominate English reading habits. Lady Linlithgow, it will be recalled from *The Eustace Diamonds*, cancelled her subscription with Mudie because every time she ordered *Adam Bede* they sent her *The Bandit Chief* (ch. xxxiv). Mudie's had become a centre of literary life by 1860, when its enlarged premises opened in New Oxford Street, and it remained a staple of middle-class leisure throughout the Victorian era.[18] Lucy Dormer of *Ayala's Angel*, which Trollope wrote in 1878, had grown used to Mudie's unnumbered volumes coming into the house 'as much a provision of nature as water, gas, and hot rolls for breakfast' (ch. ii). Such being the influence of Mudie's Select Library, it would be wise to relate the question of Trollope's rise and fall to the activities of this remarkable institution, for Trollope, according to *The Times*, was the Apollo of the circulating library.

In a survey of Mudie's holdings of work by Anthony, Thomas Adolphus and Frances Trollope, Dr Norman Gardiner took sample counts at roughly ten-year intervals between 1848 and 1935.[19] When Trollope is looked at in relation to other writers (see Appendix V) it is clear that his popularity was sustained. Apparently he reached a peak with Mudie's readers as late as 1900, with fifty-two titles listed. At the same time Charlotte Yonge had seventy-one titles, Mrs Oliphant ninety-two and Emma Marshall one hundred. Of course these figures reflect Mudie's custom in its most successful trading period, just as the fall in 1935 occurs over the whole range of stock, and points to the failure of the business. However, by examining holdings in twenty novelists from the recognised classics to the current popular best-seller I have tried to compensate for these factors. Another aspect to be borne in mind is the changing nature of the Mudie clientele, from the affluent middle class in Trollope's heyday to a far more heterogeneous group at the end of the century, who may have been inclined to abandon Trollope for the romances of Jules Verne, Baroness Orczy, Edgar Wallace and Marie Corelli. It is impossible to know which books were regularly in demand, but such shrewd businessmen as the Mudies would not have allowed unread books to take up valuable shelf-space. Arthur Mudie studied his market carefully. Popular authors like Julia Kavanagh, Anne Manning and Elizabeth Sewell had their day and were quickly dropped once their appeal had diminished. Trollope, on the other hand, is always prominent in the catalogues.

Such evidence leads me to believe that Trollope's eclipse was nothing like so great as has been suggested. Trollope indeed remained a sound commercial investment for Mudie for at least seventy years. Acknowledged classics, such as Scott and Dickens, among the twenty writers I examined, reveal little variation in holdings of their works from year to year. Lytton too, even in the 1930s, is stable, and so is Disraeli. Compared with Reade, Whyte Melville or Lever in terms of 'highs' and 'lows' in the fiction catalogues, Trollope stands out for consistent popularity over a very long time. Over the period from the late 1850s to 1935, Marryat (who belongs to an earlier era) fares badly: he is represented in 1935 by only 10 per cent of his best year's holdings. Lever does better with 20 per cent. Others register as follows: Whyte Melville, 25 per cent; Charles Reade, 33⅓ per cent; Collins, over 50 per cent. Trollope comes below Collins with about 40 per cent, and this is a remarkable level considering his enormous output.

While I cannot claim this kind of enquiry produces definitive answers to the question of Trollope's steady appeal, it certainly urges moderate views on his disappearance. It is significant that such an index of middle-class reading habits as Mudie's shows Trollope's staying power amid each decade's new favourites. The queens of the circulating library reign very briefly by comparison. Mrs Oliphant, for example, drops from over ninety titles in 1900 to four in 1935, and Miss Braddon, from seventy-five in 1920 to six in 1935. Rhoda Broughton and Ouida, writers of more sensational stamp, fall even more dramatically from public view. Mrs Henry Wood, on the other hand, seems to have lasted well, as did the writers of historical romance, G. P. R. James and Ainsworth. Without being too dogmatic about these findings, we can assume that Trollope was being steadily read during those years when he is alleged to have been forgotten. Just as at each decade of his so-called oblivion there have been readers like Harry Furniss, who told Tennyson of rediscovering Trollope in the mid-1880s, or Amelia Edwards in the mid-1890s declaring that Trollope deserved a place with Dickens and Thackeray, so his books held their place in Mudie's, outlasting each new star, from Katharine Macquoid to Conan Doyle, from Sabatini to P. G. Wodehouse.[20]

Contrary to Sadleir's observation, the *Autobiography* at its publication met with almost universal approval and long continued to be well regarded. It was certainly not the lay public to whom Trollope's 'aggressive horse sense . . . on life and book-making' was offensive.[21] It may be a mistake, as Gosse drily put it, to disclose the trade secrets in too matter-of-fact a way,[22] but on the other hand curiosity about artists' lives is insatiable, particularly in the case of so reticent a figure as Anthony Trollope. When the *Autobiography* appeared Trollope was once more in the news, and to judge from the number of reviews it seems likely that interest in the novels increased.

If the public was not shocked by the *Autiobiography*, neither was the tightly-knit circle of artists, writers and critics who knew him, for he had made no secret of his attitudes and methods. Swinburne may have shuddered, but even he could not prevent a note of admiration creeping into his reference to the *Autobiography*: 'singularly candid and interesting as well as amusing estimate of his own and other men's work'. He was impressed by the fiction, especially the creation of Crawley, the Grantlys and the Proudies – 'sketched with such lightness of hand, such an attractive ease and simplicity of manner, that the obtrusive and persistent vehemence of presentation which distinguished the style and method of Charles Reade appears by comparison inartistic and ineffectual'.[23] Trollope after death had his praises sung in unexpected quarters.

Yet so far as critical response to the *Autobiography* went Sadleir insisted that it administered the *coup de grâce* to his dying reputation. This does not seem to have been the case. Consider his disclosures about writing by the clock which were supposed to have aroused such a storm. The *Graphic* of 20 October 1883 made disapproving growls at the notion that novel-writing was like boot-making; just because Trollope was able to do it did not mean that everybody else could. *Macmillan's Magazine* (the writer was probably Frederic Harrison) objected to the needless crudity of phrase in such off-hand remarks as Trollope taking his wares to another shop, but beyond that was highly appreciative:

> Many a scribe will denounce Trollope's practice as base and mechanical, whose own best writing is a long way below Trollope's worst. The truth is that some of the greatest writers on the gravest subjects, men of the rank of Gibbon and Macaulay, have been as regular and as punctual in their work as Trollope was.

The *Atlantic Monthly* scorned the doctrine of awaiting inspiration and descanted on Trollope's indefatigable industry:

Think of that, unhappy litterateurs, who wait for the mood and weave a Penelope's web, tearing up every night the unsatisfactory pages of the day!

Even the *Westminster Review* approved Trollope's workmanlike attitude, suggesting that he occupied a position midway between Johnson and Macaulay. No fault was to be found in his business-like manner, claimed the *Edinburgh Review*, merely in the enticement he offered young men in making it all sound so easy.

By and large, then, the journals did not object to his work methods, and begged the question as to whether more revision might have produced better books. Only a whisper in *The Times* suggested this line of criticism, to be followed by the *Graphic* a week later, grumbling that he would have been fairer to his publishers if he had brought more critical judgement to his work before selling it. On the whole the critics were prepared to accept Trollope's contention that he worked best at speed and that more fallow periods would not have improved his novels. The *Saturday Review*, for example, decided, rightly in my view, that he had evolved the best technique for his own genius: 'He worked, as he played, with his whole heart'. It was by no means a property of genius, the *Graphic* acknowledged, to be erratic and unbusinesslike.[24]

Indeed there was not much to surprise in Trollope's work habits, which many writers practised, not quite with the same zeal perhaps, but in the same spirit. Only Trollope had the courage to stand up and say it out loud. Sir Walter Scott had worked by the clock, so had Dickens, Lytton and other Victorians, and in cultivating regular habits of writing Trollope followed classical precedents. *Nulla dies sine linea* was just as much Trollope's motto as Zola's and Zola could throw down his pen in mid-sentence and resume without faltering next day. Trollope's own capacity for 'quick roasting' had produced *Framley Parsonage* concurrently with *Castle Richmond* in 1860, the year which also began his association with the *Cornhill Magazine*. Certainly careful reading of the *Autobiography* makes it hard to believe that his statements on book-making were unexpected or misunderstood.

What Trollope disclosed about writing for money and social position was also unlikely to have caused much stir. All his life he had been a commercial writer, in the best sense of the term, and his activities on behalf of copyright for authors and the Royal Literary Fund, his shrewd bargaining with publishers, testified to his business sense. His 'capacity for grinding', as he called it in his Thackeray monograph, was equally well known, and frequently mentioned in reviews of the *Auto-biography*. It was a matter of physical strength, the inheritance of his mother's 'high spirits and good health'.[25]

Lastly there is the matter of Trollope's deliberate removal of the draperies of art, inspiration and genius, to expose the sullen craft itself. 'I have never fancied myself to be a genius' is the refrain of the *Autobiography*, as he talks bluntly about taking the wares to market. Some of the reasons for this I have already suggested in speaking about his life, and later on I shall examine his views in more detail to show what he was trying to achieve; the question here is simply the effect of what he said on his public and critics.

The well known analogy between his work and shoe-making which was current in Trollope circles for many years first occurs in a letter in April 1860, and should put the matter in perspective:

> I believe that the profession requires much less of what is extraordinary either in genius or knowledge than most outsiders presume to be necessary. But it requires that which all other professions require, – but which outsiders do not in general presume to be necessary in the profession of literature, – considerable training and much hard grinding industry – My belief of book writing is much the same as my belief as to shoemaking. (86, p. 57)

The metaphor had a whimsical appeal for him, and henceforth he was to be heard roaring it across the dinner table on numerous occasions. James Russell Lowell heard Trollope, in September 1861, thundering that he went to work on a novel 'just like a shoemaker on a shoe, only taking care to make honest stitches'. Asked on another occasion if he believed in inherited genius, Trollope told Cuthbert Bede 'I believe much more in cobbler's wax'. In slightly different form the sentiment reached Donald Macleod: ' "Genius," he once said to us, "is but another name for the length of time a man can sit" '.[26] At last it reached Frederic Harrison's ears at a George Eliot soirée in the way I have described (p. 19). Certainly it is one of those tales no biographer can do without, but I imagine Trollope's antic disposition was too well known in company for it to have had the shock value early biographers assumed. He was familiar by then in his role of rough country squire who had strayed into writing almost by accident. It was as much a badge of honest Trollope as George Orwell's conscious Woodbine.

Harrison, Cuthbert Bede, Viscount Morley, T. H. S. Escott, James Payn and a host of others, all part of Trollope's society, and for many years after his death influential in the world of letters, must have helped to perpetuate a true and faithful report of the man in the nineties and at the turn of the century. Morley, in fact, insisted in his *Reminiscences* on the respect due towards the industry practised by Trollope and his contemporaries.

The myth that Trollope's fame was extinguished by his *Autobiography* is as much a literary mare's nest as that Keats was snuffed out by a review. Undoubtedly some agreed with Herbert Paul in 1902

that Trollope was dead beyond all hope of resurrection, but in the same
year Stephen delivered a truer verdict when he called it merely a state
of 'suspended vitality', for within a few years new editions were being
prepared and Trollope's name was again prominent in literary journals.[27]

The first Trollope revival began in the early years of the century,
slowly gathering momentum in the First World War and reaching a
peak in the late twenties and thirties, when there were many reprints
of his work, such as the monumental series of World's Classics and
the Oxford edition. Trollope's nostalgic appeal was now uppermost and
the First World War made it especially potent. One reader observed
in these deathless lines:

> Good chronicler of Barset, weaver of genial yarns,
> Homely and unaffected as the verse of the Dorset Barnes,
> When the outlook is depressing, when journals bleat and scare,
> I turn to your kindly pages and find oblivion there.[28]

To his buoyancy and humour there was now the added charm of a
way of life that offered peace, stability and order. Major Trollope revivals have in fact coincided with the two world wars. The Archbishop
of York in 1945 is said to have nominated Trollope for first place in war-
time British reading popularity, and V. S. Pritchett has explained why:

> Since 1918 he has become one of the great air raid shelters. He
> presides over the eternal Munich of the human heart and Barset-
> shire has become one of the great Never-Never Lands of our time.
> It has been the normal country to which we all aspire.[29]

Thus Trollope criticism until very recently has tended to concentrate on
the major works, emphasising their evocation of the past and Trollope's
fidelity to a vanished era. This is noticeable among most of the tributes
of such between-wars critics as Quiller-Couch, Paul Elmer More, Hugh
Walpole, Lord David Cecil, and was eloquently phrased by Mgr Ronald
Knox:

> Or do we regret the passing of something that was not mere shadow,
> a world we were not born into, yet one that coloured for us the
> outlook of boyhood, when Archdeacons really preserved and drank
> port and quoted Horace, and country doctors dared to roll their own
> pills, and Lady Luftons brooded like a visible Providence over the
> countryside . . . Trollope's rose-hued world, like a cloistral port . . .
> is all the better for keeping; Barchester, caught once for all by the
> artist's brush in a moment of mellow sunset, lives on, uncontaminated
> by change, in that attitude.[30]

It is a potent magic still – though by no means the only one

ELBOW-GREASE OF THE MIND

It has been my argument that Trollope held his public to the end of his life. As late as 1879 *Blackwood's Magazine* could claim his name was a household word.[31] Yet the legend of his eclipse has persisted in a diffuse and lingering condescension towards him. It is in this sense, perhaps, that his candour in the *Autobiography*, in which he so plumed himself on cutting through humbug, has done his name a disservice. The view of book-making that Trollope proposed with mischievous frankness was intended to debunk elevated attitudes to art, and to stress that the seat of inspiration rested on painstaking labour at the desk. This has distracted attention from the far more important point: that he regarded himself as a professional, and that he is, perhaps of all English novelists, the one who set a standard for professionalism based upon a high degree of responsibility to his public.

Oddly enough, while he maintained a severely down-to-earth approach to his day-labour, and delighted in the most prosaic analogies he could find (the course of a story is seen in Chapter viii of the *Autobiography* in terms of a rustic driving wayward pigs to market), he indulged in the most outrageous, romantic drivel to describe his creative process. An article for *Good Words* in September 1879, entitled 'A Walk in A Wood', painted a picture of Dionysian rapture that is as far from the truth as his cobbling analogy. What he failed to make clear was that his work fell into two parts: advance preparation and actual execution. We have already seen how day-dreaming in childhood grew into the story-telling habit, a long gestation of characters and incidents – particularly characters – described in the *Autobiography*:

> I have wandered alone among the rocks and woods, crying at their grief, laughing at their absurdities, and thoroughly enjoying their joy. I have been impregnated with my own creations till it has been my only excitement to sit with the pen in my hand, and drive my team before me at as quick a pace as I could make them travel. (ch. x)

Similarly, of the Pallisers he remarks 'So much of my inner life was passed in their company' (ch. xvii). It is one more example of the dedication demanded of the novelist, the ceaseless observation and reflection, 'which work should be going on not only when he is at his desk, but in all his walks abroad, in all his movements through the world, in all his intercourse with his fellow-creatures' (ch. xii). It made him cross that anyone should think it came easily.

Plotting, which Trollope professed to find rather tedious, was less the inspiration of three hours at the desk than he implies. He was aware, when with some trepidation, he contracted with Smith & Elder to serialise *Framley Parsonage* before he had embarked upon – let alone finished – the book, that 'an artist should keep in his hand the power of fitting the beginning of his work to the end' (ch. viii), which implies a general grasp of the work before writing. And his care for plotting as part of advance preparation is borne out also by his criticism of Kate Field's novel:

The end of your story should have been the beginning.[32]

Trollope did not care, however, for the meticulous plotting of his friend Wilkie Collins, and his reasons for this are plain when one considers the primacy of characters in his imagination. His creative process seems to have worked best when he felt the relative freedom of a loose structure of story, allowing his characters to exert prompt and original pressures on his mind and to offer their own extempore direction to the plot. A revealing example of this occurs in Amelia Edwards' recollection of a conversation with the novelist:

'Why *did* you let Crosbie jilt Lily Dale?' I asked Anthony Trollope one day.
'Why did I "let" him?' he repeated. 'How could I help it? He *would* do it, confound him!'
This was not said in jest. It was earnest.[33]

With even more alacrity (and perhaps less sophisticated intention) than Thackeray, he plays up the convention of his characters as real people. But the identities of the characters do indeed seem to have been so strongly felt by him that it is not too fanciful to suggest that writing became for Trollope a species of transcription: at his desk he was like the medium hearing the spirits and recording their dictation. This is certainly one way of explaining the ambiguous comment in the *Autobiography*, that he never found himself thinking much about his work till he had to do it (ch. ix). If he functioned in a kind of mediumistic trance it is quite easy to accept the story of his anger towards his amanuensis, Florence Bland, on the occasions when she had the temerity to interrupt the flow by suggestions of her own.[34] The dialogue constantly going on in his mind produced a congruence of story-line, narrative and character development quite instinctive and largely unperceived by the author. It is impossible to know how the process worked; Trollope himself was reluctant to tamper with the bias of his mind, or to examine too closely how the thing was done: 'I am not sure that I have as yet got the rules quite settled in my own mind.'[35]

On the necessity for long preparation, ceaseless reflection and hard work, however, he was absolutely certain. His monograph on Thackeray reveals his own philosophy of literary art: 'Forethought is the elbow-grease which a novelist, – or poet, or dramatist, – requires', he declares, in one of his unhappiest metaphors. 'It is not only his plot that has to be turned and re-turned in his mind, not his plot chiefly, but he has to make himself sure of his situations, of his characters, of his effects, so that when the time comes for hitting the nail he may know where to hit it on the head, – . . . To think of a story is much harder work than to write it.' The writing he found comparatively easy: 'but to think it over as you lie in bed, or walk about, or sit cosily over your fire, to turn it all in your thoughts, and make the things fit, – that requires elbow-grease of the mind.'[36] Behind these awkward phrases lies the commitment of the writer, a figure we seldom see in the Trollope of the *Autobiography*; the artist comes out of hiding for a moment, and we catch a glimpse of the true processes of imaginative literature and the cost of the creative struggle. Escott, whose contemporary evidence is vital, declared: 'Few writers, perhaps, have taken themselves more in earnest than Trollope'.[37] It was Escott, too, who recalled the novelist's confession about life being chronically saddened by recurrent moods of indefinable gloom and despondency, part of the normal artist's birthright.[38] One does not wish to make too much of this side of the novelist, but here and there enough details can be found to balance the evidence of his role as popular novelist.

The point is that Trollope performed the intensive labour of his novels in constant reflection and dialogue with himself; it was the less taxing part to come to his desk. All he needed to do, as Ernest Baker put it, was to make his report.[39] A close friend, Sir Frederick Pollock, correcting proofs of *The Golden Lion of Granpère*, found he had little to do, so smoothly and efficiently the process of the Trollope production line worked. The words, said Pollock, seemed to have flowed from him like clear liquor from a tap.[40]

Only prodigious will, industry and training equipped Trollope for such an assembly line approach, and this he describes proudly in the *Autobiography*:

When I have commenced a new book, I have always prepared a diary, divided into weeks, and carried on for the period which I have allowed myself for the completion of the work . . . I have allotted myself so many pages a week. The average number has been about 40. It has been placed as low as 20, and has risen to 112. And as a page is an ambiguous term, my page has been made to contain 250 words; and as words, if not watched, will have a tendency to straggle, I have had every word counted as I went . . . It was my practice to be at my table every morning at 5.30 a.m.; and it was also my practice to allow myself no mercy . . . three hours a day will produce as much as a man ought to write . . . It had at this time become my custom, –

and it still is my custom, though of late I have become a little lenient to myself, – to write with my watch before me, and to require from myself 250 words every quarter of an hour. I have found that the 250 words have been forthcoming as regularly as my watch went. (ch. vii)

Such determination may have its chilling side, but it gave him a control over his creative energies few men have equalled. His long practised day-dreaming, the gestation of his stories at all hours, the fluency acquired as a civil servant, all combined to make sustained and rapid composition his mode. Half-an-hour's re-reading of the previous day's work, and weighing with his inner ear, was the vital prelude to the daily stint: warming-up of the machine so that the assembly line could work at maximum efficiency and economy.

This mechanical aspect of Trollope's methods exposed him most of all to controversy. Might the work have been better had there been less of it or if more time had been allotted to second thoughts or revision? Trollope was aware of his vulnerability on these points. 'I have never fancied myself a genius' is one way of meeting the attack, but it will not do. Certainly he was strongly opposed to revision; correction and proof-reading he found an unwelcome chore, although, as R. W. Chapman has shown, he buckled to the task more often than has been generally thought.[41] It was a question of compromise as always:

Il faut vivre. But with those of us who are highminded there is an over-riding object, one more first even than the first, – that of doing our duty; which comprehends such excellence in his work as the workman may attain, though it be attained at the expense of profit . . .
Shakespeare did his work for money, quite unconscious of its abnormal excellence. Macaulay & Carlyle have been very careful to write for money, & Tennyson is as careful to do so as any one.[42]

Or consider his comment in the Thackeray monograph about writing a novel: 'a man should write . . . because it is in him to write – the motive power being altogether in himself and coming from his desire to express himself.'[43] This is a very different proposition from cobbler's wax and taking wares to the market. It recognises that while any man may learn to mend shoes tolerably well, the writer possesses special powers.

His magazine work confirms his high sense of seriousness and duty towards letters, particularly his editing of St. *Paul's Magazine* from October 1867 until July 1870. He found being an editor thoroughly uncongenial, his very scrupulousness the biggest stumbling block. Frederic Harrison records that he read everything that came in for the magazine, and Cuthbert Bede notes: 'it was heartbreaking work to him to return a manuscript to its author, especially when the writer was one of the fairer sex, with the stereotyped "declined with thanks".'[44] For a little over three-and-a-half years Trollope endured as Thackeray had done those thorns in the editorial cushion, before he plucked up the courage to tell his publisher, James Virtue, he could no longer continue.

Trollope's attitude towards criticism and the practices of critics and fellow authors is even clearer proof of the way in which the pose of carelessness masked his true character. Towards criticism of his work in general he preserved an air of equanimity if not indifference, replying to unexpected praise with dignified reserve. 'I am always doubtful about my work,' he wrote to Charles Kent after a favourable review in the *Sun* (472, p. 278). But though he had little opinion of contemporary reviewing (witness his somewhat disenchanted estimate in the *Autobiography*, ch. xiv), he cared more than he wished to. He wrote to Anna Steele in June 1870: 'I fancy, that I am too anxious, like other authors, to see what others say about me. But now, as I know it to be hard [he had not seen a harsh piece on *The Vicar of Bullhampton* in *The Times*] I will pass it by' (464, p. 273). As usual his common sense was at command and shortly before his death he wrote to Charles Mackay: 'I fancy that we authors owe more to critics than any injustice we receive from them. I am sure that if any critic wanted to spite us, he could better do it by holding his tongue than by speaking evil of us' (827, p. 457).

As to relationships with critics Trollope was almost ridiculously high-minded, and he grew steadily more sceptical of praise from anyone likely to be known to him personally. He wrote to Alfred Austin of one eulogistic article: 'I don't like such notices, particularly when they are written by friends. I would much rather be left to the mercies of the real critics' (913, p. 496). An entire chapter of the *Autobiography* devoted to Criticism shows how seriously Trollope felt 'that there should be no intercourse at all between an author and his critic'. Such zeal led him into unfairness towards E. S. Dallas for having accepted a bound manuscript from Dickens after his review of *Our Mutual Friend*, but it also reveals once more the private Trollope behind the façade of commercially-minded scribbler.

Yet the question remains: how is this evident devotion to his art to be reconciled with his assembly line fiction? That he himself felt troubled by his compromises is clear enough. There is embarrassment as well as pride in his reply to the curious dinner guest who asked him how many books he had writen: 'I do know, but I shall not tell you'.[45] And a certain irony may be found in Cuthbert Bede's story of finding a picture of Trollope in a Birmingham shop accidentally labelled Martin Tupper. He showed it to Trollope, who laughed heartily – but possibly with inward ruefulness.[46] Throughout the *Autobiography* the gentleman in Paternoster Row who spawned three novels a year is a recurrent spectre. Again, there is Trollope's recognition of having touched the heights at certain points in his career, the natural concomitant being an awareness of how many times he had not. *The Last Chronicle of Barset*, generally acknowledged as his masterpiece (and judged so by himself) is in one respect a reproach by Trollope the artist directed at Trollope the mere craftsman.

Can we seriously accept his own defence in the *Autobiography* of his ceaseless industry, his failure to revise extensively, his deliberate concessions to the market place?

It is not on my conscience that I have ever scamped my work. My novels, whether good or bad, have been as good as I could make them. Had I taken three months of idleness between each they would have been no better. Feeling convinced of that, I finished *Doctor Thorne* on one day, and began *The Bertrams* on the next. (ch. vii)

This is begging the question. The books are as good as the time he allowed could make them; it is not the rapidity of composition one would challenge, especially in the light of the advance thought that went into them, but the failure to work on their improvement once they were done. Yet with all their imperfections the novels of Anthony Trollope are not greatly wanting. Surely some claim to genius exists for such outstanding consistency in forty-seven novels, only a handful of which are really poor and at least half a dozen are first class?

4 The Rocks and Valleys

Twice in his *Autobiography* Trollope insists there must be love in a novel. And when he tried to do without it in *Miss Mackenzie* the story bogged down so badly he had to give his rather dull spinster an elderly wooer, who brought her marriage and a ready-made family of nine children. Recalling this attempt to break from the staple of his fiction, Trollope showed his usual understanding of what the public wanted: 'It is admitted that a novel can hardly be made interesting or successful without love. Some few might be named but even in those the attempt breaks down, and the softness of love is found to be necessary to complete the story.' What else, he wondered, could a writer do but write of love, since 'every one feels it, has felt it, or expects to feel it, – or else rejects it with an eagerness which still perpetuates the interest' (ch. xii). So from his first novel, which was a tragic love story of seduction, murder and retribution, to his last, which, unfinished, left his lovers for ever fixed in mad pursuit and struggle to escape, like the figures of Keats' grecian urn, Trollope is concerned with love.

For the most part it is the youthful, passionate, romantic kind, which in thousands of volumes issued from that evergreen tree of diabolical knowledge – the circulating library. Trollope made haste to meet any charge of being a corrupter of youth, claiming with a trace of podsnappery that 'no girl has risen from the reading of my pages less modest than she was before'.[1] Critics have attacked Trollope's love stories on altogether different grounds: some interpret these remarks as a grudging acceptance of the novel's traditional subject matter, indicating that he would rather be getting on with something else; others see his submission to the public's voracious appetite for romance as a cynical evasion of artistic responsibilities. Thus post-Sadleirian criticism, intent on making a case for a more profound and serious artist, has tended to disparage what Bradford Booth called 'powderpuff romance' to a hackneyed formula of wedding bells and they-lived-happily-ever-after.[2] It comes as something of a shock reading Booth to find this ardent Trollopian alluding to the 'tragedy' of Trollope's 'capitulation to the stereotype of romantic love', regretting that he did not dare violate this unfortunate Victorian tradition, and even hinting that his preoccupation with juvenile romance is insincere. Cockshut disposes of the subject briefly, claiming that the best love scenes occur when they are there for something else. According to J. H. Wildman, love in a rose-coloured landscape characterises Trollope as the supreme writer of escapist fiction.[3]

To my mind such views are wide of the mark: Trollope is neither timid nor conventional when he deals with love. Of all his contemporaries he is the most penetrating and amusing observer of the feelings and moods of lovers, charting the strategies of Victorian courtship with a sensible, ironic and charitable narrative, remarkably free from the sentimentality which mars so much fiction of the period. His treatment of young love must be seen in all its range and depth as an integral part of his total achievement.

The gravamen of the charge against Trollope is that he capitulated to stereotypes of the romantic novel then in vogue. I should like to consider this point first, before proceeding to wider issues concerning Trollope's practice, on which I shall base an appreciation of his general ethical attitude to fiction. Clearly Trollope stands high above the level of popular romance writers such as Mrs Oliphant, Mrs Craik, Julia Kavanagh, Anne Manning, for his romances merely take the impedimenta of the genre in order to study the chemistry of personality and the vagaries of human behaviour under the influence of love. Unfortunately, what critics have found most objectionable in Trollope's romance is his use of legacies, lost wills and timely deaths, which appear to fob the reader off with a facile resolution to a human problem raised elsewhere in the novel. There *are* cases of such evasion, but they are not numerous and for this sound reason: that in most of the stories Trollope sustains a mood of optimism and serenity with such delicacy and tenderness that the illusion is not dispelled by the *deus ex machina* or the stock ending which promises wedding bells and a lifetime's felicity. They lived happily ever after is the logical and expected ending to a Trollope novel.

Even within his acceptance of the stereotype there is remarkable variety. Consider that cliché of romance, love at first sight, one of the elements in Trollope's presentation about which critics disagree. While J. Hillis Miller suggests that Trollope stresses 'what is spontaneous, irrational, and uncontrollable about falling in love', A. O. J. Cockshut maintains that love at first sight seemed 'too stagey and improbable' to Trollope.[4] As usual he evades definition. Many of his heroes and heroines do change eyes on the instant. Katie Woodward lost her heart the moment Charley pulled her from the river, and so did Lucy Robarts as soon as she set eyes on Lord Lufton. A peculiar instance of love as *coup de foudre* occurs in *Rachel Ray*, where it is presented in the sky as a cloud shaped like a human arm. In an unusually symbolic passage,

Trollope describes a beautiful Devon sunset, and the lovers, Rachel and Luke Rowan, walking home when they see the omen. Suddenly poetry and enchantment open their eyes to a world of romance and beauty, lifting them out of the sin-conscious world of Rachel's evangelical sister and the real-life problems Luke has persuading Mr Tappitt, of Bungall and Tappitt Brewery, to improve the quality of the beer. On the other hand, Fanny Clavering cannot at first stand the sight of the curate whose dogged persistence finally wins her, while Ayala Dormer's remark at the end of the story that she had loved Jonathan all along is merely an excuse for her earlier folly. She learns to love after having been a silly girl for nine-tenths of the story. 'Trollope is strangely contradictory when he deals with courtship', says Cockshut,[5] for reasons I hope to clarify.

If the stock machinery of romance damages Trollope's fiction to a lesser extent than criticism has led us to suppose, it is for a subtler reason, which has to do with two levels on which the novelist operates, balancing the romantic and the actual, and mediating between them so skilfully that significant issues worthy of our reflection are unaffected by the deployment of romantic paraphernalia. Morever, from his vantage point on middle ground Trollope secures enormous advantages for ironic comment on his material, and a warm and relaxed relationship between writer and reader that makes us say with Fitzgerald 'O, for some more brave Trollope!'[6]

Here is Trollope poking fun at his own use of the *deus ex machina*:

> But then in novels the most indifferent hero comes out right at last. Some god comes out of a theatrical cloud and leaves the poor devil ten thousand a-year and a title. He isn't much of a hero when he does go right under such inducements, but he suffices for the plot, and everything is rose-coloured.[7]

In *The Three Clerks* there is a novel within a novel. Charley Tudor is writing a romance, 'Crinoline and Macassar', which provides plenty of opportunities for satirising popular romance; but for the purposes of his own story, Charley's plot comments ironically on the actual predicament of Harry Norman, whose best friend, Alaric Tudor, is about to cut him out with Gertrude Woodward:

> 'Oh! two rival knights in love with the same lady, of course,' and Harry gave a gentle sigh as he thought of his own still unhealed grief.[8]

It may be thought that in undercutting the devices of his own plot-making Trollope is playing a dangerous game; certainly to Jamesian critics he is violating canons of artistic decorum. It is like authorial intrusions and confidences to the reader, or the breaking of the spell

James found so damaging in Thackeray, but in Trollope's case the charm remains intact. This is mainly because the genial ghost of Elizabeth Bowen's charming radio piece is for ever beside our chair, nudging us in the ribs over a particularly interesting point, inviting us to commiserate with him over the fate of one of his characters. Few writers are so palpably present in their work, or communicate so much of their involvement in it.[9] This is probably why we accept his popping in and out of the story, and the privilege he assumes of being able to satirise conventions he uses to the full.

There is further justification for authorial presence in so far as his irony towards romance as a genre embraces the extravagance and enchantment of young love. When we read the last chapter of *Framley Parsonage* – 'How they were all married, had two children, and lived happy ever after' – we are agreeably reminded of a land of make-believe, but we do not feel betrayed or let down; indeed we are made very conscious of the ironies of the chapter title as they apply to Griselda Grantly's marriage to Lord Dumbello.

Ayala's Angel, a late novel, is typical of the way Trollope both uses and satirises the romance conventions in order to indicate mature attitudes towards love and courtship. Kensington Gardens, Rome, the Tyrol, and the lake scenery of Inverness establish the mood of serenity and romantic expectation for a Beauty and the Beast fable in which the Beauty (Ayala) at first rejects the Beast (Jonathan Stubbs) who turns into the Prince. One thinks of *Ayala's Angel* as of late Shakespearean romance; the comedy has an autumnal ripeness. Indeed Trollope himself seems conscious of Shakespeare in hyperboles and romantic entanglements. Tom Tringle becomes in Ayala's mind the figure of Bottom with his ass's head. Lovers are pursued through mazes and thickets of misunderstanding reminiscent of a wood near Athens or Prospero's island, are paired as in Shakespeare, and perform an elaborate set of dances to the themes of true love versus egotism, passion and prudence, which are counterpointed by minor themes of youth and age, art versus life. In part the nostalgia derives from Trollope's consciousness of growing old. This is the last time he indulged his passion for writing about horsemanship. Indeed, the hunt in ch. xxiv, 'Rufford Cross-Roads', too long to quote, is as fine an addition to the fiction of the chase as any he ever wrote, a miniature of hunting lore, exact placing of lanes, gates and general terrain, a glimpse of the fanaticism and folly of the huntsmen, which none the less keeps the heroines in the centre of the picture. The scene of Nina and Ayala jumping Cranbury Brook together stays in the mind like an old hunting print.

While the anti-romantic elements centre on Ayala's refusal to acknowledge the ugly, red-haired and bristly Stubbs as her 'angel of light', some of the best comedy arises from the sub-plots, first Tom

Tringle's mooning after Ayala and going to the dogs in pure Wodehouse style, getting drunk with Faddle his pal at his club in Piccadilly,
assaulting a policeman, and issuing a challenge to his rival with telling
hyperbole: 'Tom was prepared to go anywhere for blood' (ch. xxx).
Then there is a delightful parody of the romantic novel in Gertrude
Tringle's pursuit of Frank Houston, a character of Jamesian ambiguity,
whose true love for Imogene Docimer is in conflict with his wish to
marry money. Partly because her father sees Frank as an opportunist,
but mostly because she regards real love as intrigue and mystery,
Gertrude proposes an elopement in an elaborate charade of secrets and
notes to which Frank, the cynic, remains wilfully obtuse. Knowing
she is watched on all sides Gertrude writes to her lover at his London
club, suggesting a tryst outside the family boundaries half-an-hour
after dusk. To baffle spies she uses no names and advises him to reply
to 'O.P.Q., Post Office, Hastings'. This Frank avoids by writing to her
at home and suggesting a meeting at her house in the afternoon.
Romance is punctured at every turn: 'Fortune' is 'altogether unfavour-
able to those perils for which her soul was longing.' When she and
Frank finally meet, poor Tom hovers like a ghost in the background, a
silent comment on unrequited love, living out the drama Gertrude is
proposing. Much of the flavour of this encounter is lost by quotation in
brief, but an extract does illustrate the judicious placing of Frank's
irritatingly bland comments which produce rising hysteria in Gertrude
as she tries to force him to elope:

'Have you ever been at Ostend?' she asked, suddenly.
'Ostend. Oh, yes. There was a man there who used to cheat
horribly at écarté. He did me out of nearly a hundred pounds one
night.'
'But there's a clergyman there, I'm told.'
'I don't think this man was in orders. But he might have been.
Parsons come out in so many shapes! This man called himself a
count. It was seven years ago.'
'I am speaking of today.'
'I've not been there since.'
'Would you like to go there, – with me?'
'It isn't a nice sort of place, I should say, for a honeymoon. But
you shall choose. When we are married you shall go where you like.'
'To be married!' she exclaimed.
'Married at Ostend! Would your mother like that?'
'Mother! Oh, dear!'
'I'll be shot if I know what you're after, Gertrude. If you've got
anything to say you'd better speak out. I want to go up to the house
now.' (ch. xxxvii)

Oscar Wilde scarcely does better. For all its concessions to his Mudie readership Trollope's novel leaves a profound impression of the healthy high spirits of true love and points to a growing-up in the characters. Ayala gets over her childishness. Frank Houston overcomes self-interest. The gentle mockery of the Tringle children proves the proposition 'That men have died from time to time, and worms have eaten them, but not for love', which suggests a touchstone for fruitful living.

TICKLISH GROUND

The first essential to an appreciation of Trollope's stories of young love is to understand his sense of responsibility towards his audience, particularly his young audience: 'the one thing of most importance to them is whether they shall love rightly or wrongly'.[10] Trollope and his contemporaries faced almost as much criticism as their predecessors in the eighteenth century on the grounds of the novel's immorality. To the whips of Victorian nonconformist wrath were added the scorns of Carlyle's sarcasm, against whose fulminations much of Trollope's defence of novel-reading is directed. Like his fellow-writers Trollope was burdened by the oppressive morality of the age, and perplexed at times by the effect this had on his freedom as an artist, and though much of what he thought about the novelist's responsibilities was trite, conventional and even contradictory, it is worth examining briefly its relation to young love in his fiction. Our main sources of information are the *Autobiography*, a lecture he gave at Edinburgh in 1870 called 'On English Prose Fiction as a Rational Amusement', an article in *Nineteenth Century* for January 1879, called 'Novel Reading', and his monograph on Thackeray published in 1880.

If his defence of the novel was timid, it was partly due to his limitations as a theorist as well as his sense of his own vulnerability as a writer of popular love stories. This goes far to explain his poor argument and its ambiguities. Recognising the novel as the popular art form of the century, he set himself to answer the question whether this coveted amusement was prone to do good or evil. It worried him that novels 'gave out a constant flow of teaching which fills the mind of all readers with continual thoughts of love'. He regretted that they fed the imagination 'too often in lieu of poetry', which he judged superior to prose for its sublimity and timelessness. 'The novelist', he said at Edinburgh, 'is bound to adapt himself to his age; and is almost forced to be ephemeral.' The fiction writer was seldom able 'to soar above the ordinary actions and ordinary language of life'.[11] Yet he insisted that, in purpose at least, the novelist stood on the same ground as the poet, impelled by the same high motives of affording pleasure and instruction.

'Novels,' he said at Liverpool Institute in November 1873, were 'the sermons of the present day, or, at any rate, the sermons which were listened to with the most rapt attention.'[12] Occasionally he varied the analogy, calling himself a professor with many pupils, and in this pedagogical strain (as though addressing a class of good young men, as Meredith described the tone of his article on Cicero)[13] he stoutly defended the artist as moralist. 'I regard him who can put himself into close communication with young people year after year without making some attempt to do them good, as a very sorry fellow indeed,' he said in *Thackeray*. For all that, Trollope's instinct led him to avoid the homiletic cadence. In the *Autobiography* entertaining is placed above teaching: 'The writer of stories must please, or he will be nothing. And he must teach whether he wish to teach or no' (ch. xii). This observation indeed comes much nearer to the total moral ambience of his work.

To what specifically does Trollope direct his moral responsibility? He tells us in some detail:

> [Novels] not only contain love stories, but they are written for the sake of the love stories . . . No social question has been so important to us as that of the great bond of matrimony . . . It is from them that girls learn what is expected from them, and what they are to expect when lovers come; and also from them that young men unconsciously learn what are, or should be, or may be, the charms of love . . . if I can make young men and women believe that truth in love will make them happy, then, if my writings be popular, I shall have a very large class of pupils . . .[14]

Trollope insists on the writer's obligation to make virtue alluring and vice ugly, but as an artist rejects Dickens' practice of making his good characters 'beautiful with unnatural virtue', and his bad characters evil caricatures.[15] Truth demanded mixed characters and also some handling of morally dubious topics. It was his treatment of the temptations facing Glencora in *Can You Forgive Her?* which produced an irate letter from a clergyman on the subject of a wife contemplating adultery. 'I was walking no doubt on ticklish ground', Trollope admitted, but his reply was masterly:

> I must in the first place beg you to believe that I do not write without thinking very much of what may be the effects of what I write, – and that I do my work with a most anxious wish & with much effort that what I produce may at least not do harm. Were I to believe that any young persons could be led into evil ways by what I have published I should be very unhappy. . . . The young girl for whom I or you are so tender is not ignorant of the sin [adultery]; – and, as I think, it would not be well that she should be ignorant of

it . . . Thinking as I do that ignorance is not innocence I do not avoid, as you would wish me to do, the mention of things which are to me more shocking in their facts than in their names. (280, pp. 173-4)

It is a splendid answer to Victorian prudery.

In the *Autobiography*, however, there is an element of disingenuousness in his defence: 'The regions of absolute vice are foul and odious . . . In these he will hardly tread. But there are outskirts on these regions, on which sweet-smelling flowers seem to grow, and grass to be green.' The temptation, he says promptly, is to linger too long in these regions, for the novelist may not be dull. 'He must please, and the flowers and the grass in these neutral territories sometimes seem to give him so easy an opportunity of pleasing!' (ch. xii). The archness betrays a certain unease but this is scarcely surprising when we consider how Victorian novelists were harassed on moral grounds. Even as late as 1879, Trollope noted that there still clung to the novel something of the bad character it had acquired many years ago. Thus one detects in him, as in his fellow-artists, tension between the pressures of the moral code and his artistic conscience, forcing him at times into compromises which mar some perceptive studies of human nature. Would Phineas, for example, swamped as he is by the glitter of metropolitan high life and consumed with parliamentary ambition, really have returned to simple Mary in County Clare, but for the demands of not only the happy, but the moral ending?

On the other hand, in view of Trollope's ethical pronouncements, it is remarkable how few failures of nerve or inconsistencies there are. He writes with fine artistic tact which avoids overt censure and obtrusive moralising, modelling himself in this respect on Scott and his beloved Thackeray. But where Thackeray leaned towards the ill side of human nature, Trollope inclined to the better, believing in man's innate tendency to virtue, the force of that conviction giving credible substance to his moral attitudes as they occur in character and action. His meliorism demands happy endings and ample worldly as well as spiritual benefits for his young heroes and heroines, but these are usually in accord with the spirit of the novel. When Harry Clavering returns dutifully to Florence Burton at the end of *The Claverings*, we hardly feel cheated; the character had been developed in such a way as to show his affinity with Julia Brabazon, and yet we recognise that he would have returned to Florence, the steadier woman. Or, to put the contrary example, does Lizzie Eustace's marriage to a vulgar Jewish confidence man turned preacher represent a false reversal of fortune to punish a worldly woman? Given her stupidity and appetite for spurious romance, the end is wholly feasible, especially as we learn later from *Phineas Redux* that she leaves her husband within a year. The value of what **Trollope** achieves through the greater proportion of a novel is seldom undermined by concessions to rewards and punishments or the conventional elements of romance. Indeed, as the example of Lizzie Eustace suggested, we have often to bear in mind a cumulative strategy of irony extending over several books.

DOWNRIGHT HONEST LOVE

With some understanding of his regard for the cheek of the young person we can venture into the complexities of romantic love as Trollope sees them. 'Who can say how his heart is moved, – and why?' he asks in *The Vicar of Bullhampton* (ch. iv). One principle at least may be settled at the outset in a line from an old Scots ballad that recurs in several novels: 'Love shall be lord of all'. This is the basis of the plot in almost every case, and the conclusion to which all rivalries, complications and setbacks lead.

The spontaneity of falling in love provided opportunities for gentle irony, but at the same time Trollope sought to convey its moments of rapture with hearty approval. Although mindful of the dangers of inflammatory scenes of passion, he made his heroes and heroines respond with healthy vigour, often recognisably sexual as well as spiritual. A total emotional excitement is there in his heroines, for example, that reminds one of Shakespeare, and so we have what Hillis Miller described as the ultimate commitment of self in love which takes us to the central importance of this topic to his fiction.[16]

To categorise the ecstatic, transfiguring excitement of love I have chosen the expression used by Mrs. Greenow in *Can You Forgive Her?* who faces a choice of suitors: the solid, dull and dependable farmer Cheesacre, who can promise her security and modest wealth, and the rather flashy, disreputable Captain Bellfield, who offers romance. Trollope thinks it a precious commodity. Widow Greenow rejects the farmer and advises him that next time he goes courting he should 'talk to her a little more about your passion and a little less about your purse'.[17] She accepts Bellfield because

> I do like a little romance . . . just a sniff, as I call it, of the rocks and valleys . . . Of course, bread-and-cheese is the real thing. The rocks and valleys are no good at all, if you haven't got that. (ch. lxiv)

This expresses very well Trollope's sense of a middle way or combination of attitudes, which is not necessarily a compromise. Real love must have its excitement, but it must produce eventual perception of one's responsibilities, one's future. The 'bread-and-cheese' does not signify a reduction of love, but rather a different phase of the relationship, an enlargement of experience, a maturing of each individual.

Trollope manages to convey the physical and emotional joys of the rocks and valleys, although proceeding according to conventions of his time. The opinion still canvassed that Trollope's stories are lack-lustre encounters between English lilies and rather limp young men does not take into account the vitality of many scenes like that between Florence Mountjoy and Harry Annesley in a late novel, *Mr. Scarborough's Family*. The two are dancing together, and Harry proposes, but Florence cannot reply because her mother is watching them carefully:

'May I not have one word,' he said; 'one word?'
What could he want with one word more? thought Florence. Her silence now was as good as any speech. But as he did want more, she would, after her own way, reply to him. So there came upon his arm the slightest possible sense of pressure from those sweet fingers, and Harry Annesley was on a sudden carried up among azure-tinted clouds into the furthest heaven of happiness. After a moment he stood still, and passed his fingers through his hair and waved his head as a god might do. She had now made to him a solemn promise than which no words could be more binding. 'Oh! Florence,' he exclaimed, 'I must have you alone with me for one moment.' For what could he want her alone for any moment? thought Florence. There was her mother still looking at them; but for her Harry did not care one straw. Nor did he hate those bright Italian lakes with nearly so strong a feeling of abhorrence. 'Florence, you are now all my own.' There came another slightest pressure; slight, but so eloquent from those fingers.

'I hate dancing. How is a fellow to dance now? I shall run against everybody. I can see no one. I should be sure to make a fool of myself. No, I don't want to dance even with you. No, certainly not! Let you dance with somebody else, and you engaged to me! Well, if I must, of course I must. I declare, Florence, you have not spoken a single word to me, though there is so much that you must have to say. What have you got to say? What a question to ask! You must tell me. Oh, you know what you have got to tell me! The sound of it will be the sweetest music that a man can possibly hear.'

'You know it all, Harry,' she whispered. . . .

When Florence had gone Harry felt that as the sun and the moon and the stars had all set, and as absolute darkness reigned through the rooms, he might as well escape into the street where there was no one but the police to watch him, as he threw his hat up into the air in his exultation.[18]

There is genuinely dual point of view here: Trollope undercuts the extravagance with 'azure-tinted clouds', and Harry's frenetic mode of speech, while preserving the exhilarating nature of the experience. The motions of fingers upon arms and fingers through hair carries the strong implication of physical delight, such slight gestures, then as now, fully as capable of conveying passion and tenderness as an embrace.

In *Framley Parsonage,* one of the best love stories Trollope ever wrote, a similar physical excitement is present, as he intimated in his description of it in the *Autobiography*:

> The story was thoroughly English. There was a little fox-hunting and a little tuft-hunting, some Christian virtue and some Christian cant. There was no heroism and no villainy. There was much Church, but more love-making. And it was downright honest love, – in which there was no pretence on the part of the lady that she was too ethereal to be fond of a man, no half-and-half inclination on the part of the man to pay a certain price and no more for a pretty toy. Each of them longed for the other, and they were not ashamed to say so. (ch. viii)

This 'downright honest love', frankly accepted, must include what Trollope cannot directly mention, its sexual joys. He himself was, I think, strongly attracted by women, and was much admired by them for a combination of charm and gruff masculinity.[19] He uses a number of methods to convey obliquely a good deal of sexual attraction, his concept of manliness for one. Violet Effingham's response to Lord Chiltern's roughness is 'You must not be so tumultuous, Oswald, or I shall have to live in a whirlwind'.[20] She is pleasantly afraid at the prospect.

A raffish and wayward manner in many of his heroes, such as Frank Greystock, Harry Clavering or John Caldigate, is a signpost to their virility. This is even more noticeable in the scamps or damaged Apollos: Crosbie, Alaric Tudor, Burgo Fitzgerald, Ralph Newton (who lived 'a useless butterfly life'), George Hotspur and Lopez. These far outweigh the prissy, mild-mannered paragons like Arthur Fletcher, Mr Arabin, John Gordon, Roger Carbury and Harry Norman. In some cases Trollope resorts to the obvious Byronic stereotype: the corsair, saturnine and black-browed, of whom George Vavasor is the perfect example, complete with flaming cicatrice which appears to light up when he is angry. The detail amuses the reader, but by resorting to such a short-hand symbol Trollope conveyed much without violating canons of propriety.

Imagery of hunting and the turf, drawing upon the medieval sense of the term venery, is another useful method of conveying sexual feeling. Lord Chiltern's wooing that so appeals to Violet Effingham's subconscious desires is like his riding, daring and violent. Perhaps this helps to account for the confusion in her own mind when she volunteers the opinion that 'a husband is very much like a house or a horse', you buy when you want to, and she has a distinct feeling that she may well finish on the wrong side of the post (ch. x). In *John Caldigate* love is simply 'riding at a fence' (ch. viii). Courtship among sporting types is inevitably confused with the joys of the chase. Captain Boodle offers Sir Hugh Clavering the benefit of his equine experience as a stratagem to impress Julia Brabazon in the words 'Let her know that you're there' (ch. xvii), while in *The Eustace Diamonds* Sir Griffin Tewett's sadistic thoughts towards Lucinda Roanoke provoke this comment: 'He'd have her, by George! There are men in whose love a good deal of hatred is mixed, – who love as the huntsman loves the fox, towards the killing of which he intends to use all his energies and intellects.'[21]

Analogies with field and turf, however, often express the finest feelings between man and woman. Compliment can strain no higher than Mr Spooner's considered opinion of Adelaide Palliser: 'He didn't think he had ever seen a girl sit a horse better.'[22] Clementina Golightly, 'a doosed fine gal', polka'd in the grasp of her partner's outstretched hand like a horse held by a bearing-rein, an art which 'must have taken as much training as a horse gets for a race'. To complete this cameo in *The Three Clerks* Trollope adds: 'But the training had in no wise injured her; and now, having gone through her gallops and run all her heats for three successive seasons, she was still sound of wind and limb, and fit to run at any moment when called upon' (ch. xvii). Much of the running is, of course, actually in the saddle. The hunt, apart from its intrinsic attraction for Trollope, offers splendid opportunities for love and flirtation, as we see in *The Kellys*, *Orley Farm* or *The American Senator*, in which Arabella Trefoil stakes everything in her pursuit of Lord Rufford on her performance in the field. These examples predominantly serve the ends of social comedy, but they are also part of the process by which Trollope implies sexual impulses. From them we may move on to a more subtle evocation of the total unfolding of the personality to love in Lucy Robarts.

In *Framley Parsonage* we are invited to consider true and false attitudes to love and their ramifications within families and society at large. We begin with Lucy's staggering admission to Fanny Robarts, her sister-in-law, that she has fallen head over heels in love with Lord Lufton. This is beautifully portrayed in a self-mocking tone which all the while bubbles with vitality and ends in almost hysterical excitement: 'He is no hero. There is nothing on earth wonderful about him. I never heard him say a single word of wisdom, or utter a thought that was akin to poetry. He devotes all his energies to riding after a fox or killing poor birds, and I never heard of his doing a single great action in my life. And yet – '[23] The lapse into silence is a neat touch. As though collecting herself Lucy continues with a picture of Lufton in moderate, banal terms – his fine legs, smooth forehead, good-humoured eye and white teeth – and then excitement rushes over her and she exclaims 'Was it possible to see such a catalogue of perfections, and not fall down, stricken to the very bone?' Fanny is bemused, and ironically, Lucy has revealed to us how fathoms deep in love she is; moreover, she has managed to convey to the reader that the ordinary qualities of the man do indeed translate him to the heroic sphere that her words are supposed to deny. But Trollope adds irony to irony, making Lucy confess ' "It was his title that killed me. I had never spoken to a lord before. Oh, me! what a fool, what a beast I have been!" And then she burst out into tears.'

Lucy is, of course, impressed by rank, as every honest person (Trollope always insists) is bound to be; but she is not drawn into love by titles and the trappings of outward appearance, unlike Griselda Grantly, who can see nothing but the coronet. The chapters entitled 'Non impulsive' and 'Impulsive' juxtapose and contrast the two women. Lucy is one of Trollope's small, brown girls; insignificant, Lady Lufton calls her. Griselda on the other hand is a great beauty, with a tall, statuesque grace and flawless white skin.

To appreciate the full flavour of a series of well-placed scenes one needs far more space for quotation, while the ironies embedded in the novel achieve their full effect only when one considers the entire Barsetshire series. Mrs Grantly, for example, prides herself upon the successful formation of her daughter's character and the management of her matrimonial campaign, but at the end of the novel is left painfully aware of her daughter's coldness:

> Mrs. Grantly kissed her and blessed her in the hall as she was about to step forward to her travelling carriage leaning on her father's arm, and the child put up her face to her mother for a last whisper. 'Mamma,' she said, 'I suppose Jane can put her hand at once on the moire antique when we reach Dover?' Mrs. Grantly smiled and nodded, and again blessed her child. There was not a tear shed – at least, not then – nor a sign of sorrow to cloud for a moment the gay splendour of the day. But the mother did bethink herself, in the solitude of her own room, of those last words, and did acknowledge a lack of something for which her heart had sighed. (ch. xlviii)

Such is Trollope's Balzacian corner of the universe; old Goriot's daughters are scarcely more savagely revealed.

Reminders of Balzac also occur in the Harding-Griselda meeting of Chapter xl, which gives a clear example of Trollope's structuring of episodes for dramatic impact. He begins with the effects of the Hartletop alliance upon the Grantlys. Mrs Grantly manages to conceal from Lady Lufton her triumph, 'hiding, as it were, her pride under a veil'. Of Griselda, Trollope observes: 'we have seen also how meekly the happy girl bore her own great fortune, applying herself humbly to the packing of her clothes, as though she ignored her own glory.' We remember that the Dumbello treaty has been arranged and ratified by the parents, and that the young people themselves have expressed little directly to each other; indeed neither seems capable of utterance, Dumbello because he is next door to imbecility and Griselda watchful, inanimate and devoid of feeling: 'a mere automaton, cold, lifeless, spiritless, and even vapid,' as Lucy has rightly said in her amusing burst of jealousy (ch. xxi). Griselda is, of course, the antithesis of all the values Trollope cares for in woman and fulfils the instructive function of the novel in the same way as Thackeray's Beatrix, who was so depicted, Trollope points out, as to make any decent girl shudder and say 'Oh! not like that; – let me not be like that!'[24]

Trollope then considers the attitude of the master of Plumstead Episcopi, Archdeacon Grantly himself, and neatly distinguishes between Mrs Grantly's foolish pride and his own. The Archdeacon has already perceived the shallowness of his daughter, and it is implied that he has withdrawn from her, preferring to build his hopes on his sons. This is in itself ironical, since in *The Last Chronicle* he is to find himself in conflict with his favourite son, Henry, who falls in love with Grace Crawley, the daughter of the poor incumbent of Hogglestock. Grantly bids Griselda love her husband and be a good wife, but is at a loss for further words. To recommend that she do her duty in that station of life to which God called her seemed to him out of place and vulgar, although it is precisely in these terms at the end of the novel that Trollope marks Lucy's marriage to Lord Lufton. The Archdeacon's worldly scale of values is thus laid bare, but this is further emphasised by the immediate reminder of his past ambitions dealt with in *Barchester Towers*. By such glances back and forward Trollope implicates his characters in a rich texture of irony. The reflections on Grantly's disappointment (renewed in this novel by fresh hopes of a bishopric) engage our sympathetic understanding of the man without affecting judgement of his misguided material philosophy. This is the true expression of his ethic in fiction, to which the *Saturday Review* (a journal inclined to severity towards him) paid tribute, noticing that his didacticism was so skilfully embedded in the fiction that one scarcely suspected its existence.[25]

The centrepiece of Chapter xl is a long description of Griselda's impending marriage epitomised by the trousseau. It is typical of Trollope that he launches his satire in this concrete way rather than resorting to metaphor. Here the wedding trousseau acts symbolically. Trollope begins with a panegyric on the importance of marriage finery to every young bride. Based on a commonplace – the old saying that the tailor makes the man has been turned into the idea that the milliner makes the bride – it gathers his female readers into a sharing of the experience. At this point Griselda displays some animation; indeed she acts with an absorbed solemnity that at once sounds a warning note: 'She even struck her mother with awe by the grandeur of her ideas and the depth of her theories'. A parody of the religious significance of the coming occasion is conveyed by references to the 'ultimate sign and mark of her status, the quintessence of her briding, the outer veil as it were, of the tabernacle – namely, her wedding-dress'. As he often does for satiric effect, Trollope ventures now quite naturally into the mock-heroic, using devotional phrases for exterior and superficial aspects of the marriage, thereby implying its complete barrenness and lack of spirituality. 'Ministers' surround her, the list of underclothing is prepared with 'sacred fervour', and so on; then to the abrupt 'Money was no object', and a torrent of references to jewels, diamonds, silks and satins, French bonnets, muslins, velvets, hats, riding-habits, artificial flowers.

Griselda's moral vacuity is then pointed beside representatives of sound values, Mrs Arabin and, more significantly, Mr Harding. Harding's introduction as a moral referent clinches the matter, and affords an example of Trollope's style at its best. Muted, reflective, free of rhetorical device, its pronounced but gentle cadences, its simple diction, echo Mr Harding's character:

> Among those of her relations who wondered much at the girl's fortune, but allowed themselves to say but little, was her grandfather, Mr. Harding. He was an old clergyman, plain and simple in his manners, and not occupying a very prominent position, seeing that he was only precentor to the chapter. He was loved by his daughter, Mrs. Grantly, and was treated by the archdeacon, if not invariably with the highest respect, at least always with consideration and regard. But, old and plain as he was, the young people at Plumstead did not hold him in any great reverence. He was poorer than their other relatives, and made no attempt to hold his head high in Barsetshire circles.

Griselda, beyond the pale of normal ties and affections, avoids physical contact with her grandfather, greeting his congratulations by touching his forehead lightly with her lips, which were now 'reserved for nobler foreheads than that of an old cathedral hack'. Her attitude is made clear to the reader in all its vanity, snobbery and self-interest. She would be ashamed that the Hartletop connection should know her grandfather chanted the litany from Sunday to Sunday, that he had 'almost disgraced his family in being, at his age, one of the working menial clergy of the cathedral'. The few words they exchange reveal an unbridgeable gulf.

'Being a Countess – that fact alone won't make you happy.'

'Lord Dumbello at present is only a viscount,' said Griselda. 'There is no earl's title in the family.'

'Oh! I did not know,' said Mr. Harding, relinquishing his grand-daughter's hand; and, after that, he troubled her with no further advice.

The last scene of this splendid chapter broadens into the comedy implied in its title 'Internecine', but also widens the irony into that dominant theme of Victorian fiction, the *mariage de convenance*. We are shown Mrs Grantly and Mrs Proudie skirmishing over the advantages of each of their daughters in the marriage market. At the end of the novel Trollope comments:

I will not say that the happiness of marriage is like the Dead Sea fruit – an apple which, when eaten, turns to bitter ashes in the mouth. Such pretended sarcasm would be very false. Nevertheless, is it not the fact that the sweetest morsel of love's feast has been eaten, that the freshest, fairest blush of the flower has been snatched and has passed away, when the ceremony at the altar has been performed, and legal possession has been given? There is an aroma of love, an undefinable delicacy of flavour, which escapes and is gone before the church portal is left, vanishing with the maiden name, and incompatible with the solid comfort appertaining to the rank of wife. To love one's own spouse, and to be loved by her, is the ordinary lot of man, and is a duty exacted under penalties. But to be allowed to love youth and beauty that is not one's own – to know that one is loved by a soft being who still hangs cowering from the eye of the world as though her love were all but illicit – can it be that a man is made happy when a state of anticipation such as this is brought to a close? No; when the husband walks back from the altar, he has already swallowed the choicest dainties of his banquet. The beef and pudding of married life are then in store for him; – or perhaps only the bread and cheese. (ch. xlviii)

Cockshut suggests that Trollope regards courtship as the period of untroubled joy after which comes the tedium and routine of marriage. It is true that Trollope's capitulations to this stereotype were frequent and perpetrated with jocose vulgarity, but the passage above is impregnated with irony. Beneath its orotund banalities and pontifical tone, the perceptive reader enjoys an elaborate joke on romantic illusions. Trollope retains a sense that beef and pudding, even bread and cheese, are very acceptable fare.

Of course the clichés are tiresome. Bachelors are always having their wings clipped and being led like garlanded bullocks to the altar; girls approach dangerous men like moths to the flame, or angle for lovers with silken nets. The worst stereotype panders outrageously to male vanity:

> When the ivy has found its tower, when the delicate creeper has found its strong wall, we know how the parasite plants grow and prosper. They were not created to stretch forth their branches alone, and endure without protection the summer's sun and the winter's storm.[26]

Trollope is seldom felicitous with metaphor and here is more than usually inept. The clinging ivy image, however chauvinistically male, remains a favourite, and is given on another occasion, inappropriately, to Mrs Euphemia Smith, who turns out to be the most persistent of creepers; we women, she confides to John Caldigate, are prehensile things, whereas she herself is as rugged and hard-boiled as the Australian gold prospectors she lives with (ch. viii). But such clichés, rather than subverting the domesticity Trollope was out to defend and celebrate, are his common denominators of expression for familiar things. They also illustrate a weakness for hoary jokes about nagging wives and mothers-in-law, and no more invalidate his views on growing up in love than the happy endings he resorts to without compunction. 'What further need be said as to Reginald and his happy bride?' he asks teasingly at the end of *The American Senator*. Indeed the fantasy world of the romantic love story *does* end there, but the real world of mature love in marriage is still to come.

PRUDENCE VERSUS PASSION

In its most obvious form, prudence versus passion is a confrontation between parents and children contributing to the entanglements of plot. Young love is a matter of the heart's own reason, but parents constantly make objections on the grounds of rank and fortune. They act to defend family honour, property and their own pride, or else scheme ineffectually to secure advantageous matches for their impecunious sons or dowerless daughters. The Earlhams of Brayboro Park manœuvre desperately to marry their precious Gus to Ralph Newton, heir to the estate of Newton Priory. Lady Lufton seeks an alliance with the Grantlys and is full of chagrin at the thought of her son marrying a doctor's daughter.

Protecting the gullible daughter against the fortune hunter, like Lopez, who made sure of Emily Wharton's money before allowing himself to love her, is a favourite complication. Members of landed families, losing their power in the mid-century scramble with men like Lopez, were also seeking alliances with wealth, and this is satirised in the attempts of Lord Nidderdale and others to win Marie Melmotte in *The Way We Live Now*. At a more comic level, in *Framley Parsonage* the common question – how a gentleman of good family and no means is to be rescued – is posed in Nathaniel Sowerby of Chaldicotes, a penniless scamp with some resemblance to Dickens' Harold Skimpole. To pay his debts it is suggested that he marry Miss Dunstable whose fortune came to her from the cosmetics industry. Miss Dunstable responds to the courtship, conducted by a proxy, Mrs Harold Smith, with her customary pithy honesty:

> Of course I am not such an ass as to expect that any gentleman should love me; and I feel that I ought to be obliged to your brother for sparing me the string of complimentary declarations which are usual on such occasions . . . I do feel grateful to him; and perhaps nothing more will be necessary than to give him a schedule of the property, and name an early day for putting him in possession. (ch. xxiv)

Here we have the apotheosis of the love as marketable commodity theme. Miss Dunstable will only marry one who expects nothing from her, and eventually finds that person in Dr Thorne.

The *Small House at Allington* sustains the love and barter analogy in a more comprehensive statement than that of *Dr. Thorne* or *Framley Parsonage*. Society endangered when love is tainted by materialism is a theme Trollope constantly explored. Here the contrasts are between the pearls of Allington, Lily and Bell Dale in the country, and a host of town-oriented people, who include the de Courcys; Griselda, now Lady Dumbello; professional men such as Butterwell and Gazebee; and in a central position the swell, Adolphus Crosbie, an ambitious public servant with a smooth tongue. Just 'a fraction of a hero', Crosbie 'was not altogether a villain'.[27] He jilts Lily for an advantageous marriage to Lady Alexandrina de Courcy, and duly gets his come-uppance. 'But in this world all valuable commodities have their price; and when men such as Crosbie aspire to obtain for themselves an alliance with noble families, they must pay the market price for the article which they purchase' (ch. xxxi). Part of the price is amusingly detailed in Chapter xl, 'Preparations for the wedding', which involve 'strapping the new husband down upon the grindstone of his matrimonial settlement', while the de Courcy ladies like cormorants devour the cash available for all the fine things that are to furnish the Crosbie house in a newly fashionable part of London, all scaffold poles and the smell of paint. The tawdry elegance and emptiness of the de Courcy world are echoed in Lady Dumbello's smiles: 'cold, unmeaning, accompanied by no special glance of the eye, and seldom addressed to the individual', (ch. xliii). Touched by a breath of scandal concerning Plantagenet Palliser's interest in her, she skilfully turns the tables on society

D

and secures from her egregious husband 'a wonderful green necklace, very rare and curious' (ch. lv).

Against this meretricious and soulless existence, Trollope places authentic living, which is centred on Lily Dale's steadfastness and Johnny Eames' devotion, and, incidentally, is one vital reason for her resolution to remain true to love. It is a good deed in a naughty world, an affirmation of the selflessness of true love against calculation and falsehood. The Dales, Johnny Eames, and Lord de Guest reaffirm the old verities of fidelity and loyalty to which the new society no longer seems strictly bound. However, it needs to be pointed out that Trollope never puts the issues so exactly; it is not merely a question of the noble, older world of Barchester invaded by the new and evil ways of the metropolis. The Dales too are obstinate, pessimistic, strongly tied to 'the good things of the world', and attached to 'the privilege of a pleasant social footing among their friends' (ch. xxxviii). Trollope is always at pains to demonstrate our involvement in the common follies of mankind.

In this matter of the prudent match Trollope comes down much harder on women than men. It can almost be taken for granted that a gentleman shall have means to enjoy a leisured existence; Trollope is extremely sympathetic to Lord Fawn, who has to keep a place in society without sufficient money. And the prudent advice Frank Greystock takes to heart is the old maxim 'Doan't thou marry for munny, but goa where munny is!'[28] But women are severely punished for making such marriages. 'That girls should not marry for money we are all agreed,' says Trollope in *Framley Parsonage*. 'A lady who can sell herself for a title or an estate, for an income or a set of family diamonds, treats herself as a farmer treats his sheep and oxen – makes hardly more of herself, of her own innerself, in which are comprised a mind and soul, than the poor wretch of her own sex who earns her bread in the lowest stages of degradation' (ch. xxi). These harsh words are put into effect in several studies of mercenary marriage, notably *The Bertrams*, *Phineas Finn* and *The Way We Live Now*. Love 'does not often run in a yoke with prudence', Trollope comments in *Phineas Finn* (ch. lxvi), and to prove it (unconvincingly in the light of his vanity and ambition) Finn runs off to marry his girl-next-door, Mary Flood Jones. Laura Standish, on the other hand, who has married for wealth and rank, suffers and comes to recognise that a woman should marry only for love. In *The Claverings* this situation is treated more comically: the widowed Julia, having dropped Harry Clavering, comes back to flutter temptingly before him and is herself the target of fortune hunters.

There is an intriguing balance of passion and prudence in the twin love stories of *The Bertrams*. Adela Gauntlet's marriage to a young clergyman, Arthur Wilkinson, is frustrated by the young man's timidity over his poor income and is 'passion nipped in its bud by a cruel prudence'.[29] The lovely Caroline Waddington on the other hand has no hesitation about having her bread well buttered:

> She would never marry – such was the creed which was to govern her own life – without love, but she would not allow herself to love where love would interfere with her high hopes. In her catalogue of human blisses love in a cottage was not entered. She was not avaricious; she did not look to money as the summum bonum; – certainly not to marry for money's sake. But she knew that no figure in the world could be made without means. (I, ch. xi)

Suddenly, with one of those unerring insights into the irrationality of human behaviour, Trollope has her marry, in a kind of self-destructive impulse, Henry Harcourt, an ambitious, wealthy lawyer. Driven almost to suicide by unhappiness she admits at last that 'determined to win the world' she had betrayed love (III, ch. v). She confides to Adela 'I was false to my own heart' (III, ch. vii), the ultimate sin in Trollope's lexicon of love.

The influence of aristocratic notions about rank, however, makes for some ambiguity in Trollope's treatment of marriage for social advantage. Although by the time of *Ralph the Heir*, the more feckless Ralph can contemplate marrying a tradesman's daughter, Trollope remains circumspect about the flouting of caste. The heart's affections are held to, but only by rigging the plot to evade the class issue. He allowed Lady Anna to marry a tailor, but packed them off to Sydney at the end of the story. His defence was spirited, however. 'Of course the girl has to marry the tailor,' he wrote to his old friend and neighbour, Lady Wood. 'It is very dreadful, but there was no other way' (520, p. 308). The interesting point to note from the rest of his letter is that Trollope wrote the story without egalitarian motives, as one of his typical moral conundrums turning on the necessity of the girl to be true either to her promise or to her lineage (the latter was only apparent long after her engagement).

Hardly more case for social mobility is made from *The Duke's Children*, in which Isabel Boncassen, though nominally an American professor's daughter, is removed from the patrician mould merely by accent, and Tregear, though impecunious, is every inch a gentleman, his seal of approval issuing from the Duke: 'I think he is a manly young man.'[30] Similar hesitancy surrounds *Marion Fay*, which makes a tentative gesture towards social change of the late Victorian period without carrying it to a convincing conclusion. Lady Frances Trafford is in love with George Roden, a Post Office clerk, a matter of great concern to her family, while her brother, Lord Hampstead, has fallen in love with a poor Quaker. Certainly the novel attempts to direct some satire against snobbery, and reveals the gap between Lord Hampstead's eccentric republicanism and his feelings as an aristocrat, for although he opposes his reactionary father on principle, he experiences acute discomfort on hearing his sister's name familiar in the mouth of a mere clerk: 'There seemed to be a sanctity about her rank which did not attach to his own. He had thought that the Post Office clerk was as good as himself; but he could not assure himself that he was as good as the ladies of his family.' Reason assured him such thinking was wrong, but reason 'though it affected his conduct, did not reach his taste'.[31] Inconsistencies of this kind Trollope greatly relished. Nevertheless he finally retreats from the problem, for he makes George Roden inherit the long-lost title of one of his Italian forebears, and as the Duca di Crinola he goes to the altar. 'There is so much in a name!' cries the bride's cousin, and with good reason, since she herself has now become Lady LLwddythlw (ch. xxi). Heavy irony does not make up for Trollope's refusal to face the consequences of raising the class issue. Hampstead's egalitarian views are never put to the test because the heroine dies of consumption. On the whole, though, I am inclined to think this is less weak evasion than attempt to flog some life into a very bad novel. *Marion Fay* ends with the most ridiculous scene of Trollope's entire work as Lord Hampstead tiptoes from the chamber of his dead love carrying his only keepsake of her: a poker she had once touched. Freudians have not, so far as I am aware, dealt with this intriguing detail.

Beyond the spiritual treachery which marriage for money or social advantage suggests, there is a whole area of prudence in love expressed by Sir Thomas Tringle in *Ayala's Angel* (ch. xxx) 'Love is all very well ... but love should be regulated by good sense.' Trollope approves a certain amount of practical wisdom in affairs of the heart, which gives his stories of young love particular distinction. All his characters hope to experience the rocks and valleys: as he puts it in the thoughts of Mary Lovelace at the beginning of that underestimated novel *Is He Popenjoy?*: 'Oh, that it might some day be her privilege to love some man with all her heart and all her strength, some man who should be, at any rate to her, the very hero of heroes, the cynosure of her world! ... There could surely nothing be so glorious as being well in love.'[32] But romantic folly is satirised. Somewhere between the magical luxury of the feelings and the sober realities of job and family, lies the ideal Trollope aims at: a compromise between the rocks and valleys and the bread and cheese of love. This is, after all, one of the crucial questions of the most detailed love story he ever wrote, that of Glencora and Plantagenet Palliser.

Nevertheless the principle remains that 'love shall be lord of all'. Older and wiser heads will forever counsel prudence and caution, but one of Trollope's great gifts was his memory of what it was like to be young. He never lost sight of his own marriage, recalled in the *Autobiography*. 'She had no fortune, nor had I any income beyond that which came from the Post Office ... We were not very rich, having about £400 a year on which to live. Many people would say that we were two fools to encounter such poverty together' (ch. iv). Trollope always decided in favour of the lovers' boldness: the jump in the dark, as he called it in *Ralph the Heir*.[33] There is a telling argument between prudence and passion in the sub-plot of *He Knew He Was Right*. Once again a heroine, Nora Rowley, faces the choice between two suitors; the worthy and high-minded Mr Glascock and the impecunious journalist Hugh Stanbury, whom she loves and finally marries. Prudence is counselled by Nora's mother :

> 'Romance is a very pretty thing,' Lady Rowley had been wont to say to her daughters, 'and I don't think life would be worth having without a little of it. I should be very sorry to think that either of my girls would marry a man only because he had money. But you can't even be romantic without something to eat and drink.'[34]

That undeniable logic is repeated many times over in the novels.

Hugh's own decision to marry Nora is amusingly done, since he is, aptly enough, puffing his pipe on top of an omnibus in Chancery Lane when he finally concludes that he has enough money for 'both shelter and clothes and bread and cheese'. Trollope then asks some questions. How should a man double his burdens if he is in want of income? How can he inflict such burdens on 'shoulders that are tender and soft'? And what will happen when children arrive? But he decides that if the girl is prepared for all these burdens, why should a man fear what she does not fear?

> Of course there is a risk; but what excitement is there in anything in which there is none? So on the Tuesday he speaks his mind to the young lady, and tells her candidly that there will be potatoes for the two of them, – sufficient, as he hopes, of potatoes, but no more. As a matter of course the young lady replies that she for her part will be quite content to take the parings for her own eating. Then they rush deliciously into each other's arms and the matter is settled. For, though the convictions arising from the former line of argument may be set aside as often as need be, those reached from the latter are generally conclusive. (ch. xxxiii)

And so, with mild irony and great sympathy, Trollope settles the question of prudence and passion. The lovers seldom if ever have to exist on potatoes, but this does not invalidate the sentiments expressed in praise of wholehearted commitment.

ILLUSION AND REALITY

To see how Trollope's lessons in love are formed in tender and delicate stories, how the dream is made reality and the fairy tale imbued with values which strengthen and animate, involves a little more of his theories about fiction, particularly where they relate to the genre of romance as distinct from the general term by which he denotes young people's attitudes to love.

It is generally agreed that Trollope achieved the highest degree of actuality in his scenes and characters; less readily acknowledged perhaps is that he transmuted the raw materials of life and that his imagination had a quality of daring and vivacity we may properly call romantic. He himself assisted in later depreciation of his work by persistently under-valuing a visionary side of his nature (which appears in his Irish books, for example). It was Hawthorne's praise Trollope most valued and quoted with such pride in the *Autobiography*: 'I have always desired,' he wrote, 'to "hew out some lump of the earth", and to make men and women walk upon it just as they do walk here among us, with not more of ex-cellence, nor with exaggerated baseness, – so that readers might recognize human beings like to themselves, and not feel themselves to be carried away among gods or demons' (ch. vii). From the time of the successful *Dr. Thorne* (1858), Trollope was a dedicated realist, seeing the novel as 'a picture of common life . . . the canvas . . . crowded with real portraits', his praises reserved for those writers, like Charlotte Brontë and Thackeray, who portrayed life as naturally as possible, while his criticisms were directed at writers untrue to nature, as he saw it, particularly Disraeli with his 'paste diamonds', and to a lesser extent Dickens, with his exaggerations and grotesqueries.[35]

Truth may be stranger than fiction, but Trollope preferred to seek it in the broad highroad of life and present an average view of it rather than one heightened and concentrated as Dickens' so often was. Indeed, he seems to have totally failed to see that by seizing on peculiarities Dickens gave them a resonance which fixed with unforgettable exactness those very common traits of humanity which he himself sought to cap-ture, nor that by looking long enough it was possible to find a man who actually did swallow eggs, shell and all. As a sober civil servant, Trollope kept his eyes on the ground before him and his imagination well in check. Yet this is not the whole truth. Tennyson might grumble that his novels were prosaic and dull with 'never a touch of poetry',[36] but it can be argued that Trollope's concentration makes a kind of poetry of the actual, and that on occasions he too is a writer of bold colour and grand effect.[37]

Poetic utterance, the striving for grand effects, was not, after all, what he was after, and we see from his literary observations just those weak-nesses of his perception which in the end limit his achievement. Towards poetry, of which he appreciated little beyond *vers de société*, he adopted a tone of awe-struck politeness. Tennyson he admired, as all Englishmen did, but Browning he thought a 'stodger',[38] and Arnold was doubtless alien to his temperament. He found a correlation between poetry and fiction only when the novel in highly skilled hands rose to the challenge of the tragic experience, or what he called the sublime. 'As in poetry, so in prose, he who can deal adequately with tragic elements is a greater artist and reaches a higher aim than the writer whose efforts never carry him above the mild walks of everyday life.'[39] Touches of the sublime were to be found in *Jane Eyre*, *The Bride of Lammermoor* and *Guy Mannering*, the scene between Meg Merrilies and Mr Bertram in particular : 'That is romance, and reaches the very height of the sublime'.[40] Notice this use of the word 'romance', which suggests a height of creativity in fiction to which he would not aspire. He detached himself from the transcendental and sublime, the metaphysical and the occult, from much of the mysterious energies of dream, fantasy and fancy, choosing to concern himself with ordinary life and behaviour. 'I have shorn my fiction of all romance', he wrote proudly to George Eliot of *Rachel Ray* (207, p. 138), evidence enough, from that very dull novel, of a certain limitation in his theory.

At the opposite pole to himself was a writer like Hawthorne, dreaming dreams which, Trollope pointed out in an essay in the *North American Review*, raised people for a while into 'something higher than the common needs of common life',[41] a singularly inadequate judgement. Whenever he volunteered an opinion on non-realistic approaches to the novel, he was out of his depth. The sublime in novels, he said, represented an attempt 'to soar above the ordinary actions and ordinary language of life', and, while he respected this, it was not for him central to the novel. Scott was occasionally betrayed by it, 'failing with things in their common course', and dialogue which sometimes departed from the natural and appropriate. Romance in its gothic form he had little time for. He found *Udolpho* stilted and up in the clouds, while Bulwer's *Pelham* was a novel in which 'no word is ever spoken as it would have been spoken;—no detail is ever narrated as it would have occurred'. In prose the sublime had a way of becoming 'cold, stilted and unsatisfactory'. What was worse, the romance was often half-way to lies. The fault of *Udolpho* was that it was unreal, unlife-like : 'It is not true'.[42]

It is by this kind of admission that Trollope limits his apprehension of the novel. It accounts also for the appallingly inadequate view of Dickens; he had no sense of the essentially poetic nature of Dickens' writing with its symbolic charge. Yet he remained as conscious as Dickens of the infinite variety of mankind, simply using his imagination in a different fashion, rejecting any colouring or effect that did not fit the detailed literary genre painting at which he aimed. The absolute criterion became truth to ordinary life, which he found in Maria Edgeworth and Jane Austen.

This anti-romantic stance was mitigated by a strong point of his literary theory which enabled him to carry off some grand effects time and time again: that is his belief in the author's power to draw men and women of flesh and blood. He had the gist of the matter after all, summed up in the admirable passage of the *Autobiography* that crowns his discussion of his own methods and Wilkie Collins': 'Truth let there be, – truth of description, truth of character, human truth as to men and women. If there be such truth, I do not know that a novel can be too sensational' (ch. xii). For 'sensational' we may easily substitute the word 'romantic', and see an alteration in the hard line between realism and romance. Trollope is admitting that the novel must contain both elements. As he said of Collins, speaking of sensational (romantic) novels and his own anti-sensational (realistic) novels: 'A good novel should be both, and both in the highest degree' (ch. xii). But what he is also saying is that the vital principle is unity within the convention, the degree of felt life which goes to produce that sense of actuality which will convince. Or, put another way in his monograph on Thackeray: 'And yet in every truth the realistic must not be too true, but just so far removed from the truth as to suit the erroneous idea of truth which the reader may be supposed to entertain' (p. 185). What mattered was the effect of actuality within whatever convention. Collins had it; Disraeli emphatically had not. Trollope's comments on his fellow novelists are interesting in this respect, since they turn upon the truly imaginative and creative act (exemplified by Charlotte Brontë's human truth) and the resultant evocation of a world detailed and accurate at every point. As usual with Trollope there is compromise, a middle ground from which to operate, an instinct for the right thing, however inadequate the theory.

The pose is set in *The Bertrams* (I, ch. xiii): 'Castles with unknown passages are not compatible with my homely muse', and yet he exploits stock materials of romance: lost wills, missing heirs, blackmail and murder. Sudden shocks, he maintains, have no interest for him as a storyteller, for they belong to sensational fiction. 'Our doctrine', he says in *Barchester Towers* 'is, that the author and the reader should move along together in full confidence with each other' (ch. xv). Such comments are only partially true. Although he is sparing of melodramatic scenes in a genuine attempt to get at authentic experience, he is acutely aware of the need for incident. As he told John Blackwood while *The Last Chronicle of Barset* was appearing in instalments: 'A weekly novel should perhaps have at least an attempt at murder in every number. I never get beyond giving my people an attack of fever or a broken leg' (321, p. 193).

Disclaiming the labels 'hero' and 'heroine' is another instance of how he mediates between realism and romance. The stance, in this example from *The Three Clerks*, is again that of honest broker reluctantly following a pattern: the public expects heroes and heroines, but he would prefer to cut out such nonsense:

> he [the author] professes to do his work without any such appendages [as hero and heroine] to his story – heroism there may be, and he hopes there is – more or less of it there should be in a true picture of most characters; but heroes and heroines, as so called, are not commonly met with in our daily walks of life. (ch. xlvii)

This helps to guarantee his reliability, and at the same time distract us, like the conjuror's patter, while he works in as much romantic excitement as he wishes.

Framley Parsonage also provides an example of this sleight of hand. As I said earlier it is a Cinderella story in which Lucy is recognised by the handsome prince and after a series of misadventures united with him. The archetypes of fairytale lie behind most of Trollope's stories of young love. As usual he surrounds the fantasy with minute detail of parish, parsonage and country house, investing the story with such matter-of-fact realism that he conveys the impression that a poor girl's marriage to a lord is an everyday occurrence. Part of his technique lies in disposing of the grand titles of hero and heroine in a rigmarole of charming playfulness:

> I know it will be said of Lord Lufton himself that, putting aside his peerage and broad acres, and handsome, sonsy face, he was not worth a girl's care and love. That will be said because people think that heroes in books should be so much better than heroes got up for the world's common wear and tear. I may as well confess that of absolute, true heroism there was only a moderate admixture in Lord Lufton's composition; but what would the world come to if none but absolute true heroes were to be thought worthy of women's love? What would the men do? and what – oh! what would become of the women?

And what, the reader may well ask, would become of the novelist? This confession is Trollope's declaration of his own honesty and directness which he caps by moving again along on his scale:

> Lucy Robarts in her heart did not give her dismissed lover credit for much more heroism than did truly appertain to him; – did not, perhaps, give him full credit for a certain amount of heroism which did really appertain to him; but, nevertheless, she would have been very glad to take him could she have done so without wounding her pride. (ch. xxi)

is light, airy, nonsensical, but done with such finesse. Lord Lufton ɔcomes a Prince Charming in everyday clothes, and the solid ground of

Barsetshire a land where dreams come true. It is well to remind ourselves of the romance in Trollope's fiction which tends to be forgotten in the praise lavished on his roast-beef-and-ale realism. In many ways Trollope's young love stories are the prose idylls of the century. Hester Caldigate is Mariana in her moated grange, and Lily Dale is a Griselda. The knights confront their trials and sinful selves in quest of the grace, virtue and chivalry of Victoria's England.

But although the young heroes eventually slay some dragons or rescue the princess they spend a good deal of their time wallowing in temptation and surrendering to their vices. Being young men at the threshold of life they are uncertain, insecure, inexperienced and terribly prone to getting into scrapes over horses, cards, drink, investments, the wrong sort of men or – more especially – women. Parsons, politicians, scions of noble stock, clerks or lawyers, journalists or men with no need to work at all, they all go off the rails temporarily, like Mark Robarts with the moneylenders, Alaric Tudor with his tin mines or Paul Montague with the South General Pacific and Mexican Railways. And usually there is a woman in the case to whom these warm-blooded heroes are particularly susceptible. This allows Trollope ample scope for titillating the reader's palate with his hero's wicked ways, having apologised for him beforehand : 'It will, perhaps, be complained of him', he says archly of Harry Clavering, 'that he is fickle, vain, easily led, and almost as easily led to evil as to good' (ch. x). Walpole found Clavering 'one of the feeblest, most vacillating, and least interesting of all the Trollope heroes'.[43] This is entirely to miss the point; that very vacillating makes Clavering the typical Trollopian hero. It is the equivocal nature of the hero's thought and conduct that holds our interest and Trollope uses it to depict 'real' life and satisfy his readers' demand for romance. Harry Clavering fulfils this purpose admirably, and is, indeed, one of Trollope's best studies of growth from hobbledehoy to man. We sympathise with him at first over Julia, but we deplore his attitude to the Burtons and positively loathe him when he treats Florence so abominably. This is what Trollope wants and in the splendid chapter 'The Sheep Returns to the fold' we enjoy the spectacle of his uncomfortable hour in the Burton drawing-room as everyone else decides how the good news of his forthcoming marriage to Florence is to be broken to Julia and Harry is passed from hand to hand, as it were, like a brown-paper parcel.

Trollope similarly apologises for Frank Greystock in Chapter xxxv – 'Too bad for sympathy' – of The Eustace Diamonds, taking the fullest advantage of his midway position between romance and realism. Frank is an even more ambiguous hero than Harry Clavering, older and more intelligent, and the strength of Trollope's mock horror at his goings-on makes one wonder if he felt that he might have let his hero stray too far among those borderlands of vice. At any rate the narrative very well illustrates how Trollope could pretend to show 'real' life and deploy his romantic materials, venture into dubious moral territory yet hedge off his censors' wrath and round the story off happily. Frank is trembling on the brink of playing false to Lucy Morris with his cousin. Trollope affects dismay and assumes the reader's horror:

> One does not willingly grovel in gutters, or breathe fetid atmospheres, or live upon garbage . . . With whom are we to sympathise? says the reader, who not unnaturally imagines that a hero should be heroic.

Yet says Trollope, playing the anxious novelist, it woud be so easy to depict 'a man absolutely stainless, perfect as an Arthur' (it is interesting that he draws on this standard of medieval chivalry), but human nature is mixed of good and evil: 'The Ivanhoe that you know, did he not press Rebecca's hand?' He concludes:

> The true picture of life as it is, if it could be adequately painted, would show men what they are, and how they might rise, not, indeed to perfection, but one step first, and then another on the ladder.

Thus at a stroke Trollope establishes Frank's genuineness as a character, and his right to misbehave; he absolves himself from condemnation for immorality, and clears the way for the uplifting ending.

By taking a middle position, his own 'romantic realism', Trollope illustrates the axiom 'love shall be lord of all' without making disastrous compromises between his ethical responsibilities and his wish to be a popular entertainer. While fulfilling the expectations of day-dream and delight for milliner, countess or millionaire's daughter, his novels are also founded on the normal and representative in everyone's experience. But reproducing the cycle of ordinary events can cause the occasional dullness that Tennyson complained of. It is also, along with the length and quantity of Trollope's work, responsible for the fact that the novels do not stay clearly before us. Raymond Mortimer was right when he likened our acquaintance with Trollope characters to people met on a cruise, in which sharp, intense friendships or dislikes may blaze, but are soon forgotten after the passengers have disembarked.[44] A price has to be paid for avoiding high peaks of incident and emotion. Trollope, of course, is aware of the danger, and speaks often of the need to avoid being dull; for this reason he often supports his leading characters with slightly odd and memorable minor figures: Priscilla Stanbury, Lucinda Roanoke, Mr Moulder, Clementina Golightly, Captain Boodle; there are a few in nearly every novel, not to mention characters like Mrs Proudie, Sophie Gordeloup, Chaffanbrass, who are immortal. But many of his young heroes and heroines (Phineas Finn excepted) do fade from the memory rather quickly.

Accepting then a certain loss of clarity as the inevitable consequence of Trollope's art of the commonplace, we can recognise certain compensations. To re-read one of his novels is to enjoy recognising the familiar, and the host of details and characters compel our attention and affection at once. Trollope's art depends on fullness of detail, like the painting of his friend Frith. What he lacks in the intense moment or taut expression that goes to the heart (although these too are present in his work), he makes up for in an impressive unfolding of human response to the pressures of day-to-day living. He makes us acknowledge and re-examine what we normally take for granted; he rediscovers the familiar and our lives are the richer for it. Though it is not what we remember most vividly, most of our lives happen this way and it has made us what we are. It is an art that depends on time, space and cumulative effect, and this is why he makes a diffident gesture in his *Autobiography* towards inviting us to read his works as *romans fleuves*. It is the length of our acquaintance with Glencora Palliser which makes her unforgettable among his heroines; it is the sense of lives unfolding in a gradually changing Barsetshire that is most satisfying. In this respect Trollope amply sustains Henry James' admiration for his complete appreciation of reality.[45]

The Trollopian mode of undramatic disclosure is a process of gradual revelation through many insignificant actions and a host of tiny observations which, with the author's genial presence as commentator and host, creates a sense of well-being and ease, like opening one's own front door. It is to be found in *The Claverings* where Fanny Clavering, against all the misgivings of her family (and some of her own), is finally won by the persistence of the rather down-at-heel and eccentric curate, Mr Saul, a fictional cousin of the obstinate Mr Crawley. Saul is presented in Chapter ii, first through the eyes of Mr Clavering, and then by third-person narration :

> Mr. Saul was very tall and very thin, with a tall thin head, and weak eyes, and a sharp, well-cut nose, and, so to say, no lips, and very white teeth, with no beard, and a well-cut chin. His face was so thin that his cheekbones obtruded themselves unpleasantly. He wore a long rusty black coat, and a high rusty black waistcoat, and trousers that were brown with dirty roads and general ill-usage.

Trollope allows him few pleasant features, drawing us into sympathetic alliance with Fanny, who is vaguely insulted when he proposes to her. Everything is awkward and misplaced about Saul; even his proposal is ill-timed as they splash along a muddy lane in drizzling rain :

'Upon my word,' said the rector, 'I think it was very impertinent.'
Fanny would not have liked to use that word herself, but she loved
her father for using it. (ch. vi)

Soon, however, Trollope turns our amusement at the cadaverous clergyman into sympathy, by showing the petty snobbery that lies behind
the Claverings' attitude, and Fanny herself gradually comes to recognise
Saul's worth. In a final chapter worthy of Jane Austen Trollope has the
family resigned to the inevitable as 'Mr. Saul came, punctual as the
church clock, of which he had the regulating himself.' Mrs Clavering,
in place of her indolent husband, makes a case for prudence that would
be calculation but for its grain of commonsense. Trollope, as usual, is
being fair to both sides:

> My idea is that a child should be allowed to consult her own heart,
> and to indulge her own choice, – provided that in doing so she does
> not prepare for herself a life of indigence, which must be a life of
> misery; and of course providing also that there be no strong personal
> objection.

There is a distinct barb here as in so much of the book which gives a
pleasingly sharp flavour. None of the Claverings really likes Mr Saul;
even Harry declares 'He isn't quite one of our sort'. The curate knows
he is disliked too, and this makes him accept Mrs Clavering's insult
with urbanity:

> 'A life of indigence need not be a life of misery,' said Mr. Saul
> with that obstinacy which formed so great a part of his character.
> 'Well, well.'
> 'I am very indigent, but I am not at all miserable. If we are to
> be made miserable by that, what is the use of all our teaching?'
> 'But, at any rate, a competence is comfortable.'
> 'Too comfortable!' As Mr. Saul made this exclamation, Mrs.
> Clavering could not but wonder at her daughter's taste. But the
> matter had gone too far now for any possibility of receding.

Clearly, Mr Saul's round. The engagement is announced and plans made
for Saul to take over Mr Clavering's parish.

> 'Ah, I see how it is to be,' said the old rector to his wife. 'There are
> to be no more cakes and ale in the parish.' Then his wife reminded
> him of what he himself had said of the change which would take
> place in Mr. Saul's ways when he should have a lot of children
> running about his feet. 'Then I can only hope that they'll begin to
> run about very soon,' said the old rector.

This clear-sighted reflection points to an intriguing future. Knowing
how spirited Fanny is and how inflexible Mr Saul, we are left in little

doubt that conflict will arise when the ideals Fanny now admires in him have an uncomfortable effect upon day-to-day living. The bread and cheese of married life will not easily be digested. This is one of those minor love stories everywhere to be found in Trollope's fiction which do justice to the actual in life. Marriage is the conventional optimistic ending, but who would dare add 'they lived happily ever after'?

ANGELS OF LIGHT AND SMALL BROWN GIRLS

Trollope centres all his ideals of love in his heroines, accepting in the conventional manner that love is their whole existence. As he puts it in *The Duke's Children* :

> It does not come to a man that to be separated from a woman is to be dislocated from his very self. A man has but one centre, and that is himself. A woman has two. Though the second may never be seen by her, may live in the arms of another, may do all for that other that man can do for woman, – still, still, though he be half the globe asunder from her, still he is to her the half of her existence. (ch. lxxiii)

This ideal, like most of his beliefs, is hedged about with qualifications and inconsistencies. Like Lord George Carruthers in *The Eustace Diamonds* Trollope takes people as he finds them, forever deciding 'They're a queer lot; – ain't they, – the sort of people one meets about in the world?' (ch. lxxv), and Trollope's presentation of the heroine is a briar hedge of contradiction, incongruity and sometimes fatal error. Yet more than any of his contemporaries he has the power of drawing lifelike women in credible situations, of intuitively sympathising with their point of view. Women were continually surprised at this:

> I understand, Mr. Trollope, your knowing what a young gentleman and a young lady say to each other when they are alone together;

wrote an unknown diarist,

> 'but how can you possibly know the way that two young ladies talk to each other while brushing their hair?' Mr. Trollope only laughed and said: 'It's not by listening at the keyhole, I assure you!'[46]

This may well remind us that Trollope's characters were personages created from acute and pertinacious observation; Archdeacon Grantly was 'the simple result of an effort of my moral consciousness'.[47]

Trollope's infallible grasp of the female psyche guaranteed him a large public when *Barchester Towers* caught the mood of a generation avid for light entertainment after the emphatic propaganda of social problem novels. If George Eliot was the only novelist to write convincing dialogue for men when there were no women present, then Trollope was the only man to write good scenes for women without men. Consider the many scenes of confidences between mother and daughter in Trollope; between girl friends or rivals. How well he manages the sparring between Laura and Violet Effingham over Phineas, or between Glencora and Madame Marie Goesler concerning the tendency of the old Duke's affections; and what exquisite comedy is extracted from the meeting between Mrs Proudie and Lady de Courcy, two great ships of the line aiming their batteries in the direction of Madeline Vesey Stanhope Neroni. Trollope seemed to know by instinct not only how women felt, but how they spoke and acted. As Henry James said, he took over the English girl and made her his own.[48]

Yet there are often failures, where the strain existing between what he postulates as a desirable norm of behaviour and his artistic conscience results in the collapse of a character's integrity and reality. Where moral responsibility conflicts with artistic responsibility Trollope often chooses compromises which destroy his novel. The reason for this lies in ready acceptance of the concept of ideal womanhood that we find in much poetry of the time, from Tennyson's 'The Princess' to Coventry Patmore's 'The Angel in the House', an ideal which Trollope demolishes in nearly every heroine who stirs his deepest creative imagination. Woman in the abstract is placed on a pedestal, endowed with angelic virtues, worshipped from afar, as Charley Tudor worships Katie Woodward, referred to in *The Three Clerks* as 'angel' and 'child of heaven'. She is the traditional redemptive symbol for fallen man, who 'by instinct desires in his wife something softer, sweeter, more refined than himself' (ch. xxxi). Charley has 'visions' of a 'sweet home, and a sweeter, sweetest, lovely wife' (ch. xvii) – and Trollope sinks into sickly superlative. Charley's declaration of love takes place, appropriately enough, in a garden hot-house at Chiswick; and later the expulsion from Katie's side depicts him with 'large globules of sorrow' splashing in the dust, walking away 'as Adam did when he was driven out of Paradise' (ch. xxx). Whereupon Katie falls into the conventional decline, urging her mother to let her speak to Charley before she dies in one last bid to make him reform: 'Mamma, it will be as though one came unto him from the dead' (ch. xlii). Trollope can seldom get much worse.

The ideal woman occurs again and again and is nearly always an artistic failure, a disembodied spirit like Mary Bonner in *Ralph the Heir*, who could have been 'a model for any female saint or martyr' (ch. iv). But even the ideal woman shows sparks of life on occasion. The juxtaposition of angel and temptress is amusingly employed in *The*

Eustace Diamonds, where irony rescues the pure girl, Lucy Morris, from being the usual stereotype, and a fair amount of pugnacity towards the domineering Fawns gives the character more credible angularity. Having the mischievous Lizzie Eustace as a contrast enables Trollope to play with some useful thematic imagery, as this description of Lucy shows:

> She was but a little thing; – and it cannot be said of her, as of Lady Eustace, that she was a beauty. The charm of her face consisted of the peculiar, watery brightness of her eyes, – in the corner of which it would always seem that a diamond of a tear was lurking whenever any matter of excitement was afoot. (ch. iii)

Here is true diamond against paste imitation, though unfortunately Trollope later allows this sharp brilliance to be absorbed in the familiar light from the angel.

Fidelity unto death is one of the conventions Trollope constantly upholds, with a personal eccentricity difficult to fathom. The celebrated case is Lily Dale's stubborn persistence in love after she has been jilted by Adolphus Crosbie: she refuses Johnny Eames' proposal in *The Last Chronicle* and remains an old maid. Some critics have called it a shrewd gauging of public taste by confounding romantic expectation; or it may be another manifestation of the headstrong, stubborn quality we find in several of his heroines, that tendency of Trollope's, as Mario Praz noted, to draw masochistic women.[49] My own view is that by being true to Crosbie, Lily is made to serve that lofty, symbolic love which Trollope is continually upholding as a holy grail.

Trollope repeats this unusual posture in other novels. In *The Prime Minister* Emily Wharton marries the scoundrel, Lopez, who throws himself under a train. Considering herself tainted by this marriage, she repulses Arthur Fletcher and only with great reluctance does Trollope allow them to marry. In *Sir Harry Hotspur* Trollope pursues the theme to its ultimate conclusion, making Emily Hotspur faithful to the point of suicide by wasting away. Love apparently demands wholehearted sacrifice once it has been accepted, and his heroines are expected to endure being jilted or not loved in return. Both Emily in *The Prime Minister* and Lady Anna, in the novel of that title, succumb to the conventional decline. Certainly there are grounds for thinking that plot interest demands such melodramatic gestures, but the more important reason is that they testify to the strength of true love. Whatever happens love must remain an ever fixed mark. This is summed up by Emily's view of George: 'his untruths would not justify hers'.[50]

Sir Harry Hotspur is a really interesting example, in fact, of the disastrous collision between truth to life and demands of the ideal, in the question of fidelity to love. Apart from *The Warden*, Trollope seldom did well with the short novel in one volume, but *Sir Harry Hotspur* is a little gem, taut and tart on the tongue. The plot is quite simple, unencumbered by side issues and counterpointing subplots. Sir Harry is anxious about leaving the estates of Humblethwaite in Cumberland in good hands, but the heir to the title, his nephew George Hotspur, is a rake. Sir Harry would prefer his only daughter, Emily, to marry somebody decent like Lord Alfred Gresley, and he would gladly make over the estate accordingly. But Emily falls in love with George, who is eventually exposed as a liar. Knowing how worthless he is, she still refuses to abandon him. So the story ends unhappily, Sir Harry's hopes dashed, the family happiness ruined, and Emily a martyr to love. This dark ending is forecast early on when so much of the novel's theme is clearly being centred on Emily's powerful nature: 'How terrible was the danger of her loving amiss, when so much depended on her loving wisely! The whole fate of the House of Hotspur was in her hands, – to do with as she thought fit!' (ch. ii). As in *The Vicar of Bullhampton* the innocent and lovely heroine is the agent of catastrophe, surrounded at the end by several ruined lives, in this case her own as well. The story also makes the point that wisdom in love is seldom if ever possible.

In synopsis it sounds absurdly melodramatic, but in fact its cumulative power is totally credible, and depends on the tight relationship of the Hotspurs and the insights we get into the family. Sir Harry is one of Trollope's ideal country gentlemen, whose conscience is racked by love of his daughter, concern for her welfare, and duty to the estate; his plight grows steadily more poignant towards the end of the novel, as he discovers more and more damning evidence about his nephew, and finds himself impelled towards a course he knows will destroy Emily's happiness. He is an immensely generous, loving man, forlornly hoping that some miracle will rescue him from the dilemma, even sneakingly drawn to the scapegrace heir, and not in the least impressed by the 'walking sticks' (as Emily calls them) brought in to take her mind off the renegade. He scolds and upbraids, but in his heart he longs for peace; and it is a hard blow when his precious Emily gradually withdraws her little touches of affection. Gloom reigns in the hall as evidence against George accumulates, and the force of the estrangement is felt in the suspension of one of Sir Harry's customary treats:

It was her custom of a morning to spread butter on a bit of toast for her father to eat. This she still did, and brought it to him as was her wont, but she did not bring it with her old manner. It was a thing still done, simply because not to do it would be an omission to be remarked. 'Never mind it,' said her father the fourth or fifth morning after his return. 'I'd sooner do it for myself.' She did not say a word, but on the next morning the little ceremony, which had once been so full of pleasant affection, was discontinued. (ch. xvi)

It is hard to say who is the more wounded by this little exchange. This is the imaginative touch at which Trollope excels, a small detail of the domestic fabric beautifully observed and interpreted.

Part of the tangled situation, we soon realise, stems from the pride Emily has inherited from her father, as he recognises with admiration and dread. Her mother, Lady Elizabeth, is the buffer between them, bullied or cajoled, but fully aware of her own weakness and of what is going on within the family. Tension depends on the family's gentle warfare, upon Emily's intransigence and Sir Harry's vacillation, which give George a chance to win right up to the last minute, and the novel is especially memorable for its perception of emotional ties within the family. One has the impression of boundless love among the Hotspurs that becomes helpless and painful, of the impossibility of saying what one feels, of understanding much yet being incapable of giving it voice. Indeed, there is great emotion beneath the blandness and reticence of this novel. In Chapter ii Emily's disinclination to consider Lord Alfred Gresley as a suitor is implied in the seemingly casual exchange between father and mother, which follows the hints about her interest in Cousin George, a man she hardly knows.

'Is she pleased that he is coming?' he said to his wife, the evening before the arrival of their guest. [Lord Alfred]

'Certainly she is pleased. She knows that we both like him.'

'I remember when she used to talk about him – often,' said Sir Harry.

'That was when she was child.'

'But a year or two ago,' said Sir Harry.

'Three or four years, perhaps; and with her that is a long time. It is not likely that she should talk much of him now. Of course she knows what it is that we wish.'

'Does she think about her cousin at all?' he said some hours afterwards.

'Yes, she thinks of him. That is only natural, you know.'

'It would be unnatural that she should think of him much.'

'I do not see that,' said the mother, keen to defend her daughter from what might seem to be an implied reproach.

'George Hotspur is a man who will make himself thought of wherever he goes. He is clever, and very amusing; – there is no denying that. And then he has the Hotspur look all over.'

'I wish he had never set his foot within the house,' said the father. (ch. ii)

What Trollope achieves here is a poignant combination of parental soli-
citude, wishful thinking, faint irritation with each other occasioned by
their mutual anxiety; in all, a masterly rendering of the relationship
between man and wife.

When Lord Alfred arrives, not yet in love with Emily but ready to
fall, there is a total lack of communication; no one mentions how Emily is
to behave towards him: 'Of the thing to be done, neither father nor
mother said a word to the girl; and she, though she knew so well that the
doing of it was intended, said not a word to her mother. Had Lady Elizabeth known how to speak, had she dared to be free with her own child,
Emily would soon have told her that there was no chance for Lord
Alfred.' It is this inability to bridge the gap, the sheer bad luck of a
missed opportunity, that makes its trenchant comment on our lives.

The crucial issue in this book arises from Emily's stubborn refusal to
get over the shock of being denied the right to marry George, bad as he
is, and her ultimate death. Is it a disastrous collapse of character, a
concession to the public's appetite for sensation, or some quirk of
Trollope's own feelings? Most modern critics would recognise it as a
serious blemish on an otherwise splendid tale. It is scarcely thinkable
that a strong-minded, sensible girl as this would simply pine away. She
might well become an old maid, or more likely a Miss Havisham,
mouldering away in Humblethwaite Hall alone with her bitter memories,
but surely it is too melodramatic to have her expire from love? Trollope
tries hard to justify his ending by suggestions in the earlier part of the
book as to her pride and stubbornness, which are clearly subconscious
defiance of parental authority. And Emily's argument for constancy
is very telling in the mid-section: it becomes a matter of religious
devotion, bound up with ideals of sacrifice and salvation dear to the
Victorian heart. Trollope preaches on the text of Christian hope for
the sinner, and Emily changes before our eyes into that abstraction of
purifying angel so often at war with the human truth. Had he spared
her life all might have been well with *Sir Harry Hotspur*.

Similar problems crop up in other novels. Cecilia Holt, in *Kept in the
Dark*, finds herself unable to confess a prior relationship with a cad once
the highly respectable Mr Western has proposed. She too has come to
regard herself as tainted by this earlier liaison. Florence Burton will
allow no possibility of marriage when she thinks Harry Clavering has
deserted her. In *Cousin Henry*, Isabel Broderick faces a dilemma, for,
having once refused a minor canon of Hereford Cathedral on the extraordinary grounds of her expectations as an heiress, she cannot go back
on her word when she discovers that she is not to be a great lady after
all. Exquisite scruple also occupies Mary Lawrie in *An Old Man's
Love*, who feels honour bound to keep her word to old Mr Whittlestaff, although her true love begs her to break the engagement. All

these ingenious impediments to true love provide Trollope with necessary, sometimes forced, complications of plot, but at the same time bear witness to love as an ideal. Devotion, even to an utterly unworthy man, makes a statement on the sacredness of love, however it may seem to us to reveal perversity or masochism in the heroine. And love in all its purity and permanence is the moral centre of Trollope's work.

For this reason the jilt is very harshly treated. Julia Brabazon ruthlessly casts Harry Clavering aside, and is punished in the early stages of the novel by marriage to the wealthy debauchee, Lord Ongar. Where money and social ambition govern a girl's choice, as we have already seen, Trollope is highly critical. As Miss Dunstable remarks in *Dr. Thorne* to Frank Gresham, who has been urged to marry money:

> Never let them talk you out of your own true, honest, hearty feelings . . . Greshamsbury is a very nice place, I am sure; and I hope I shall see it some day; but all its green knolls are not half so nice, should not be half so precious as the pulses of your own heart.[51]

Having jilted John Grey, not from material motives, but merely doubts about her own nature, Alice Vavasor, in *Can You Forgive Her?*, is made to say: 'I am a fallen creature . . . There are things which, if a woman does them, should never be forgotten; – which she should never permit herself to forget' (ch. lxxiv). Men are let off more easily for being light of love, and are even expected to engage in a little philandering before they settle down. But for men too a price is paid for dishonesty in love. Lying is the unpardonable sin and this is what puts George Hotspur beyond the pale. Lizzie Eustace is to be judged severely as one who subverts human relationships by her enjoyment of lies. Truth in love, therefore, becomes a major concern in *The Eustace Diamonds* (a book concerned indeed with the whole theme of honesty), and it is embodied in Lucy Morris, through whom Frank Greystock learns that 'truth to his sweetheart is the first duty of man' (ch. lxxvi). Similarly the true-love idea runs through *Barchester Towers* in the refrain mockingly sung by Madeline Vesey Stanhope to the discomfiture of Mr Slope:

> It's gude to be merry and wise, Mr. Slope;
>   It's gude to be honest and true;
> It's gude to be off with the old love – Mr. Slope,
>   Before you are on with the new.[52]

A woman's awakening to love is another complicated topic. 'No woman ought to marry a man unless she feels that she loves him,'[53] but finding out if she does can be a problem, since she is expected to be unaware of her feelings until her lover declares an interest. She may, of course, entertain vague fancies of future happiness with the right man, as Mary Lovelace does in the beginning of *Is He Popenjoy?*, but her affection sleeps until the hero awakens it. 'A girl loves most often because she is loved, – not from choice on her part', declares Trollope in *Ayala's Angel*. 'She is won by the flattery of the man's desire.' So for Lucy Dormer it is Isadore's plaintive 'Am I to lose you again?' which tells her that she can no longer do as she pleases with her heart (ch. xvii). Similarly in *Castle Richmond* Lady Clara feels powerless at Owen Fitzgerald's declaration of love 'almost fierce in its energy'.[54]

For a woman to offer her love first is cheap and degrading; Lizzie Eustace does, of course, and we immediately know what to make of her. Mrs Smith, the attractive widow in *John Caldigate*, is unmistakably dangerous once she has openly encouraged the hero's advances on board ship. The female is to be attentive, submissive, docile and properly ignorant of the male's intentions. To reverse the roles and become the huntress is unforgivable. Or nearly always so. Finn can barely get over the shock when Marie Goesler breaks with convention and admits she loves him, but in this case Trollope strongly enlists our liking for her courage. She is older, however. Young girls are advised not to love until the hero has committed himself, as though it were possible to control their hearts (an impossible task, as Trollope will admit on occasion), and Fanny Robarts is greatly perturbed to find Lucy has allowed herself to love without due notice of Lord Lufton's intentions: 'I should have thought that you would have been too guarded to have – have cared for any gentleman till – till he had shown that he cared for you.'[55] The word 'love' is too significant to be bandied about and has to be avoided.

The incidental love story of Mary Wortle and young Lord Carstairs in *Dr. Wortle's School*, quite irrelevant to the main plot, sets out these conventions perfectly. Expelled from Eton, the young rip travels on the continent for a year, and then at eighteen comes under the jurisdiction of Dr Wortle at Bowick School. Mrs Wortle is immediately anxious about her daughter's heart. Lawn tennis in the rectory garden is inevitable, but 'Mrs. Wortle was always there to see fair-play'.[56] On one occasion some months later, however, when the watchful mother is absent during one of the tennis games, Lord Carstairs asks Mary to marry him, if she could love him:

> It was a most decided way of declaring his purpose, and one which made Mary feel that a great difficulty was at once thrown upon her. She really did not know whether she could love him or not. Why shouldn't she have been able to love him? Was it not natural that she should be able? But she knew that she ought not to love him, whether able

or not. There were various reasons which were apparent enough to her though it might be very difficult to make him see them. He was little more than a boy, and had not yet finished his education. His father and mother would not expect him to fall in love, at any rate till he had taken his degree. And they certainly would not expect him to fall in love with the daughter of his tutor. She had an idea that, circumstanced as she was, she was bound by loyalty both to her own father and to the lad's father not to be able to love him. She thought that she would find it easy enough to say that she did not love him; but that was not the question. As for being able to love him, – she could not answer that at all. (Part V, ch. iv)

Mary Wortle is curiously innocent and naïve about her feelings, a mixture of prudent common sense and maidenly modesty. When the young man's father writes to the Wortles, agreeing to the match but suggesting that the couple wait until his son finishes his degree, Dr Wortle is delighted: 'How could she possibly fail to love the young man if encouraged to do so?' (Part V, ch. viii). For the mother there is much anxiety in the thought of a long engagement and conversation with her daughter turns on the awful prospect 'If he were to change his mind?' As Mrs Wortle says: 'But if there were to be no regular engagement, and you were to let him have your heart, – and then things were to go wrong!' The difference in attitudes to love between man and woman is summed up by the Doctor:

A man throws himself into it headlong, – as my Lord Carstairs seems to have done. At least all the best young men do . . . A young woman on the other hand, if she is such as I think you are, waits till she is asked. Then it has to begin. (Part V, ch. x)

Having repulsed the young man Mary was still heart-whole, but once his feelings have been sanctioned by virtue of his father's letter she then feels love. It is an oddly Trollopian view of the onset of love advanced to meet conventional Victorian ideals of pure womanhood.

True heroes propose impetuously like Will Belton, clumsily like Lord Chiltern, or incoherently like Dr Crofts – sometimes, as in *Ayala's Angel*, the recognition of love is wordless – but when cads like Crosbie propose they rise to the occasion with a cluster of well-turned compliments. The usual response has to be one of utter astonishment. Faced with Mr Arabin's declaration, Mrs Bold, belying her name, fled like a roe from the chamber. The true declaration is often unpremeditated. As Trollope says in *Barchester Towers*, a gentleman usually proposes 'without any absolutely defined determination' of doing so (ch. xlviii), and his light-hearted instructions in *Orley Farm* are:

Dance with a girl three times, and if you like the light of her eye and the tone of voice with which she, breathless, answers your little questions about horseflesh and music – about affairs masculine and feminine, – then take the leap in the dark. (ch. xxxiii)

For women love enjoins stricter and more complex rules. The demure Clarissa Underwood, in *Ralph the Heir*, has no conception of the risks she runs when Ralph moors his skiff against the bank of Popham Villa, Fulham, and she even enjoys some flirting on the villa lawn. But when he steals a kiss she bursts into tears from shock. Her feelings, half of shame and half of pleasure, are amusingly portrayed:

Wicked and heartless man, who had robbed her of so much! And yet how charming he had been to her as he looked into her eyes, and told her that he could do very much better than fall in love with her West Indian cousin. Then she thought of the offence again. Ah, if only a time might come in which they should be engaged together as man and wife with the consent of everybody! Then there would be no more offences. (ch. iii)

As Victorian prudery begins to relax, female response is less restricted. Young girls are no longer quite so answerable to parental control or hemmed in by the conventions; flirtations proceed more openly on croquet lawn or tennis court. In *Dr. Wortle's School* Trollope is even able to show the lovers at the end of the story walking out alone together in Bowick woods, and embracing in the presence of the girl's parents.

Animation and high spirits are the trademarks of the heroine, and these healthy attributes (with strong implication as to sex appeal) are conveyed with much skill. The trick is to heighten a particular feature – nose, teeth, lips, neck, but most often eyes – and to stress the ordinariness of the subject at the same time. This is done by negative recommendation: she is not this, she is not that, she is not the other, but . . . and then comes the detail that turns an apparently plain woman into a striking one:

Miss Thorne wanted one attribute which many consider essential to feminine beauty. She had no brilliancy of complexion, no pearly whiteness, no vivid carnation; nor, indeed, did she possess the dark brilliance of a brunette. But there was a speaking earnestness in her face; an expression of mental faculty which the squire now for the first time perceived to be charming.[57]

It is a variation of that sleight of hand Trollope used to dispose of the terms hero and heroine, and then let the characters act just as heroically as need be. Of course the demonstration of inner resources and spiritual beauty is conveyed in the whole course of the novel, but Trollope's invariable practice is also to give thumbnail sketches of his men and women, usually as part of the exposition at the beginning which he affects to chafe under.[58] The end Trollope has always in view with such descriptions is to prove that true beauty comes from the soul. Thus he sets off his heroine against a flawless beauty who is patently silly, vain or cold like la Neroni or Griselda Grantly. A Venus is either a mantrap or a fraud, and statuesque Junos have headstrong wills that get them into trouble. Of the Lady Amaldina, daughter of Lord Persiflage in *Marion Fay*, Trollope writes 'as beautiful in colour, shape, and proportion as wax could make a Venus' (I, ch. xii). La Neroni recumbent on her chaise-longue is also a Venus whose dashing Italianate beauty is immediately apparent. Beside her Eleanor Bold has the sort of beauty of which 'the truth and intensity' strike you only later. Trollope often satirises the physical charms of 'bosoms for show, but not for use'.[59]

Some discrepancy seems to exist in his mind between the gentle maiden fair and assertive heroines like Lucy Robarts and Mary Thorne, between the often childlike heroine and one with almost matriarchal decisiveness. Of Mary compared with Frank Gresham we are told 'Though she was a grown woman, he was still a boy' (ch. vii), and Violet Effingham, it will be recalled, 'lacked that sweet, clinging feminine softness, which made Mary Flood Jones so pre-eminently the most charming of her sex.'[60] The point to notice is that Mary Flood Jones is silenced for ever at the end of the novel, for truth to life and the expression of absolutes, in love as anything else, cannot be made to correspond. Trollope's artistic sense tells him that the angel of light does not exist; and if she did Trollope probably would not like her.

There is a basic model of feminine beauty for Trollope: his small brown girls of the Barsetshire novels, whose primary qualities are reserve without dullness, candour without pertness and freshness without art. Consider Lucy Robarts taking charge of the Crawley infants in *Framley Parsonage*, or Grace Crawley standing up to the formidable Archdeacon. Both are hardy, decisive young women who run rings round the men. Energetic females emerge from the doll's house. Emily Trevelyan, feeling herself in the right over an argument with her husband, is not going to back down, and taunts her sister in *He Knew He Was Right* for her counsels of self-abnegation and patience: 'You yourself, – you would be a Griselda, I suppose' (ch. xi). Likewise, improvident young men continue to find ginger hot in the mouth despite what the preacher warns. So we have fine mixed portrayals in Frank Greystock, Harry Clavering, John Caldigate and Phineas Finn, who is without doubt one of Trollope's ablest characterisations, a case of a character outstripping the author's intention, since he emerges as a nasty, philandering young man whose true nature seems to have baffled people in the story as well as generations of readers.

Truth breaks through the tissue and tinsel of popular romance or the rough brown paper of moral efficacy. Florence Burton triumphs in womanly spite over Julia Ongar, arms herself with female pride to visit the Claverings, and fusses over her appearance. Lucy Robarts spits angry denunciations of Griselda Grantly. Where the reality of female psychology gets the better of the idealising process we get a number of astonishingly complex characters, as Pamela Hansford Johnson has remarked.[61] In Julia Brabazon, Lizzie Eustace and Arabella Trefoil amongst others, we sense human sexuality, rather than passionless purity. Glencora's passionate nature is brought out in the first Palliser novel in which she is separated from Burgo Fitzgerald; later the damming-up of this physical side of her nature is partly responsible for the difficulty of her relationship with Plantagenet Palliser. Sexual deprivation is strongly hinted at in Laura Kennedy's marriage to the puritanical Kennedy and her attraction for the very masculine Finn. A good deal of the physical appetites is conveyed in this novel, as they are in *The Bertrams* and *Castle Richmond*.

These are some of the realities against which the angel of light seems fragile and ineffectual. Trollope as artist knew that it represented a dream and, more significantly, that it did not bear much relation to the obligations of real life. As one reads of the marriages in his work, of the Furnivals, the older Claverings, the Grantlys, the Greshams as they appear in *Framley Parsonage*, even the Proudies, one can only ask where the angel of light has gone. Here are real people, bickering, confiding, nagging, separating and sometimes reuniting.

Yet we cannot discard the ideals I have been discussing of loyalty, fidelity, meekness, in the young girl as a misjudgement in art. For the rocks and valleys are not mere apparatus of romance but an expression of joyous anticipation to which ideals of womanhood are tied, and to which Trollope's ethic of fiction is firmly committed. There are unresolved tensions between his artistic and ethical attitudes, but in many cases a synthesis is achieved between what gives life dignity and beauty through love, and the realities of human fallibility. The result in the case of the Barset heroines, for example, is a successful integration of Cordelia's simplicity and steadfast love with the angularities and idiosyncracies that go to make up average humanity. In them it seems that tropological significance coincides with realism of portrayal. By the same token, without jarring our sensibilities or unduly straining our credulity, Trollope often brings high romance and truth to life into peaceful co-existence.

5 The Bread and Cheese

A man's love, till it has been chastened and fastened by the feeling of duty which marriage brings with it, is instigated mainly by the difficulty of pursuit.[1]

When it suits him, as we have seen, Trollope adopts the conventions of romance and stands them on end for gentle mockery of puppy love, all the while exploiting the fairy tale so engagingly that his readers are willing participants in the game of make-believe. We follow lovers' adventures, mistakes and partings up to the grand moment when all problems are solved and the lovers are clasped in each other's arms. What follows in a page or two is perfunctory tidying up of the loose threads until every Jack has his Jill. Some critics scorn this frivolity. But young love is important preparation for later relationships against the stable background of marriage, home, work and satisfying avocations. Perhaps youthful pangs and ecstasies occupy more space than what comes after. This is only to be expected, for pursuit and capture offer such scope to the writer. But in Trollope's case they are only part of the matter; and despite their preponderance in his fiction the less significant part. It is his studies of mature love in marriage through which moral problems are examined, complex characters are explored, and much of the chaotic and disturbing pattern of human life is set before us.

The central plot in every Trollope novel concerns despised or thwarted love, but this must be seen in the context of many other types of love; that within the family, for example, which impinges on the fortunes and decisions of the lovers; or that within other marriages which makes indirect comment or implies standards of behaviour. Almost every book extols the domestic hearth, and speaks of the duties and responsibilities to which the young lovers eventually come as the lasting values of love – its bread and cheese, a useful metaphor suggesting wholesome sustenance. The lovers have to come down from starry heights to grapple with the realities of family and home. Alaric Tudor's maturity is bound up with realisation of the bond between Gertrude and himself that can be honoured only by working for the welfare of his family in Australia. Likewise, if Frank Houston and Imogene Docimer are to find happiness it will come from steady work and a cradle filled annually.[2] One would like to think some irony is intended, since Trollope often mocks the awakening to the harsh realities of married life, but it is not. Trollope is thoroughly committed to the Victorian ideals of family life and the responsibilities of the bread-winner.

I intend to show in the course of this discussion that his ideals of man and wife went further than one might suppose from descriptions of feminine submissiveness and dependence offered as ideals in his stories of young love. Possibly he sees his subjects more clearly, or else, feeling more intensely involved with his material, is less prone to com-promise and arbitrary changes in character. But the chief reason for the more coherent and unified studies of mature love is surely the com-patibility of aims with the situations and characters he creates: he upholds a credible doctrine, rather than an ideal; one that is concerned with the reasonable expectation the individual should have of marriage. 'Bread and cheese' expresses exactly this concept of a workable partner-ship, in which adjustments and allowances must be made. The benefits are considerable but not exciting: mutual encouragement and succour, companionship against the blows of fate or the disastrous consequences of one's own folly and the insults of old age. 'Uphill together have ye walked peaceably labouring'; he writes in one of the more extravagant flights in *The Bertrams*, 'and now arm-in-arm ye shall go down the gradual slope which ends below there in the green churchyard' (III, ch. ix).

Home and its joys figure in Trollope's stories, therefore, as refuge from the hurly-burly of industrial England, creating that ordered back-ground of serenity and confidence behind so many of his novels. Nor does this reflect an ivory tower existence, for the refuge may be breached, or even sometimes mined from within, by irrational human acts. Indeed, unhappiness in marriage is a more common subject than happiness. Honesty compels Trollope to look at conflicts of personalities bound together by the closest of unions; and thus, besides being a sanc-tuary, the home is frequently a battleground of clashing wills and desires. Men abuse their position and become sadists, and women retaliate by trials of strength in which they nag and scold. Mrs Proudie as well as being the traditional Xanthippe has some relevance to the serious question of marital cruelty. Studies in marital collapse stand out in Trollope's fiction: the Kennedys' mortal combat, the Trevelyans' deliberate self-destruction, the Furnivals' slow decay. Trollope's analysis of marriage more closely resembles Meredith's 'Modern Love' than Patmore's 'The Angel in the House'. The angel belongs to love's young dream, not to the realities of making a marriage work.

Yet the ideal is always there. In this respect Patricia Thomson correctly viewed Trollope as the high priest of marriage, but she oversimplified the matter in suggesting that his novels merely flattered Victorian prejudices about the relations between the sexes: 'It was on reading Trollope that Victorians must have felt their ideal of wifely submission was in its finest hour'.³ Not by any means. With discretion and subtlety, Trollope often undermines the shibboleth of male domination, even though by today's standards of female liberation his subversion of the Victorian citadel is extremely tentative. The strong-minded heroine as prototype Women's Libber is made to suffer for rebelling against the conventionally feminine sphere. Though Trollope sympathises with her frustration the most he will allow Lady Laura is to influence politics by helping Phineas in his career. Other girls who long for self-realisation outside the home have to work off their frustrations on horseback after the fox. Typical of Trollope's Junos – they are alike in being imperious, statuesque and aggressive – Caroline Waddington in *The Bertrams* can only fume and dream:

> I have always thought that there was much in this world worth the living for besides love. Ambition needs not be a closed book for women, unless they choose to close it. (II, ch. vii)

On the other hand, his depiction of vigorous young women deferring to masculine leadership is often ironic; his wives soothe, placate and manipulate in a way that shows their superior tact and intellect. Consider Mrs Grantly's adroitness with the Archdeacon, or Lady Hotspur's manipulation of her husband's feelings over their daughter's fondness for George Hotspur. In matters of feeling, women are superior but also in sheer intellect and wit they often outclass the men they humour. The Reverend Mark Robarts and his bright little wife are an obvious example. By implication at least, Trollope is sympathising with women's situation in a man's world. The downtrodden, obedient, adoring female with a vacant mind and an aptitude for water-colouring has no place in Trollope's view of the sound marriage.

If he remained all his life an opponent of the female rights movement, he was close at least to the spirit of what Mill advocated for women.⁴ His anti-feminism results merely in tiresome caricatures such as the Baroness Banman. Where he is more seriously engaged in the nature and problems of women his thinking is nearly always judicious and helpful. In presenting marriage he shows his typical balance and compromise, envisaging a relationship which gives credit both to female intelligence and male pride, involves the faculties and special endowments of either sex, and depends upon mutual concessions and hard work, as the Pallisers come to recognise. As he puts it in *He Knew He*

Was Right, 'When people are married, they must put up with something; – at least, most always.'[5]

One principle Trollope obviously valued was that like should mate with like, particularly in regard to social level. Frequently the marriage theme touches caste and social compatibility, and provides a comment on social changes Trollope observed around him. When he achieved fame in the late fifties everyone was acutely conscious of social mobility and prey to anxieties it engendered. Sudden losses of fortune and rank and equally rapid elevations were commonplace, and a vast public existed for novels of high life, manuals of etiquette, social registers, and the like. The social calendar, gossip, balls and levees, dress and decorum, were the staple of fiction by Mrs Gore, Bulwer Lytton and the young Disraeli. Trollope's novels contain, of course, a much more profound social analysis than is common to the novel of manners, but his fiction is full of observation that reflects his age's preoccupation with social behaviour. One change that fascinated him was the interaction of conservatism and tradition with capitalism and commerce, sometimes vulgar and uncivilised but often full of vitality : the clash of opposites Dickens depicted in Sir Leicester Dedlock and Mr Rouncewell. The de Guests, the Luftons, the de Courcys, or Miss Marrable of *The Vicar of Bullhampton*, are pictured with kindly irony as fossils of the old order. Initially Trollope's fiction deals with them as eccentric oddities, guilty of old-fashioned exclusiveness like Lady Lufton; the only reason Mary Thorne, Lucy Robarts and Grace Crawley are not suitable wives is the insurmountable class barrier. How can the son of a noble house, or even of an archdeacon, ally himself with an apothecary's niece or the child of a lowly curate? The attitude persists into late works. George Roden doubts whether he should marry into a peer's family, since they were 'in truth of a different race; as much so as the negro is different from the white man'. Mrs Roden agrees : 'Unequal marriages never make happy either the one side or the other.'[6] Uneasiness over flouting of caste remains, even though a more flexible society is evolving.

The adjustment of landed families to commercial enterprise is seen in the Barsetshire novels, especially in *Dr. Thorne*, where the old symbols of landed power (Greshamsbury) meet the challenge of a new age. Past and present contrast in the lineage of Dr Thorne and the mushroom title of Sir Roger Scatcherd. The problems of the Greshams epitomise the clash of cultures. Frank 'must marry money', while Augusta, his sister, is engaged to one of the new men of the age, Mr Moffat, 'a young man of very large fortune, in parliament, inclined to business, and in every way recommendable' (ch. iv). Superlative pride of family rests in the de Courcys, especially the Lady Amelia, to whom it appears that the union of birth and trade is 'diluting the best blood of the country, and paving the way for revolutions' (ch. vi), and when her friend, Augusta, asks her advice as to the suit of a promising attorney, Mortimer Gazebee, she receives a broadside :

> Neither money nor position can atone to me for low birth. But the world, alas ! is retrograding; and, according to the new-fangled doctrines of the day, a lady of blood is not disgraced by allying herself to a man of wealth, and what may be called quasi-aristocratic position, I wish it were otherwise; but so it is. (ch. xxxviii)

Lady Amelia, a character in the Jane Austen tradition, is splendidly memorable in her hauteur and inconsistency. Though she would not for worlds see the de Courcy blood defiled, 'gold she thought could not defile' (ch. vii), and for fear of being left on the shelf she obligingly accepts Gazebee as her own husband.

HOME TRUTHS

Marriage between people of different social backgrounds intrigues Trollope, and he certainly does not underestimate its difficulties. In *The American Senator* the attorney, Gregory Masters, is plagued by a nagging second wife, whose social inferiority is part of her resentment towards her stepdaughter, Mary, who has acquired dignity and grace through long association with Lady Ushant of Bragton Hall. 'Ushanting', says Mrs Masters in a moment of inspired nastiness, is what leads the girl to put on airs and bring dissension into the family. Mrs Masters has already been soured by envy and social inferiority when the story opens, for the first Mrs Masters had been the daughter of a clergyman, while her own father was only an ironmonger. Since she could not gain entry into local society, 'she took to hating gentry instead' (ch. iii). The focus of her rancour, however, becomes her husband and the daughter of his first marriage, Mary, and controversy soon erupts over the choice of a husband for her. Mary is in love with a gentleman of scholarly habit, Reginald Morton, and is pursued by a local farmer, Larry Twentyman. Mrs Masters supports the farmer and subjects Mary to a prolonged barrage of sneers and bullying. Chapter xxxiii, 'The Beginning of Persecution', in which the step-mother tries moral blackmail, innuendo, false statement, and all her armoury of prejudice without success, is a study in the power of womankind in domestic situations that is far from the common concept of Trollopian females, a disturbing picture of insidious nagging unrelieved by comic elements.

In Chapter xviii, 'The attorney's family is disturbed', the problem for Mary is whether she should accept an invitation to stay with Lady Ushant which will put her in close proximity with Reginald Morton, a question which is bound up with tensions at home. These tensions are then dramatised in a dialogue between husband and wife in which Mrs Masters' vulgarity brings painful reminders to the husband of his gentle first wife. Next Mrs Morton launches an onslaught on Mary and the chapter ends with a vivid account of the step-mother's self-pity and bitterness. Where Trollope succeeds so well is in capturing the humiliations, the self-absorption and stubbornness of the guilty party, the hurtful nature of the accusations, the inarticulate misery of those not involved, above all the atmosphere while the trouble lasts. Mary and her father naturally draw closer together, and we sympathise with the husband, tight-lipped with disgust and indignation as the tide of blame rolls over his head. But Trollope also secures our understanding of, if not our sympathy for, the wife's sense of inferiority, and genuine wish to act well according to her own lights. The Trollope world is one which for ever seeks to give due regard to the best intention of the worst of us and the fallibility of the most virtuous.

Mrs Masters is an embodiment of the dominant female, and represents for Trollope an unhealthy reversal of roles. Strong-minded girls in love are well enough, but he wants it clearly understood that in marriage there should be mutual agreement, collaboration and sharing of obligations, with voluntary restraint of the will to power. The tyrannous will of either party in marriage is what leads to disaster. It is not that man shall control and women obey, but that a husband tends to lead, initiate and exercise final authority. Violet Effingham is right to fear that marriage with Lord Chiltern will be stormy: 'We are too much alike. Each is too violent, too headstrong, and too masterful'. In fact she curbs her headstrong spirit and the marriage works very well. The Marquess of Hartletop, like Bishop Proudie, is unmanned by lack of spirit: 'the senior lacquey in his wife's train'. The natural state of affairs, on the other hand, is embodied in Marion Fay, who yields to authority, decisiveness, even a little harshness. Mabel Grex vacillates over Lord Silverbridge because of his apparent subservience: 'But I could never feel him to be my superior. That is what a wife ought in truth to feel.'[7] It is worth noting that this doctrine conflicts with the idealising of woman and is part of Victorian ambiguity towards women in general.

Trollope's sympathies were frequently with the woman because she was so often the loser in marriage. If matrimony involved sacrifices for men, for women it meant the bondage of child-rearing, domestic trivia, and few interests outside the home environment other than charity work and the consolations of religion, all of which led to psychological strains few Victorian males cared to contemplate. Trollope shows insight nto this problem. Charity bazaars and good work have little appeal to he spirited heroine of *Is He Popenjoy?* The tedium of marriage for the

woman is implied in much of this novel, especially through Mrs
Adelaide Houghton who found excitement in an outrageous flirtation
with a married man, Lord George Germain. This underestimated novel
has prejudiced many by its title, which I find quite *à propos*, since it
reflects the absurdities over birth and rank with which the story is
most concerned. Unusually for Trollope the story begins with a
marriage. Under the worldly tuition of her father, Dean Lovelace, the
heroine, Mary, is drawn to accepting Lord George Germain, for, as the
Dean observes sagely, 'marquises do not grow on every hedge' (ch. ii).
So, slightly against the dictates of her own heart, Mary marries Lord
George. Twelve months earlier Adelaide De Baron, Lord George's first
love, had suddenly married the wealthy Mr Houghton. It was not long
before Adelaide decided that she had been forced to marry a stupid old
man and needed some freedom as compensation. There is a hint of sup-
pressed sexual deprivation here, revealed in her wish to rival Mary by
having a flirtation with her former admirer. While George, weak-willed
and at the same time high-minded, slips further into Adelaide's clutches,
his own wife receives the flattering attentions of Jack De Baron. 'He was
the source of all the fun that ever came in her way; and fun was very
dear to her' (ch. xxxiii). It seems as if Trollope is setting up a Feydeau
farce in his neat interweaving of characters. And in one scene he
dabbles in material heavily spiced with erotic undertones (for a Victorian reader at any rate) in which Adelaide vamps her lover in front
of her sleeping husband, while a game of bagatelle is going on in the
other room :

'Has she – quarrelled with you, George?' At the sound of his
christian-name from the wife's lips he looked round at the sleeping
husband. He was quite sure that Mr. Houghton would not like to
hear his wife call him George. 'He sleeps like a church,' said Mrs.
Houghton, in a low voice. The two were sitting close together, and
Mr. Houghton's armchair was at a considerable distance. The occasional knocking of the balls, and the continued sound of voices,
was to be heard from the other room. 'If you have separated from
her I think you ought to tell me.'
'I saw her to-day as I came through.'
'But she does not go to Manor Cross?'
'She has been at the Deanery since she went down'.
Of course this woman knew of the quarrel which had taken place
in London. Of course she had been aware that Lady George had
stayed behind in opposition to her husband's wishes. Of course she
had learned every detail as to the Kappa-kappa. She took it for granted
that Mary was in love with Jack De Baron, and thought it quite
natural that she should be so. 'She never understood you as I should

1   Anthony Trollope (drawn by R. Birch, after
     a photograph by Sarony)

2a Waltham House (in 1900)

2b Harting Grange, North Front

"IT'S DOGGED AS DOES IT."

3   A Trollopian maxim from *The Last Chronicle of Barset,*
    illustrated by George Thomas

4   Lord Lufton and Lucy Robarts in *Framley Parsonage,* illustrated
by J. E. Millais

Christmas at Noningsby. — Morning.

Christmas at Noningsby. — Evening.

5   Illustrations by J. E. Millais from *Orley Farm*

Trevelyan and child

Jemima Stanbury

Caroline Spalding

Bozzle

Mr Gibson and Arabelle French

6   Vignettes by Marcus Stone from *He Knew He Was Right*

'When the letter was completed, she found it to be one which she could not send.'

Mary Lowther writes to Walter Marrable.

7 Agonies at the writing desk: from *The Vicar of Bullhampton*, illustrated by H. Woods (left) and frontispiece to *Kept in the Dark* by J. E. Millais (right)

"You, I think, are Miss Melmotte."

8 Illustration by Luke Fildes from *The Way We Live Now*

have done, George,' whispered the lady. Lord George again looked at the sleeping man, who grunted and moved. 'He would hardly hear a pistol go off.'

'Shouldn't I?' said the sleeping man, rubbing away the flies from his nose. Lord George wished himself back at his club. (ch. xlvii)

Of course, sanity is restored in the nick of time, husbands and wives discover they loved each other all along, and the curtain is rung down on this charming comedy with the birth of a little Popenjoy, whose destiny has had little if anything to do with the novel.

Is He Popenjoy? comments forcibly on the hyprocrisy of one set of rules for husbands and another for wives, and the absurdity of contemporary ideas of feminine propriety, according to which slang, bagatelle and fortune-telling were unacceptable. Mary, egged on by Mrs Montacute Jones, an emancipated and colourful socialite, commits the dreadful gaffe of taking to the floor with Jack and dancing the Kappakappa. Mrs Jones, a splendid Dame Edith Evans character, echoes the Dean's common sense, and offsets the absurd spokeswomen for Female Rights, Dr Olivia Q. Fleabody, the Baroness Banman and Aunt Ju.

Much trenchant irony in the novel is directed against male egotism, itself a form of tyranny in marriage. As Lady Chiltern drily remarks to Phineas Finn, 'What man thinks of changing himself so as to suit his wife?'[8] For Trollope a successful marriage demands that each must learn to respect the other's feelings and, above all, be tolerant; as the Dean tells his daughter 'whatever you do, make the best of your husband' (ch. xviii). His advice concerning her domestic responsibilities is amusing:

Men, he had assured her, were to be won by such comforts as he described. A wife should provide that a man's dinner was such as he liked to eat, his bed such as he liked to lie on, his clothes arranged as he liked to wear them, and the household hours fixed to suit his convenience.

The doctrine of expediency in the mouth of a churchman also exposes a male vanity Trollope laughs at, for the passage continues:

She should learn and indulge his habits, should suit herself to him in external things of life, and could thus win from him a liking and a reverence which would wear better than the feeling generally called love, and would at last give the woman her proper influence. The Dean had meant to teach his child how she was to rule her husband, but of course had been too wise to speak of dominion.

Not that the kindly old dean has got it wrong, but he perpetuates the idea of marriage as the survival of the fittest, and entirely discounts the mutual understanding which makes for harmonious consultations

E

and decisions. By seeking to arm his daughter against the mastery of the husband he points to the great issue in Victorian marriage, the subjection of women. Trollope does not dispute the role of paterfamilias by any means – and makes this clear in *He Knew He Was Right* – but the male despot 'should make his mastery palatable, equitable, smooth, soft to the touch, a thing almost unfelt' (ch. v). George disappoints in this respect. Weak-minded and hypercritical, his view of matrimony is summed up in one phrase, 'What a man does is different' (ch. xxxix). Trollope disagrees, and provides hero and heroine with parallel temptations, whereby George is seen to be by far the most blameworthy. Not only does he fall for Adelaide's blandishments, but he is deceitful into the bargain, and Trollope enjoys showing him up. Some fine narrative passages exploit his mixed feelings and misconceptions about marriage. As he toys with the idea of a flirtation, vanity is uppermost: having kissed Adelaide,

> He was so moved by his various feelings, that he could only walk by himself and consider things. To her that final embrace had meant very little. What did it signify? He had taken her in his arms and kissed her forehead. It might have been her lips had he so pleased. But to him it had seemed to mean very much indeed. There was a luxury in it which almost intoxicated him, and a horror in it which almost quelled him. That she should so love him, as to be actually subdued by her love, could not but charm him. He had none of that strength which arms a man against flatterers – none of that experience which strengthens a man against female cajolery. It was to him very serious, and very solemn. There might, perhaps, have been exaggeration in her mode of describing her feelings, but there could be no doubt in this, that he had held her in his arms, and that she was another man's wife. (ch. xix)

Is He Popenjoy? is a useful example of how Trollope steered close to the wind without offending sensibilities.

Through George's carelessness with a love note the shabby romance is unmasked, and the prospect he has most dreaded, not being able to lord it over his wife, becomes a reality. However, male ego is safeguarded by the salutary experience of begging his wife's forgiveness, and Mary has the novel pleasure of being able to offer her pardon:

> Then, and not till then, he is her equal; and equality is necessary for comfortable love. But the man, till he be well used to it, does not like to be pardoned. He has assumed divine superiority, and is bound to maintain it. Then, at last, he comes home some night with a little too much wine, or he cannot pay the weekly bills because he has lost too much money at cards, or he has got into trouble at his office and

is in doubt for a fortnight about his place, or perhaps a letter from a lady falls into wrong hands. Then he has to tell himself that he has been 'found out'. The feeling is at first very uncomfortable; but it is, I think, a step almost necessary in reaching true matrimonial comfort. Hunting men say that hard rain settles the ground. A good scold with a 'kiss and be friends' after it, perhaps, does the same (ch. xxxii)

The viewpoint is male, and the expression arch, but the idea behind it is basically sound, and the bon mot at the beginning exactly captures Trollope's cheerful good sense: 'equality is necessary for comfortable love'.

THE PALLISER MARRIAGE

Trollope's most detailed study of marriage is the Pallisers. As a *mariage de convenance* of two utterly dissimilar natures it should, according to what we have seen so far, have been disastrous. It began unpropitiously when Glencora McCluskie, a Scots heiress, was compelled to marry, against her heart's persuasion, the rising politician Plantagenet Palliser, heir to the Duke of Omnium. Glencora had fallen deeply in love with a charming wastrel, Burgo Fitzgerald, and once, in anger, saw her marriage with Palliser as a vile betrayal of her nature: 'I did it like a beast that is driven as its owner chooses'.[9] A woman who marries without love will break her heart, Trollope has said so often. But the long study of Cora's life with Planty over the Palliser novels shows how she survives and grows in stature: instead of tragedy we have a study of evolving grandeur which expresses Trollope's ideas of the mutual respect and obligation essential to a working marriage. The Palliser marriage also shows the kind of partnership many people experience, full of regrets, unfulfilled dreams and petty irritations, but one which lasts, and even achieves a kind of quiet happiness. It is the perfect expression of what Trollope means by the bread and cheese of love, and in Glencora's development he evokes exquisite pathos.

Their story really begins with the Barsetshire chronicles and the old Duke of Omnium, an immensely rich Whig potentate, remote, bored, mysterious and with a decided whiff of corruption about him. His ruthlessness is suggested in *Framley Parsonage*, in which his agent and manager, Fothergill, acts for him to dispossess Sowerby and absorb Chaldicotes into his estates. His power is so great, we learn from *Dr. Thorne*, that he rivalled the Queen herself in his revenues and disdained relationships with royalty. Everyone (except Lady Lufton) kow-tows to his ducal magnificence at Gatherum Castle, a quarter-of-a-million-pound stage set, in which unsavoury tycoons like Lord Boanerges are entertained and cabals plot future Whig strategy. Though he separates himself from all this, the old Duke is rumoured to be a debauchee, and his closeness to the Dowager Marchioness of Hartletop in *Framley Parsonage* and proposal to Marie Goesler in *Phineas Finn* bear this out. In every way he is the opposite of his nephew and heir, Plantagenet, who first appears in *The Small House at Allington*, at twenty-five 'a man of mark in the world', diligently pursuing his parliamentary career but in society 'quiet, reserved, and very often silent' (ch. xxiii). Foolishly involved in a flirtation with Lady Dumbello, he is cautioned by his uncle, who reminds him of his high destiny, and so in course of time he is married to a suitable lady.

Glencora McCluskie, when we first meet her in *Can You Forgive Her?*, a novel of restlessness and tension, is wayward and dissatisfied. Her life runs a parallel course with that of her unhappy cousin, Alice Vavasor, who, by jilting her lover, acts out what threatens Cora's marriage. Glencora is innocent and vulnerable, but never quite succeeds in quelling that streak of wildness in her nature which so captivated both men and continues after marriage to break out now and then. Early in *Can You Forgive Her?* she becomes Lady Glencora Palliser 'with all the propriety in the world', but she has married, as her cousin expresses it, against the code which demands one 'to be true to her love if her love was in itself true' (ch. xviii). Inevitably she must pay a price in shame at her own nature and guilt over both men's lives, and Trollope shows her very clearly at times a prey to misery and nervous excitement.

She and Planty are entirely different in temperament and interests. He is silent; she is a talker. He is shy, melancholy, slow to anger, orderly, and completely dedicated to his work; she is volatile, gregarious, gay and given to flashes of vulgarity which are the opposite of his gravity and decorum. There is a splendid example of their difference in the account of the visit to Europe towards the end of *Can You Forgive Her?*

They went into no society at Paris, and at the end of a week, were all glad to leave it.

'I don't know that Baden will be any better,' Lady Glencora said; 'but, you know, we can leave that again after a bit, – and so we shall go on getting nearer to the Kurds.'

To this, Mr. Palliser demurred. 'I think we had better make up our mind to stay a month at Baden.'

'But why should we make up our minds at all?' his wife pleaded

'I like to have a plan,' said Mr. Palliser.

'And so do I,' said his wife, – 'if only for the sake of not keeping it.'

'There's nothing I hate so much as not carrying out my intentions,' said Mr. Palliser (ch. lxviii)

It is easy to see why these characters grew so large in Trollope's mind and why they remained his favourites. They charm the reader with total reality embodying a common stock of illogicality and cross-grained emotional and psychological density.

Cora is the livelier and more waspish, and through the series torments her quiet husband, but she suffers more, for beneath her gaiety and sparkle she is a bewildered and eventually disenchanted woman. Putting that wild love episode behind her she sets herself to make her marriage work, but Burgo cannot be forgotten, and indeed comes back to haunt her. Planty is not a brilliant man, and certainly not an impressive politician, and his dullness in Parliament or at Matching serves to in-flame Cora's longing for sexual fulfilment. His satisfaction lies in his career, and once he has tidied up his private life by a judicious match (as he thinks) he gets on with his work, so wholeheartedly indeed that he commits the heinous crime in *Phineas Redux* of neglecting the coverts. But he neglects his wife above all. Unlike Burgo, he is a very unromantic man, inhibited by shyness, and details in the story clearly imply his sexual inadequacy and Cora's physical frustration. His dry nature 'realised neither the delights nor the dangers of love' (ch. xliii). Greeting her after a short absence, he takes her hand and kisses her, 'but it was the embrace of a brother rather than of a lover or a husband' (ch. xlii). Even when making his admission of love, Planty omits the physical contact she yearns for:

> She followed him and took hold of him as he went, so that he was forced to turn to her once again. She managed to get hold of both his hands, and pressed them closely, looking up into his face with her eyes laden with tears. He smiled at her gently, returned the pressure of the hands, and then left her, – without kissing her. It was not that he was minded not to kiss her. He would have kissed her will-ingly enough had he thought that the occasion required it. 'He says that he loves me,' said Lady Glencora to herself, 'but he does not know what love means.' (ch. lix)

This and the scene at the end of the previous chapter are two of the rare moments of actual love-making in Trollope and are quite free from the mawkishness of sensational romance.

In contrast with Planty's lack of sexual motivation, Burgo's is highly apparent; he responds to Cora's beauty in a way she desires, and although Trollope makes ambiguous references to his want of money, the evidence points to strong physical desire:

And among other things, he wanted the woman's beauty of the woman whom he coveted. He wanted to kiss her again as he had once kissed her, and to feel that she was soft, and lovely, and loving for him. (ch. lxvi)

Cora's attachment to the priory ruins are as symbolic of her physical needs as the Basle river scene, much later in the novel, when the sight of swimmers borne helpless in the flood wrings from her the heartfelt sentiment, more to be expected in Lawrence than Trollope: 'how beautiful to be carried along so quickly; and to go on, and on, and on! I suppose we couldn't try it?' (ch. lxix). The note of lost joy, impermanence, and happiness never quite achieved, runs through the entire Palliser series, and has its apotheosis in *The Duke's Children*, where the problem is seen through the eyes of Plantagenet, an old man troubled by the past.

What Glencora and Plantagenet have in common – integrity, pride, conscience and generosity of soul – only serves to increase their problems in *Can You Forgive Her?*, and they drift further apart. She grows more tormented in spirit and more reckless, harbouring a letter from Burgo in secret and even encouraging his attentions for a while. Being childless is another focus of her guilt and sense of failure. Trollope manages to convey desperate gaiety cloaking a growing sense of futility. A petty row over the arrangements to attend Lady Monk's party splendidly depicts frayed nerves and mutual irritation. Cora seizes by instinct on what will aggravate her fastidious husband:

On the morning of Lady Monk's party a few very uncomfortable words passed between Mr. Palliser and his wife.
'Your cousin is not going, then?' said he.
'Alice is not going.'
'Then you can give Mrs. Marsham a seat in your carriage?'
'Impossible, Plantagenet. I thought I had told you that I had promised my cousin Jane.'
'But you can take three.'
'Indeed I can't, – unless you would like me to sit out with the coachman.'
There was something in this, – a tone of loudness, a touch of what he called to himself vulgarity, – which made him very angry. So he turned away from her, and looked as black as a thunder-cloud.
'You must know, Plantagenet,' she went on, 'that it is impossible for three women dressed to go out in one carriage. I am sure you wouldn't like to see me afterwards if I had been one of them.'
'You need not have said anything to Lady Jane when Miss Vavasor refused. I had asked you before that.'

'And I had told you that I liked going with young women, and
not with old ones. That's the long and the short of it.'
'Glencora, I wish you would not use such expressions.'
'What! not the long and the short? It's good English. Quite as
good as Mr. Bott's, when he said in the House the other night that
the Government kept their accounts in a higgledy-piggledy way.
You see, I have been studying the debates, and you shouldn't be
angry with me.' (ch. xlix)

This passage is dense with covert gibes and undercurrents. The reader
is already aware that Planty is hostile towards Alice, and he begins by
avoiding her name. Cora, on the other hand, regards Mrs Marsham and
Mr Bott as duenna and spy respectively, and she presses home her
advantage until her husband is reduced to picking her up for a speech
mannerism. Even then she rallies and strikes again with a sarcastic
reference to her assumed interest in politics, and in one area, finance,
particularly mortifying to him. Cora discharges a fusillade, hitting her
bird on both wings and breast as well. Her sharp tongue and quick wit
will always overcome his scrupulous sensitivity, and at the Baden casino
she is very spiteful indeed. This early seeding in Palliser's mind of her
tendency to vulgarity continues in other novels, especially *The Prime
Minister*, and increases soreness of spirit for each of them. In this way
Trollope shows how small irritations can become fixed patterns of
grievance.

Lady Monk's party provides Burgo's opportunity to ask Cora to
elope, and in one of those elaborate set-pieces frequent in Victorian
novels, Cora takes the floor with Burgo. Trollope conveys her feeling of
recklessness and unreality as she waltzes; she seems to be standing outside herself as she dances, looking at her cavalier, then at Mrs Marsham
and other reproachful eyes. In one of his fine dramatic touches Trollope
breaks the spell by Burgo's injudicious reference to the 'old days' which
brings Cora out of her dream. Burgo makes his proposal, and Cora,
lacking the strength to refuse him outright, temporises by agreeing
to see him again. The even more powerful confrontation with Plantagenet in 'The Pallisers at Breakfast' (ch. lviii), in which she admits she
loves Burgo is a turning-point, however, in that her husband awkwardly
tries to reach out to her by offering to take her abroad. This unselfish
act is indeed a token of his love, as it prevents him from becoming
Chancellor of the Exchequer, and it is the beginning of a mature relationship. He must acknowledge her as a woman with all her faults,
and she must learn to curb her impetuous follies and consider his happiness. The European journey is difficult and fraught with tensions.
Cora often acts childishly, but drawing on his reserves of patience and
the love which she has now begun to perceive, he accepts her freakish

outbreak of gambling, and in their chance encounter with the destitute Burgo gently offers to help him. Then Cora discovers she is pregnant and the couple draw closer together. The icy Palliser blood is being thawed, and Cora has begun to come to terms with herself.

In *Phineas Finn* she has thrown herself into the role of Whig hostess, threatening to outdo Planty himself in pride of family. When the old Duke of Omnium at seventy pays court to Marie Goesler, her dynastic sense rebels and she acts to safeguard the line of inheritance for her own little Silverbridge. She has lost some of her innocence learning the harsher ways of the world: 'Mr. Palliser knew well how thoroughly the cunning of the serpent was joined to the purity of the dove in the person of his wife' (ch. lvii), and this shows in her somewhat disenchanted view: 'the world was right, and that grooves were best' (ch. lxii). Thus the old Duke will be made to toe the line and forgo his little romance, just as she had done many years ago. Trollope's triumph in the Pallisers is to convey how the past is always with them and, indeed, confronts Planty a second time when his daughter wishes to make an imprudent match with Frank Tregear. Throughout the series we are conscious of a growing comradeship in the Pallisers, despite their dissimilar natures, and possibly because of the conscious efforts each has had to make to accommodate the past. This is particularly so in Cora's case. She will always feel a hankering for lost romance, and we see her now punishing Planty with her sharp tongue, now defying convention in outbursts of her pent-up spirit. Sacrifices and retribution form a major part of the Palliser marriage for both parties. While Planty grows ever more devoted to parliamentary blue books and his precious decimal coinage, Cora rashly befriends the dangerous Lizzie Eustace and interests herself in the scandalous affair of the diamonds. Later she champions a worthier cause, but no less impetuously when she takes up the cudgels for Finn in *Phineas Redux.* But her greatest follies are reserved for *The Prime Minister,* when her zeal to make her husband a popular political leader rebounds disastrously and awakens all the old wounds of her early life.

The last two Palliser novels, *The Prime Minister* and *The Duke's Children,* were not the most successful of the series, for Trollope was no longer the doyen of domestic studies he had been. Yet these graceful works best express the love and marriage theme. In striving and recovery after misjudgement on both sides, the Pallisers seem to reach a bond of reciprocal awareness that fully expresses for Trollope a state of positive human experience to which his energies as a writer were directed. *The Prime Minister* is a novel of purposes mistook, fall'n on the inventors' heads, a gentle exposure of motives and a study of the tender consciences and pride of both husband and wife. We come to another crisis in the marriage. Cora's injudicious meddling in *Phineas*

Redux, when she tried to assist Finn to a post, and used her influence to discredit Bonteen as a potential cabinet member, is again a feature of the plot. As her authority, energy and power over the Duke have increased, so has the magnitude of her blunders. To advance her husband's position when he has at last become Prime Minister, and, as she thinks, to mitigate his austere and retiring manner, she becomes a kind of campaign manager, committing two major indiscretions, both of which cause much inconvenience and embarrassment. To begin with, Plantagenet is a reluctant Prime Minister, impelled by his strong sense of duty to assume the office and entirely unmoved by personal ambition.[10] Glencora, on the other hand, is excited, greedy and opportunistic, and resolves at once to remedy his excess of scruple by her own powers. Trollope amusingly describes her feeling a little like Lady Macbeth as she schemes to consolidate his power.

At this point, what has been throughout the series the triumph of Trollope's art in characterising Plantagenet, a sense of inadequacy, an over-active conscience, and morbid distrust of his own motives, produces secret suffering in him, and the disparity of view between husband and wife is most noticeable. Embarking on a round of sumptuous receptions and banquets, Cora decides that Gatherum Castle must lower its hospitality on all those who can in any way promote the popularity of the Prime Minister. Members of the press, influential city men, rising barristers and representatives of the arts are systematically cultivated, among them the entrepreneur with political aspirations, Ferdinand Lopez, who is to cause Cora's second tactical blunder.

This social coruscation at Gatherum Castle, described with great relish, is the climax of Cora's promotion of the Prime Minister. It provides a series of cameos illustrating the tangle of emotions between husband and wife, as the Duke, aware of his inadequacy in parliament, begins to suspect that it is due to his wife's public relations campaign that his position remains secure. This mortifying and totally false impression intensifies his misery, just as his dislike of show increases at the massive alterations Glencora is effecting at Gatherum, of which he was unaware. In his anger, he stings his wife with the reproach that her attempts to exploit their rank and wealth are vulgar, but Glencora obstinately persists and, to make matters worse, proposes that her husband should assist her protégé, Lopez, to a vacant constituency. The round of entertainments continues through the autumn and to Christmas, the Duke, increasingly aware that he is neither gregarious nor communicative, growing steadily more uncertain. His friend, the Duke of St Bungay, sees him as the prey of 'a certain nervous sensitiveness' (ch. xxvii), and later in the story recognises that Palliser has not the kind of thick-skinned resilience that the premiership demands: 'he is a little too conscientious, a little too scrupulous' (ch. lxvii).

Escaping for a few moments from the press of ambitious politicians and sycophants at Gatherum Castle, the Duke takes a stroll with Lady Rosina de Courcy, and we get a vivid impression of his loneliness and misery. Their conversation, as distant as it can be from public affairs, is about the weather and the efficacy of good boots with cork soles. It is one of those simple illuminating moments at which Trollope excels: 'I think I owe my life to cork soles' said Lady Rosina enthusiastically,' and for a moment the Duke is lifted from his gloomy isolation, as he reflects on his liking for her: 'She was natural, and she wanted nothing from him' (ch. xxvii). This oasis of calm evaporates like a mirage when the egregious Major Pountney catches him by the stables and baldly asks for the vacant parliamentary seat at Silverbridge. For once the Duke loses his temper, and stalks off to brood on the vexations his wife has brought him. In the altercation that inevitably follows Cora displays that disregard of principle which makes her such an intriguing opposite to her husband: 'Anything is constitutional, or anything is unconstitutional, just as you choose to look at it', insisting that Plantagenet may dispose of Silverbridge in the manner of his ancestors with their pocket boroughs (ch. xxvii). On the other hand, the yardstick of her husband's behaviour (as it is of Trollope's) is that honesty cannot admit of any deviation, and when, through Cora's interference in the election on behalf of Lopez, a taint of irregularity attaches to him, he is utterly prostrated.

The intricacies of their relationship at this point are beautifully rendered in 'What business is it of yours?' (ch. xxxii): the slightly guilty mockery she displays in defending her own course of action, her changes of tactics, and his impotent anger, his sense of injustice and self-pity – and all the while a sense of their underlying affection for each other. Yet the depth of sorrow comes only later, when Lopez, having lost the election, writes a letter demanding his expenses as the candidate openly supported by the Duchess. As always, quotation cannot capture the fullness of statement that means so much in Trollope. But Trollope's eye misses nothing, from Cora's reading slowly, playing for time, under Planty's concentrated glance to her typical explosion, 'the man is a blackguard, – of course'. When he gently reminds her that Lopez had been her friend, she hedges: 'he was my acquaintance'. The Duke tries to remain calm, but cannot resist upbraiding her, and her temper flares: 'Do you want to make me roll in the gutter because I mistook him for a gentleman?' Her husband's despairing response stuns her momentarily:

That was not all, – nor half. In your eagerness to serve such a miserable creature as this you forgot my entreaties, my commands my position! I explained to you why I, of all men, and you, of a women, as a part of me, should not do this thing; and yet you did it, mistaking such a cur as that for a man! What am I to do? How am I to free myself from the impediments which you make for me? My enemies I can overcome, – but I cannot escape the pitfalls which are made for me by my own wife. I can only retire into private life and hope to console myself with my children and my books. (ch. xxxii)

A tinge of self-pity imperceptibly leads the reader's sympathy towards Cora, for even in despair the Duke is stiltedly aloof. Nevertheless, for the moment Glencora is abashed:

> There was a reality of tragedy about him which for the moment overcame her. She had no joke ready, no sarcasm, no feminine counter-grumble. Little as she agreed with him when he spoke of the necessity of retiring into private life because a man had written to him such a letter as this, incapable as she was of understanding fully the nature of the irritation which tormented him, still she knew that he was suffering, and acknowledged to herself that she had been the cause of the agony. 'I am sorry,' she ejaculated at last. 'What more can I say?' (ch. xlii)

To end the affair the Duke does pay Lopez, but the incident is taken up by the gutter press and mentioned in the House.

At this point Trollope emphasises Glencora's remorseful following of the news. This is an important shift, since it crystallises her latent response to the Duke's character, and subtly reintroduces those strands of her early life which have tied her into this complex pattern of behaviour. She contemplates irreconcilable differences between their natures with a determined objectivity. Yet the strength of their relationship is consolidated by the very heartaches and struggles they have endured. Her confidante is Mrs Finn:

> 'Though in manner he is as dry as a stick, though all his pursuits are opposite to the very idea of romance, though he passes his days and nights in thinking how he may take a halfpenny in the pound off the taxes of the people without robbing the revenue, there is a dash of chivalry about him worthy of the old poets. To him a woman, particularly his own woman, is a thing so fine and so precious that the winds of heaven should hardly be allowed to blow upon her. He cannot bear to think that people should even talk of his wife . . . He is all trust, even when he knows that he is being deceived. He is honour complete from head to foot. Ah, it was before you knew me when I tried him the hardest. I never could quite tell you that story, and I won't try it now; but he behaved like a god. I could never tell him what I felt, – but I felt it.'

'You ought to love him.'

'I do; – but what's the use of it? He is a god, but I am not a goddess; – and then, though he is a god, he is a dry, silent, uncongenial and uncomfortable god. It would have suited me much better to have married a sinner. But then the sinner that I would have married was so irredeemable a scapegrace.' (ch. lvi)

Sentimentality is avoided by self-mockery and the reassertion of what still separates; this is Trollope's triumph, for while each learns to reverence the other's spirit, there is still no escape from the necessities of their natures. Thus the Duke of Omnium at the moment of grieving over Cora's death is mindful 'that in the exuberance of her spirits she had been a trouble rather than a support to him'.[11] Cora is still wryly scornful of Planty's impossibly pure nature. In the course of *The Prime Minister*, through her newly-awoken devotion to him, she arrives at mature perspective. The old Duke of St Bungay observed 'that though she had failed to love the man, she had given her entire heart to the Prime Minister' (ch. lxvi), assuaging the loss of a romantic love with something, less sweet perhaps, but durable and sustaining – the bread and cheese of love. This is no facile evading of the real problems of married life, for Cora remains moody, silent, angry at her husband for withdrawing from political life after his failure as Prime Minister. She blames him, and in vindicating her own course of action sounds the familiar note of self-justification that makes Trollope's characters so true to life. 'I was right' is the cry that issues from the inmost souls of all Trollope's most interesting people.

In *The Duke's Children* Trollope showed the same ruthless hand which despatched Mrs Proudie in *The Last Chronicle*. This time no gossiping clergymen overheard in the Athenaeum prompted the fatal blow, but the novelist's sense that his greatest hero, the Duke, should now be tried to the utmost. It is a fitting coda to the series. So the first sentence reads: 'No one, probably, ever felt himself to be more alone in the world than our old friend, the Duke of Omnium, when the Duchess died.' One can imagine with what qualms Trollope began in this way, for Glencora had been one of his favourite characters. Mrs Proudie's death was majestic and bizarre, Glencora's commonplace but equally appropriate: the vital, incomparable Cora snuffed out by a sudden bout of influenza. 'When she left town the Duchess was complaining of cold, sore throat, and debility. A week after their arrival at Matching she was dead' (ch. i). There is an awful irony here that runs through the book and, indeed, the whole series, drawing attention to the arbitrary events which confound human endeavour.

Attention is focused on the Duke in old age, alone as never before and poised on the brink of new misfortunes. Yet though the Duchess is dead her presence is palpable, and results in a rich texture of past and present. True to her nature she has left a legacy of disturbance and disorder, for she has encouraged her daughter, Lady Mary Palliser, to entertain imprudent love for an irresponsible young Cornishman of limited means, Frank Tregear. She has done so secretly, and her role in the affair naturally causes the Duke much pain, not least because the situation appears a deliberate reliving through her daughter of that lost romance many years ago with Burgo Fitzgerald. The scrupulous old Duke must remember what he has tried to forget, the guilt and remorse, together with the added pain that Burgo's love had touched her as his had failed to do. The past has returned with a vengeance, particularly as Lady Mary looks like her mother. By this ingenious direction of the plot Trollope draws out a thread of anguish and pathos like the dying notes of Mr Harding's violoncello.

The Duke's sorrows come not single spies but in battalions. His son, Lord Silverbridge, shocks him by his political apostasy in joining the Conservatives, while the younger, Gerald, is expelled from Cambridge. Then Silverbridge falls in love with an American, Isabel Boncassen, having led his father to believe that he would make a prudent match with Lady Mabel Grex. This reinforces the love versus prudence theme touched upon in Lady Mary's love for Tregear. Much of the novel confronts the Duke's reserve and pride, handicaps which age has increased. Embittered by Cora's last indiscretion he quarrels with Mrs Finn, whom he wrongly suspects of having abetted Mary in her secret affair, and mortified at his son's lack of feeling for rank and duty he is overwhelmed by loneliness. This grief is described, in a moment that reveals, in a most Trollopian way, the infinite feeling that can be expressed in a usually commonplace action, and those inalterable aspects of Planty's character that hampered his relationship with Cora when she was alive:

> In spite of all her faults her name was so holy to him that it had never once passed his lips since her death, except in low whispers to himself, – low whispers made in the perfect, double-guarded seclusion of his own chamber. 'Cora, Cora,' he had murmured, so that the sense of the sound and not the sound itself had come to him from his own lips. (ch. xv)

Characterisation of the Duke reaches its height in this novel, both as symbol of moral excellence and as psychological study in the ordinary conflicts of human character. The Duke is torn between his love of his children and the code to which his whole life has owed allegiance. He is also a man stranded by old age in a changing society: the generation gap is very noticeable, for example, in his comic-sad lecture to the sons he does not understand, and their hedonistic response to his high-toned oratory. One striking detail – the habitual emphatic gesture with his hands – revives in the reader's mind the disappointment that severance from public life had brought him :

> 'Isn't it a great grind, sir?' asked Silverbridge.
> 'A very great grind, as you call it. And there may be the grind and not the success. But –' He had now got up from his seat at the table and was standing with his back against the chimney-piece, and as he went on with his lecture, – as the word 'But' came from his lips – he struck the fingers on one hand lightly on the palm of the other as he had been known to do at some happy flight of oratory in the House of Commons. 'But it is the grind that makes the happiness. To feel that your hours are filled to overflowing, that you can barely steal minutes enough for sleep, that the welfare of many is entrusted to you, that the world looks on and approves, that some good is always being done to others, – above all things some good to your country; – that is happiness. For myself I can conceive none other.' (ch. xxv)

Having lived by such an ethic, the Duke is utterly perplexed by the frivolousness of his children.

Echoes of the past from time to time not only make this novel an effective summing up of the series, rather in the manner of *The Last Chronicle*, but also convey the idea that the Duke must make the effort to move forward without sacrificing his principles. Details are added to make the continuum of the Duke's life apparent, and to cause him to effect a stocktaking of his experience. One result of this is to fill out the reader's knowledge of the Palliser marriage: how he first became acquainted with Glencora, and the old Duke, his uncle, whispered approval in the young man's ear. This kind of reality in depth is one of the great strengths of Trollope's writing. A cyclical pattern of events contributes striking irony: the sons' gambling is reprehensible to the Duke not only in its flouting of his principles but because it echoes Glencora's temptation at the casino in Baden Baden (in *Can You Forgive Her?*); and the Duke's journey to Vienna with Lady Mary, in a futile attempt to make her forget Tregear, is a reminder of that journey with Glencora many years ago. Always the play of time augments the novel's pathos: 'time, they say, cures all sorrows' (ch. xli). And in one sense it does. The 'wrong' done to Glencora by her repressive guardians forcing her into a loveless match is absolved a generation later when Lady Mary is allowed to marry Frank Tregear. Once again love shall be lord of all. The sin is expiated, and the harmony of a new generation of Pallisers is promised. Likewise in the Silverbridge/Boncassen union an optimistic future is envisaged in the alliance of feudal aristocracy and the new world.

Towards the end of the novel, Trollope reiterates those values which have been embodied in Plantagenet Palliser in a powerful scene between father and son, 'Bone of my bone' (ch. lxi), which signifies the continuity of the family and the leavening of the Duke's personality with greater compassion and warmth. It begins with the unpleasant news that Silverbridge has broken with Lady Mabel Grex and fallen in love with Isabel Boncassen. True to his nature, the Duke brushes aside the boy's inclination to marry for love and reminds him peremptorily of his duty:

> Do you recognize no duty but what the laws impose upon you? Should you be disposed to eat and drink in bestial excess, because the laws would not hinder you? Should you lie and sleep all the day, the law would say nothing! Should you neglect every duty which your position imposes on you, the law could not interfere! To such a one as you the law can be no guide. You should so live as not to come near the law, – or to have the law to come near to you. From all evil against which the law bars you, you should be barred, at an infinite distance by honour, by conscience, and nobility. Does the law require patriotism, philanthropy, self-abnegation, public service, purity of purpose, devotion to the needs of others who have been placed in the world below you? The law is a great thing, – because men are poor and weak, and bad. And it is great, because where it exists in its strength, no tyrant can be above it. But between you and me there should be no mention of law as the guide of conduct. Speak to me of honour, of duty, and of nobility; and tell me what they require of you. (ch. lxi)

It is a fine statement of the patrician ethic, and Silverbridge is right to listen with some admiration. But at the same time it is a touching irony, for this is the case for personal discipline that the Duke spent his life trying to impress on Glencora, and it lacks a human dimension which has all along been the man's handicap. The doctrine has an uncomfortable austerity and coldness, and fails to make sufficient allowance for human fallibility and the generous bonds of family, although Plantagenet is supremely aware of his children's alienation and his need of them. Furthermore he is using his argument rather underhandedly, to divert Silverbridge from an honourable and worthy love which the father thinks should be resisted solely because of rank. It is an uneasy defence of a fine set set of principles applied in an inappropriate context and without regard for what Hutton so aptly called 'the moral hooks and eyes of life';[12] in fact it is just the kind of situation Trollope relishes, and the chapter ends with a reinforcement of the Duke's unease and imperfect philosophy by a neat juxtaposition of inconsistent attitudes. 'Yes, – he liked Isabel Boncassen. But how different was that liking from a desire that she should be bone of his bone, and flesh of his flesh !'

In the last phase of the novel the Duke achieves greater self-knowledge. By giving way he opens his heart to his family, and moves into closer ties with his son by reason of political affairs. The conquest over his pride is seen in his agreement to re-enter politics. This is a significant aspect of his growth in wisdom, for he had vowed, after his disappointments as Prime Minister, never to serve in office again. 'He had much to do to overcome this promise to himself; – but when he had brought himself to submit he was certainly a happier man' (ch. lxxviii).

Trollope's allegedly cavalier attitude to his fiction is belied by the care he gave to the creation of the Pallisers. Rather wistfully he hoped some of his readers would work through the whole series and by doing so would savour the characters, and presumably his art, more fully. Like his Duke of Omnium he was at heart a shy man, too modest by half, and ever prey to self-doubt. Certainly the whole series in chronological order contains a staggering amplitude of reference. Cross references, recurring motifs, the reintroduction of minor characters, give a dimension of reality to the Pallisers unmatched in nineteenth-century English fiction. It is intriguing, for example, to see Glencora as Duchess of Omnium playing the grand dame in *Phineas Redux*, and to recall the bewildered, frightened, rebellious creature in *Can You Forgive Her?* Lecturing Gerald Maule on the realities of marriage her wisdom carries ironies not to be missed in the light of her own subjugation of passionate longings, and the discerning reader will catch an undertone of sadness beneath her flippancy :

'The truth, is, Mr. Maule, you are a very lucky man to find twenty thousand pounds and more going begging about the country in that way.'

'Indeed I am, Duchess.'

'And Adelaide is lucky, too, for I doubt whether either of you are given to any very penetrating economies. I am told that you like hunting.'

'I have sent my horses to Tattersall's.'

'There is enough now for a little hunting, I suppose, unless you have a dozen children. And now you and Adelaide must settle when it's to be. I hate things to be delayed. People go on quarrelling and fancying this and that, and thinking that the world is full of romance and poetry. When they get married they know better.'

'I hope the romance and poetry do not all vanish.'

'Romance and poetry are for the most part lies, Mr. Maule, and are very apt to bring people into difficulty. I have seen something of them in my time, and I much prefer downright honest figures. Two

and two make four; idleness is the root of all evil; love your neighbour like yourself, and the rest of it. Pray remember that Adelaide
is to be married from here, and that we shall be very happy that you
should make every use you like of our house until then.' (ch. lxxvi)

Much the same kind of richness comes from the kaleidoscope of past
and present in the Grantly history, especially *The Last Chronicle*, in
which Henry's imprudent attachment to Grace Crawley revives painful
memories of Griselda, who so assiduously cultivated the Grantly
doctrine of prudent calculation that she turned her heart to stone.
Indeed, both mighty rivers of narrative, Barset and Palliser, come
together briefly in *Can You Forgive Her?* to provide ironic perspective
on passion and prudence. At the crucial moment of Lady Monk's
splendid party an impressive tableau is constructed. Cora, ascending the
staircase, is above Burgo, who leans against the wall watching her
intently, and against her will she has to look back from the top of the
stairs before passing along the upper gallery to Lady Monk's reception
room, where she meets Griselda, Marchioness of Hartletop. The narrative contrasts the two women, and by ironically approving the discretion,
hauteur and coldness of Griselda increases our liking for Glencora.

The consistency in these novels, written over a twelve-year period, is
one of Trollope's great achievements. The Pallisers remain locked in a
marital situation which is both sanctuary and struggle: always striving,
they are never quite whole; needing each other they are constantly at
odds. Their confrontations are of genuine passion rather than the contrived and perfervid encounters of the contemporary love story, and
their sorrows and disappointments infinitely more moving and credible
than one might suppose from reading just one of the series. The
dominant feeling is always one of pathos, for although the Pallisers
move towards each other in a spirit of mutual affection, there is always
the sense that neither has altogether perceived the full extent of each
other's sweetness and worth, that their marriage is one long act of
atonement for a crime against love, in which both were implicated
though innocent. There is an element, too, of that mysterious proximity
of pain in love arising from their dissimilar natures. Failure is nearly
always at hand in some shape or other to alloy their relationship. Each
is denied the complete fulfilment Trollope upholds as an ideal of
marriage, for the compact between them to bury the past poses the
eternal condition of striving for a unity that is always intermittent and
elusive. The two natures can never be completely reconciled, although
after her death the Duke in his grief recalls that 'there had been no
other human soul to whom he could open himself'.[13] The saddest words
in the language – 'If only . . .' are the basis of Trollope's creation of
the Pallisers and the source of their perennial appeal to readers.

THE RAVAGES OF LOVE

Is He Popenjoy? is the comic rendering of la Neroni's hard-boiled remark in *Barchester Towers*: 'Marriage means tyranny on one side, and deceit on the other' (ch. xv). Her own disability was said to have been the result of her husband's physical cruelty. Elsewhere Trollope treats this hidden evil of Victorian family life in several characters: Lord de Courcy, the old Duke of Omnium, the Marquis of Trowbridge and the Earl of Lovel in *Lady Anna*, 'a man who had never yet spared a woman in his lust' (ch. i). Male paranoia is a notable element in *He Knew He Was Right*, the Phineas novels, and *Kept in the Dark*.

Small wonder that so often Trollope's wives are browbeaten creatures like Lady Hermione Clavering. In Chapter xx of *The Claverings* she listens intently and fearfully for Sir Hugh's arrival – 'her ears were acute with sorrow' – after the death of their only child, the one link that kept this austere, selfish man in some sort of tolerant relationship with his wife. We get a sense of the awful silence and tangible misery of the cold house, Hermy's pathetic attempt to reach out and comfort her husband, and his brutal turning away from her; he cannot bear even her touch and she must yield in dumb agony. Later, he abruptly announces that he is going sailing to Norway. 'He took, I think, a delight in being thus over-harsh in his harshness to her. He proved to himself thus not only that he was master, but that he would be master without any let or drawback, without compunctions, and even without excuses for his ill-conduct.' Her feeble remonstrances are met with sneers and the threat of banishment from Clavering to a grimmer house on the edge of Dartmoor. Trollope explains the tangle of her emotions, insisting, as he often does, that though she is cruelly used she cannot hate him. 'We very rarely, I fancy, love those whose love we have not either possessed or expected', Trollope notes, ' – or at any rate for whose love we have not hoped; but when it has once existed, ill-usage will seldom destroy it.' This is Hermione's case, and her suffering is expressed in a commonplace act. Hugh rises early to avoid a farewell:

> but she, – poor fool, – was up by times [sic] in the morning, and, peeping out between her curtains as the early summer sun glanced upon her eyelids, saw him come forth from the porch and descend the great steps, and get into his dog-cart and drive himself away. Then, when the sound of the gig could be no longer heard, and when her eyes could no longer catch the last expiring speck of his hat, the poor fool took herself to bed again and cried herself to sleep. (ch. xxxv)

Thackeray would have dealt with this far more harshly, but Trollope makes more of the human feeling. Within such small compass Trollope gives us the anatomy of a failed marriage, the woman racked by intense love and hurt beyond expression, the husband wretchedly aware of her dependence but unable to overcome his loathing. Oddly enough the sequel to this little scene comes at the end of the novel. Sir Hugh has been drowned off Heligoland, Lady Clavering is now freed from her tyrant husband, but

Ah ! what falsehoods she told herself now of her love to him, and of his goodness to her; pious falsehoods which would surely tend to bring some comfort to her wounded spirit. (ch. xlv)

A similar burden of sorrow and self-delusion is imposed on Lady Scatcherd, relict of the late Sir Roger, the Barchester stonemason. This marriage, and that of the Greshams, are set out amusingly as cautionary examples to Dr Thorne, in Chapter xxxix of *Framley Parsonage*, when he is anxiously debating whether to propose to Miss Dunstable. He quizzes himself on the pros and cons of matrimony, with that over-active conscience which is the burden of nearly every character Trollope is fond of. On horseback he makes his way to Greshamsbury to call on two of his patients : the wife of the squire, Lady Arabella Gresham, and Lady Scatcherd. First he is waylaid by the squire, who 'was very hard set for occupation in these summer months'. A vignette follows of the unoccupied man, bored out of his wits, prolonging conversation as long as possible, harping on the past and then turning sulkily away when the doctor refuses to stay to dinner and insists on going up to the house. Here the performance is repeated by Lady Arabella, with much querulousness and carping about her husband. We get the sense of the doctor's irritation beneath his determined cheerfulness, and the pathos of the woman's confinement in the tedium of her recital of 'such prosy gaieties as came from time to time in the way of her prosy life'. It is brilliant observation of the ordinary affairs of married life and can be read today as relevant to the plight of the retired couple who suddenly find themselves in closer proximity than ever before, and in a sense displaced persons in their society. The circular, random nature of the conversation, the fidgety and disagreeable manner of Lady Arabella, demonstrate Trollope's skill in conveying undercurrents of feeling :

'It frets me dreadfully that I cannot get to see Mary,' Lady Arabella said, as soon as the first ordinary question as to her ailments had been asked and answered.
'She's quite well, and will be over to see you before long.'
'Now I beg that she won't. She never thinks of coming when there can be no possible objection, and travelling, at the present moment,

would be – ' Whereupon the Lady Arabella shook her head very gravely.

'Only think of the importance of it, doctor,' she said. 'Remember the enormous stake there is to be considered.'

'It would not do her a ha'porth of harm if the stake were twice as large.'

'Nonsense, doctor, don't tell me; as if I didn't know myself. I was very much against her going to London this spring, but of course what I said was overruled. It always is. I do believe Mr. Gresham went over to Boxall Hill, on purpose to induce her to go. But what does he care? He's fond of Frank; but he never thinks of looking beyond the present day. He never did, as you know well enough, doctor.'

'The trip did her all the good in the world,' said Dr. Thorne, preferring anything to a conversation respecting the squire's sins.

'I very well remember that when I was in that way it wasn't thought that such trips would do me any good. But, perhaps, things are altered since then.'

'Yes, they are,' said the doctor. 'We don't interfere so much nowadays.'

'I know I never asked for such amusements when so much depended on quietness. I remember before Frank was born – and, indeed, when all of them were born – But, as you say, things were different then; and I can easily believe that Mary is a person quite determined to have her own way.'

'Things were different then' : the phrase echoes, like a long sigh, down the ages. The scene, as vivid now as ever, represents a triumph of Trollope's art of the commonplace, a permanent record of the sad and imperfect but durable partnership of the Greshams.

Next the doctor calls on Lady Scatcherd who can think of nothing but the dead husband whom she has made into a paragon but 'who in his life had ever been to her imperious and harsh, and had sometimes been cruel and unjust'. Despite such strong arguments against marriage, Dr Thorne, in a letter as romantic as a chemist's prescription and far from the rocks and valleys, does propose to Miss Dunstable, and she accepts. This is a fine multiple view of the marriage tie. Lady Scatcherd in particular reminds one of the splendid *coup* Trollope brings off with the Proudies. Better than the well-known scene in which Mrs Proudie is found rigid in death clutching the bedpost is its aftermath, when the bishop experiences a moment of dreadful horror mingled with his relief in the stillness that has descended upon the palace. He is free, alone – and awful misery engulfs him There had been a kind of comfort even in the company of a termagant.

By the time he wrote the Phineas novels Trollope had a surer touch with scenes of marital discord, and the scenes of male cruelty blaze with imaginative intensity rather than theatrical sentiment. *Phineas Finn* and *Phineas Redux* depict one of those introverted and suicidal natures which occur from time to time in Trollope's novels, and which probably derive from the character of his strange, unlovable father, the failed lawyer. Robert Kennedy is a wealthy landowner who keeps a huge estate in Scotland and represents a number of Scottish boroughs in Parliament. A situation similar to that of *The Bertrams* occurs as Laura Standish, another strong-minded, intelligent woman keenly interested in politics, who made the young Phineas her protégé and then married Kennedy for wealth and power, discovers her husband is a tyrant. Kennedy is an interesting study in monomania, meticulous in all he does, fastidious in his habits, snobbish about his place in society and rigidly puritan in his moral attitudes. A tendency to melancholia, noticeable from the start, gradually increases under the stress of his jealousy of Finn, deepens into pathological hatred and brings him to mental collapse. In Laura Kennedy he meets formidable spirit and intellect refusing to submit to the Victorian martinet:

'There are moments, Robert, when even a married woman must be herself rather than her husband's wife. It is so, though you cannot understand it.'
'I certainly do not understand it.'
'You cannot make a woman subject to you as a dog is so. You may have all the outside and as much of the inside as you can master. With a dog you may be sure of both.' (ch. xxxix)

In an age which placed such severe restraints on woman and until the legislation of 1881, denied her, within marriage, control even over her own property, it is interesting to see Trollope reacting so sympathetically. The problem behind the Kennedy situation is that of the married woman without rights treated by the husband as an item of the household establishment; Laura's reaction is an instinctive reaching out for Phineas, who releases her passionate feeling and generosity.

Male insensitivity to the rights and needs of women is frequent and incurs Trollope's profound disapproval. Where the natural, healthy impulses of the wife are thwarted, or where the husband has crudely asserted dominance to disguise his vanity, egotism or weakness, we have scenes of marital disturbance. In the little-known novel, *Kept in the Dark*, the balance is disturbed by the pride of George Western, who magnifies a trivial error of judgement by his wife and treats her with prolonged mental cruelty which comes close to destroying the marriage. In one way or another all the characters succumb to pride. Sir Francis Geraldine represents pride of birth, characterised by selfishness and snobbery instead of dignity and manliness. When the story opens he ungraciously deigns to accept Cecilia Holt as his future bride in order to prevent his cousin succeeding to his title. Neglected and humiliated by the baronet, and ragged past endurance by Francesca Altifiorla, a man-hating spinster, Cecilia jilts Sir Francis, who salves his pride by letting it be known that he terminated the engagement. The affair is gradually forgotten, and in due time Cecilia meets George Western, 'a silent, shy, almost middle-aged man'.[14] Learning that he too has been jilted in the past, Cecilia decides not to tell him about her relationship with Sir Francis, but after their marriage George discovers the secret, and exacts a terrible punishment, refusing to accept her explanations and abandoning her, furious at having been kept in the dark for so long.

Thus a situation develops like that of *He Knew He was Right*, with George wallowing in rancorous self-pity and behaving like the conventional tyrant. Cecilia grows angry when her attempt at reconciliation is rebuffed, and in the latter part of the story Trollope shows each of them adamant. Of the two, George is certainly the more reprehensible, his pride like that of Sir Francis the expression of unworthy masculine egotism : 'But still, – but still his honour must be saved' (ch. xxi). On the other hand, Cecilia's position is not wholly admirable, for as the gulf widens she sees herself contending for mastery in the relationship, an attitude underscored by Trollope's satire against the women's rights movement. Eventually Cecilia concludes that 'He had a right to command, a right to be obeyed, a right to be master' (ch. xxii), and does in fact capitulate, even though she feels herself innocent. Admittedly she has the last word, but she also assumes the correct posture of clinging wife. Such an ending is not ironical and weakens the otherwise telling criticism of male tyranny.

It is apparent, however, from the aggregate of his work that Trollope, far from acting as apologist for the stereotype of Victorian domesticity, is bent on exposing its less worthy aspects. It may be argued, of course, that in stressing the unseemly and sensational elements of marriage he is writing for the market : the happy marriage does not sell books. But on the other hand his appreciation of variety and contradiction in human nature was bound to draw him into areas which gave scope for depicting the collision of wills. His imagination is kindled by a vein of perversity in human nature, and even the casual reader of Trollope's novels soon becomes aware that the bread and cheese of marriage often turns out to be very hard tack after the sweetmeats of courtship. The perennial problem was the inability of one party to the contract to make sufficient effort to overcome will, pride or vanity. It provided him with the material of a dozen novels, and among the best in this vein is *He Knew He Was Right* (1869) a mordant analysis of unhappy marriage. Contemporary critics looked askance at husband and wife in this novel, and Trollope himself after the fact was apt to recoil from the creatures he had summoned from recesses of his imagination.

The novel stands at a pivotal moment in Trollope's life. Begun three months after his resignation from the Post Office, it heralds more complex psychological works like *Cousin Henry* or *Kept in the Dark*. In the Kennedys or the Harcourts he had already ventured into what Henry James called 'the ravages of love',[15] but now mental pressures are probed more deeply and motive dissected with greater precision:

> They who do not understand that a man may be brought to hope that which of all things is the most grievous to him, have not observed with sufficient closeness the perversity of the human mind. (ch. xxxviii)

To those readers accustomed to Barsetshire sunshine, this low-toned comment ushers in a dark, unfamiliar area of Trollope's work, but it is central to this novel, which exploits with appalled relish the delight a young couple take in destroying love. What makes *He Knew He Was Right* so memorable is the *schadenfreude* of the Trevelyans, as indeed of the watching social chorus. We begin with a love match, with all the benefits of wealth and leisure, and see it degenerate into a ruinous power struggle encouraged by a jaded society represented at one level by the cynical private detective, Bozzle, who battens on human misery, and at the other by Lady Milborough, who can only counsel the unhappy husband to take his wife abroad. Colonel Osborne, the family friend, is an amoral mischief-maker who precipitates Trevelyan's jealousy and stands back to watch the spectacle. Aunt Stanbury turns out to be a vindictive shrew. Priscilla Stanbury is a morbid man-hater, the Reverend Gibson a philandering hypocrite.

This bleak novel presents a disoriented society deficient in sustaining values and beliefs, blown this way and that by forces that individuals seem unable to control. As Mr Gibson puts it:

> I fancy sometimes that some mysterious agency interferes with the affairs of a man and drives him on, – and on, – and on, – almost, – till he doesn't know where it drives him. (ch. lxv)

This exactly expresses the Trevelyan situation. From misunderstanding over his wife's liaison with Osborne, as much due to his innate jealousy as to her pique at his very suspicion, Louis is embarked on a downhill course that leads to mental collapse amid the arid landscape of Siena, in a scene that earned James' respect. Certainly there is much to praise in Trollope's evocation of a harsh landscape in tune with Trevelyan's wild hilarity. A slow atmospheric passage full of details – lizards under a blazing sun, brittle vegetation, silence and oppressive heat – point to the misery of the man's condition. Trevelyan appears on his verandah in bizarre Italian costume, hair dishevelled and beard neglected, as dislocated from his environment as from the processes of normal reason. It is a moving scene in which his hymn to freedom rings out in sublime irony over the hills, the abject cry of a man broken under the rigidity of his own moral egotism and the pressures of the social code he worshipped.

But what is even more intriguing about this novel is the way Trollope involves Emily in the process of Trevelyan's downfall and at the same time makes us consider the pressures society puts upon the individual. Society is the real villain in this novel. From the start rumours about Emily's behaviour produce a spreading infection implicating nearly everyone. Appearances are made the bases of judgements again and again, and it becomes apparent that the unity of the novel resides in the judgement Trollope tempts us to make of the destructive powers of society as much as of the follies of the central characters. Gossip, spying and false counsel mislead the Trevelyans. The social chorus at Exeter led by Aunt Stanbury judges without charity or knowledge. The society to which man and wife constantly refer is shallow and dangerous – indeed, the chit-chat of its salons is fed by their plight. Reference to the social norm is almost fatal to the Spalding-Glascock match which provides a sub-plot, while events involving Hugh Stanbury and Brooke Burgess – both 'bohemian' characters in a sense, showing a healthy scepticism towards society and convention – counterpoint the main action. Nora Rowley resists the world to marry against all material considerations, while the marriage of English aristocrat and American democrat (the Glascock-Spalding affair) is a similar triumph of personal integrity over convention. In this respect one has to compare Nora's view of marriage as sharing responsibilities with the more conventional Victorian concept of submission and male domination. As Nora declares: 'I don't mean to submit to him at all, Lady Milborough; – of course not. I am going to marry for liberty' (ch. xcv). It is in the light of this authorial subversiveness that we have to view Trevelyan's repudiation of English society – 'the most damnable, puritanical, God-forgotten, and stupid country on the face of the globe' (ch. xcii).

The balanced attitude of the minor characters fulfils the moral drive of the story, but, of course, it is the struggle embodied in the title that fills our horizons. Certainly what hits hardest is the psychological depth of Emily and Louis and the stages of their power struggle. If in many ways Emily forfeits sympathy early on for being so headstrong, Louis shows himself repugnant in his tyranny and pettiness, becoming the very opposite of manly in his need to bolster his ego by dominating his wife. He becomes obsessed (like George Western in *Kept in the Dark*) by the need to secure his wife's total surrender. As it happens Emily is the stronger soul. We see this in the half-playful sparring before intransigence hardens into self-dramatising hostility. What Trollope shows so superbly is how a delicious, dangerous game becomes a perversion. From the outset Emily 'had a dim perception that she was standing on the edge of a precipice . . . she liked the excitement of the fear' (ch. xx). Louis positively gloats over his misery and returns to Bozzle like the drinker to his dram. When Glascock visits him he remains conscious of his role: 'There he stood gazing at the pale, cloudless, heat-laden, motionless sky, thinking of his own sorrows, and remembering too, doubtless, with the vanity of a madman, that he was probably being watched in his reverie' (ch. lxxxvi). The minds of the combatants are laid bare as the novel proceeds and each stage of the quarrel is vividly realised: the exaggerations, privately rehearsed grievances, preposterous attudinising before an audience, stilted conversations and elaborately planned counter-attacks – a comprehensive analysis of marital break-down.

The novel was intended as a study in obsession, and Trollope's own comment stressed the husband's errors of self-righteousness. Louis shows himself a tyrant to Lady Rowley (ch. lxii), while Lady Milborough undoubtedly knew he was *wrong*. So in his heart, of course, did Louis: 'But he was jealous of authority, fearful of slights, self-conscious, afraid of the world, and utterly ignorant of the nature of a woman's mind' (ch. xxvii). One is tempted to ask who with this kind of burden could possibly survive any kind of marriage, but the theme of the novel in terms of mutual respect and self-abnegation is not in-validated. Louis is the more guilty in his lust for power: at one point he craves that Emily shall admit to adultery to prove him right: 'Say that you have sinned; – and that you will sin no more' (ch. lxvii). Yet he knew that 'he himself, had consummated the evil by his own folly' (ch. lxxiv). Some may say that this is Trollopian ambiguity at its best and perhaps they will be right, for Louis gives Emily only partial ab-solution at the end, when she finds the courage to ask the question that turns the knife in the wound: 'I have not been a harlot to you; – have I?' The answer she needs would be her salvation and in a sense his defeat, and it is a masterstroke of Trollope's to give his reply as 'What name is that?' She urges him to kiss her hand as a sign that he acknowledges his false suspicions, and this he fails to do. Returning to Nora she herself reports what she interprets as his message:

'He declared to me at last that he trusted me,' she said, – almost believing that real words had come from his lips to that effect. Then she fell into a flood of tears, and after a while she also slept. (ch. xcviii)

Technically, it is a masterly ambiguity, but it is also an appropriate finale to a relationship in which both man and woman failed to observe that consciousness of each other's spirit which is the cornerstone of the true marriage.

NONINGSBY

Defending the wholesome tone of English fiction in 1863, a critic for the *National Review* thought that *Orley Farm* reflected 'the precise standard of English taste, sentiment, and conviction'. Anthony Trollope was now 'almost a national institution'.[16] The *Saturday Review*, usually grudging in its praise, declared that 'no one has ever drawn English families better'.[17] *Orley Farm* is a remarkable novel for many qualities, but its presentation of the domestic scene is particularly apt for showing Trollope's concern with the bread and cheese of love in varied settings, including London, Yorkshire and the Home Counties around Orley Farm itself (the Julians Hill, Harrow, of Trollope's boyhood). In London we are taken to the haunts of lawyers, Lincoln's Inn, Bedford Row, and the Furnival household in Harley Street, as well as to humbler neighbourhoods like Red Lion Square and Peckham, where Mary Snow is groomed to be the perfect wife. At Groby Park, seven miles from Leeds, we encounter Joseph Mason and his wife, two of Trollope's great comic creations. In Leeds too are the commercial travellers led by the outsize Mr. Moulder, who lives at St Helens. Orley Farm is set in an area called 'Hamworth', within thirty miles of London, in which lies also the estate of Sir Peregrine Orme, lord of the manor. In the market town of Hamworth, Samuel Dockwrath runs his legal business, and in the vicinity is Noningsby, near Alston, the home of Judge Staveley and his family. The range of these settings contributes to what Walpole most prized in the novel: 'All rural England is here, it is the perfect and final symbol of everything that Trollope tried to secure in his art'.[18] The novel has an altogether finer edge than this suggests; its restless movement from one town to another, from south to north and back again, are the true register of a changing society and the clash between rootlessness as a fact of urban life and peace within the rural setting. These are matters I shall explore more fully in my final chapter. Here my interests lie in questions of personal fulfilments within home and marriage, represented chiefly by ironical contrasts among the family groups, the Ormes, the Staveleys, the Masons, the Furnivals.

Architecture, seldom of interest to Trollope, has to be noted carefully in the background of each group. Sir Peregrine's home, 'The Cleeve', is 'old, venerable, and picturesque' and inspires Trollope to a delightful sketch of romantic landscape. Joseph Mason's house at Groby Park is comfortless and chill, and barely described at all, for he is ruthless and unprincipled, out of place in his surroundings and cut off from nourishing links with the past. Between the two is Noningsby, Judge Staveley's home, representing balance, compromise and fairness in thoroughly Trollopian fashion. Noningsby is new from cellar to ceiling, with all mod. cons. as it were, a place of sanctuary in tasteful comfortable design. Trollope points out that it 'lacked that something, in appearance rather than in fact, which age alone can give to the residence of a gentleman in the country' (ch. xxii). The faint note of regret is sounded, but Trollope is stating firmly that what matters most is the spirit within. Here is order in tune with progressive attitudes, free from the rigid conservatism of Sir Peregrine Orme, yet untainted by the shoddy commercialism of the Masons. The Judge looks to the future, while Sir Peregrine is trapped in the past. It is worth noting that although The Cleeve has its symbolic role in resisting the flux and crudity of the encroaching commercial world – rather like Sir Thomas Bertram's estate in *Mansfield Park*, it 'has not been a gay house' (ch. iii); it is inflexible, limited and therefore doomed. Thus Sir Peregrine cannot take the necessary human step towards forgiving Lady Mason for forging a cheque, the crime which is the focus of the melodramatic plot. Judge Staveley, by contrast, shows great warmth and sympathy. A Christian without cant, he is compassionate and generous to all, particularly the young. That the Staveleys embody an ideal of marriage and domesticity is clear in the scene between father and daughter, 'Miss Staveley declines to eat minced veal' (ch. lviii) when the judge urges his daughter to marry only for love.

By juxtaposing several scenes of Christmas festivity Trollope emphasises the symbolic importance of the Staveley household as a cell of good living. At Noningsby (drawn probably from Trollope's own family gatherings at Waltham Cross) there are walks, games and feasting, in direct contrast with the austerity of Sir Peregrine's mansion or the hilarious discomforts of Groby Park. Christmas at Great St Helens is portrayed, perhaps inevitably after Dickens, with the conventional trappings of 'wittles and drink' (ch. xxv). Again as in Dickens, feasting is an index of goodwill, and Moulder, whose 'body had been overcome by eating, but not yet his spirit' (ch. vi), is a generous host. Christmas at Groby Park, however, is a sorry affair. We have already met Mrs Mason in action : 'Portions of meat would become infinitesimal. When standing with viands before her, she had not free will over her hands' (ch viii). Her parsimony over the Christmas fare is only surpassed by her gift to the curate and his wife in recompense for two years' free singing lessons for her daughters. Having obtained a set of 'Louey Catorse furniture' at less than cost price because they have been 'strained' in demonstrations, she has stowed them in one of the bedrooms. Here in all their trumpery glory they exert a fatal fascination. First she abstracts two chairs for her own use. Then, after church on Christmas morning adding a third to her store, she reflects that there are still six, counting a rocking chair – quite ample for the curate's small living-room. It is one of Trollope's best comic scenes, and certainly his finest study of pathological meanness.

Another vignette, easily missed, adds to the cumulative picture of what ought to be the bread and cheese of love by providing a negative example. By diligent effort Thomas Furnival has become an eminent barrister, but has moved out of the sphere of his comfortable wife, Kitty:

> Men who had risen in the world as Mr. Furnival had done do find it sometimes difficult to dispose of their wives. It is not that the ladies are in themselves more unfit for rising than their lords, or that if occasion demanded they would not as readily adapt themselves to new spheres. But they do not rise, and occasion does not demand it. A man elevates his wife to his own rank, and when Mr. Brown, on becoming solicitor-general, becomes Sir Jacob, Mrs. Brown also becomes my lady. But the whole set among whom Brown must be more or less thrown do not want her ladyship. On Brown's promotion she did not become part of the bargain. Brown must henceforth have two existences – a public and a private existence; and it will be well for Lady Brown, and well also for Sir Jacob, if the latter be not allowed to dwindle down to a minimum. (ch. xi)

Poor Mrs Furnival, taking tea alone in Harley Street, dreams of their early days in Keppel Street (where Trollope was born) and muses bitterly on her husband as a devotee of port wine and – worse – a follower after strange goddesses (he has succumbed to the charms of Lady Mason). It is typical of Trollope that the woman's plight should be expressed by a mock heroic threnody on hot buttered toast:

> In the course of the evening the footman in livery brought in tea, handing it round on a big silver salver, which also added to Mrs. Furnival's unhappiness. She would have liked to sit behind her tea-tray as she used to do in the good old hard-working days, with a small pile of buttered toast on the slop-bowl, kept warm by hot water below. In those dear old hard-working days, buttered toast had been a much-loved delicacy with Furnival; and she, kind woman, had never begrudged her eyes, as she sat making it for him over the parlour fire. Nor would she have begrudged them now, neither her eyes nor the work of her hands, nor all the thoughts of her heart, if he would have consented to accept of her handiwork; but in these days Mr. Furnival had learned a relish for other delicacies. (ch. xi)

Christmas in Harley Street, different again from the others, is a skirmishing ground of passive resistance and flaring tempers, an important element of the strategy by which Trollope advances the case for Noningsby values, the healthy norms of behaviour to which an evolving society must aspire. Madeline Staveley is spontaneous and natural alongside Sophia Furnival, a creature of studied attitudes like Griselda Grantly: where Sophia needs the carriage, Madeline goes on foot; while Madeline decorates the village church, Sophia looks on (ch. xxii). By such ironic parallels Trollope directs the paths of narrative to the central landmark, Noningsby, a comfortable home born of a comfortable love, the solid ground of his fictional ethic which the young may hope to discover when they leave the rocks and valleys for a different landscape of experience.

6 Single Life

A woman's life is not perfect or whole till she has added herself to a husband. Nor is a man's life perfect or whole till he has added to himself a wife.[1]

All Trollope's fiction revolves on this axiom of Victorian felicity. So far I have traced it through young love and married life. The pursuit of love is also my main concern in this chapter, among those characters who for one reason or another are deprived of marriage, or who for reasons of temperament or psychological difficulty are denied the comforts of family life. Trollope's fiction depicts dozens of single people on the fringe of the family circle or the social world: the widow struggling to bring up her family, or shyly looking at the possibilities of matrimony; the gay old stagers and half-pay officers making their pensions go a long way and enjoying flirtations with married women; the spinster aunts and bachelor uncles for whom the family makes room at times with a sigh of impatience. Trollope's sympathy is also directed towards the bereaved, the outstanding example being Plantagenet Palliser after the death of Glencora. Trollope's emphasis in later books falls upon loneliness as a problem of the elderly, quite naturally, since he felt keenly the limitations old age imposed upon himself. That unfortunate foray into science fiction, *The Fixed Period*, is interesting solely for its sense of weariness in old age fused with masochistic contemplation of the ultimate solitude.

The intractable qualities of personality which isolated some men and women clearly fascinated Trollope. Some are just unlucky in love, like Harry Gilmore. Some like Kennedy and Trevelyan almost seem to welcome the solitude they bring upon themselves, and some, like Lucinda Roanoke and Priscilla Stanbury, reveal fascinating psychological traits. Lucinda, for example, is doomed to isolation by sexual forces she does not understand. Indeed few of his female characters equal her in sexual ferocity. She appears in the later stages of *The Eustace Diamonds*, seemingly a pawn in the mercenary marriage game which is part of Trollope's exposure of 'this degenerate age' (ch. xxiv), in which money rather than love is lord of all. But the psychological force of her role goes far beyond this. Her entry in the novel is sudden, mysterious and totally unexplained, her relationship with Sir Griffin Tewett the most bizarre in all Trollope's exploration of courtship. No reason is given for her implacable hostility towards him, but her actions strongly point to a homosexual nature. In an age of such taboos it is an outstandingly frank portrait of a girl in conflict with her own nature. Lucinda is racked with guilt and morbid fears:

> it had seemed to her that all the men who came near her were men whom she could not fail to dislike. She was hurried here and hurried there, and knew nothing of real social intimacies . . . There was a savageness of antipathy in her to the mode of life which her circumstances had produced for her, It was that very savageness which made her ride so hard, and which forbade her to smile and be pleasant to people whom she could not like. And yet she knew that something must be done. (ch. xxxix)

In appearance she is one of Trollope's Junos, with a passion for horse-riding which may be a symptom of the sexuality she cannot fathom or come to terms with. Riding is both an expression of desire to escape her feminine nature and a death wish: 'I like hunting because, perhaps some day I may break my neck . . . If I could break my neck it would be the best thing for me' (ch. xli). The outburst is left unexplained. Other hints about her are dropped from time to time: 'When a man does come near you, you're as savage and cross as a bear' (ibid.). One witness of her engagement observes: 'I hope Griff will understand her, – that's all . . . If they come to blows Lucinda will thrash him, I don't doubt' (ibid.). And later Mrs Carbuncle, her aunt, and Lizzie Eustace tacitly agree she would be sure to hate any man she might accept, her nature is so peculiar.

Lucinda's horror at a man's touch is described in terms clear enough to the modern reader:

> What did it matter, even though he should embrace her? It was her lot to undergo misery, and as she had not chosen to take poison, the misery must be endured. (ch. xlii)

When Sir Griffin takes her in his arms the parody of romance becomes almost obscene:

> On a sudden she made up her mind, and absolutely did kiss him. She would sooner have leaped at the blackest darkest, dirtiest river in the county. 'There,' she said, 'that will do,' gently extricating herself from his arms. 'Some girls are different, I know; but you must take me as I am, Sir Griffin, – that is if you do take me.' (ch. xlii)

Now that the marriage has been arranged Lucinda begins to show signs of acute mental disorder. She begs Lady Eustace to make Sir Griffin abandon her: 'Tell him that I am thoroughly bad, and that he will repent it to the last day of his life' (ch. lxvi), and she confesses 'I don't think I could feel to any man as though I loved him' (ch. lxix). But the marriage is inevitable, and Lucinda, in an almost catatonic state, accuses her aunt 'You have destroyed me' (ibid.). Beyond doubt Lucinda Roanoke is one of the most extraordinary pictures of the isolated woman in all Trollope's fiction.

The unmarried woman was a cause of public concern throughout Trollope's life. Trollope was prepared to accept without irony Jane Austen's aphorism about young ladies being in want of husbands. It was a fact of Victorian life as well as a simple man's belief in the companionship and security which he had craved in youth and found in his own marriage. Thus the opening of *Rachel Ray*, with its sentimental rendering of women's lot has to be swallowed in all its oleaginous sincerity before we come to grips with a charming little tale of family squabbles and evangelical measliness, snob values and small town goings-on in the West Country Trollope loved. This was the tale which George Eliot described, to Trollope's delight, as juicy and complete as a nut on a stem,[2] but its opening holds little promise:

> There are women who cannot grow alone as standard trees; – for whom the support and warmth of the wall, some paling, some post, is absolutely necessary; – who, in their growth, will bend and incline themselves towards some such prop for their life, creeping with their tendrils along the ground till they reach it when the circumstances of life have brought no such prop within their natural and immediate reach.[3]

Such a beginning belies the novel's charm, for although there is no more startling event in the story than Luke Rowan's attempt to gain control of a brewery and marry Rachel against the wishes of his snobbish mother, the story is thoroughly Trollopian, full of delightful comment and insights into ordinary life.

The widowed daughter of the Ray family, Dorothea Prime, is a harshly evangelical woman like the odious Mrs Bolton in *John Caldigate*. Grimly dedicated to the Dorcas society and the pursuit of virtue 'she had taught herself to believe that cheerfulness was a sin' (ch. i), allying herself with the Reverend Samuel Prong, whose presentation owes a great deal to the immortal Slope. It was the heavy-handed satire against evangelicalism that frightened the editor of *Good Words*, who had commissioned a story from Trollope, into breaking the contract Trollope scornfully wrote to Millais that he was proved 'altogether un suited to the regenerated!' He trusted to remain so, 'wishing to pre serve a character for honest intentions' (193, p. 131). Certainly the story makes its point well about the gulf between Christian good will and an oppressive, joyless orthodoxy next door to cant and humbug.

Although a conventional young love story is central to *Rachel Ray*, the more interesting character is the heroine's sweet-natured mother. Widowed after ten years of marriage, Mrs Ray, now in her fifties, wants to enjoy life, but is dominated by her elder daughter, Dorothea. Rachel is sunny and affectionate, but a source of anxiety since she has formed an attachment to a young man. Her mother broods over her responsibilities, confused by Dorothea's formidable catechising. The question for Mrs Ray is whether Rachel should engage in normal pursuits like attending Mrs Butler Cornbury's party, choosing a pretty dress and waltzing in public, or whether she should accept the Dorcas society and Mrs Prime's joyless regimen in the name of salvation. In a society like that of Cranford, watchful eyes and wagging tongues add to Mrs Ray's problems, as she treads warily between her children's wishes and the minefields of rank and social proprieties. She comes through her ordeal with dignity, confronting Dorothea splendidly in Chapter xii for the sake of Rachel's freedom. 'Maternal Eloquence' (ch. xv) is also a scene strongly reminiscent of Mrs Gaskell, in which Mrs Ray quietly asserts her daughter's merits against the combined snobbery of Mrs Tappitt and Mrs Rowan.

The mother-daughter situation in *Rachel Ray* is unusual. A more typical family relationship is that of the child dominated by either parent, often a source of comedy, though in some novels of rather darker significance. In *Castle Richmond*, for example, the Countess of Desmond is actually her daughter's rival in love. Lady Lovel virtually imprisons her daughter to prevent a match between her and the tailor, Daniel Thwaites, in *Lady Anna*, and when this fails tries to murder the young man. Incarceration is also attempted by Mrs Bolton in *John Caldigate* to keep her daughter, Hester, from the hero. Mrs Bolton is a fascinating character who rises above the melodramatic exigencies of the plot, for her possessiveness is revealed as one of those studies in monomania peculiar to Trollope. Her tyranny is sexually based and combined with religious mania as is apparent from the chapter entitled 'Men are so wicked' (xix), and her perversity turns her into a monster as she tries to break Hester's spirit (ch. xxxvi). As so often in Trollope the demon of the absolute destroys. When Hester remains immovably loyal to John Caldigate her mother's spirit begins to dissolve, and when at last her own husband resists her, loses the will to live. Delving into abnormal states, as Henry James was among the first to recognise, Trollope showed unexpected powers.

Sons too are not exempt from maternal dominance. In the short stories 'La Mère Bauche' and 'The Lady of Launay', domineering mothers actively hinder their sons' happiness, the former, indeed,

F

driving the poor girl in question to suicide. Widowed Lady Lufton's harassment of her only son over Lucy Robarts is perhaps redeemed by her queenly condescension towards the end of the novel, but there is nothing to be said on behalf of the Marchioness of Kingsbury in *Marion Fay* who tried to stand in the way of both her step-children's happiness. Perhaps Lizzie Woodstock needed a strong disciplinarian to curb her flightiness, but she was certainly unlucky to have fallen under the tutelage of her maiden aunt, Lady Linlithgow, who engineered her marriage to Sir Florian Eustace; and Lucinda Roanoke was equally unfortunate in her widowed aunt, Mrs Carbuncle, who trapped her into the engagement with Sir Griffin. Wealth and social position confer the prescriptive right on widow or maiden aunt to meddle and manipulate.

Usually such a character is little more than an outline with a strongly caricatured element, a trick of speech or oddity of appearance. Miss Marrable in *The Vicar of Bullhampton*, 'thought a good deal about blood', adored the eighteenth-century novelists, and loathed Dickens for manufacturing 'a kind of life that had never existed, and never could exist'.[4] Aunt Jemima Stanbury in *He Knew He Was Right* is a thoroughgoing Tory of the old school, whose tastes are summed up in the categorical: 'All change was to her hateful and unnecessary' (ch. vii). Four pages describe her politics, reading, appearance, daily routine, her robust likes and dislikes, all in the most precise detail, down to the name of the servant who cleans her boots. By this close rendering of even the most minor characters Trollope peoples his world. Possibly such characters as Miss Stanbury and Miss Marrable were based on Trollope's mother's great friend, an eccentric and lovable 'aunt', Fanny Bent. Miss Stanbury's attachment to George III and the glories of the subsequent reign is a characteristic of other spinsters, such as Lady Rosina de Courcy and, of course, Miss Thorne of Ullathorne, providing Trollope with comparisons between the old world and the new. Miss Thorne's attempts to recapture the chivalries of bygone ages reflect the old-fashioned Barsetshire with some irony, but they also prick the conscience with reminders of what is being lost in the scramble for modernism.

At a lower social level another kind of spinster performs a useful function. Miss Sally Todd is a good example, an outspoken, vigorously active, independent maiden lady who has made a success of single life by establishing herself in the Paragon at Littlebath. She too may well reflect an actual character: the humanitarian and anti-vivisectionist, Frances Power Cobbe.[5] Miss Todd appears in *The Bertrams* and *Miss Mackenzie* with her great friend Mary Baker, who is pursued by the old soldier Sir Lionel Bertram. In scenes of pump room and vicarage garden, at whist in the drawing-room and making morning calls, single women are an essential part of the ordinariness of Trollope's novels, but we glimpse at times their unhappiness. Mid-way through *He Knew He Was Right*, in a violent outburst of bitterness and self-pity, Miss Stanbury, speaking of lonely people generally, puts the plight of any spinster like herself:

They are not anything particular to anybody, and so they go on living till they die. You know what I mean, Mr. Burgess. A man who is a nobody can perhaps make himself somebody, – or, at any rate, he can try; but a woman has no means of trying. She is a nobody and a nobody she must remain. She has her clothes and her food, but she isn't wanted anywhere. People put up with her, and that is about the best of her luck. If she were to die somebody perhaps would be sorry for her, but nobody would be worse off. She doesn't earn anything or do any good. She is just there and that's all. (ch. li)

In *Miss Mackenzie* the heroine is generally regarded by a cruel indifferent society as 'a silent, stupid old maid' (ch. i). Having devoted herself to nursing her selfish father and brother, she comes into a small fortune, and is immediately pursued by impecunious suitors, notably the squint-eyed curate of Littlebath, the Reverend Jeremiah Maguire. One of the pleasing aspects of this novel is the way in which Miss Mackenzie grows in self-respect and confidence, aided by her friends Miss Baker and Miss Todd. The interaction of the three makes an eloquent case for women who have to survive without the support of husbands. Miss Todd's practical wisdom is not only commendable as a way of facing up to loneliness but superior to the censoriousness of her exclusively religious neighbours in Littlebath. As Miss Todd exclaims:

Tell me why are cards wicked? Drinking, and stealing, and lying, and back biting, and naughty love-making – but especially back-biting – back biting – back biting – those are the things that the Bible says are wicked. I shall go on playing cards, my dear, till Mr. Stumfold can send me chapter and verse forbidding it. (ch. ix)

The vehemence of her remarks is both comic and touching.

The author's comment on capitulating to romance to provide Miss Mackenzie with a lover is unimportant in face of the developing maturity of the central figure which, to my mind, is the novel's singular virtue. Originally titled 'The Modern Griselda', it was clearly intended to make much of the heroine's pluck enduring the label 'old maid', an existence 'sad, sombre, and, we may almost say, silent' (ch. ii) and with the help of her friends making her life worthwhile. How superficial by comparison is the scene in *The Last Chronicle* where Lily Dale writes in her diary her future destiny as Old Maid. As Miss Todd expresses it :

> We single women have to be solitary sometimes – and sometimes sad . . . Have you never heard there are some animals, that when they're sick, crawl into holes, and don't ever show themselves among the other animals? Though it is only the animals that do it, there's a pride in that which I like. What's the good of complaining if one's down in the mouth? When one gets old and heavy and stupid, one can't go about as one did when one was young; and other people won't care to come to you as they did then. (ch. xiv)

One of the defining marks of Trollope's fiction is an intuitive sympathy with those forced to live life outside its most comfortable run.

If the spinster has means, she can move in society, like Miss Dunstable, occupying herself with the social round. If not she must find happiness at home in caring for a father or mother, as Dorothy Grey does in *Mr. Scarborough's Family*. So happy was Dorothy that she refused to marry her father's partner. Perhaps, like Miss Sarah Jack of Spanish Town, Jamaica, in the short story, she can enjoy love and marriage by proxy, as it were, sublimating her own needs in matchmaking. Otherwise she can fill her time by ruling her little kingdom as Miss Stanbury does, or plunge into soul-saving and good works like Mrs Prime in *Rachel Ray*. In *Is He Popenjoy?* the unmarried sisters of Lord George Germain, led by Lady Sarah, who 'was never idle and never wanted to be amused' (ch. iii), make petticoats for the poor as the sole outlet for their energies, an activity Trollope ridicules since it is carried on with no relevance to an actual human situation. *Is He Popenjoy?*, one of the novels reflecting greater concern with the role of women in the late sixties and seventies, offers several examples of the conditions which encouraged bored wives to flirt and single women to scheme for husbands. Few spinsters are as contented as Hetta Houghton, who has managed to come to terms with her existence. 'She has lots of money, and lives all alone . . . She goes everywhere, and is up to everything,' declares her sister-in-law proudly (ch. xii). The plight of Augusta Mildmay is more common : like Arabella Trefoil in *The American Senator* she has to work desperately hard and against time to secure a husband. Brilliantly deploying the irony of her wanting to be in love and also to add to her fortune, Trollope shows that succes on her terms is not worth having.

Trollope pities the designing female none the less, however frankly he exposes her duplicity and punishes her, and the frequency of thi type in his stories reiterates the imperative of marriage in the Victoria period. For a young girl denied matrimony the future is grim indeed

Georgiana Longestaffe in the closing chapters of *The Way We Live Now* exclaims to her mother in horror at her failure to secure a husband:

> What is to become of me? Is is not enough to drive me mad to be going about here by myself, without any prospect of anything?[6]

And having lost the financier, Mr Brehgert, she flings herself into the arms of the curate, Mr Batherbolt, with whom she elopes. Spinsterhood is so dreaded that a woman is prepared to pursue a potential husband around the world, as happens in the story, 'The Journey to Panama'. Jokes are directed about the predicament of the old maid, but Trollope more often shows the real misery of such a situation.

The elaborate campaign of Arabella Trefoil to ensnare Lord Rufford in *The American Senator* is conceived with a vigour and sympathy that redeem the novel from its tedious contrasting of English and American customs. The memorable scenes of the novel are where Arabella shows her paces on a spirited horse (ch. xxii), contrives a rendezvous with Rufford in the shrubbery (ch. xxxviii), and advances her love affair by a shrewd letter (ch. xliv). Trollope's fictional letters are superb, and he makes Arabella's gems of flattery, apparent artlessness and wistful earnestness. Each stage of her campaign intensifies aggression towards her mother. Lacking the financial resources to compete successfully in aristocratic circles, she is terrified at the prize eluding her, and at one point almost breaks down in bitter complaint:

> 'I've been at it till I'm nearly broken down. I must settle somewhere; – or else die; – or else run away. I can't stand this any longer, and I won't. Talk of work, – men's work! What man ever has to work as I do? (ch. xiii)

Trollope is critical of her morality, but he understands her, and she wins our admiration by her grit and determination. There is a haunting scene the night before the hunt in which Arabella hopes to distinguish herself in Lord Rufford's eyes (ch. xxxix). She leans from her window in the moonlight almost praying that there will be no frost in the morning. As the novel moves towards her failure, and far less glittering match with Mounser Green of the Foreign Office, her demoralisation is conveyed by growing hatred of her mother. 'We shall kill each other,' she shrieks in a scene of great intensity (ch. lxii); the mental strain of pretence and watchfulness has brought her near collapse. Like the actress who is never off stage, she has little sense of her own identity at last. As Trollope drily observes of one of her performances:

> She had taken great trouble with her face, so that she was able to burst out into tears. (ch. l)

But it takes an actress of stronger nerves, like Lizzie Eustace, to survive in such a campaign.

Trollope's treatment of such victims of the marriage lottery reveals the inadequacies of the Victorian stereotype of relations between the sexes, and results in some of his strongest characterisations. Certainly criticism is levelled at the system which compels women like Arabella, Caroline Waddington, Julia Brabazon, even Lizzie Eustace, to scheme their way to matrimony. Lady Mabel Grex in *The Duke's Children* is a woman of tremendous vitality and intellect wasted among inferior men. Well-born, elegant, a splendid, scornful character, she has tried to suppress her feelings for her cousin, Arthur Tregear, and must pretend to sympathise with his attachment for Lady Mary Palliser; she is mocked by her insensitive father, Lord Grex, for not marrying, and at the back of her mind lurks a fear of being left on the shelf. We see her chafing at the situation which demands that a woman secure a husband before her looks are gone, and squirming under the hypocrisy of welcoming advances from stupid suitors. 'Sometimes,' Trollope has her remark acidly to one of them, 'Mr. Longstaff, I deny myself the pleasure of saying what I think.' And to her friend and companion, Miss Cassewary, she exclaims wrathfully about men in general, – 'those stupid do-nothing fools that one meets everywhere' (ch. xx).

Isabel Boncassen, the American girl who finally marries Lord Silverbridge, finds herself similarly vexed by male attentions, and feels her intellect insulted by Longstaff's proposal. She makes a blistering statement:

> Young men are pretty much the same everywhere, I guess. They never have their wits about them. They never mean what they say, because they don't understand the use of words. They are generally half impudent and half timid. When in love they do not at all understand what has befallen them. What they want they try to compass as a cow does when it stands stretching out its head towards a stack of hay which it cannot reach. Indeed there is no such thing as a young man, for a man is not really a man till he is middle-aged. But take them at their worst they are a deal too good for us, for they become men some day, whereas we must only be women to the end. (ch. xxxiii).

It is true this is exaggeration for comic effect, and Isabel herself does come round to loving Lord Silverbridge in the end, but there is no denying her superior wit and intelligence. So far as he is concerned, she is in the same category as Lady Mabel, to whom he earlier pays court and whose great drawback, he felt, was that as his wife she would be his superior, 'and in some degree his master' (ch. xix). Trollope conveniently lessens the gap between the lovers at the end. But for Mabel

Grex there is no fortunate resolution, and a vein of bitterness in her character deepens as she loses her chances one by one with the lords of creation. A complicated state of mind is exposed in her chagrin at the prospect of losing even Silverbridge: pride in not wheedling a proposal from him, natural jealousy of the other woman, a hint of self-pity at her isolation. Trollope is adept at combining authorial comment and analysis of state of mind to bring out the nuances of character and situation.

The Duke's Children, a very quiet, reflective book, offers many examples of this narrative technique, notably in Chapter xl. The method is to give an illusion of the character thinking the matter over, going into all the pros and cons, talking it out with herself, as we all tend to do when confronting problems and decisions. Trollope shuffles around the ideas in slightly different patterns and words, giving different emphases, qualifications, distinctions, so that we get all the complications of choice. It is a method which produces fullness of statement, amplitude and cumulative power. It is not succinct and it would not succeed if it were, but it gives great strength and breadth to the narrative and makes for our complete involvement with, and knowledge of, character. It often meanders, but it is seldom tedious or off the point. Usually it follows or heralds a brief dramatic scene or piece of dialogue and is signalled by some such formula as 'Then, when the evening was over she spoke to herself again about him . . .' (ch. xvi). Sometimes a direct question is posed: 'But could she love him?' (ch. xvi). Such narrative reflection is very prominent in Trollope.

Later there is much pathos in the way Lady Mabel is reduced to vamping Silverbridge despite her principles. Grotesquely, and with a sense of self-disgust, she throws herself at him, knowing that in her heart she still loves Tregear. It is a raw and painful scene. Suddenly she realises that the game is lost and the dreary, empty life of an old maid awaits her. In her disappointment she becomes spiteful and thoroughly embittered, salving her pride by blaming both Silverbridge and Tregear for their weakness and inconsistency. By the end of the novel she has begun to look old. 'A girl unless she marries becomes nothing, as I have become nothing now' (ch. lxxvii). Her consciousness of this is well portrayed in the final renunciation of Silverbridge. Reminded that in course of time her memories will be less painful, Lady Mabel launches an excoriating rebuke against the male sex which vividly expresses her fear of remaining single:

Yes; time, – that brings wrinkles and rouge-pots and rheumatism. Though I have so hated those men as to be unable to endure them, still I want some man's house, and his name, – some man's bread and wine, – some man's jewels and titles and woods and parks and gardens, – if I can get them. Time can help a man in his sorrow. If he begins at forty to make speeches, or to win races, or to breed oxen, he can yet live a prosperous life. Time is but a poor consoler for a young woman who has to be married. (ch. lxxiii)

In Lady Mabel Grex Trollope came near to making a tragic heroine.

A WOMAN'S ONE CAREER

Although the headstrong woman in a Trollope novel is often mercenary and ambitious, the underlying theme of her deprivation always draws our sympathetic interest, and redeems the character from the sensational circumstances of her role. Miss Dawkins, in that very slight tale, 'An Unprotected Female at the Pyramids', is presented as a wily campaigner hovering on the fringes of any company, and waiting to pounce on any available male. Trollope suggests that such women soon lose their feminine delicacy, and become strident, cynical, even masculine in their manners; at this point sympathy gives way to prejudice. Lady Laura Standish in *Phineas Finn* is described in terms that seem calculated to make the reader's attitude equivocal :

> She would lean forward when sitting, as a man does, and would use her arms in talking, and would put her hand over her face, and pass her fingers through her hair, – after the fashion of men rather than of women; . . . (ch. iv)

The suggestion of hormone imbalance looks like a rather mean piece of male chauvinism, and in one sense, of course, it is, for when it comes to the question of women vying with men in spheres of intellect and affairs, the prejudices of his generation work against Trollope's personal appreciation that women deserve better than to be treated as pretty toys or domestic paragons. To the question he tentatively raises, of woman's fulfilment beyond the pleasures of her family and home life, he has no answer, and withdraws in baffled irresolution. Clearly there is something wrong in a society that fails to provide for the intellectual needs of Lady Laura and Violet Effingham, but at the same time emotional prejudice causes Trollope to fall back on the conventional picture of womanly dependence.

He is similarly confused over the issue of the working woman. While he admires the courage of such independent souls as Miss Todd, he prefers to pity those like Miss MacNulty or Miss Casseway who accept subservience as companions – frequently the only avenue open to women of slender means. In *North America* (I, ch. xviii), for example, he shows marked sympathy for those forced to seek employment as governesses, separating them from the crusaders for women's rights, to which he remained implacably opposed. His position is made clear in *Miss Mackenzie*:

> I believe that a desire to get married is the natural state of a woman at the age of – say from twenty-five to thirty-five, and I think also that it is good for the world in general that it should be so. I am now speaking, not of the female population at large, but of women whose position in the world does not subject them to the necessity of earning their bread by the labour of their hands. There is, I know, a feeling abroad among women that this desire is one of which it is expedient that they should become ashamed; that it will be well for them to alter their natures in this respect, and learn to take delight in the single state. Many of the most worthy women of the day are now teaching this doctrine, and are intent on showing by precept and practice that an unmarried woman may have as sure a hold on the world, and a position within it as ascertained, as may an unmarried man. (ch. xi)

To Trollope such doctrine was merely crying for the moon, but his contempt for the feminist movement went deeper, for he found it repugnant to his cherished ideas about the harmony between men and women on which healthy society should be based. Calling upon women to march, secure the vote, compete with men in jobs and generally involve themselves in male pursuits (other than hunting, of course) seemed to Trollope, as to the majority of his contemporaries, a subversion of the natural law. Tennyson was expressing a widely held view in 'The Princess' when his emancipated young ladies of the Academy pledged themselves at last to the discovery that 'woman is not undevelopt man, / But diverse . . . Not like to like but like in difference'. As for sex equality Trollope agreed with Tennyson:

> Seeing either sex alone
> Is half itself, and in true marriage lies
> Nor equal, nor unequal.
>
> (7,283)

How much Trollope's attitude represented Victorian prejudice against female usurpation of male prerogative, rather than philosophical judgement, is open to question, but in depiction of the female rights movement his usual fair-mindedness is markedly absent. Before I go on to illustrate this prejudice, however, it is well to note that it was shared by the vast majority. In an age increasingly beset by change, hearth and home became, even more than religious faith, the safest anchorage, so is easy to appreciate how sinister the feminist movement appeared. It was not solely male chauvinism that made Parliament howl with derision at J. S. Mill's regular pleas for female suffrage, but fear at any threat to order and security in a world where stabilities were harder to find. Thus the domestic values Trollope's fiction upheld were not illusions but sustaining realities that fitted most people's needs.

In point of fact, Trollope supported Mill's advocacy of more opportunities for women's education and greater availability of jobs to single women. But marriage was uppermost in his mind for the young girl, and he deplored any idea that a career should divert her from her destiny as a wife and mother. This is clear from his correspondence with Kate Field, whose views on the emancipation of women never failed to elicit a response from the novelist. At one point she saw herself as a popular lecturer, and received this rebuke from Trollope:

> You do not, I think, catch the objections which are made; – that oratory is connected deeply with forensic, parliamentary, and pulpit pursuits for which women are unfitted because they are wanted elsewhere; because in such pursuits a man is taken from his home, and because she is wanted at home. (641, p. 363)

One of Trollope's comments on women's role occurs in *The Vicar of Bullhampton*, 'Female Martyrdom' (ch. xxxvii), the martyr in question being Mary Lowther, who is grappling with the problem of her preference for Walter Marrable whom she cannot marry and Harry Gilmore whom she can. There is nothing more natural, says Trollope, than a young girl's wish to get married: 'It is a woman's one career – let women rebel against the edict as they may.' All women know this, he goes on, and yet 'Saturday Reviewers and others blame them for their lack of modesty.' What Trollope has in mind is clearly the widespread currency of an article by Mrs Lynn Linton called 'The Girl of the Period'[7] in which the writer had suggested that girls had become so immodest of late as to tease, flirt and generally go to any lengths to attract a man. Trollope was incensed by the slur on womankind and by the implication that young girls should mend their ways for the sake of appearance and mock-modesty.

> Our daughters should be educated to be wives, but, forsooth, they should never wish to be wooed! The very idea is but a remnant of the tawdry sentimentality of an age in which the mawkish insipidity of the women was the reaction from the vice of that preceding it. That our girls are in quest of husbands, and know well in what way their lines in life should be laid, is a fact which none can dispute. Let men be taught to recognize the same truth as regards themselves, and we shall cease to hear of the necessity of a new career for women. (ch. xxxvii)

With this knock-down argument satisfactorily concluded Trollope resumes his narrative.

Comically inadequate as it is, however, it does show why he was so ambivalent towards his strong-minded heroines, admiring their spirit but drawing back from that dangerous 'over-fed craving for independence' he described in Alice Vavasor in *Can You Forgive Her?* (ch. xi). Caroline Waddington, even more the new woman, made speeches about female independence in *The Bertrams*, announcing early on that she was not the type who would 'ever grow into a piece of domestic furniture' (I, ch. ix). Such women miss the point in Trollope's eyes, for by their obduracy they injure their natures, and grow embittered in a struggle they cannot hope to win. The situation, unlike other social issues such as education and the franchise, about which he was a declared progressive, seemed to admit of no solution. It was unfortunate, but had to be endured. As he wrote to an American friend, Adrian Joline, in 1879:

> You cannot by Act of Congress or Parliament make the woman's arm as strong as the man's or deprive her of her position as the bearer of children. We may trouble ourselves much by debating a question which superior power has settled for us, but we cannot alter the law . . . The necessity of the supremacy of man is as certain to me as the eternity of the soul. (740, pp. 417–18)

The distinction Trollope wishes to make between supremacy and superiority is clear enough. It is true that the question of a wife's mental fulfilment and its effect upon her psychological well-being is often sympathetically depicted in the novels, as the idea of equal though different is propounded as the basis of good marriage.

Outside his fiction, he is much more conventional. His views on the education of women, on which he lectured in several cities and published a pamphlet, probably in 1868, are shallow, and expose his weakness as a thinker. Flattering his audience and edging round the subject, he at last ventures the safe assertion that women's education has made remarkable progress in two hundred years. He regrets that it stops too soon, due partially to a lack of that 'persistent energy by which he [a man] does perform, and has been intended to perform, the work of the world'.[8] This gratuitous point enables him to by-pass any really significant plea for university or other higher education for women, and leads him to the feminist movement, whose militancy he brands as the work of females who 'grudge the other sex the superior privileges of manhood', falling back again upon the comfortable cliché of the man's strong right arm.

The lecture attacks co-education, the same syllabus for boys and girls, and the dangers of over-indulgence in novels. To clinch his argument, Trollope draws a picture of an emancipated girl in the un-disciplined atmosphere of the modern home, succumbing to novels, abandoning her German dictionary, and at last becoming 'too languid for walking' (p. 84). On the other hand his picture of educational opportunities proper for the young lady is hardly more invigorating: study in foreign languages; unspecified critical training (doubtless to offset the insidious effects of the Mudie novels); instrumental accom-plishment; painting; study of birds and insects; and the old stand-by of philanthropy and social work. Finally, he calls for a spirit of high resolution, industry and conscientious attention to the house-work.

The interest of such a half-baked statement on a serious social problem is not so much what it reveals of Trollope's inadequacy as a theorist, but that it is so far beneath his abilities to deal with the same issues in his fiction where he expounds a far wiser and truer perception of the problems confronting young women in and out of marriage.

His remarks on women in *North America* are even more prejudiced. Chapter xviii of this intriguing and often amusing travel book is devoted to the Rights of Women, and its argument is freighted with non sequiturs, false analogies and loaded evidence. The central thesis is that 'the best right a woman has is the right to a husband'. For those who cannot secure a husband, he declares, let more job oppor-tunities be found, but he is firmly opposed to the militant feminists who are encouraging women to establish independence through their careers and not to marry.

An odd little essay in *St. Paul's Magazine* in February 1868, an un-signed, but with the hallmarks of Trollope's heavily playful style, may sum up this brief account of his non-fiction writing about women's rights. The article purports to be written by 'an old maid', and offers hints on matrimony for young ladies. They are warned neither to dis-guise their ignorance, nor on the other hand to play the 'jeune ingenue with gushing emotions and impulsive affections', but to ask intelligent questions of the man they sit next to at dinner. The 'old maid' advises her readers:

> Your proper study is to make yourself the best possible wife for your best possible husband, by educating your soul and mind and body to the best of your abilities.[9]

As one might expect from all this, the feminist agitator in his novels is an outrageous caricature, like Baroness Banman in *Is He Popenjoy?*, ugly, dictatorial, often hypocritical, and motivated entirely by un-reasonable dislike of the male sex. The baroness, a Bavarian lady, is 'a very stout woman, about fifty, with a double chin, a considerable moustache, a low broad forehead, and bright, round, black eyes very far apart' (ch. xvii). She is matched by Olivia Q. Fleabody from Vermont, who wrests control from her of an Institute in the Marylebone Road 'established for the Relief of the Disabilities of Females' and irreverently known as the 'Disabilities'. Trollope enjoys his spoof, especially of the American feminist, giving Miss Fleabody enormous pebble glasses, a thick, nasal accent and the notorious bloomers. The directness and lack of reticence in the American character (to which he gives ample praise in *He Knew He Was Right*, *The American Senator* and *The Duke's Children*) both fascinated and disconcerted him.[10] Much as he admired Americans, he could not forgive them many things: double-talk, the Fenian movement, and women's rights. Olivia Q. Fleabody, aided and abetted by Lady Selina Protest, intrigues to gain power over the Institute, while the Baroness is driven to found a rival establishment in Lisson Grove. Motivated by financial greed, both batten on the gullibility of gentle souls like Lady Germain, and dotty eccentrics like Aunt Ju.

Trollope is just as unfair to the American poetess and advocate of women's rights, Wallachia Petrie, the Republican Browning, who tries to wean Caroline Spalding away from Mr Glascock in *He Knew He Was Right*. Brought in as makeweight, one suspects, a good way through the novel, she adds comic relief, and by her impregnable sense of her own rightness is not out of harmony with the book's general theme. She has more to do than Trollope's other feminists, being first and foremost a poet, with a gorgeous pseudo-poetic diction which she delivers in a strongly cultivated nasal accent as a token of her national pride:

> 'Caroline,' said the poetess with severe eloquence, 'can you put your hand upon your heart and say that this inherited title, this tinkling cymbal as I call it, has no attraction for you or yours? Is it the unadorned simple man that you welcome to your bosom, or a thing of stars and garters, a patch of parchment, the minion of a throne, the lordling of twenty descents, in which each has been weaker than that before it, the hero of a scutcheon, whose glory is in his quarterings, and whose worldly wealth comes from the sweat of serfs whom the euphemism of an effete country has learned to decorate with the name of tenants?' (ch. lv)

Wally is a bigot and a bore, with a characteristic Trollope ascribes to many Americans of making 'that too visible effort of the intellect' (ch. lvi) to persuade and impress. Much of her undoubted intelligence is directed to the status of women, in which the ferocious eloquence and enthusiasm of her manner provide an amusing counterpoint to the marriage plans of Carry and the future Lord Peterborough (ch. lxxvii). As usual Trollope makes nonsense of Wally's advocacy of women's rights, reducing her to 'a republican virago, with a red nose' (ch. lxxvii), whose motivation is the resentment of an unattractive woman unable to get a husband.

Invariably Trollope's resolution of the question of women's rights comes down to the complacent statement which begins Chapter lxxvii:

> We in England are not usually favourably disposed to women who take a pride in a certain antagonism to men in general, and who are anxious to shew the world that they can get on very well without male assistance; but there are many such in America who have noble aspirations, good intellects, much energy, and who are by no means unworthy of friendship. The hope in regard to all such women, – the hope entertained not by themselves, but by those who are solicitous for them, – is that they will be cured at last by a husband and half-a-dozen children.

A last fling at the feminist in *Kept in the Dark* is no less patronising and exaggerated. Francesca Altifiorla turns out not only a she-dragon but an apostate. Born 'in poor circumstances, but with an exalted opinion as to her own blood' (ch. i), Francesca congratulates Cecilia Holt on avoiding 'the common quagmire of marriage' (ch. iii) after the collapse of her engagement to Sir Francis Geraldine. When Cecilia falls in love with Mr Western, Francesca is eloquent about a future devoted to 'the mending of his stockings and the feeding of his babies'. Marriage, she maintains, is no more than being 'a man's toy and then his slave' (ch. v). Better by far to remain, like her, an independent spinster. But having met Sir Francis she begins to reflect upon 'the chill of her present life, of its want of interest, of its insipid loneliness' (II, ch. xv), abandons female rights and plumps for marriage, confident that she will know 'how to be the master'. Sir Francis, of course, eludes her, while Cecilia exercises her own 'mastery', by true love and tactful flattery reestablishing harmony with her husband; in Trollope's opinion, the proper exercise of women's rights.

Trollope draws the frustrations of highly-strung intellectual women with mixed feelings of pity, admiration and dislike. Headstrong women are Junos destined for unhappiness, whether inside marriage or out, and their rebellion against male hegemony ends in capitulation or destruction. Part of Violet Effingham's attitude towards her domineering fiancé is tinged with resentment at woman's restricted sphere:

> 'A man should try to be something,' said Phineas.
> 'And a woman must be content to be nothing, – unless Mr. Mill can pull us through!' (ch. lix)

but she knuckles under to Oswald Chiltern and finds peace of mind – wishful thinking on Trollope's part rather than truth to life and character. Her friend, Lady Laura Standish, however, who wanted to lead a salon and influence political events, is broken on the wheel of her restless ambition, the element of masculinity in her character explaining her deep discontent, as I have indicated. Lady Glencora, wiser than both, limits her ambition by succeeding as hostess, as in life the wives of leading politicians chose to do.[11] It is impossible to rebel against the man's world. Even Madame Max Goesler, though asserting the joys of independence, clutches at the chance of marriage which comes her way.

As in Trollope's depiction of young love, one is conscious of tension and ambiguity, as an artist's perception of human truth comes into conflict with convention. Crusaders for women's rights are caricatured, the ideal of sweet, self-sacrificing motherhood is upheld, but the Trollopian domestic scene is seething with disturbed, anxious, rebellious womankind, sex-pots and icebergs, strangely distraught anti-males like Priscilla Stanbury and Lucinda Roanoke, others manifestly compensating for tedious, boring domestic rituals in bursts of energetic horseriding or, worse, mischievous gossip and flirtation. Clara Amedroz in *The Belton Estate* is like many other heroines in chafing under the limitations of behaviour society prescribes for women.[12] Even the looseliving Mrs Smith in *John Caldigate* has Trollope's sympathy when she grumbles about the world for men and for women. Less inclined to prevailing censoriousness about moral error he calls for charity towards the victims of masculine egotism and infidelity. Both Mrs Askerton of *The Belton Estate* and Carry Brattle in *The Vicar of Bullhampton* come in for a good deal of compassion. As Trollope put it to his friend Anna Steele: 'Fathers and mothers will forgive anything in a son, debauchery, gambling, lying – even the worst dishonesty and fraud – but the "fallen" daughter is too often regarded as an outcast for whom no hope can be entertained.' (*Letters*, 461, p. 272). Moreover, women themselves, he points out in *An Eye For An Eye*, are too often prone in cases of moral lapse to think 'that the woman should be punished as the sinner and that the man should be assisted to escape'.[13] He makes a plea in the *Letters* for Arabella Trefoil:

> Will such a one as Arabella Trefoil be damned, and if so why? Think of her virtues; how she works, how true she is to her vocation, how little there is of self indulgence or idleness. I think that she will go to a kind of third class heaven in which she will always be getting third class husbands. (644, p. 364)

Madame Max (Marie Goesler), on the other hand, is guaranteed a first-class heaven from her very first appearance in *Phineas Finn*. Rich, widowed, a dark-eyed Viennese, she maintains her own salon in a stylish Park Lane house, outside which the Duke of Omnium's plain green brougham (the one without a coat of arms) is regularly seen. However, in such an equivocal position Madame Max retains her reputation. No wonder Lady Glencora fears a threat to the prospects of her son as heir to the Duke's estates. Few scenes among women equal those in *Phineas Finn* in which these two fence with such delicacy and propriety over the Duke's possible remarriage.

To begin with Marie is a woman of rare beauty and social charm, exercising her attraction over a number of men, notably the old Duke, who asks her to be his mistress but is so besotted that he is even willing to marry her. Lord Fawn, old Maule and finally Phineas Finn come under her spell. She grows in the reader's mind as the series proceeds, errors increasing her wisdom, sadness ennobling her character, experience adding to her gentleness and softening her humour. There is a scene in *Phineas Redux* which shows all Trollope's skill in presenting character amid delicate human situations. The old duke is dying (ch. xxv) and has asked for Marie. Every insignificant detail is directed towards the uneasy relationship of the two women, Glencora and Marie, at the side of the dying man. Cora is careworn, agitated, watchful; we are constantly aware of what has gone on in the past, what might ensue. The Duke wishes to be alone with Marie, and the reader is invited to share Cora's anxiety: what might he say, or promise, when she is out of the room? The Duke's mind goes back inevitably to that one sweetmeat his power and money had failed to secure for him: 'It is a pity you did not take the coronet when I offered it you'. By a simple touch or a brief observation such as this Trollope has always the power to engulf his characters in a flow of remembrance. But Marie stands firm: 'Nay, Duke, it was no pity. Had I done so, you could not have had us both'. She has the nobility now, as she kisses him gently on the forehead, and he, sipping his spoonful of broth, is a fretful child balked of his prize. Lady Glencora's curiosity cannot be contained once they are alone: 'I suppose he whispered something very gracious to you'. The old rift in their relationship is still evident.

Other details etch the scene in the memory. Sir Omicron Pie, now retired from general practice but in constant attendance, appears briefly with an unforgettable line: 'The vital spark is on the spring', as he waves 'a gesture heavenward with his hand'. Then comes the Marchioness of Hartletop, an old flame, reviving memories Omnium would sooner forget, but Trollope allows *her* remembrances of her own, stark, and clear, of an incident of many years past which had become precious to her. She is not allowed to see the Duke despite her journey:

She had submitted herself to discomfort, indignity, fatigue, and disappointment; and it had all been done for love. With her broad face, and her double chin, and her heavy jowl, and the beard that was growing round her lips, she did not look like a romantic woman; but, in spite of appearances, romance and a duck-like waddle may go together. The memory of those forty years had been strong upon her, and her heart was heavy because she could not see that old man once again. Men will love to the last, but they love what is fresh and new. A woman's love can live on the recollection of the past. (ch. xxv)

As usual, a homely and trite observation gains fresh vitality from a trick of presentation such as this.

Next there is a reminder of the Eustace diamonds scandal that amused the Duke in his dotage, heralding a mockingly ironic repetition: an awkward legacy to Marie of jewellery and twenty thousand pounds, which arouses Cora's uncontrollable jealousy: 'You had better be careful. There is no knowing what they are worth. He spent half his income on them, I believe, during part of his life' (ch. xxvi). Marie quietly replies that all she wants is one small ring as a keepsake. Now her triumph comes in a last test of pride and independence; it is her nobility of soul which enables her to meet Cora at last on grounds of equality. 'When once she had made up her mind not to marry the Duke, the Duke had been safe from her; – as his jewels and money should be safe now that he was dead' (ch. xxx). So despite huffing and puffing from Plantagenet, she devotes the legacy to helping Adelaide Palliser and Jeffrey Maule marry and begin life together.

Marie Goesler is ready for a worthy love, and it comes from her devotion to Phineas under the accusation of having murdered Mr Bonteen. Steadily she grows more beautiful; Lady Laura is jealous of her now, and 'hated her as a fair woman who has lost her beauty can hate the dark woman who keeps it' (ch. lxv). Exonerated at his trial by evidence that Madame Goesler miraculously unearths in Prague, a more mature, disenchanted and less self-centred Phineas is now a fit husband for her.

In *The Prime Minister* Marie and Phineas fade into the background, although she is closer than ever before to Glencora, who is sustained as the wife of a prime minister by Marie's strong heart. All this makes more affecting the separation that occurs with Cora's death, and Plantagenet's unjust accusations in the last of the series, *The Duke's Children*, which bring reminders of the gulf of birth which separates her from the nobility. Throughout the Palliser series the conception of Marie Goesler in its vivacity and truth to nature is almost as bewitching as that of Glencora herself.

BACHELORHOOD

Trollope's single men, usually less interesting than his single women, perform fairly mechanical roles as foils and confidants. Adopting the drama's pairing of young men to display the virtues of the hero, Trollope found his most useful foil in the man-about-town leading the hero astray in mild dissipations and youthful indiscretions: Sowerby and Mark Robarts, Laurence Fitzgibbon and Phineas Finn, Dot Blake and Frank Ballindine, Isadore Hamel and Jonathan Stubbs. Their value is in complicating the fortunes of the central figure by drawing him into debt or damaging his reputation. Sowerby seriously affects Mark Robarts' position in the parish and with Lady Lufton, by getting him to sign a bill and by involving him with the racing fraternity and the Duke of Omnium. Fitzgibbon offers a selfish and irresponsible standard in political life which is meant to contrast with Finn's ideals of service. Of the two Cambridge men in *John Caldigate* it is Dick Shand 'the very imp of imprudence' (ch. vii), who encourages the hero to emigrate to Australia in search of gold. Unfortunately this promising minor character soon fades from the story. Other notable male pairings include Will Belton and Captain Aylmer in *The Belton Estate*, Lucius Mason and Perry Orme in *Orley Farm*, and the Newton cousins in *Ralph the Heir*. The secondary leading males, as they might be called, often compete for the heroine's affections, and in so doing emphasise the hero's qualities by their inadequacies or delinquencies.

Trollope adopted the practice of providing his central figure with a foil in his second novel, *The Kellys and the O'Kellys*, creating in Dot Blake not only the reckless ally of Lord Ballindine, but also the gay bachelor, who crops up in many later novels and spends his time gambling, riding, playing whist and making up the numbers at house-parties. Quite often Trollope draws this type as an eccentric aristocrat, like Lord Popplecourt in *The Duke's Children*, whose attitude to girls is expressed thus:

> His idea of marriage had as yet gone no farther than a conviction that girls generally were things which would be pressed on him, and against which he must arm himself with some shield. (ch. xxxv)

Trollope is unsurpassed among nineteenth-century novelists for a splendid gallery of weak-minded oafs. The doyen of them all is Bertie Stanhope. Bertie is a shade brighter, and a master in the art of pleasing himself and living on credit. His interview with Bishop Proudie in Chapter xi of *Barchester Towers* is one of the funniest scenes in the novel. Down the social scale come Major Tifto, Captain Green and the odious Major Pountney, representatives of the shabby-genteel world of toadying ex-military men, seedy foreigners of mysterious background like Count Pateroff, failed attorneys, clerks and shady men of business like Sexty Parker, who cluster like flies around the leading figures.

In Trollope's later fiction the bachelor becomes increasingly a character of intriguing ambiguities rather than a stooge or foil. Emphasis falls on his moral inadequacies and inability to act from any fixed basis of duty, honour or social obligation. Trollope's heroes in the later books reflect a greater insecurity and inability to control events, which point to a failure of inner resources and possibly a widespread cultural dilemma of the later Victorian period. The weak-spirited lover, caught up in a chain of events arising from an initial act of fraud in *Cousin Henry*, driven by self-deception to further intrigues, and all the while racked by guilt, indicates the direction taken by Trollope's imagination in the increasingly complex world of late Victorian England. Jack De Baron in *Is He Popenjoy?* and Dick Ross in *Kept in the Dark* both function in a strangely disorientated society, looking on scenes of moral conflict with a compound of self-conscious world weariness and hedonism. This is very noticeable in the character of Frank Houston in *Ayala's Angel* whose unabashed avarice and egotism is displayed in pursuit of Gertrude Tringle whom he finally abandons without a qualm for his first love, Imogene Docimer. Where once the hero's devotion admitted no more than a little straying from the paths of virtue, and caddishness could be rewarded simply and effectively by a well-timed punch on the nose, the new world offers fewer certainties and remedies for wrong-doing; the moral life grows more complicated and the derelictions of Henry Jones or the wily John Scarborough more resistant to moral judgement. Fred Neville, the central figure in *An Eye For an Eye* is typical, perplexed by obligations of rank which draw him to Sophia Mellerby and powerless to withstand the lust which draws him to Kate O'Hara. Neville is 'a self-indulgent spoiled young man who had realised to himself no idea of duty in life' (I, ch. xii). After seducing Kate he ruthlessly tries to cast her off once he comes into his inheritance. Kate is unfit by birth to become the Countess of Scroope, although under pressure Neville offers her the opportunity of a secret marriage abroad. Incensed by his treachery, Kate's mother pushes him over the cliffs of Mohill. Full of insecurity and guilt Fred Neville is a very modern hero, a victim of the glands, devoid of moral stability, driven beyond his meagre emotional and spiritual capital:

> There was an unconquerable feeling on his own part that he was altogether unfitted for the kind of life that was expected of him. (II, ch. viii)

Another and more intriguing example of the young man, basically decent and yet somehow destined to take the wrong path either through some inherent weakness or mere fluke is Harry Gilmore in *The Vicar of Bullhampton*. A far more interesting character than Fred Neville simply because he is more ordinary and part of a far less melodramatic plot, Harry is unlucky in love, and for not much more reason than that he is just not very likeable. Larry Twentyman in *The American Senator*, the gentleman farmer and sportsman, is similarly (without being unpleasant) just unamiable, although Trollope at least allows him to acquire a wife by the time he reappears in *Ayala's Angel*. Harry Gilmore, on the other hand, remains the martyr to unrequited love, and it does peculiar things to his character. As the 'other man' in Mary Lowther's life he has every right to feel aggrieved at her rejection of him in favour of Walter Marrable; he is, after all, the squire of Bullhampton, who has done rather well at Harrow and Oxford, a man with a thoroughly good heart, good-looking and with teeth 'almost too white and too perfect for a man'. What more could a girl ask in those preorthodontic days? But Mary simply cannot bring herself to love him and that is that. What happens is typical of Trollope's eye for the gloomier paths a man may follow. When a marriage of convenience looms for Marrable, Mary allows herself to slide into a dubious engagement with Harry from which she subsequently withdraws. Harry is torn between vindictiveness and a stubborn hope that Mary may change, and Trollope shows the thoughts churning in his mind, rankling and damaging his nature. In the depiction of this character ruined by suspicion and self-doubt we realise again how greatness as a novelist of subtle psychological turns was within Trollope's grasp:

> Then by degrees there grew upon him a fear that she still meant to escape from him, and he swore to himself, – without any tenderness, – that this should not be so. Let her once be his wife and she should be treated with all consideration, – with all affection, if she would accept it; but she should not make a fool of him now. (ch. lxiv)

Told in the novelist's customary dry, undemonstrative narrative, the sad transformation of this gentle person might easily be missed. Yet the implications about the changes love, disappointment, betrayal occasionally effect are both true and disturbing. The confrontation between Harry and Mary is a fraction melodramatic, but no less telling on the reader's nerves, as he, beside himself with anger and frustration, almost calls her a whore. Walter wins Mary, of course, and poor Harry Gilmore embarks on a solitary cruise reflecting upon his shame and failure.

Older men are seldom of major importance in Trollope's stories, and generally fulfil the role of confidant or cautionary example to the hero. Such a figure is the lawyer, Mr Prendergast, in *Castle Richmond*. Another is the prebendary of Salisbury Cathedral, the Reverend

Henry Fitzackerley Chamberlaine in *The Vicar of Bullhampton*, who is the perfect rendering of a clerical type Trollope had already made his own in the Barsetshire novels, the indolent clergyman of private means:

> He was a very handsome man, about six feet high, with large light grey eyes, a straight nose, and a well cut chin. His lips were thin, but his teeth were perfect, – only that they had been supplied by a dentist. His grey hair encircled his head, coming round upon his forehead in little wavy curls, in a manner that had conquered the hearts of spinsters by the dozen in the cathedral. It was whispered, indeed, that married ladies would sometimes succumb, and rave about the beauty, and the dignity, and the white hands, and the deep rolling voice of the Rev. Henry Fitzackerley Chamberlaine. (ch. xxiv)

With details such as these Trollope portrays a familiar figure of the mid-Victorian social scene, the clergyman whose natural endowments smooth his way to preferment.

Few of Trollope's older bachelors are as comfortable with the world, although they strive for an air of contentment and well-being. Captain Cuttwater, thrown up on the shores of life like one of Dickens' old salts, has nothing to do in *The Three Clerks* but voice Trollope's complaints about competitive examinations for the Civil Service and provide the cash for Alaric Tudor's career. Sir Lionel, in *The Bertrams*, scrounges from his son and brother, and makes up to two ladies in the hope that at least one will be foolish enough to let him get his hands on her fortune. Worst of all is the repellent figure of Colonel Osborne in *He Knew He Was Right* who takes perverse pleasure in sowing discontent between a young married couple. Altogether these portraits of the bachelor reveal the impoverished and self-absorbed existence of men without the anchor of love, marriage and family life. This is the significance such characters have in relation to Trollope's love ethic and total commentary on human affairs. To a great extent, however, they are peripheral and like the spinster aunts are called upon for effects in the plot, parading before the reader sometimes like pantomime wicked uncles. Maurice Maule, paying court to Madame Max in *Phineas Redux*, 'an idler, a man of luxury, and then a spendthrift' (ch. xxi), struts like a gander, inviolable in his self-satisfaction and devoted to his own comfort:

> No one knew better than Mr. Maule that the continual bloom of lasting summer which he affected requires great accuracy in living. Late hours, nocturnal cigars, and midnight drinkings, pleasurable though they may be, consume too quickly the free-flowing lamps of youth, and are fatal at once to the husbanded candle-ends of age. ch. xxi)

Even more suggestive of pantomime, Colonel Marrable in *The Vicar of Bullhampton* clings desperately to his youthful appearance by tinting his beard and wearing padded coats. Quickly captured in a paragraph, such men reveal a finicky introversion and excessive fear of growing old that are telling points in Trollope's depiction of the solitary man.

It is in studies of the loneliness of old age that Trollope finds scope for pathos and deeper analysis of character. The bereaved husband has already been mentioned in connection with the Pallisers and *The Duke's Children*. There are other haunting studies of age and loneliness. In *Ralph the Heir*, which begins that fine ten-year period of creativity from 1870, the central figure is Sir Thomas Underwood, who becomes unwillingly embroiled in the rigmarole surrounding Newton Priory and its rightful heir. From the start Sir Thomas shows himself by nature unable to communicate or make close friends, a born solitary, yet encumbered with irksome responsibilities. Now sixty and a widower, he prefers living alone in his chambers in Southampton Buildings and dining at his Pall Mall club to the society of his two daughters at their Fulham villa, who eagerly await his coming at weekends. He frets about his absence from them, however, as he does about the arrival of his niece, Mary Bonner, from the West Indies, and his failure to discharge his guardianship properly to Ralph Newton.

Trollope develops a complex character in Sir Thomas, for allied with his inertia and lack of will-power is a fundamental guilt about not having made more of his abilities as a lawyer. He is generous and sweet-natured, but slothful and irresolute. Procrastination, much disliked by Trollope, is treated here with great sympathy, especially towards the end of the book, when Sir Thomas' preoccupation with his *magnum opus*, a life of Bacon, is revealed as the symbol of his timid evasion of life. For many years he has compiled materials for his projected study, of which he has not yet written a line. Trollope's understanding of this kind of psychological case is conveyed in a passage of tender insight:

There are men who never dream of great work, who never realise to themselves the need of work so great as to demand a lifetime, but who themselves never fail in accomplishing those second-class tasks with which they satisfy their own energies. Men these are who to the world are very useful. Some few there are, who seeing the beauty of a great work and believing in its accomplishment within the years allotted to man, are contented to struggle for success, and struggling, fail. Here and there comes one who struggles and succeeds. But the men are many who see the beauty, who adopt the task, who promise themselves the triumph, and then never struggle at all. The task is never abandoned; but days go by and weeks; – and then

months and years, – and nothing is done. The dream of youth becomes the doubt of middle life, and then the despair of age. (ch. xl)

There is much of Trollope's inner self here, a vindication of his own
industry at a crucial point in his life. Unlike Trollope, however, Sir
Thomas is a loser, who has grown into the habit of regarding himself
as an unlucky man. Piqued by the brevity of his career as Solicitor-
General over only four months of one administration, he is lured by the
residue of his ambition into contesting Percycross at a general election,
a wry account of Trollope's own dismal experience. The venality of the
electorate and the aftermath of his election success disgust Sir Thomas,
and he turns once more to the refuge of his great work. Now we see
its significance :

> By Bacon he had justified to himself, – or rather had failed to justify
> to himself, – a seclusion from his family and from the world which
> had been intended for strenuous work, but had been devoted to
> dilettante idleness. . . . He was for ever doubting, for ever intending,
> and for ever despising himself for his doubts and unaccomplished in-
> tentions. (ch. xl)

It is all an illusion protecting him from a world he would not face.
Chapter li, 'Music has charms', is a splendid evocation of the man's
helplessness and immobility. Alone in his room he sits with his papers,
which have become his solace and his curse, racked by guilty knowledge
of his self-deception, and at the same time resigned; failure hangs
heavily in the air-like dank grass, sweet to his nostrils. Outside a boy
is playing a melancholy flute, and this exacerbates his wretchedness,
prompting an angry outburst against his servant. His precious books
must be packed without delay. He will move to Fulham and begin
work there immediately. Trollope allows him his comforting illusions :
'Let us hope that the great Life of Bacon may yet be written' (ch.
lviii).

Pictures of the solitary man outside marriage are seldom so detailed.
This being so, it is odd that Trollope's last completed novel should
tackle the subject of an old bachelor's love for a young girl. In point
of fact, *An Old Man's Love* is not the study of lonely old age it was
intended to be, so much as a low-powered comedy involving a devoted
but domineering housekeeper, Mrs Baggett, and a triangular love plot,
in which the old man, William Whittlestaff, rather half-heartedly
attempts to win Mary Lawrie from her childhood sweetheart, John
Gordon. Whether or not Trollope can be thought of as reliving some
of his feelings over Kate Field, as Sadleir suggests, the result is a disappointing tale and there is very little in the study of Whittlestaff.[14]
His stiffness and pomposity never adequately mask his shyness, and

the ending of the affair by his saintly renunciation of Mary, even though she had engaged herself to him, is novelettish stuff. One is reminded with some irritation of another self-sacrificing bachelor, Roger Carbury, in *The Way We Live Now*. Both make noble gestures with florid farewells embarrassing to the modern reader. Of course, *An Old Man's Love* was written only six months before Trollope died and shows his exhaustion. One may conjecture that had he written it at the height of his powers it might have been his major study of the solitary man.

LIZZIE EUSTACE

Next to Glencora Palliser the outstanding female character of Trollope's fiction is the heroine of *The Eustace Diamonds*, and although her role lacks the pathos of yearning and loneliness in such characters as Mabel Grex she is such a splendid solitary as to provide a fitting conclusion to this discussion. Lizzie Eustace embodies the themes of greed, vulgarity and delusion that run through the novel. Just as the necklace is the talisman of a jaded materialistic society (one is reminded of the symbolic role played by Wilkie Collins' moonstone), Lizzie Eustace is its reigning deity and at the same time its indictment. But she is human and fascinating; one of the great heroines like Emma Bovary and Becky Sharp. Thackeray's heroine is the obvious comparison, and Trollope took pains in the *Autobiography* to distinguish between them. That he should anticipate the comparison at all is evidence that he knew how well he had drawn Lizzie, and although we may question his assertion that without Becky his heroine would have been no different, it is fair to say that she is by no means a second Becky. She has her own unique style in the novel she dominates both as huntress and intended victim of greedy adventurers and impoverished aristocrats like Lord Fawn. She is abominable and pitiful in her stratagems to retain the jewels acquired through her marriage to Sir Florian Eustace.

Something of her duality is implied in the first two chapters, 'Lizzie Greystock' and 'Lady Eustace', the names themselves suggestive of Trollope's conception and of her difference from Thackeray's heroine. Lizzie Eustace is in limbo, a displaced person, empty-headed as well as empty-hearted, a doomed exile in the society she so much wants to conquer. Had the book been conceived in tragic terms, her condition might have been described as truly hellish, for she is a ghost seeking to establish her identity. As it is a social comedy, she is merely an actress in a succession of roles she does not feel or understand: Lizzie Greystock and Lady Eustace, with innumerable changes of costume, scene and script. Trollope describes her with a wealth of adjectives. She is hard, mendacious, 'clever, sharp and greedy' (ch. ii), but unintelligent and ignorant. Her cleverness is an instinct to change colour like the chameleon; her adaptation to other people's moods the quickness of a lizard (ch. x). She dreams of having what by nature she is incapable of having – real feelings: 'I do not know that she cared very much. As she was utterly devoid of true tenderness, so also was she devoid of conscience' (ch. i).

Early in life she had known loneliness; her father, old Admiral Greystock, died when she was nineteen, and she was put in the care of her aunt, Lady Linlithgow. A better start than Becky's, perhaps, and like Becky she made resolutely for the haven of marriage, only to lose Sir Florian within the year. Her personal fortune was at least comfortable, but 'through it all, there was a sense of loneliness that nearly killed her' (ch. ii). She is to remain isolated throughout the story, for it is the very essence of her nature not to be fulfilled. She has no centre, in contrast to Lucy Morris 'who had a well-formed idea of her own identity' (ch. iii). This is Lizzie's tragedy, the cause of her plotting, recklessness and wandering. She has no anchorage and therefore no real substance, unlike Lucy who appears to Frank to have 'a reality and a truth about her . . . as firm rocks which could not be shaken' (ch. xiii). Hence Lizzie's unassuageable hunger for friendship, romance, poetry: 'There existed in her bosom a sort of craving after confidential friendship' (ch. xiv), and her stunted feelings are almost touched by Lady Glencora's interest in her. Her wish to possess the diamonds, dreams of a Corsair lover, attempts to wrest Frank from Lucy and other liaisons are pathetic bids to establish identity. Ironically she seeks solitude among the rocks at Portray; she is least able to be alone. Although the widow of Sir Florian Eustace she has no place, no actual position in society: there is 'still too much of the mushroom' about her (ch. xxi). She is described as a cat, a solitary predator, but one lacking the strength of other preying animals. Her hard, glittering presence in society suggests the anomalous role of the wealthy courtesan, notorious in London society when this novel was gestating in Trollope's mind. Indeed the character is a disguised rendering of a familiar figure of the mid-Victorian scene.[15]

All this points up the real difference between Lizzie and Thackeray's heroine. Where Becky, overreaching herself, making mistakes, is majestic and terrifying in her calculated movement towards a goal, Lizzie combines resourcefulness with immense folly. More the forerunner of the modern cinema's dumb blonde with the cash register mind, she acts wildly, improvising from minute to minute, and an amusing gulf opens for the reader between her aspirations and her intellect. Trollope's heroine is, in some ways, the more subtle study, a woman adrift on a sea of impulses she has no way of understanding. Becky is always fully conscious of going to the devil, scattering the debris of unpaid bills and broken hearts behind her. Knowing what she wants so clearly, she can school herself not to feel; Lizzie simply does not have any feelings at all, only nerve endings.

> The reader, perhaps, by this time, has not a high opinion of Lady Eustace, and may believe that among other drawbacks on her character there is especially this, – that she was heartless. But that was by no means her own opinion of herself. She would have described herself, – and would have meant to do so with truth, – as being all heart. (ch. xxvi)

Trollope fastens here on a facet of character which produces skilful actors and actresses, and sometimes schizophrenics. She entertains, in her boundless egotism, an entirely false belief in herself; it is not surprising that Trollope gives full measure to her talents as an actress. This contrived love scene is no more than a stage performance:

> She ran up to him and grasped his hand, and hung on his arm, and looked up into his face, and then burst into tears. But the tears were not violent tears. There were just three sobs, and two bright eyes full of water, and a lace handkerchief, – and then a smile. 'Oh Frank,' she said, 'it does make one think so of old times.' (ch. xiv)

A heavy price often exacted by the acting profession is losing contact with personality, and this is what happens to Lizzie. As one set of illusions follows another she flounders in bewilderment, with just enough self-knowledge left to make her uncomfortable: 'She was never at ease. There was no green spot in her life with which she could be contented' (ch. xxi). One of her illusions is that the grand passion of her life is just around the corner:

> She had a grand idea, – this selfish, hard-fisted little woman, . . . of surrendering herself and all her possessions to a great passion . . . Now she desired to be so in love that she could surrender everything to her love. (ch. v)

But her lack of contact with reality and want of feeling deprive her of any chance of happiness, so she drifts from one lover to another. Frank she would win merely as an exercise of her allure:

> She would carry on the battle, using every wile she knew, straining every nerve to be victorious, encountering any and all dangers, and yet she had no definite aim before her. She herself did not know what she would be at . . . the guiding motive of her conduct was the desire to make things seem to be other than they were. To be alway

acting a part rather than living her own life was to her everything. (ch. xix)

Marriage to Lord Fawn promises rank and social standing – and awful dullness. Lord George de Bruce Carruthers, a shady gentleman living on his wits, at least offers danger and excitement, a certain Byronic fascination, but her lying is too much even for him. He finds her at last 'such a mass of deceit, that he was afraid of her' (ch. lxiii).

One of the triumphs of characterisation Trollope achieves in Lizzie is in adapting his ideas about romance and reality, sham and true feeling, to the diamonds Lizzie believes in and flaunts in public until they acquire symbolic value. They are even made to disappear – illusions again, like Lizzie's feelings and her dreams: 'If I had a Corsair of my own how I would sit on watch for my lover's boat by the seashore!' (ch. v). Her literary aspirations are appropriately part of her chronic self-deception, and an essential part of the truth-falsehood dichotomy traced through the novel. Poetry is a marketable commodity to increase her stock among cultivated people; she reads well to the dying Sir Florian. She flourishes her volumes of Shelley, but wants lines 'good for quoting' (ch. xxi). When Lady Glencora comes to call on her in her bedchamber Tennyson's poems are prominently displayed. The verses of the laureate appeal to her, partly because he is the literary lion of the day, but also because she sees herself without a knight loyal and true.

In this respect Shelley is even more important, for he suggests an elevated state that serves as a substitute for feeling. Even Miss MacNulty sees through this falsity and sticks honestly to her romantic novels. But Lizzie, who most of all needs people to fill the vacuum in herself, persists in regarding herself as a solitary; Chapter xxi is a masterly evocation of her inconsistencies. On her first morning at Portray Castle on the Firth of Clyde, she takes her copy of *Queen Mab* and makes her way down to the rocks and to one pinnacle in particular 'as a place appropriate to solitude and Shelley'. Here reality begins to intervene: her rocky perch is in full sunlight, so she retreats to the summerhouse where the bench is too narrow and the snails cannot be ignored, but she presses on with her reading. Seeing herself as Ianthe, the pure spirit, she rejects the world's falseness (although not long since she has begged Lucy to spy for her at Fawn Court), and she burbles on to herself about her unspotted soul while toying with the idea of seducing her cousin. Lines from the poem interspersed with snatches of her practical concerns show the hollowness of her pretension; she does commit some lines to memory, and returns to the house to try them out on Miss MacNulty. Value for the allowance she pays her companion is hardly forthcoming, Lizzie decides, since the older woman fails to be awed by Lizzie's cultural accomplishments, and indeed, as the fortnight wears on, she herself finds that poetry taxes her mind too much, and she joins Miss MacNulty in devouring French novels.

All this poetic posturing is, of course, central to Lizzie's character, and relevant to her play-acting, her materialism and her inability to face real life. Poetry she later equates with lies (ch. lxxiii), finding it in her last lover, the Reverend Joseph Emilius, a Bohemian Jew with a foothold in society as a preacher. Lord Fawn, she has decided, has not a grain of poetry in him, 'and poetry was what her very soul craved; – poetry, together with houses, champagne, jewels, and admiration' (ch. lxviii). Greasy Mr Emilius, on the other hand, has 'a dash of poetry about him; and poetry, as she thought, was not compatible with humdrum truth' (ch. lxxiii). He wins her with a pastiche of Shelleyan diction, using words like 'adamantine', 'queen of my soul' and 'empress', which, although half-recognised as flattery, gives Lizzie the frisson of romantic experience she enjoys most.

Trollope leaves us in no doubt as to her falsity and vulgarity, yet manages to invest the character with pathos, suggesting all along that she acted without self-knowledge or purpose. In the end Becky Sharp is a harpy and more detestable, since she acted consciously and deliberately in ruthless pursuit of the vanities she worshipped. We can hardly feel sorry for Becky who is so much more intelligent than everybody else; but poor Lizzie is never mistress of events, and from the start doomed to lose the gamble for the diamonds because of her stupidity. Had Trollope the qualities of a Balzac or Dostoievski, Lizzie Eustace might have been a tragic heroine rather than the 'cunning little woman of pseudo-fashion'[16] he is content to make her. It is sometimes sad to reflect on Trollope's near-misses of greatness.

7 Trollope and Ireland

And now I went ashore . . . happy also to know that
I was once more in Ireland.[1]

Trollope's lifelong involvement with Ireland produced several novels,
all of which have come to be regarded as aberrations from the main
course of his fiction. Indeed, one of the most fascinating aspects of the
'chaos of criticism' surrounding Trollope is the unwarranted neglect of
his Irish stories. Apart from several reviews in his lifetime and scattered
comments in surveys of his work, generally favourable, there is no
adequate treatment of this area of his fiction. One article in recent
years paid tribute to the first two novels, both failures in Trollope's own
day, but its very title – 'Trollope's Prentice Work' (taking up a phrase
of Sadleir's) – betrays a quite unnecessary hesitancy.[2] Yet his first novel,
The Macdermots of Ballycloran, published by T. C. Newby in 1847 on
the half-profits system, does in fact show that by this year Trollope
had already arrived at competence in story-telling and characterisation.
But to Sadleir it was a false dawn in his career,[3] as was his second
novel, The Kellys and the O'Kellys, published by Henry Colburn in
1848. The other two Irish novels, Castle Richmond (Chapman & Hall,
1860), and The Landleaguers (Chatto & Windus, 1883), which Trollope
left unfinished at his death, seemed to Sadleir scarcely novels at all,
but documented pamphlets. This judgement is quite inadequate but
has not been seriously challenged.

Since Sadleir, the commonly accepted view has been that Trollope's
literary inspiration flowered not on the rocky, windswept headlands
of Moher, but in the purlieus of Salisbury, an impression Trollope himself perpetuated with his own account of his career. Even today it is
taken for granted that Trollope's oeuvre really begins with The Warden
in 1855. Ireland produced the man, Sadleir declared, but England made
the novelist. What had the creator of Lily Dale to do with absentee
landlords, Ribbonmen or tenant rights? Such an attitude has tended
to limit our understanding of Trollope's art in particular ways, not to
mention helping deny us access to some remarkable novels. For the
Irish books have become collector's items. The Landleaguers has not

been reprinted since its publication, while *The Macdermots* survived only until 1906, in the John Lane New Pocket Library series. *The Kellys* figured in the monumental World's Classics collection of Trollope novels begun in the 1920s, last appearing in 1929. *Castle Richmond* went out of print in 1906.

In Trollope's lifetime, however, the Irish novels were popular and critically acclaimed. The *Dublin Review* in 1872 praised him for 'the unembarrassed judgement of a critical spectator who had no "side" in the social, political, and religious questions which distracted Ireland'; fair comment on the middle ground so characteristic of this writer. The *Athenaeum* suggested that he treated Irish life with more earnestness than Lever, while the *Academy* felt he was one of the few non-Irish writers who could convey local colour without strain. Alexander Innes Shand in the *Edinburgh Review* commended his shrewdness and perception in the early novels set in Ireland.[4] Irish critics, such as Stephen Gwynn and Stephen Brown, were also impressed. Brown appreciated the accuracy of landscape in *The Macdermots* and *The Landleaguers*, and Gwynn called *Castle Richmond* the *locus classicus* for a fictional description of the Great Hunger. *Douglas Jerrold's Weekly* found *The Kellys* 'free from that outrageous exaggeration which is so common in sketches of Irish life and character'; another pertinent observation on the verisimilitude which was Trollope's forte.[5] Modern scholars have established that contemporary criticism by no means disparaged Trollope's first novel when it appeared.[6] *The Macdermots*, said T. H. S. Escott, gave 'a true picture of the country, a correct insight into its people'.[7] G. S. Saintsbury found a remarkable quality in *The Landleaguers*.[8] So a body of opinion did exist, prior to Sadleir's *Commentary*, that Trollope represented Irish life truthfully, and that the novels set in Ireland were worth considering as an integral part of his total output. The *Spectator* critic (probably R. H. Hutton) went so far as to declare 'the Irish novels will be regarded as the high-water mark of his ability'.[9] Such a judgement is unlikely, for they have many inadequacies. At the same time they deserve a great deal more consideration than they have had. No study of Trollope can fail to take into account either the Irish novels or the total significance of the time he spent in Ireland to his development.

Trollope went to Ireland in September 1841, at the age of twenty-six, undisciplined, unfulfilled, yet at the same time half-inclined to redeem the past with his new job as deputy surveyor's clerk for country posts in Southern Ireland. He was stationed at Banagher. Bad report pursued him from St Martin's le Grand, but within a year, as he tells us in the *Autobiography*, he had gained 'the character of a thoroughly good public servant' (ch. iv). The most helpful contribution of Trollope's latest biographer, James Pope Hennessy, has been to supplement the novelist's comments in the *Autobiography* on these years in Ireland.

At the same time as his career took shape he found his personal salvation in marriage and family life. The paucity of details we have about his marriage to Rose Heseltine in 1844 has been mentioned, but we can safely assume that falling in love was the turning point in his fortunes, and the key to his impulses both as post office servant and subsequently as writer. At Clonmel, to which he had been moved from Banagher, his sons were born. Frequently moved in the course of his duties, he had to settle his family for eighteen months at Belfast, and then at Donnybrook, outside Dublin. By the time he left Ireland, in 1859, he had risen to the rank of surveyor, with considerable responsibility for postal services over the whole country, and much prestige at St Martin's le Grand, which was happy to capitalise on his grasp of affairs and prepared to overlook his often overbearing manner in return for the efficient expansion of the postal service overseas.

Trollope was to look back on his Irish life with the deepest affection, and to retain the fondest memories of its people:

> My life in England for twenty-six years from the time of my birth to the day on which I left it, had been wretched. I had been poor, friendless and joyless. In Ireland it had constantly been happy.[10]

The Irish have a saying, praise a boy and he will prosper, and in this lies the key to Anthony's transformation. He came to the country gloomily preoccupied with his inertia and failure, but bearing down upon country post offices, and the casual encounters with priests and peasants and tenant farmers, forced him into social initiatives that ripened into acquaintance. Soon after his arrival he took up hunting, and quickly won the respect of his rough, good-natured hosts. Riding with the Galway Blazers he acquired a reputation for courage in the saddle. The mere fact of gaining a foothold socially was enough to liberate his sense of fun. Irish goodwill and hospitality did the rest. Trollope puts his feelings on this point in the *Autobiography*, contrasting his existence in London, where he was clearly a rudderless soul, with the roistering life in Ireland, where to his astonishment he was liked and respected. 'Irish acquaintances I have by dozens', he was to recall in *Castle Richmond*, 'and Irish friends, also, by twos and threes, whom I can love and cherish.'[11] One of the most influential was Sir William Gregory, who had occupied the next desk to Trollope at Harrow.[12] At Coole Park, Co. Galway, the Tory MP for Dublin entertained the best society, and here Trollope widened his acquaintance. He became friendly with Charles Lever and other writers, as well as men eminent in politics and law. Thus, first by travel among the common people and then through association with society, Trollope acquired broad understanding of his adopted country.

In fact Ireland was in many ways more Trollope's spiritual home than England, for here he established his identity. He once claimed

> It has been my fate to have so close an intimacy with Ireland, that when I meet an Irishman abroad, I always recognize in him more of a kinsman that I do in an Englishman.[13]

This is a surprising comment for one so closely associated with the fabric of English middle-class life. Yet he spent one third of his working life – about eighteen years in all – in Ireland, which exerted its influence upon him at a crucial time, affecting not only his character but his imagination. Clearly his love of Ireland went beyond mere gratitude for his second chance. There was something in the land, something in the people, that went straight to his heart and called to qualities buried in his soul; Lord Dunsany once spoke of the near-mystic experience the stranger has, coming to the country of mist and bog and mountain : soil and air, he said, seeming to be at one, bringing back the bog to its own, wherever man has lifted the spade against it. 'The soil seems to work for the bog, while the damp air fights against man. And so the spade is laid by, and the bog steals softly back; and in a few years there it is again, as though man had never troubled its ancient stillness.'[14] Trollope, the stranger, heard the voice of the endemic ruin, and went on to express it in *The Macdermots of Bally-cloran*. Feeling the anarchic strains within the Irish, Trollope exulted. He too had known alienation, defeat, poverty; he had seen himself an outcast. Moreover he could find it in himself to welcome disaster and decay with the same fatalistic pleasure as the Irish peasant moving in the black shadow of his cabin or caught in the flickering light of the peat fire. Among the people, Escott conjectured, Trollope saw at once 'a certain congeniality between his own lot, present or future, and the dismal destinies, the depressing sights and sounds surrounding him'.[15] Certainly he depicts, with painful realism in *The Macdermots* and *Castle Richmond*, the actualities of hunger and suffering. But Escott has not gone far enough. Something in Ireland was balm to Trollope's soul, and led to an instinctive love of the land; by the time he came to write his first novel, that long-postponed bid to self-assertion within a family of writers, he knew how Ireland's ruin floated on the wind, and how its soil seems to bear a grudge against civilisation.[16]

There were happier influences too. Much in the Irish people he was drawn to : their rough good nature and carefree attitude to life despite its hardships, their gusto and lively sense of fun, quick temper and all. Even their roguery and impossible sense of time went to his heart. He enjoyed the Irish gift for the tale, spicy, irreverent and black, and what Elizabeth Bowen called 'peasant toughness',[17] which came to his notice as he journeyed by Bianconi car or horseback over the rough roads of the south. 'It was altogether a very jolly life', he says in the *Autobiography* (ch. iv).

The basic requirement for the potential writer is character. In Ireland, Trollope was deluged with raw material. 'The hunting, the whisky punch, the rattling Irish life' gave him, he says, the stuff of a whole volume of stories.[18] *Tales of All Countries* I (1861) and *Lotta Schmidt: and Other Stories* (1867) contain stories of the kind he heard from people with natural fluency, whose lives were full of folklore passed on by close-knit family groups. According to *Blackwood's Magazine*, Trollope had a fund of Irish anecdotes.[19] He listened with a stranger's intentness; he trained himself in accurate, rapid observation; he assimilated celtic romance. It was truly said of him by a Dublin woman that his Irish novels struck her as having the close scrutiny of a customer in a shop looking at materials for a new dress.[20] His practice, as Hawthorne later put it, of hewing out some lump of earth and depicting humanity scurrying about their work and not realising they were being made a show of, was born in Ireland. His Irish novels offer a variety of character: slightly raffish and down-at-heel aristocracy like Lord Ballindine; the ragged, poor farmer, Thady Macdermot; the expatriate English landowner, Mr Jones of Morony Castle, County Galway; the vicious murderer Lax, in *The Landleaguers*. In style they differ from his other work in being touched with the mingled exuberance and pathos of the Irish. A corpse rising from the coffin to sing a chorus or two would not, one feels, be out of place in *The Landleaguers*, or, indeed, in *The Macdermots*, both of which have their moments of black comedy. Several minor roles have immediate and unforgettable sharpness: Dr Colligan doing the rounds of his patients in *The Kellys* with dirt-grimed fingernails; Denis M'Govery in *The Macdermots*, slyly weighing up the values of a wife or a good strong sow. Such types were the quarry of his sojourn in Ireland, where time and the land, jogging across country for days at a stretch, brought substance for Trollope's castles in the air. The small boy's habit of escaping from an ugly world, now a fixed practice of his adult life, fused with realities of the Irish scene, and somehow the 'world altogether outside the world of my own material life'[21] seemed more solid and real among the Connemara hills or the harsh landscape of County Leitrim. At any rate, it was here in Leitrim, with his friend John Merivale, that a ruined house called up the immemorial voice of inspiraton:

> We wandered about the place, suggesting to each other causes for the misery we saw there, and while I was still among the ruined walls and decayed beams I fabricated the plot of *The Macdermots*

G

of Ballycloran . . . When my friend left me, I set to work and wrote
the first chapter or two. Up to this time I had continued the practice
of castle-building of which I have spoken; but now the castle I
built was among the ruins of that old house.[22]

This is where I suggest the most significant direction to the novelist's
temperament and imagination is to be found. It is a critical commonplace to speak of Trollope's earthy realism, rooted in observation of
the ordinary matters of English social life. In the Irish novels there is
a vein of strange excitement, sadness and vivacity that his adherence
to Barchester curbed and controlled, yet did not wholly quell. It is the
strain of romance which the mists of the Shannon breathed into his
work that gives a shimmering haze to the dusty roads travelled by Mr
Crawley on the way to the Bishop's palace. The romance of Ireland
went deep with him, and not only gave the Irish novels a peculiar
intensity of their own, but inspired his greatest scenes, in which higher
reaches of imagination transcend mundane social realism. Likewise a
sense of ambiguity in character, a fusion of the colourful and the drab,
the absurd and the sober, the human weakness in the ideal, owes much
to the period Trollope spent in Ireland. Commenting on the Irish with
words like 'perverse', 'irrational' and 'irregularity', Trollope perceived
turmoil and contradiction in the celtic temperament. All this was to be
reflected in memorable characters like Harding or Crawley, and those
drawn to failure and irrationality.

In the Irish novels themselves, we meet such contrarieties in exotic
colourings, and this makes them worth our attention. If, as Ruth ap
Roberts has said, 'he is as little symbolic as an artist in words can be',
it is the Irish novels that call this generally valid assertion into
question.[23] *The Macdermots*, for example, has a highly symbolic level.
But symbolism and romance have been generally ruled out of court
when dealing with the chronicler of Barset, so it is not surprising that
the Irish novels have found few supporters. 'The Irish character', Trollope declared, 'is particularly well fitted for romance', and Stephen
Gwynn was expressing a fairly widespread bewilderment of the post-
Sadleir school when he grumbled, what had Anthony Trollope to do
with romance?[24] But Gwynn was wrong. Trollope's art is more protean,
and at the same time more orthodox, in being a combination of romantic impulse and down-to-earth observation. England taught Trollope to
anchor his imagination in the semi-factual and unheroic, but Ireland
gave him the power of idealising that transforms the Barsetshire landscape. There was more of the poet in Trollope than meets the eye, and
more of his mind was nourished by dreams engendered by Ireland than
critics have so far perceived.

One instance of his romantic susceptibility was noted by his friend and neighbour in Montagu Square, Lady Pollock. In 1869 Trollope told her of a visit to Killarney soon after he had arrived in the country. At the famous beauty spot a woman had been drowned, the incident providing the subject of a best-seller Trollope much admired, Gerald Griffin's *The Collegians*. Trollope became very excited, exclaiming that hereabouts was the spot where Hardress committed his foul murder, whereupon his guide shuddered and said: 'Hardress was my first cousin, and I stood on the steps of the scaffold when he was hung'.[25] Trollope obviously relished the anecdote. The English, as V. S. Pritchett has said, can become very light-headed in Ireland.[26]

TWO NATIONS

Trollope's four Irish novels[27] are grounded on significant events of history: the agricultural distress and Ribbonism of the thirties (*The Macdermots*); O'Connell and the movement for Repeal during the forties (*The Kellys*); the Famine of 1847–8 (*Castle Richmond*); and the agrarian outrages of 1879–82 (*The Landleaguers*). With the exception of *The Kellys*, each makes an attempt at social analysis and becomes partially a *tendenzroman* in rather unTrollopian fashion, but only the first and last achieve the difficult synthesis of social problem and human interest which makes them worth considering at length. *The Macdermots* is both a 'condition of Ireland' novel, and Trollope's *Wuthering Heights* (it appeared in the same year as Emily Brontë's classic), for it satisfies both as social and domestic tragedy. Certainly it is the best of the four and, if Trollope is to have his due, deserves to be thought of as a dynamic beginning to his career.

'Twenty years ago', said the *Athenaeum*, 'The Macdermots* would have made a reputation for its author'.[28] Yet it is the most neglected first novel of any English author of recognised achievement. It seems inconceivable that this far from negligible work is accessible even today only in scarce copies dating from its last edition in 1906. To add to the singular fate of this unlucky book, it escaped Sadleir's notice that Trollope excised one hundred pages of the original story, reducing it from thirty-six to thirty-three chapters for a new edition by Chapman & Hall in 1861.[29]

Its publishing history has long been a mystery, and critics have speculated on Trollope's apparent ignorance of the favourable reviews it received on publication. Could an aspiring author, one of a family of writers, have really been ignorant of opinions voiced by the *Athenaeum* and the *Spectator*? Was it the shame of having to admit to his famous mother that the book had sold no more than fifty copies that led him to discount several encouraging reviews? In his *Auto-biography* he recalled the book's appearance as utterly disastrous:

> If there was any notice taken of it by any critic of the day, I did not see it. I never asked any questions about it or wrote a single letter on the subject to the publisher . . . It is probable that he [Newby] did not sell fifty copies of the work; – but of what he did sell he gave me no account. (ch. iv)

Trollope's second novel, *The Kellys*, was equally unsuccessful. The publisher suggested that Irish stories were a drug on the market and that the author had better abandon novel-writing altogether. This was indeed a slap in the face, since tales of authentic Irish background were much in vogue.[30] Turning to other literary ventures Trollope wrote a series of letters on the Irish famine for the *Examiner*,[31] a historical romance, *La Vendée* (1850), and a play, *The Noble Jilt* (1850), later to provide material for the first of his Palliser novels, *Can You Forgive Her?* Next he tried his hand at a guidebook on Ireland, working at it steadily during 1850 and 1851, returning to Ireland for material from his new base in the south of England. These were years of toil and disappointment that would have crushed a weaker man, for it was not until 1857 with the publication of *Barchester Towers* that Trollope began to feel his powers as a novelist were recognised.

Given the favourable reviews and the current vogue for social problem stories and for Irish novels generally, it is hard to understand why Trollope was so unfortunate with *The Macdermots*, but after a second appearance in 1848, when the publisher tried to drum up a little more interest by labelling it 'A Historical Romance', the novel languished until Trollope's fame in 1859–60 assured a steady and continuing sale. Then after the early years of this century it disappeared.

The Macdermots of Ballycloran is no lost masterpiece, but it has elements of the mystical and phantasmagoric that make comparison with Emily Brontë not altogether inappropriate, and that certainly bear some relevance to the destructive passions to be found in characters of later novels. *The Macdermots* achieves grandeur on the personal level against the sweep and scale of a national calamity, fusing individual tragedy and broad social misery with an assurance and technical mastery that matches Disraeli's best efforts. Everywhere there is vivacity of imagination and, amid dark, sensational events, eruptions of humour and vivid transcriptions of racy Irish vernacular. The first six or seven chapters of peasant comedy are not unlike Maria Edgeworth's tales of Sir Condy Rackrent, while Denis McGovery's courtship might have come from Carleton's *Traits and Stories of the Irish Peasantry*. Trollope's ear has caught the idiom of the people, and he seldom overplays his hand or falters into stage Irish. The dialogue is picturesque without strain: 'we'll hole him till there ar'nt a bit left in him to hole'.[32] Nor does Trollope miss a vein of poetry in the utterance of common folk: Joe Reynolds, an outlaw, comments with bitter glee after the death of the hated symbol of oppression, Myles Ussher, the Protestant Revenue Officer:

> Ussher's black soul has gone to hell this night with more curses on it than there are stones on these shingles. (II, ch. x)

Pat Brady, the treacherous estate manager who has great talent for acting, is an exquisitely lyrical rogue:

> 'D——n Flannelly!' was Brady's easy solution of the family difficulties. 'Let him take the house he built, and be d——d to him; and if we can't build a better one for the masthur and Miss Feemy and you, without his help, may praties choke me!' (I, ch. iii)

In narration Trollope adopts a more stilted phraseology, a literary voice he never entirely abandoned, although practice gave his prose a felicitous swing and cadence which makes it admirable for reading aloud or broadcasting. At the start, for instance, Trollope adopts the device of the story within the story, describing the ruined house in a picturesque manner:

> I crept out of the demi-door again, and down the ruined steps, and walked round the mansion; not only was there not a pane of glass in the whole, but the window frames were all gone; everything that wanted keeping was gone; everything that required care to preserve it had perished. Time had not touched it. Time had evidently not yet had leisure to do his work. He is sure, but slow; Ruin works fast enough unaided, where once he put his foot. Time would have pulled down the chimneys, Ruin had taken off the slates; Time would have bulged the walls, Ruin brought in the rain, rotted the timbers, and assisted the thieves. (I, ch. i)

This attempt at lofty style, grandiose and not altogether logical has, nevertheless, plain and simple diction. When Trollope comes down to earth and trusts his eye, we get rubbish heaps invading the gardens and cabins built up against the wall, 'as jackdaws do their nests in a super-annuated chimney' (I, ch. i), or a knot of ragged children, saucer-eyed at the man's intrusion, and a loquacious peasant who begins the tale by identifying Ballycloran House and its occupants of six or seven years ago, the Macdermots. Trollope next asks the guide of the Boyle coach whether he knows what caused the ruin:

' 'Deed then, sir, and I do,' said he, 'and good reason have I to know; and well I knew those that lived in it, ruined, and black, and desolate as Ballycloran is now.' (I, ch. i)

Immediately the story comes to life.

Yet the preamble is not mere decoration. Ruin is at the heart of Ireland's misery, as it is at the centre of the novel – ruin engendered by mismanagement and violence; and the action of the story unfolds a cycle of destructive passions in the Macdermots. True to Irish temperament, wild actions continually confound all the family. At the outset Thady is a well-intentioned fellow, but he is driven to violence both by external events and the faults of his own irresolution and blood. Trollope has placed his hero in an equivocal position which sets up all kinds of moral and social reverberations; it was a technique he used for the rest of his life. As titular master of tumbledown Ballycloran Thady is little better off than the peasants, who doff their hats in a mockery of familiar subservience. Many of his tenants engage in illicit distilling in the hills, and are linked with the Ribbon societies plaguing County Leitrim. Thady's senile father despises him, while his agent, Brady, is leagued with both Ribbonmen and the family's enemy, the lawyer, Keegan. To add to his wretchedness, his sister Feemy is in love with Captain Ussher, who seduces her and half-heartedly encourages her to elope. Thady surprises them in this attempt and, overwhelmed by his blood, he kills Ussher. Ribbonmen hide him in the mountains, but he is tormented by guilt and returns to face trial, is convicted and hanged.

As melodrama the book moves along grooves of renegade and guilt tales popularised by Godwin, Bulwer Lytton and Griffin, whose influence is strongly felt in the brooding atmosphere. There is a touch of Hardress Cregan's weakness in Thady, and some resemblance between Feemy and Eily O'Connor. The stress on Thady's agony of repentance is a conventional element too, to be found in *Caleb Williams*, *Eugene Aram* or *Paul Clifford*.

Trollope was fond of his plot and rightly so. Its unity stems from the violence which engulfs the main characters: Feemy, with her headstrong passion for the Byronic villain, Ussher; Thady, unwillingly drawn into a blood feud; and his father, old Larry, finally insane at the collapse of all his dreams of property and power. When early in the novel Keegan comes to bargain for control of Ballycloran, Larry screams at his son:

'Kick him out, Thady – kick him out, will ye? – have ye none of the owld blood left round your heart, that you'll not kick him out of the house, for a d——d pettifogging, schaming black-guard!'
(I, ch. x)

Blood is the main issue; the Irish heritage of passion, indolence, illusion, error and extravagance, exacerbated by English misrule: a deadly combination which sealed the country's ruin. This was Larry's inheritance from his own father, who had built the mansion in a style befitting the descendant of a Connaught prince, but without the money to support it. Then there is the legacy of blood uniting the people. The local priest, Father John McGrath, has a hard time keeping peace in the community. In Chapter vii he warns Feemy about bad blood between families and the danger of her association with Ussher, who represents the oppressors and is a Protestant to boot. Feemy, the first of Trollope's self-willed heroines, refuses to listen, and is admonished: 'Then your sins and your sorrows be on your own head!' (I, ch. viii). An outburst in Chapter x from Thady, consumed with his own trials, is more foreshadowing of bloodshed. As he becomes enmeshed in the plotting of Joe Reynolds and the Ribbon conspirators, the atmosphere grows more ominous. Keegan is waylaid and his leg severed as a reprisal for oppressing the tenantry, and after Ussher's murder Thady flees to the hills of Aughacashel.

Now comes the most interesting section of the book. One hesitates to use the word phantasmagoria in connection with Anthony Trollope, but it aptly conveys the scene in which Thady is haunted by Andy McEvoy, Death's emissary, it seems, in a bleak and barren place. Here public and private themes combine as Thady, in undeserved personal suffering, driven to a murder of honour, becomes the emblem of the misery in which the people exist. Our attention is caught by the strange beauty of Loch Sheen and the Aughacashel by moonlight, and the sudden black shape of Corney Dolan's cabin on the edge of the bog. We are at the spot where Ussher had arrested Joe Reynold's brother for selling spirits, a reminder of tyrant and subject people. Thady is taken further on the slopes of Aughacashel, where the inhabitants are 'a lawless, reckless set of people'. There is 'no road or sign of a road' within miles of this desolate region. The people exist 'without the common blessings or restraints of civilisation', and at the limits of endurance Thady stumbles into a cabin to meet life at its most animal level (II, ch. x). He appears to be among ghosts or demons. There is Dan Kennedy and his wife, the girl, Meg, in whom all feeling appears to be dead, and the silent, watching McEvoy. The cabin is like a tomb where time is suspended, and the silent man becomes for Thady 'his enemy' (II, ch. xi). From this limbo he makes a second escape, returning to the cruel world of English law to pay his penalty, thus triumphing over anarchy and passion within himself, and at the same time becoming a martyr for Ireland. Joe Reynolds and Corney Dolan are outside Carrick gaol, like Eliot's chorus in *Murder in the Cathedral*, a folk motif, when Thady's execution takes place.

What is so remarkable about this novel is the harmonising of private and public themes. The three-cornered conflict involving Thady, Feemy and Ussher, is never irrelevant to the destiny of Ireland, and much of the novel dwells on what has goaded a people to madness, as well as what lies deep within the national life to produce ruin and anarchy. So, as well as domestic melodrama, the story is a *roman à thèse*, not unlike Disraeli's *Sybil*. Behind the struggles of the protagonists lie the oppressed people, victims of absentee landlords, informers, spies and bullies among their own people, yet resilient and indestructible. Ragged men sprawl in Mrs Mulready's shebeen or stand like spectres in the doorways of their derelict cabins. Several scenes evoke the Leitrim tenantry, one of the most memorable a Gaelic wedding, in which reckless feasting curiously creates an atmosphere of tension : the men eat and drink with the frenzy of those whose bellies are often empty; and though Father John reproves them for drinking like animals, he has compassion for them. The scene is detailed so that public and private themes coalesce without strain. We are in the midst of a typically Irish party with fiddle, laughter and dancing. But Trollope, cutting skilfully between character and event, reminds us of the charged situation affecting the main characters : amid the gaiety, Denis M'Govery, the bridegroom, warns Ussher of threats against his life, and Ussher, in genuine feeling for Thady, warns him to keep an eye on Brady. The noise grows louder, the company more drunk, and tensions erupt in angry exchanges. Thady succumbs to Brady and his cronies, and half-drunk agrees to take the Ribbon oath. Outside he quarrels with Ussher. By stressing the darkness at this point Trollope heightens the premonitory quality of the event, for being drawn into personal vendetta and public conspiracy, Thady sentences himself to death.

The revelry of Mary Brady's wedding is contrasted with the ostentatious *fête champêtre* for the wealthy landowners :

> The ladies began to unpack the treasures with which the wells of their cars had been loaded – cold hams – shoulders of mutton – pigeon pies – bottles of sherry – and dozens of porter soon made their appearance. (II, ch. vii)

The meagre table spread by Father John, or Thady's bacon scraps on the mountain-side are ironic counterparts to such luxury. Such contrasting is, I think, intentional, for there is constant oscillation between the simple lives of the poor, and the grossness of the rich. This may well excuse some of the apparently extraneous comic interludes of the novel, such as the duel, the Carrick ball and the race. Certainly there is much sarcasm directed towards Jonas Brown who was 'careful to see that he got the full twelve hours' work from the unfortunate men whom he hired at five pence a day, and who had out of that to feed themselves and families, and pay their rent' (II, ch. vii). Police methods, the evils of spying and informers, con-acre farming, rack-renting, absenteeism, Catholic disabilities and the English tyranny in general come under a critical eye. Never again was Trollope so strong a tribune of the people. Intending a social purpose from the first page, his florid description of Ballycloran is linked with the 'wrong, oppression, misery and despair to which someone had been subjected' (I, ch. i). Thady's wrong is also the people's wrong, symbolised by the town of Mohill which breeds men like Joe Reynolds. Mohill is like Lord Marney's town in *Sybil*. Its owner, Lord Birmingham, is an absentee, whose tenants live in hovels like neglected dung-heaps. Indignation leads Trollope to attempt to copy his mother's satire in *Michael Armstrong*, and he overplays his hand in rhetorical question. In a passage reminiscent of Dickens' 'high stilted irony'[33] he impales the absentee landlord:

> Look at his name on all the lists of gifts for unfortunates of every description. Is he not the presiding genius of the company for relieving the Poles, a vice-presiding genius for relieving destitute authors, destitute actors, destitute clergymen's widows, destitute half-pay officers' widows? Is he not patron of the Mendicity Society, patron of the Lying-In—Small Pox—Lock and Fever Hospital? Is his name not down for large amounts in aid of funds of every description for lessening human wants and pangs? . . . 'Tis true he lives in England, was rarely in his life in Ireland, never in Mohill: could he be blamed for this? Could he live in two countries at once? . . . Yet shall no one be blamed, at [sic] the misery which belonged to him; at the squalid sources of the wealth with which Poles were fed, and literary paupers clothed, was no one answerable for the grim despair of that half-starved wretch, whom but now we saw, looking down so sadly on the young sufferers, to whom he had given birth and poverty? that can hardly be. And if we feel the difficulty which, among his numerous philanthropic works, Lord Birmingham must experience in attending to the state of his numerous dependants, it only makes us reflect more often, that from him to whom much is given, much indeed will be required. (I, ch. ix)

This is the most outspoken passage of social criticism in all of Trollope. However clumsy it may appear alongside Dickens' onslaughts on misplaced philanthropy or misguided charity – the horrified sensibility, the look of facts got up to make a case, the moral exordium – it is none the less sincere, and avoids the patronising to be found, for example, in parts of Kingsley's *Alton Locke*. At least the sympathies are keen and true. Irresponsible landlordism and officialdom are the culprits, and Joe Reynolds is the product of bad environment. Thady, as society's victim, is an emblem of the people's misery, and Ussher is a symbol of the system's corrupt authority.

'In certain details,' Escott said, 'as well as in general idea, *The Macdermots* formed the microcosm of an entire people.'[34] This is true. The characters embody representative qualities without losing sharpness of outline; a remarkable achievement for an inexperienced novelist. Old Larry is the very type of improvident native landowner whose *folie de grandeur* brings the family to ruin. Feemy is in part the immortal Cathleen, possessed of dark, fiery beauty and peasant durability. Brady is that monster created by the Encumbered Estates Act of 1849, the local land agent, robbing his employer, gouging the tenants, and always serving his own ends. Equally representative is Father John, the ubiquitous friend of the poor, playing in the original version a much larger role than Trollope later allowed in revising the book for reissue in 1861. The parish priest, as Trollope soon learned, was patriarch, adviser, and often sole custodian of the law among the common people. An instance of Trollope's independence is his firm sympathy with Catholics at a time when Englishmen were chiefly embittered and intransigent. Throughout his life Trollope remained tolerant to the Catholic viewpoint. He wrote from Strabane, Northern Ireland, in 1854, that he preferred Southern Ireland to the North, liking better 'on the whole papistical to presbyterian tendencies' (39, p. 23), and in *Castle Richmond* he applauded Catholic missionary work among the starving, while exposing the bigotry behind some Protestant attitudes. *The Macdermots* recognises the efficacy of the priesthood, and at one point speaks in favour of Maynooth, then a controversial subject, on the score of public support for Catholic education :

> It is alleged that the priests of the present day are dangerous men – enthusiasts – political fanatics and bigots; if it is so are these faults most likely to be found in an imperfectly, or in a highly educated character? if in the former, sure the more that is done for the priests of the next generation, the less likely are they to be imbued with the crimes which are now attributed to their predecessors. (III, ch. ii)

Father John with his learning, dignity and goodness, is clearly a moral centre of the novel. However, the above passage and much else relating to Father John was excised when the book went into single volume issue.

The Macdermots is remarkable for its technique in ways other than characterisation. Despite considerable length it possesses a pleasing rhythm of rising tensions relaxed every now and then by comic interludes. In the first volume the impending tragedy is balanced by

Chapter v, 'Father John', and Chapter xii, 'The Wedding'; in the second, 'Sport in the West' (ch. v), and 'The Races' (ch. vii) – Trollope's first attempt at horses and riders, thereafter a staple of his fiction – relieve the grim subject of Ussher's death; and in the third volume, three chapters dealing with Father John's journey to Dublin, and 'The Duel' (ch. iv), only the last of which was retained in the single-volume issue, provide comic relief. These are not unrelated episodes, but part of the unity of mood in the novel, alternating farce and tragedy and producing a counterpoint between the gaiety of a whole people, driven to violence by inner compulsions and exigent circumstances, and a personal tragedy bearing on the larger issues of national wrong. In the end Thady, sentenced by Baron Hamilton, 'an immovable figure or statue placed beneath the dusky canopy' (III, ch. x) and the custodian of English law, has become the scapegoat of the muddle of the system, and this is appropriately summed up in the legal wrangle which allows Ballycloran to fall into ruin.

How strange it is that the virtuoso performance of this novel should have been ignored.

His second novel, *The Kellys and the O'Kellys*, shows more familiar Trollopian touches. The hovel and shebeen have been exchanged for the comforts of Handicap Lodge and Grey Abbey, and already one can discern themes that came to dominate his fiction: the strategies of courtship, intricate moral choices, the endlessly fascinating nuances of social behaviour, money, family rivalry, the generation gap, and the ageless antagonism of class distinction. The book was a resounding failure and like its predecessor has been virtually ignored.

Trollope sub-titled it 'Landlords and Tenants, A Tale of Irish Life', but its connection with social affairs is slight. It is Trollope's foray into the broad comedy of Lever and Maria Edgeworth and not bad at that; the *Athenaeum*, cordial but patronising, remarked on its 'true "emerald" humour'.[35] Instead of the single action Trollope tried a double plot structure (subsequently his basic plot device) with two sets of lovers whose happiness was threatened by parental, family and material complications. The O'Kelly plot concerning Lord Frank Ballindine and Fanny Wyndham, rich ward of the Earl of Cashel, has at times the sparkle of eighteenth-century comedy, while the Kelly episodes concerning Martin Kelly, Anastasia Lynch and her wicked brother Barry are robust black humour. Obviously a comic replica of Thackeray's Barry Lyndon (one is immediately struck by the similarity of names), Barry Lynch has an Elizabethan villain's gusto in his schemes to wrest from his sister a half-share in the family property. From hoping she will die he turns to assaulting her, and thence to persuading his lawyer, Daly, that she is not right in the head. In traditional comic fashion his own cunning brings about his

ruin again and again. Preparing for the interview with Daly he
primes himself with punch until he is so pickled he cannot match the
lawyer's skill. Driven at last to desperation he suggests that Dr Colligan should poison his sister while treating her for the illness brought
on by his own persecution. Colligan promptly knocks Lynch across
the room and then finishes him off by revealing his villainy.

There is much to enjoy, too, in the Ballindine plot, particularly in
the confrontations between youth and age. Lord Adolphus Kilcullen,
a dandy with a streak of common sense (a type Trollope was to special-
ise in), is required by his father, the Earl of Cashel, to pay court to
Fanny, the Barset heroine in outline. Cocooned in self-righteous dignity, the earl tries to force his will upon the young people, as deluded
about his motives as Barry Lynch is about his; Barry needs his dutch
courage, the earl his puffy eloquence. In one scene Trollope skilfully
deploys the separate trains of thought of father and son. Kilcullen
is trying to extort money to pay gambling debts, while his father is
trying to persuade him to pay court to Fanny. As they skirmish and
parry, secretly priding themselves on their manoeuvres, the contrast
is well made between the old man's platitudes and the son's directness. Kilcullen drives a hard bargain before agreeing to set his cap at
Fanny and the earl is left ruefully reflecting that 'the generation was
deteriorating' (I, ch. xi). But Fanny, of course, rejects the young man,
who faces his father once more, coolly asking for five hundred pounds so
that he can flee his creditors and settle in France. The old earl fumes
and frets, but pays up. With the scatterbrained insouciance of his
type Kilcullen reflects on the interview later:

> I have no doubt an alligator on the banks of the Nile is a fearful
> creature; – a shark when one's bathing, or a jungle tiger when one's
> out shooting, ought, I'm sure, be avoided; but no creature yet
> created, however hungry, or however savage, can equal in ferocity
> a governor who has to shell out the cash ! (III, ch. iii)

Thus *The Kellys* shows both a derivative element of the Irish broad
comic novel, but also something uniquely Trollopian in its genial tolerance and understanding. Here in the relations between parents and
children, young and old, lovers and their rivals, Trollope found his
model for future comedy and pathos.

FAMINE AND REBELLION

Of *Castle Richmond* there is little to be said. Its melodramatic plot is
ill-adapted to its commentary on the great famine, and the feeling for
the social issues vitiated by being used to support the sensational
materials of the story which is primarily a conventional Trollopian

romance. Long passages from Trollope's memories of the tragedy are genre paintings, carefully arranged tableaux of suffering, like the description of mother and children midway through the book:

> A woman was standing there, of whom you could hardly say that she was clothed, though she was involved in a mass of rags which covered her nakedness. Her head was uncovered, and her wild black hair was streaming round her face. Behind her back hung two children enveloped among the rags in some mysterious way; and round about her on the road stood three others, of whom the two younger were absolutely naked. The eldest of the five was not above seven. They all had the same wild black eyes, and wild elfish straggling locks; but neither the mother nor the children were comely. (II, ch. ii)

Trollope is consciously playing up the scene, like the modern journalist intent on 'human interest'. This kind of over-emphatic quality mars a great deal of social problem writing in the mid-Victorian period. Kingsley, for example, is particularly prone to it, Disraeli a little less so, Dickens least of all, where involvement in the human elements of his material nearly always comes to his rescue. As a civil servant Trollope characteristically saw the complexity of the government's role, to which he was sympathetic. His villains were unscrupulous land speculators and rack-renters after the Act of Union had produced a social upheaval. The Irish aristocracy had deserted the country, while ill-educated farmers had rapidly become gentry or squireens. The absentees, as Maria Edgeworth pictured them, had lost contact with the land and people, employing agents, many of whom were extortioners and rogues, and few as upright as Somers of the Castle Richmond estate.

> The fault had been the lowness of education and consequent want of principle among the middle classes; and this fault had been found as strongly marked among the Protestants as it had been among the Roman Catholics. Young men were brought up to do nothing. Property was regarded as having no duties attached to it. Men became rapacious, and determined to extract the uttermost farthing out of the land within their power, let the consequences to the people on that land be what they might . . . And thus a state of things was engendered in Ireland which discouraged labour, which discouraged improvements in farming, which discouraged any produce from the land except the potato crop; which maintained one class of men in what they considered to be the gentility of idleness, and another class, the people of the country, in the abjectness of poverty. (I, ch. vii)

From this two nations analysis one would have expected Trollope to have made more of Herbert Fitzgerald's awakening responsibility (as Disraeli would have done) and treated the Countess of Desmond more satirically. But Trollope lacked the passionate indignation that makes the social problem novelist, and while this saves him from polemical writing it does not make for conviction, and it lays him open to charges of evasion and timidity. Patently Trollope was not a timid writer, so we must assume that his treatment of the famine deliberately sought to give a broad picture simply because his imagination, unlike Reade's, for example, is geared to the general human implications of event. What is most worthwhile in *Castle Richmond* is a broad humanity compensating for the limited perspectives. As a novel, however, it must be consigned with other failures such as *Marion Fay* and *The Fixed Period*.

The *Landleaguers* (1883) is a condition of Ireland novel like *The Macdermots of Ballycloran*. Scarcely anyone has spoken well in modern times of this unfinished last work, and indeed it has glaring deficiencies, but it has compelling moments, too, and no study of Trollope and Ireland can disregard it. Basically it has two faults. Whereas in *The Macdermots* Trollope was stirred by the ruins of the old house to create a fiction which embodied certain truths about the country, in *The Landleaguers* he was crusading against land reform agitation, and made up a story to fit his thesis. He broke his cardinal rule, writing not because he had a story to tell, but because he had to tell a story. In the first two Irish tales he had immersed himself in the real and imaginary worlds of Thady and Anty Lynch. Now he had a mission: to expose Gladstone and the iniquities of the Land League. But the issues were too complex and he had to make excuses:

> In the pages of a novel the novelist can hardly do more than in-
> dicate the source of the troubles which have fallen upon the coun-
> try, and can hardly venture to deal with the names and characters
> of those who have been concerned.[36]

In desperation he interpolates an analysis of the situation totally sep-parate from the action of the novel. Not that such an insertion is without precedent in his work; prejudices about the entrance examin-ation for the Civil Service, some thirty years previously, had led him to include one in *The Three Clerks*. But discretion as an artist had prevailed and he had withdrawn it from the single volume issue. On this occasion time did not allow second thoughts; Trollope died with eleven chapters unwritten. From internal evidence there are strong indications that he would have made revisions, since this book was to be his last tribute to the country he loved, but as its stands it is a broken-backed novel. However, to correct Sadleir's criticism, the chief flaw is not so much that 'characterisation is submerged in floods of almost literal fact',[37] as that the plot (unlike that of *The Macdermots*) is sometimes inappropriate for his serious intentions. It was unwise, for example, to have focused tragic events between Catholics and Protestants on the conversion of Florian Jones, a seven-year-old boy; but worse to have put his death roughly on the same level as his family's having to do without servants or sleeping on unironed sheets.

The Landleaguers is plainly the work of a tired man, although it is not without merit. What can be claimed for it? Chiefly, I think, its overall mood and breadth: Ireland in the grip of anarchic strains as it entered a crucial period of the struggle with England. That is why I call it the least technically accomplished, but in some ways the truest in spirit of the novels set in Ireland. It has a cumulative tension, despite ill-judged elements of plotting and the interpolated essay, and once again a range of incidents and minor characters convey a society in turmoil. It develops the classic form of an outmoded political structure meeting revolutionary activity, and studies the breakdown of law and order with timeless relevance. Even today it can be read with reference to the situation in Northern Ireland. An intensely prophetic book, it makes its point about the effects of revolution upon human lives with far more impact than George Moore's *A Woman in Muslin* (1886), dealing with the same troubled period. Moore produces the aesthetically purer fiction, but Trollope's account is more keenly felt. With Trollope the effect of the masks and shootings is palpably present and claustrophobic. With Moore the agrarian troubles are a drab background to a story of female emancipation, Ibsenite and objective, from the Victorian prison. The heroine's sprained ankle is more real than a shot through a farm window, and even though an improvident, self-centred upper class is under the microscope, the people's world is blurred and unreal, whereas in Trollope it is threateningly present; Moore's novel exists in only one dimension with the life of the Dublin season, the tennis party and the panoply of the Viceregal Lodge.

Keeping closely to the period of political events between autumn 1880 and 1882, Trollope exploits his narrative to show up weaknesses of English policy and the unhappy consequences of the Land League agitation which it exacerbated. It is the closest he ever came to writing a documentary fiction: the rendering of complex social and political issues is well done, but for a disastrous error in plotting which divides the action between the main plot, set in Ireland, and the sub-plot, intended as comic relief, set in England. Philip Jones, a widowed English Protestant, has farmed four hundred acres of the Morony Castle and Ballintubber estates for thirty years, gradually reclaiming the land from bog and waste by means of sluices and drainage systems, and winning the affection of local tenantry and labour. But when the story opens crop failure has caused the tenants, spurred on by malcontents, to withhold rents. One night the sluice gates are opened, causing serious flooding, and Jones is suddenly aware of gathering hostility. To make matters worse his younger son, Florian, is implicated. As a Catholic convert and witness to the flooding, he has been compelled into deception by the conspirators:

> 'You see that jintl'man there?' And Carroll pointed to the man in the mask.
> 'I see him,' said poor Florian, almost in tears.
> 'You'd better mark him, that's all. If he cotches a hould o'ye he'd tear ye to tatthers, that's all. Not that he'd do ye the laist harum in life if ye'd just hould yer pace, and say nothin' to nobody.'
> 'Not a word I'll say, Pat.' (I, ch. ii)

Eventually, however, Florian does speak, and is murdered for doing so. From this time violence accelerates. The apparatus of terror is well conveyed, not only by the secret notes, masks and veils, and sudden hideous acts – incendiarism, cattle-maiming and murder – but by the suggestion of unidentifiable evil at work enmeshing the innocent:

> There must be some terrible understanding among them, some compact for evil, when twenty men are afraid to tell what one man has been seen to do. (I, ch. iv)

Fear keeps people silent as trust breaks down in families. Old feuds are resurrected under the cloak of revolutionary ideals, and the cause of the League becomes subsumed in a more basic love of violence, an insight into illegal action which is relevant today. The rapid decline of moral sense is well done. The rebels change from a set of boisterous ruffians to a sinister mafia practising executions in broad daylight. There is at first a sense of high spirits among the rabble who disrupt the hunt, among them Kit Mooney, one of those cheeky rogues Trollope draws so well:

> 'The boys are just taking their pleasure themselves this fine Christmas morning,' said Kit, who had not moved from the bank on which he had been found sitting. 'Begorra, you'll find 'em all out about the counthry intirely, Mr. Daly. They're out to make your honour welcome.' (I, ch. xi)

This is passive resistance, but soon the men begin to organise. Trollope depicts the unchanging pattern of totalitarian methods: 'A new and terrible aristocracy was growing up among them, – the aristocracy of hidden firearms' (III, ch. xlvi). The people become frightened, inert, unwilling to face facts; it is an Orwellian picture of society breaking up.

Finally, however, the murder of an entire family triggers off deeply overlaid conscience among the people, who awake from their trance and start to resume their old occupations. This is wishful thinking on Trollope's part, but all along his skill has been to convey a sense of nightmare for which the awakening is appropriate in terms of his narrative, if not history. The depredations of the League and dangerous teachings imported from America have bewitched the people and released demons among them. Yet the suggestion of supernatural impulse to the spreading evil is true to the soil of Ireland, and is shown validly through Lax, the fierce masked conspirator, whose escapades have a touch of fantasy in the eyes of the common people. 'All the want of evidence in this country', mutters Captain Yorke Clayton, despairingly trying to enforce the law, 'comes from belief in the marvellous' (III, ch. xxxix). Touches like this reveal Trollope's sensitivity to the land.

It is in the last volume that the political matter stands out most prominently from the main story, although in itself it is interesting for what it says, forcefully and frankly, of Trollope's opinions, shared by a wide section of the English public, Irish landowners and small independent farmers. Unlike *The Macdermots*, which showed a humane and radical outlook, *The Landleaguers* has a reactionary tone which can be explained only by reference to current events. In the first place Trollope was out of touch with the aspirations of the common people, and failed to perceive what the land agitation really was: the beginnings of a movement towards national liberty. In the second place he was prejudiced in favour of the ruling class in Ireland, among whom he had so many friends. Thus, as Thady Macdermot had represented the sufferings of the people thirty years previously, now Philip Jones was the voice of all the honest landlords, plagued by terrorists and vexed by Gladstone's administration: 'Everybody has to get his own, except an Irish landlord,' says Jones mournfully (III, ch. xl).

For all his love of Ireland, Trollope had little understanding of the common people's hopes. He had loved and pitied them in the years of the great famine, but persisted in regarding them as children. As early as 1848, in a letter to his mother, he had drawn this kind of distinction between the English and Irish working class:

Here in Ireland the meaning of the word Communism – or even social revolution – is not understood. The people have not the remotest notion of attempting to improve their worldly condition by making the difference between the employer and the employed less marked. Revolution here means a row . . . My own idea is that there is no ground to fear any general rising either in England or Ireland. I think there is too much intelligence in England for any large body of men to look for any sudden improvement; and not enough intelligence in Ireland for any body of men at all to conceive the possibility of social improvement. (14, pp. 6–7)

He began *The Landleaguers*: 'Never were a people less fitted to exercise such dominion without control. Generous, kindly, impulsive, and docile, they have been willing to follow any recognised leader' (I, ch. i). The people were easy prey to demagogues, amongst whom Parnell was chief – a political opportunist of the worst kind. 'My own idea,' Trollope wrote to Rose from Limerick, in May 1882, 'is that we ought to see the Parnell set put down' (884, p. 481). Trollope had no inkling of Parnell's greatness, no sense of the love aroused by patriots like Davitt and Stephens,[38] and no grasp of the realities of nationalism. His thinking was thirty years out of date; he had but one remedy for Ireland's ills – the English panacea of emigration.

But it must be remembered that he voiced the feelings of his class, and several reasons can be found to account for Trollope's attitude and that of a good many liberals. His friendship with Sir William Gregory, whom he regarded as a sensible Irish landowner and an extremely knowledgeable politician, certainly influenced his thinking. In London clubs, his acquaintance with men such as Frederick Leveson Gower, whose family had Irish estates, made him sympathetic to the landlords' case. Most significantly, he was a close friend of W. E. Forster, the predecessor of Lord Frederick Cavendish as Secretary for Ireland and Parnell's implacable foe. Trollope's thinking on the Land Question is largely Forster's thinking, particularly with regard to repressive measures against the League. But even George Moore, a staunch patriot, felt as a landowner extreme repugnance both for the Land League and Gladstone's policies on land reform, and it is interesting that his pamphlet, *Parnell and his Island* (1887), some five years after Trollope's novel, puts in semi-documentary form many of the points that look so insensitive in Trollope.

As outrage and unrest gathered momentum in Ireland, English middle-class feeling grew less and less sympathetic towards Gladstone's pacific stance, until one devastating incident sent a wave of horror and indignation throughout England and spelled disaster to Gladstone's Irish policy. This was the Phoenix Park murders on 6 May 1882, when gunmen shot down Lord Frederick Cavendish, the Chief Secretary for Ireland, and Thomas Henry Burke, the Permanent Under-Secretary. To many this proved the folly of tolerating the Parnell party at Westminster, the inevitable consequence of concessions under the Land Act of 1881, and Gladstone's truckling to gangsters and revolutionaries, as the fiery Tory MP, Bromley Davenport, put it.[39] The Phoenix Park murders polarised feeling between hawks and doves on Irish affairs.[40] Trollope was solidly behind Forster, who had long advocated force, and had a good deal of support in the country. When Forster pressed for Parnell's arrest early in 1881, he had the 'almost universal approval of Englishmen, appalled by the mounting tale of horror and defiance in Ireland'.[41] But, as we know from the lessons of empire over the past fifty years, no country's will for independence can be broken by coercion and penal legislation. Recognising this, and containing the Parnell group, Gladstone forged ahead with his Land Act of 1881, which Trollope anathematised as 'robbing five million Irishmen of their liberties' (II, ch. xvi). Pressing his policy of no concessions, fortified by the knowledge that the Land Act did not bring peace to Ireland, Forster made the great error of his career in the winter of 1881 by proclaiming the Land League a criminal organisation. This produced new groupings of terrorists and increased activities among the Ladies' Land League, the 'Moonlighters', and the notorious Invincibles, responsible for the Phoenix Park murders the following spring. Gladstone sensed, at this supreme moment of tragedy, that his policy was sowing dragon's teeth, and turning now to Home Rule he met Forster's demand for more coercion in bold terms:

> If we say we must postpone the question [of relieving Great Britain from the enormous weight of the government of Ireland unaided by the people] till the status of the country is more fit for it, I should answer that the least danger is in going forward at once. It is liberty alone which fits men for liberty.[42]

Such vision was unheeded by Trollope, who now finally broke with the Liberals. He concluded:

> It cannot be denied that the promoters of the Land Laws are weak, and that the disciples of the Landleague are strong. In order that the truth of this may be seen and made apparent, the present story is told. (III, ch. xii)

The crux of Trollope's political attitude is in Chapter xli, 'The State of Ireland'. Essentially, Trollope applies the same arguments he raises in the chapter on the people and their rulers in *The New Zealander* – the role of guardianship, which had special force to the Irish situation: 'Property has its duties as well as its rights', Thomas Drummond, Under Secretary for Ireland, had observed in the thirties. The principle of *noblesse oblige* had been propounded throughout Trollope's career in the Palliser ideal. In practical terms this meant seeing that labour was decently employed, housed, fed and taught. Already, by the time he came to write *The New Zealander*, Trollope had concluded that in Ireland the guardians had failed; thus the good land-lord had found himself increasingly cut off from the government and his own people. Bad legislation had made this separation worse, and after a year's functioning of the Land Act, Trollope throws himself into this final battle of his career.

His case is one-sided and bears hard on the labouring poor, who, Trollope implies, are being encouraged to expect venison from gold spoons. The new legislation has catered to human greed, he declares, for once the tenant is in possession he will fatten himself by selling once the price is right. This section of *The Landleaguers* shows an un-appealing harshness in Trollope at the end of his life. Totally unable to see the relationship between land agitation and political aspiration, he blames the Land Act for encouraging unrest among the people, who are a great deal better off than in 1842; he sees the government's soft handling of the Parnell group at Westminster as playing into the hands of malcontents; above all he traces the past link between America and Fenianism, revived Ribandism and Home Rule. For his political thinking is not marked by Gladstone's daring, still less by Bright's moral duty. Thus he totally failed to understand the new spirit fired by Parnell and trained revolutionaries from across the water. Behind the novel one senses the westering sun of empire. Grow-ing industrial strength in America and Germany threatened England's trade supremacy; a potential rival on the doorstep was the last thing English merchants wanted. Similarly, though no bigot in religion, Trollope shared anxieties about the implications of opening a back door for Rome. These were not perhaps in the forefront of his mind, but they permeated the clubs in which he moved. Acknowledging these facts one is admitting that, once again, Trollope is the most repre-sentative author of the Victorian middle class; his views must be seen in the light of conventional thinking of his time. Only a Dickens or a Tolstoi could have surmounted such a weight of national self-interest; Trollope merely showed that another forty years of bloodshed were inevitable.

Alongside the main story there is an extraordinary farrago con-cerning Philip Jones' daughter, Edith, courted by Captain Clayton when he is not chasing landleaguers, and Frank Jones, the elder son, in love with an Irish–American opera singer, Rachel O'Mahony, who goes to London to become a star, chaperoned by her father, Gerald O'Mahony, 'the Galway incendiary'.[43] O'Mahony, member for County Cavan, cuts a swathe through Westminster in a parody of the extreme national-ists. It is a thin device for tying two disparate stories together and the discontinuity of scene causes Trollope immense technical difficulty.

The sub-plot has some good comic scenes, however. In London, Rachel is pestered by her manager, Mahomet M. Moss, and by naughty Lord Castlewell, a stage-door johnny who wishes her to become his mistress. Forced to spend much time in her dressing-room, her father is 'constantly on the watch, like a Newfoundland dog, without an object' (II, ch. xvii), while Moss conducts an importunate wooing that supplies fine comedy in this otherwise depressing book.

Rachel O'Mahony is Trollope's only full-length study of a new type of woman emerging in late Victorian society, the career girl. Despite his love of the drama, Trollope seldom drew theatrical types without succumbing to conventional prejudices against actresses. Euphemia Smith in *John Caldigate* is an example. But Rachel is highly respectable, not to say prudish, rewarding stolen kisses with slaps, and at one time drawing a knife on the ardent Mr Moss. Level-headed and practical, she decides for herself that marriage with the impecunious Frank is out of the question, and orders him not to follow her to London. But there is more than a hint in Rachel of the struggle between domesticity and dedication to stardom: 'Love is not to be lord of all with me . . . Gas is the atmosphere in which I am destined to glitter' (II, ch. xviii). It is burlesque and it is fun, for we know she loves Frank and will eventually marry him, and it reminds us that Gilbert and Sullivan were then in vogue.[44] The happy ending is in fact brought off with a theatrical *coup*, for Rachel suddenly loses her voice and must stop singing for a year. Unable to speak, she scrawls on her slate the name of her lover, who comes post-haste to her side.

While Rachel remains pure, the world of show business is thoroughly debased. Her enemy, Madame Socani, tries to procure her as Moss mistress, while Lord Castlewell frankly attempts to get her into his bed. Above all there is Moss with his reptilian charm. In one hilarious scene he attempts to win her with the wildest promises of a showbiz entrepreneur:

'Only think! Before long we would have a house on the Fifth Avenue so furnished that all the world should wonder; and another at Newport, where the world should not be admitted to wonder. Only think!'

'And Madame Socani to look after the furniture!' said Rachel.

'Madame Socani would be nowheres.'

'And I also will be nowheres . . . Father, don't you think Mr. Moss might go away?' (II, ch. xix)

Nothing daunted, for Moss is supremely confident in his power over women – 'They have been my study up from my cradle' – he continues his courtship via Mr O'Mahony, in a scene notable for its closeness to Victorian stage comedy (II, ch. xix). Even in his last months, utterly exhausted and ill, Trollope could still write some extremely telling lines.

In the last third of the novel the atmosphere becomes claustrophobic. Old Mr Jones is passively depressed, Frank desperately think-ing of emigration. Even the woodcock, Clayton, a square-jawed hero of the new adventure story tradition, a prototype Bulldog Drummond, begins to lose vitality. When he is shot and wounded, in Chapter xlvi, Trollope promises we shall see him in action no more. One feels the book grinding to a halt. It is, indeed, a gloomy novel, marred by a sourness alien to Barset. Age and illness sharpened Trollope's tongue in this book to an unusual degree: the Protestant bigot takes meat to the poor house Catholics on Fridays; the lawyer, Trollope notes acidly, 'is absolved from all the laws common to humanity' (II, ch. xxii); the modern girl sacrifices purity in pursuit of women's rights. These familiar crotchets, playfully displayed in earlier books, now raise his spleen. Sadly, his last novel is far from crowning his career as a novelist. But, saddest of all, it fails to convey the love of Ireland he so much wanted to express.

8 The Outside World

Cum vivere ipsum turpe sit nobis

When even to draw the breath of life at
such a time is a disgrace to us![1]

There lies at the core of the Trollopian world in the heyday of Victorianism an earnest enquiry into what should constitute the good life
in a just and equitable society. In all his books Trollope propounds
a simple creed of good nature, honesty and love as the basis of self-
fulfilment and social health. The foregoing chapters have shown how
the individual is nourished and invigorated through the domestic ties
of marriage and family. In the broader sphere of his social life and
career – the world outside rectory and drawing-room window – man
is exposed to greater strains and temptations, in which his natural
pride, ambition and vanity cause more urgent crises of conscience. Here
the conflict between ideals and practice is posed in its most acute
form; here Trollope explores most fruitfully the concept of the moral
life.

On the face of it the supreme *biedermeyer* novelist of his generation, Trollope shows himself sturdily independent on occasion, his
honesty and common sense driving him against the contemporary
stream, with here a defiant riposte against narrowness and orthodoxy,
there an enlightened cosmopolitanism running against the grain of
Victorian complacency. He once wrote to Kate Field: 'One's country
has no right to demand everything. There is much that is higher &
better & greater than one's country. One is patriotic only because
one is too small & too weak to be cosmopolitan' (178, pp. 118–19). At
a time of increasing anti-Americanism, Trollope praised the young
nation for its energy and confidence, frequently attempting to interpret the Americans to his countrymen. His political position he defined in the *Autobiography*: 'an advanced, but still a conservative
liberal' (ch. xvi), a not uncommon position of the time, which accords
well with a prevailing taste among Englishmen for the reconciliation
of opposites and gradual legislation. Such attitudes Walter Bagehot
found the strength of English law and social change.

As an instance of Trollopian caution and compromise, the article in *St. Paul's Magazine*, I, March 1868, 'Our Programme for the Liberals', is typical. Edward Dicey wrote most of the political articles, but this one has distinctly Trollopian characteristics as does 'The New Cabinet, and what it will do for us'.[2] His statement of legislative priorities is moderate and conventional: a state system of education and no further extension of the franchise; an attempt to solve the Ireland problem; a series of reforms to the criminal code, game laws, poor laws, the army and navy, municipal government and the land, with particular reference to entail. It is not that Trollope was politically un-educated; moving among a wide circle of intellectuals in society he was fully aware of the views and writings of men like Fitzjames Stephen or Mill, Carlyle and Morley. He was a man who took the trouble to be up with affairs, to read and study, but he brought to public affairs no more than the sceptical awareness of the well-informed gentleman amateur characteristic of mid-Victorian England, and typified by Thackeray's friend Matthew Higgins (Jacob Omnium), that indefatigable writer to *The Times* and occasional contributor to the *Pall Mall Gazette*.

Because there is little actual politics in his novels, critics are often tempted to see Trollope as a less competent observer of the political scene than Disraeli, who had the advantage of being on the inside. Getting it right was, of course, an essential both for Trollope's ethic and his art, and from an early period he felt keenly criticisms of in-accuracies, over legal points particularly. Hence the lengths he went to in seeking legal opinions over matters connected with the plotting of *Cousin Henry*. Having burned his fingers over legal issues in *Orley Farm* he grew more inclined to offer elaborate apologies, as in *Phineas Finn*:

> The poor fictionist very frequently finds himself to have been wrong in his description of things in general, and is told so roughly by the critics, and tenderly by the friends of his bosom. He is moved to tell of things of which he omits to learn the nature be-fore he tells of them, – as should be done by a strictly honest fiction-ist. He catches salmon in October; or shoots his partridges in March. His dahlias bloom in June, and his birds sing in the autumn. He opens the opera-houses before Easter, and makes Parliament sit on a Wednesday evening. And then those terrible meshes of the Law! (ch. xxix)

The ensuing scene, a cabinet meeting, demonstrates just the inhibi-tions one might expect from such a disclaimer. It is strong on imagined touches deriving from the clear picture in Trollope's mind of each character, but weak in depicting an actual policy meeting

They are a poor lot, these Cabinet ministers, when it comes down to real debate in the inner sanctum. The scene is full of promise and preparation, but nothing actually happens, beyond the expected announcement from Mr Mildmay of his intention to resign. What the scene does show, however, is the ordinariness of men in office. Trollope resists any temptation to glamorise the occasion. He opens with a subdued description of the dark and dingy chamber overlooking St James's Park, and then passes to the decrepit messenger fiddling unnecessarily with the chairs and papers and hearing the ministers' voices, 'men with whom it seemed, from their tone, that things were doing well in the world'. The witness is subsumed in the narrative voice as Trollope gives a deft portrait of each arrival, and the reader is permitted to eavesdrop, as it were, from the vacant armchair which should have gone to the errant Mr Turnbull. Jaunty narration and telling observation of character is what counts: Sir Marmaduke Morecombe, Chancellor of the Duchy of Lancaster, is pliable but probably loyal to Mr Mildmay, which is why he has kept his seat in the cabinet for three years. The 'probably' almost slips by unnoticed. Then there is the Duke of St Bungay, the Talleyrand of several administrations, 'a man who has been thrice spoken of as Prime Minister, and who really might have filled the office had he not known himself to be unfit for it'. The phrase points to Mildmay's downfall and also, in reference to Plantagenet Palliser's career (he is the next person introduced), conveys a strong irony. Glimpsing the future direction of his saga Trollope continues: 'If industry, rectitude of purpose, and a certain clearness of intellect may prevail, Planty Pall, as he is familiarly called, may become a great Minister'. One by one the ministers are introduced. Sir Harry Coldfoot reveals none of the strains of Home Office affairs under the daily scrutiny of the press. Viscount Thrift performs his dedicated work for the Admiralty while dreaming of translating Homer and wearing the Garter. By such details, Trollope reveals the contending forces within a cabinet and the uneasy undercurrents beneath the calm as these men face a crisis and balance personal ambition with loyalty to chief and party.

There is more artifice in the scene than first appears, the dialogue, made up of deliberately casual conventionalities in the aftermath of Mr Turnbull's sabotaging of Mildmay's Reform Bill, undercut by anxious smiles, silences, the very postures. The taking-up of positions is interesting and strikes a note of disquiet: the Privy Seal is described as 'moving about uneasily for a while' before taking a seat, and the empty chair – Turnbull's – focuses on the source of their troubles. Gresham, whose star is in the ascendant after a brilliant speech in the House, stands at the corner of the fireplace furthest from Mr Mildmay. The difference between the two is well brought out and one can see how parallels between Palmerston and Gladstone suggested themselves to contemporary readers:

> For Mr. Gresham is a man with no feelings for the past, void of historical association, hardly with memories, – living altogether for the future which he is anxious to fashion anew out of the vigour of his own brain. Whereas, with Mr. Mildmay, even his love of reform is an inherited passion for an old-world Liberalism.

Something of Trollope's own ambivalent political allegiances is felt here.

This account of the Cabinet amply demonstrates that Trollope did not need, as Disraeli did, the impetus of actual event to achieve verisimilitude, although he, as much as any of his contemporaries, could utilise event for endless improvisation without distorting his plot. Historical and political facts abound in his novels, but they are seldom as crucial to the narrative as they are in Disraeli. He is, in any case, a novelist who eschews the polemic of political novels. He merely takes his fling at the political doings of the day; the phrase accurately suggests the degree to which actual politics enters the world of his novels. He writes as a man committed to men not measures (in contrast with the doctrine of Monk, Finn and Palliser), and as his depiction of clergymen avoids dogma so his political novels – more properly called 'Palliser novels' – avoid specifics. Quite apart from the difficulty he felt in making politics interesting in view of its essentially mundane, day-to-day operation, his vital concern was always character, which he considered the highest merit of a novel. And in the elucidation of the political mind and motive, particularly the nature of power and ambition, he was every bit as good as Disraeli. In the Pallisers, he said:

> I have endeavoured to depict the faults and frailties and vices, – as also the virtues, the graces, and the strength of our highest classes; . . .[3]

He rightly sensed that in politics, just as in theology, the proper vehicle for discussion of doctrine was the periodical and not the novel; hence his discussion of current affairs and social problems is limited to journalism. His views on this point are summarised at the end of *The Last Chronicle of Barset*:

> I would plead, . . . that my object has been to paint the social and not the professional lives of clergymen; and that I have been led to do so, firstly, by a feeling that as no men affect more strongly, by their own character, the society of those around than do country clergymen, so, therefore, their social habits have been worth the labour necessary for painting them; and secondly, by a feeling that

though I, as a novelist, may feel myself entitled to write of clergy-men out of their pulpits, as I may also write of lawyers and doctors, I have no such liberty to write of them in their pulpits.[4]

He thought of his writing about politicians in similar terms.

A comment on *The Prime Minister* in the *Autobiography* directs attention to the principal qualities needed in a public figure: dedica-tion, integrity and love of country (ch. xx) – qualities Trollope dis-cerned in Lord Palmerston, who remained his political ideal, and on whom he wrote a graceful monograph.[5] This was written while he was engaged on *Phineas Finn* during a period of intense political thought and activity between 1866 and 1868. Some of his reading and journalism, his book on Palmerston, and his essays on Cicero, provide the clearest evidence on his ideas about the ethics of public life and the role of the individual in society.

POLITICS AND THE MAN OF CONSCIENCE

Towards the end of his life, when Trollope was reviewing his experi-ence for the *Autobiography*, he published two essays, 'Cicero as a Politician', and 'Cicero as a Man of Letters', in the *Fortnightly Review* on 1 April and 1 September 1877 (subsequently *The Life of Cicero*, in two volumes, in 1880). The Roman statesman and poet had held a lifelong interest for Trollope. One of his earliest publications, a review of Charles Merivale's *The History of the Romans Under the Empire* for the *Dublin University Magazine* (June 1851), had included an apology for Cicero which he had been obliged to omit because of its length. Publication of Froude's sketch of Caesar's life (1879) provided further impetus to vindicate the Roman patriot from 'one prolonged censure' in Froude's work.[6]

The reasons for Trollope's advocacy, and the relationship between Trollope's ethical views and those of Cicero, have been well explored by Ruth ap Roberts, who draws parallels between English social life and Caesar's Rome that have a bearing on such novels as *The Way We Live Now*. To some extent an analogy could also be made between Trollope's own career and that of his subject. Cicero had been a *novus homo*, who competed for a career with great zeal and without stain to his honour. This similarity of origin and temperament may have led Trollope to speculate on the nature of the economic and political structure in his own time, which he formulated in a series of propositions for his fiction concerning the conflict between ambition and moral principle. Success is as much a goal today, he maintains, as it was in Cicero's time, and the same moral delinquencies work against a just and equitable society in Victorian England as they did in Rome. Great men will bend the knee and bargain for ribands, lieuten-ancies and titles; there is, moreover, 'a growing feeling in favour of Caesarism and success which has ceased to be shocked at means'.[7]

Trollope's highest praise for Cicero is that he devoted his life to justice, honesty and the rule of law in a period of monstrous corrup-tion, and that he did it without isolating himself. Cato was pure, but kept from places of sin; 'Cicero did go where men defile themselves; but he kept himself clean'.[8] 'A man no doubt may teach virtue and live viciously, as Sallust did. But it was not so with Cicero.'[9] Trollope relished Cicero's weaknesses as well as his strengths, picturing him as vain, mercurial and morbidly sensitive to criticism; in this latter re-spect like his own statesman, Plantagenet Palliser. At heart there was a division in the Roman orator, between the public figure and the man, the scrupulous upholder of truth and the waverer, between the political opponent of tyranny and misgovernment and the man avid for public acclaim. Ruth ap Roberts accurately perceived the link between Trol-lope's interpretation of the ambiguity of Cicero's nature and his own novels as an awareness of moral relativism and the difficulties of the moral life. As the *Cicero* has it:

> The man who saw his duty clearly on this side in the morning shall, before the evening come, recognize it on the other; and then again, and again, and yet again the vane shall go round. (I, ch. i)

Perhaps the most significant of all the consistencies in Trollope's work is expressed in the *Cicero*: the variety of human impulse leading to inconsistent action:

> But the same man may, at various periods of his life, and on various days at the same period, be scrupulous and unscrupulous, impractical and practical, as the circumstances of the occasion may affect him. At one moment the rule of simple honesty will prevail with him. *Fiat justitia, ruat coelum. Si fractus illabatur orbis Impavidum ferient ruinae.* At another he will see the necessity of a compromise for the good of the many. (Ibid.)

One has only to consider the multiple viewpoints on moral acts in the stories of Mr Harding and John Bold, in Grantly, or in the dilemma of Mr Crawley, to recognise it as one of Trollope's lifelong interests. Indeed, later books explore with a humour and detachment much like that in Cicero's moral essays the conflicts of duty and desire, and the pressures upon moral integrity. Novels like *Cousin Henry, Dr Wortle's School* or *Kept in the Dark*, are earnest jokes of this kind. To give one example: it may appear that for the man who loves justice and honesty, truth must be stronger than friendship. But there are cases in which charity and compassion take precedence, as in the Askerton situation of *The Belton Estate*, or the Lady Mason–Sir Peregrine dilemma in *Orley Farm*, and certainly in the case of the Peacockes in *Dr Wortle's School*. Pillars of rectitude in the novels are always gently mocked for self-righteousness; justice is explored with a wary eye to the absolutism that diminishes the spirit rather than enhances it; certain vices are shown to have mitigating circumstances; only the sin of lying thunders in the index.

Trollope dwells, in a comment on *De Officiis* that Mrs ap Roberts rightly stresses, on the principle of *honestum* as all that is 'manly, graceful, honest and decorous' (II, ch. xiii). Since this is tempered by a keen awareness of the complexity of right action, however, he is saved from dogmatism. The peaceful surface of his fiction which mirrors the calm and commonplace in upper-middle-class life conceals the eddies and drifts and undertow of multiple ironies. Being at 'the mercy of a divided mind', as John Hagan once described it, has advantages.[10]

In most of Trollope's fiction young men must make an essentially Ciceronian choice between *honestum* and *utile*. Phineas is a case in point. He starts out a callow, self-centred, unpleasant youth with strong ambitions in Parliament, learns the terms in which he can expect to function effectively (after much suffering and disappointment), and finally reaches cabinet rank. The long process of maturing makes of the Palliser novels a *bildungsroman* almost as much for Finn as for Glencora and Plantagenet. One of the significant events of Finn's growth is clear on reflection, in a fragment of *The Prime Minister*, when he is silent after Quintus Slide's attacks in the gutter press. His growth is only meaningful and apparent when one recalls the impetuous member for Loughshane who so alarmed Barrington Erle in the first of the series by his talk of measures not men.

The choice Finn is called upon to make between principle and expediency poses one of those moral conundrums Trollope savoured in his *Cicero*, but here, I think, Trollope owes more to another source. The question for Phineas is this. Should he, as a reforming Liberal of the younger generation, stand for Loughton as the nominee of Lord Brentford? Finn reasons that he should not be over-scrupulous:

> You must take the world as you find it, with a struggle to be something more honest than those around you. Phineas, as he preached to himself this sermon, declared to himself that they who attempted more than this flew too high in the clouds to be of service to men and women upon earth.[11]

He does stand, and is duly elected. Trollope is putting in very simple terms the *real-politik* of Henry Taylor's *The Statesman* (1836), which he surely knew since he was on good terms with the author.[12] It seems

highly likely that while preparing for his novels of parliamentary life
Trollope would have refreshed his knowledge of this well-known
manual, in which there is a chapter (xvi) 'On the ethics of politics',
which goes to the heart of Trollope's own writing about principle and
expediency. Taylor maintains that the legislator's difficulty lies in
reconciling individual morality with public life: 'The law of truth
stands first in the code of private morality',[13] but in the context of
law-making such rigid morality produces only stalemate. A compromise has always to be made:

> For when a member of a government, advocating a particular measure which he does not sincerely approve, is believed by himself, or
> by others, to be committing the same violation of the principle of
> truth as if he were telling a falsehood in private life, then indeed he
> himself incurs the guilt of such a falsehood and the corruption of
> conscience attending it, and the cause of truth suffers by his example and his impunity. But if, on the other hand, he advocates
> what he does not approve with a clear conscience, and stands, *quâ*
> statesman, in his own apprehension and in that of others, under a
> well understood absolution from speaking the truth in particular
> cases, then there is in reality no more violation of the principle
> of truth at large than there is of his own conscience. For falsehood ceases to be falsehood when it is understood on all hands that
> the truth is not expected to be spoken. (Ibid.)

Well might Taylor add that 'A statesman is engaged, certainly, in a
field of action which is one of great danger to truthfulness and sincerity', for his serpentine prose reeks of policy and equivocation. He concludes that moralists must allow statesmen:

> a free judgment namely, though a most responsible one, in the
> weighing of specific against general evil, and in the perception of
> perfect or imperfect analogies between public and private transactions, in respect of the moral rules by which they are to be governed. (p. 85)

If intellectually Trollope accepted the reasoning, his spirit must have
revolted from the machiavellianism of this appendix to Bacon, another
writer whose expediency disgusted him.[14] Certainly Finn's perplexity
over means and ends which occupies the professional debate in the first
half of the novel, and his capitulation to a dubious moral stance when he
accepts the role of Lord Brentford's nominee, reflects one side of Taylor's
approach. But later principle and expediency are more acutely opposed
when loyalty to party conflicts with obligations of personal conscience
Finn, increasingly troubled by his acceptance of patronage, decides, when
Mr Turnbull brings in a bill to disfranchise seven boroughs, to vote

with him, even though his party will suffer. Monk, who is throughout
the parliamentary novels a norm of reasonable conduct and a mentor
for the young member, is angry:

> telling him that his conscience was of that restless, uneasy sort which
> is neither useful nor manly . . . 'There must be compromises, and
> you should trust to others who have studied the matter more thor-
> oughly than you, to say how far the compromise should go at the
> present moment.'[15]

This sentiment is very close to Taylor's reasoning in Chapter lx of
his manual, 'Concerning the conscience of a statesman', and we recall that the Achilles heel of Plantagenet's career, especially in his
brief reign as Prime Minister, is an exquisite conscience, which
makes him unable to trim and cut corners. As the Duke of St Bungay reflects sadly:

> One wants in a Prime Minister a good many things, but not very
> great things. He should be clever but need not be a genius; he
> should be conscientious but by no means strait-laced; he should
> be cautious but never timid, bold but never venturesome; he should
> have a good digestion, genial manners, and, above all, a thick
> skin.[16]

Finn begins by disliking Palliser for his aloofness, but discovers at
last his scrupulous sense of truth and honour, and comes to respect
him. Mr Monk, who has acted as devil's advocate in the exchange
just quoted, is able to work within the framework of checks and
balances without damage to his code of ethics. He exemplifies the
practical application of the Taylor doctrine. But it is typical of
Trollope's feeling for counterpoise that Monk should be spiritually
impoverished. Like Tom Towers, the eagle of the *Jupiter*, alone in
his eyrie above Temple Gardens, Monk is cut off from domestic ties
and involvements, which count so much in Trollope's work for the
fructifying energies of the spirit. When, in a crucial scene of
Phineas Redux, the hero, under suspicion of murder, most needs
Monk's friendship and support, the older, wiser man abandons him
with a degree of ruthlessness which comes as a shock. Through such
a minor character Trollope illuminates much more of the human
landscape than mere manners.

Yet in terms of the political dilemma with which the two Phineas
novels deal, it is Monk, a maverick among his party, who champions
legislation for tenant-right in Ireland while urging Finn to look to
his own interests. Finn may well be committing political suicide by
following Monk, in what Barrington Erle, the suave party-manager,
calls 'a bad cause', one which Lord Cantrip likewise opposes in

Chapter lxviii, in very much the manner of Taylor's manual, but it is a crisis in the hero's life. So he acts with Monk, and Mr Gresham dissolves the House. The hero's action proves to have been quixotic, and merely puts him in the political wilderness, but clearly Trollope sees his act as praiseworthy; it is part of a moral growth, in conjunction with his political education, which will be continued in *Phineas Redux*.

Nearly four years separate *Phineas Finn* and *Phineas Redux*, but with that extraordinary memory spanning many years of his characters' lives which constitutes one of his strengths, Trollope traces the final stages in his hero's development. Possibly because he had become more uneasy about including too much political discussion, Trollope concentrates on Finn's social adventures, but nevertheless in the background the debate between principle and expediency continues, revealed not only in Finn's conscience, but in party skirmishing and the characters of the two party leaders, Daubeny and Gresham.

The Conservatives have a premium on manoeuvre and opportunism, acting out the *real politik* advocated by Taylor under a ruthless leader, Daubeny, who 'had achieved his place by skill, rather than principle' (ch. v). It is Daubeny, in an attempt to dish the Whigs, who introduces a disestablishment bill to keep his party in power. As is commonly known, the character embodies Trollope's distaste for Disraeli, whose apparent willingness to sacrifice allegiances to ambition represented a deterioration in public life. If Peel had deserved branding in *The Three Clerks* for changing his mind about the Corn Laws, then Disraeli was doubly guilty of political apostasy. Daubeny, then, is harshly presented, as is the Conservative party in general in *Phineas Redux*. 'A party has to be practical' declares Trollope at one point (ch. viii), as the discomfited Whigs see the bread and butter taken out of their mouths once again. Yet there are failures of nerve and principle on both sides, as Trollope is careful to point out.

This does not necessarily mean that Trollope was thoroughly disenchanted with the political process, as Cockshut implies when he suggests that Parliament appears in the novels as 'fundamentally futile', or that 'politics were a sham and settled nothing'.[17] Of Dickens this estimate is valid, but for Trollope it is too strong a judgement. Rather did he accept the party system with all its faults, the clinging to power, the slow pace of drafting bills, the factitious independence of a Turnbull, and the cumbersome apparatus of the civil service behind Parliament, as representative of the necessary sifting and weighing of information, the accommodation of personalities and prejudices. Trollope respected the balancing of attitudes which make up the spectrum of public life, even the chance and muddle which seemed futile and time-wasting to the uninitiated. He remained true to his civil-service training, in short. Dickens, looking strictly from the outside, stormed at the bureaucratic operation with a passionate dismay at its errors and delay, and with abundant reason for doing so, but Trollope brought to the day-to-day problems of administration and decision-making a professional understanding.

As always in his fiction, moderation and fairmindedness are evident. One small issue – individual independence versus the party machine – is weighed and explored through a variety of viewpoints. Finn's integrity contrasts with Turnbull's self-centred independence. Fitzgibbon's casual allegiance to the party may be compared with Bonteen's, or even Browborough's, where a high degree of selfishness is involved. Trollope shows in the Phineas novels the fallibility of all men engaged in government, but he does so without cynicism or disenchantment. If he fears a deterioration from the highest standards of political ethics, he takes comfort that political honesty is far greater than in previous generations – an attitude firmly opposed to Carlyle's which Trollope often satirised. The Palliser novels plainly show that despite individual lapses society is evolving slowly in the right direction. Realistically, he even allows the necessity of men like Sir Orlando Drought and Sir Timothy Beeswax. He would prefer, like St Bungay, that the legislators came from the Whig aristocracy, but he is sufficiently able to move with the times to realise that the system must accommodate men like Bonteen and the odious Bott.

Tolerance and broadmindedness at once come to Trollope's aid. The traditionalism of Parliament, its forms and conventions, remain its great strength, and somehow its loose and irregular constitution is proof against demagoguery and corruption. Rogues like Undecimus Scott and Vavasor will be eventually unmasked and turfed out; Melmotte will overreach himself. Somehow the work is done, and Trollope is as generous towards amateurs, like Lord Fawn and Laurence Fitzgibbon, as he is devoted to work-horses like his excellent cabinet minister, the young Lord Cantrip, and, of course, Plantagenet. All this is very English, and part of Trollope's indefinable agreeableness. Visitors like Elias Gotobed, the Senator from Mickewa, can only throw up their hands in bafflement at the seeming inefficiency of the British parliamentary system.

Like Planty Palliser, Phineas Finn fails to reconcile principle and expediency, and his resignation at the end of *Phineas Redux* is similar to Palliser's failure in *The Prime Minister*. Finn is, of course, the lesser man, and his reasons for giving up the struggle (setting aside the personal issue regarding Marie Goesler) are self-indulgent. He has been wounded by seeing 'a man whom he despised promoted', and 'evil words

H

between men who should have been quiet and dignified' (ch. lxxvii). So he has the triumph of refusing Mr Gresham's invitation to join his administration, but it is a triumph we are meant to view ironically.

Palliser is more complex and carries the author's investigation into the ethics of public life a stage further. Unlike Finn he does not allow himself the luxury of gestures of independence: he has been content to serve as Chancellor of the Exchequer with modest views of what is possible. His case for statesmanship in *The Duke's Children* is perhaps Trollope's most effective riposte to the political opportunism in the Taylor manual. It takes the form of a contrast between the old political generation and the younger. The new men of politics are Sir Timothy Beeswax, the first man in the Commons, and Lord Drummond, who is Prime Minister in the House of Lords. These two are great party managers rather than statesmen, knowledgeable in all the arts of staying in power expounded by Taylor. Where the Duke of Omnium was a silent man, 'Sir Timothy was a fluent speaker, and when there was nothing to be said was possessed of great plenty of words' (ch. xxvi). Evasion, hypocrisy, expediency and absence of principle are reflected in every sphere of political and social life. As Finn says, 'Turveydrop and deportment will suffice for us against any odds' (Ibid.) Against such signs of deterioration the Duke holds steadfastly to his ideals, and decides at the end of the novel to re-enter political life, taking office aptly under the man of high principle, Mr Monk, as President of the Council. Was this his favourite office? asks Silverbridge. Not exactly, the Duke replies, and his son guesses that being Prime Minister had been the Duke's highest pleasure. Typically the Duke replies:

> No, Silverbridge, if I could have my way, – which is of course impossible, for I cannot put off my honours, – I would return to my old place. I would return to the Exchequer where the work is hard and certain, where a man can do, or at any rate attempt to do, some special thing. A man there if he stick to that and does not travel beyond it, need not be popular, need not be a partisan, need not be eloquent, need not be a courtier. He should understand his profession, as should a lawyer or a doctor. If he does that thoroughly he can serve his country without recourse to that parliamentary strategy for which I know that I am unfit. (ch. lxxviii)

Palliser starts out with the advantages of rank and an inbred consciousness of the aristocratic function, and through him Trollope registers qualities he revered in Cicero. At the same time his 'faults' or flaws as a politician are very much those Taylor warns about; his scrupulous conscience, his shyness, and his pride continually obstruct his success. His rage at Pountney's impertinent enquiry about the Silverbridge vacancy is both the laudable reaction of the honest man and the statesman's failure to find the right stance towards his adherents. For the bad characters in the novels there is no wavering and no adherence to principle: Burgo Fitzgerald 'lived ever without conscience';[18] George Vavasor launched upon a political career cynically indifferent to parliamentary ideals, and fought Chelsea Districts on a trumped-up issue; Harcourt, driven by egotism and ambition, propelled himself swiftly to the post of Solicitor-General; Lopez used all the resources of flattery and blackmail to succeed in politics. All such men have great self-assurance, while honest men like Sir Thomas Underwood agonise over their own motives. Taylor's manual saw the politician's over-acute conscience 'as a quagmire, in which the faculty of action shall stick fast at every step' (ch. ix, p. 47). The irony of Palliser's situation is that 'a man altogether without guile, and entirely devoted to his country'[19] is at the same time filled with political ambition and fascinated by the power of his position as Prime Minister once he sees it slipping away.

THE PRESS

Scant attention has been paid to Trollope's attitude towards the press in his fiction, although it is a vital aspect of his concern with the quality of living. Like Thackeray, he was closely associated all his life with journalism, from the time of his earliest work – a series of letters on the Irish famine in the *Examiner* – to his contributions to the *Fortnightly Review*, the *Pall Mall Gazette* and the *Daily Telegraph*. Yet in writing about the Press he stressed its triviality, power-seeking and dishonesty: two of his fictional papers are the *Daily Tell-Tale* and *Everybody's Business*. As one of the *Fortnightly's* founders he recalled in the *Autobiography*, 'I was craving after some increase in literary honesty' (ch. x), and he campaigned for signed articles for that reason. The passion for truth is paramount as in all his fiction and with only one exception pressmen are shown as treacherous and deceitful. That exception is Hugh Stanbury in *He Knew He Was Right*, and even his job at the *Daily Record* is treated sceptically – 'a deal honester than defending thieves, and bamboozling juries' (ch. iv). Through him Trollope expresses his dislike of irresponsibility:

'Mr. Stanbury, I won't have irreligion. I hope that doesn't come from writing for the newspapers.'

'Certainly not with me, Mrs. Trevelyan. I have never been put on to take that branch yet. Scruby does that with us, and does it excellently. It was he who touched up the Ritualists, and then the Commission, and then the Low Church bishops, till he didn't leave one of them a leg to stand upon.'

'What is it, then, that the Daily Record upholds?'
'It upholds the Daily Record. Believe in that and you will surely be saved'. (ch. vi)

A similarly ponderous irony is voiced by Charley Tudor in *The Three Clerks* about the *Daily Delight*: 'always to hold up a career of virtue to the lower orders as the thing that pays. Honesty, high wages, and hot dinners. Those are our principles' (ch. xxii).

The Times bears the brunt of Trollope's attack on the press in *The Bertrams*, *The Struggles of Brown, Jones and Robinson* and notably in the Barsetshire novels. That recently unearthed quarry for Trollopians, *The New Zealander*, sets out (in sub-Carlylean polemic) the case against the press: monopoly power, irresponsible reporting, character assassination and interference with the due process of government and law. It is tedious reading; Trollope is a poor debater. In fiction he makes his objections far more effective through two memorable characters, Tom Towers and later Quintus Slide. Towers wields 'the tomahawk of the dread Editor' in *The Warden*, and comes into the story over the Hiram's Hospital affair which, thanks to John Bold's campaign, is taken up by his paper the *Jupiter*, clearly meant to represent *The Times*. Trollope was in fact drawing upon some charity exposure stories with which his audience was familiar.[20] An interesting juxtaposition of views follows the initial flurry of publicity: Bold is flattered, the attorney, Finney, thinks of his widened scope for business, Harding is shocked by the invasion of his privacy and wants to reply to the attack, the Archdeacon with his habitual practicality puts his foot down: 'In such matters it is omnipotent' (ch. vii). 'Does not every one know that it [the *Jupiter*] would take up any case of the kind, right or wrong, false or true, with known justice or known injustice, if by doing so it could further its own views?' (ch. ix).

The vehemence of Trollope's satire here, and consistently in his novels, suggests more than neutral observation, possibly the civil servant's sensitivity to criticism on public matters, possibly a personal experience about which we know nothing, because *The Times* under John Delane from 1841 to 1877, though prone to *ex cathedra* pronouncements, did exercise considerable judiciousness and responsibility, witness the reporting of the Crimean War by Russell and others. Russell, indeed, became Trollope's staunch friend in the sixties, as did Delane, whose fulminations against business corruption provided material for *The Way We Live Now*. All of which makes Trollope's unfairness to journalism hard to understand. However, *The Times*' leaders apparently offended the novelist, who could not resist trying to capture their moral indignation and self-satisfaction in the philippic addressed to Mr Harding in *The Warden* (ch. xiii). Harding's mortification is all the greater since he cannot refute any of the paper's charges, and his mute despair is Trollope's eloquent plea against personality journalism. The climax of Trollope's satire is the embarrassed confrontation of John Bold and Tom Towers in Chapter xiv, in which Trollope hurls some thunderbolts of his own on the general theme 'the *Jupiter* is never wrong'. Were it not for the fact that Trollope genuinely feels his attitude is warranted, this diatribe would be better forgotten, but it demonstrates that the freedom of the press is in fact the tyranny of an irresponsible élite pursuing its own ends, the symbol of which is Tom Towers, an all-seeing Olympian, inaccessible and unaccountable to the public which supports him. The implications of this are so horrendous to Trollope that anger swamps his normal fair-mindedness, and breaks out in personal remonstrance as he visualises a frightening, totalitarian power:

> The discretion of Tom Towers was boundless: there was no contradicting what he said, no arguing against such propositions. He took such high ground that there was no getting on it. 'The public is defrauded,' said he, 'whenever private considerations are allowed to have weight.' Quite true, thou greatest oracle of the middle of the nineteenth century, thou sententious proclaimer of the purity of the press – the public is defrauded when it is purposely misled! against what a world of fraud has it to contend.' (ch. xv)

Tom Towers reappears in *Barchester Towers* in the context of Mr Slope's campaign to become the new dean. It seems fitting to Trollope that his spongy-nosed chaplain should ally himself with the public press, and regard it 'as the great arranger and distributor of all future British terrestrial affairs whatever' (ch. xliii). Trollope seems to be saying that such a monolithic power is inimical to democracy. 'No man who uses a pen can do other than desire power', he claimed in *The New Zealander* (ch. iii), and the monopolistic *Times* now sought not only to be politically strong but politically supreme. In *Barchester Towers* Slope wants to harness the press to his own chariot, and through his acquaintance with Towers he is puffed in sixty thousand clarions as the most able successor to the late Dean Trefoil. Parodying the unctuous platform manner of the *Jupiter*, Trollope demolishes its claim to sincerity by commenting that the Slope crusade was due to lack of copy at the time. He also provides, in this and Chapter ii of *Barchester Towers*, an ironical conclusion to the Hiram's Hospital scandal. Subject always to the vagaries of fashion, the *Jupiter* (not long after Mr Harding had been congratulated by the Archbishop of Canterbury on his resignation as Warden) wrote eulogistically of him, having discovered that he was the author of 'Harding's Church music'. For a while Mr Harding had to suffer the encomia of the press as in the past he had suffered its excoriations; although, Trollope adds, the old man's one vanity on the subject of his music was gratified before the *Jupiter* took up other names – 'the undying fame promised to our friend was clearly intended to be posthumous'. The last word, as Trollope well knew, was always had by the press, and so the *Jupiter* plumed itself on having brought about a happy ending to the Hiram's Hospital affair.

The charges levelled in *The New Zealander* are not fraud and dishonesty so much as misuse of power, for which Trollope blames the public almost as much as journalists themselves. In his fiction, however, his most urgent and most often levied judgement on the press was that it distorted and muddied the very issues upon which the public needed unbiased presentation of facts. Falsity in journalism was much in Trollope's mind in *The Way We Live Now* when he created Alf, Booker and Broune and *The Evening Pulpit*. Their dishonesty was in puffing particular authors with whom they had connections in the fashionable world, a contemporary vice Trollope particularly disliked. Through them Lady Carbury establishes her reputation as a writer.

The plan of the novel makes it clear that Trollope had in mind far greater concentration on Lady Carbury and the editors than finally occurred. Lady Carbury is described in Trollope's layout as 'an authoress, very handsome, 43 – trying all schemes with editors etc. to get puffed'. The character may well have suggested itself from several friends who were urging him to read their work and, doubtless, put a word in the right ear now and then. As regards the editors, his notes supply possible identities only for two. Mr Nicholas Broune, editor of the *Morning Breakfast Table*, who is 'Fond of ladies', has two additional bracketed comments: the name 'Morrish' and the location 'Pall Mall office in Trafalgar Square'. He plays the largest role in *The Way We Live Now*, occupies rooms in Pall Mall East and proceeds daily to his office in Trafalgar Square. One of the lighter strands of the novel consists of his flirtation with Lady Carbury. Who 'Morrish' was remains a mystery. The second editor, Mr Booker of the *Literary Chronicle*, has the bracketed name Alfred Shand; as Donald Smalley has pointed out, a link with Alexander Innes Shand, a regular contributor to the *Edinburgh Review*. Doubtless Shand remained ignorant of the possible connection for in 1877 he wrote a warm appreciation of Trollope's fiction for the *Edinburgh Review*.[21] The third editor, Mr Ferdinand Alf of the *Evening Pulpit*, described in Trollope's rough note as a 'great swell', has no name attached to puzzle over. Part-proprietor of the *Evening Pulpit*, Alf is the conventional muck-raking journalist, power-hungry and omniscient, a latter-day Tom Towers who becomes Melmotte's rival for the Westminster constituency. This improvisation enables Trollope to broaden his satire in keeping with the overall social ends of the novel, and leads him to the indictment of press morality which accompanies Melmotte's downfall. The *Mob* a new farthing paper, is introduced which, in championing Melmotte, declares that 'magnitude in affairs is a valid defence for certain irregularities' (ch. lxix).

Monumental dishonesty is the keynote of Trollope's other journalistic scorpion, Quintus Slide, through whose machinations in the *Phineas* novels and *The Prime Minister* Trollope continues his examination of the press and public life. Whereas Tom Towers had a certain respect for his profession and a gentlemanly exterior at least, Quintus Slide is a vulgar, thoroughly vicious trouble-maker, brought to life with Dickensian gusto from the moment he adopts Finn as useful political capital: 'there's nothing like having a horgan to back you. What is the most you can do in the 'Ouse? Nothing, if you're not reported. You're speaking to the country; – ain't you? And you can't do that without a horgan, Mr. Finn.'[22] Mr Turnbull in *Phineas Finn* is a radical politician and tribune of the people; some say a demagogue and a rabble-rouser. So, too, is Slide, though with far less altruism than Turnbull, who was modelled loosely on John Bright, the great independent liberal of Gladstone's party.

> It was Mr. Slide's taste to be an advanced reformer, and in all his operations on behalf of the People's Banner he was a reformer very much advanced. No man could do an article on the people's indefeasible rights with more pronounced vigour than Mr. Slide. But it had never occurred to him as yet that he ought to care for anything else than the fight, – than the advantage of having a good subject on which to write slashing articles. (ch. xxvi)

At the time of Slide's conception Trollope was associated with the *Pall Mall Gazette*, contributing, as well as his admirable hunting sketches, 'some imitations of Captain Sterling's political thunder (once so telling in *The Times*)' still largely unidentified.[23] There is no question of relating the odious Slide to Edward Sterling, but the slashing style evidently lingered in Trollope's memory. Slide is the embodiment of malicious personality journalism, and despite his misplaced aspirates 'a well-known and not undistinguished member of a powerful class of men' (ch. xxvi). While urging some sincerity for him, Trollope damns him for his political ignorance and venality: 'To be a "people's friend" suited the turn of his ambition, and he was a "people's friend" ' (ch. xxvi). Inevitably, Slide turns against Finn, and in *Phineas Redux* makes at least three attempts to ruin him. On the first occasion Finn has stopped the *People's Banner* printing Robert Kennedy's letter proclaiming his wife's desertion, and is admonished by Slide: 'We go in for morals and purity of life, and we mean to do our duty by the public without fear or favour' (ch. xxii). This is a reminder of that high moral tone which so thoroughly irked Trollope in *The Times*. Indeed the criticism of the *People's Banner* is the same as that of *The Times* in most respects: immense power, subversive of democracy and wielded without responsibility.

Slide is again active in *The Prime Minister*, with the *People's Banner*, in one of its frequent changes of allegiance, attacking the Duke of Omnium's coalition government. The Duke himself is under fire as a result of his connection with Ferdinand Lopez. Attacks on the Prime Minister, motivated largely by Slide's resentment at being refused entry to the Duke's house, highlight the psychological conflict at the very heart of the story. It is ironical that the Duke, a man of fierce integrity, should be accused of dishonest practices, and the press campaign against him emphasises the gulf between political principle and unscrupulous journalism, at the same time bringing out Plantagenet's vulnerability:

> In his old happy days two papers a day, one in the morning and the other before dinner, sufficed to tell him all that he wanted to know. Now he felt it necessary to see almost every rag that was published. And he would skim through them all till he found the lines in which he himself was maligned, and then, with sore heart and irritated nerves, would pause over every contumelious word. (ch. xxxviii)

Largely through this failure to cope with Slide's attacks, Plantagenet is shown to be too sensitive to criticism for office. To make matters worse, in a cabinet reshuffle Plantagenet appoints Finn to the Admiralty, reawakening Slide's animosity to his former enemy. Slide publishes an outrageous libel denouncing Finn as the Duke's lackey and blaming the Prime Minister for hounding Lopez to his death, a calculated move to boost the paper's circulation which misfires, since neither of Slide's victims will launch an action. One of the central issues in the novel – the chivalric code associated with the old world of Whig aristocrats assailed by modern aggressive politics tainted by commercialism – is thus brought into focus. Plantagenet, the pattern gentleman, cannot stoop to retaliate, while Finn has matured enough to exercise restraint: 'It had not been so with him always, but now, at last, he was hardened against Mr. Quintus Slide' (ch. lxii).

Trollope's aversion to the press becomes more noticeable in his later work. In *Is He Popenjoy?* the Dean of Brotherton's passion for hunting attracts newspaper gossip, while in *John Caldigate* the press gloats on the allegations of bigamy surrounding the hero. In *Dr. Wortle's School* Trollope invents a London weekly paper called *Everybody's Business* which prints a burlesque on ' "Amo" in the cool of the evening', almost provoking Dr Wortle to sue. The hypocrisy underlying much press activity is always material for satire. Mr Maguire, the evangelical cleryman, sermonises on the evil of riches in the *Christian Examiner* while wooing Margaret Mackenzie to secure her supposed fortune. Almost without exception Trollope's presentation of journalism is hostile, for he saw how it could undermine the honesty and integrity of those who could influence public life. Remembering his many friendships with journalists, and the indirect power of such men among publishers, one cannot but respect the novelist for speaking out so boldly when the consequences might well have harmed his career. *Fiat justitia ruat coelum.*

GENTLEMEN AND OTHERS

The basis of Trollope's approach to a man's actions in the social and public sphere is the meaning he attaches to the word 'gentleman'. The general conduct of society – business enterprise, parliamentary affairs, the management of the estate, parish or cathedral precinct, the practice of the law and of medicine – revolves on a single criterion of conduct embodied in this very English concept. And it is the impact of social change upon a code with chivalric origins that provides the tension and enjoyment of Trollope's best fiction. In politics we see expediency and hucksterism professed by men who have broken with the past or who have spurious claims to gentility. Old Amedroz in *The Belton Estate* is right to lament that instead of gentlemen 'none but brewers, and tallow-chandlers, and lawyers go into Parliament now' (ch. xv), and a similar complaint is voiced in *The Duke's Children*. Parliament and society have been invaded by the arrivistes. 'There used to be a feeling in favour of gentlemen', remarks Lady Cantrip bitterly (ch. xxxv); Archdeacon Grantly sees properties in the cathedral close leased to retired merchants instead of elderly prebendaries; Ralph Newton can justify marrying Polly Neefit, the breechesmaker's daughter, on the grounds that 'Everybody is doing it now' (ch. v). But much as Trollope regrets what is being lost in grace, good manners, and a reliable ethic, he takes up his characteristic mid-position of ironic perspective, looking sceptically into the future, and critically into the past; to what is fusty, authoritarian, rigid and outmoded in Barchester or Ullathorne or Carbury Manor, as well as what is shoddy in Leeds or the new London surburbia.

To miss this ambivalence is to mistake Trollope for a Victorian Colonel Blimp. In fact, he stands on much the same ground as his contemporaries, particularly the Tennyson of the *Idylls*, for he advances

Arthurian chivalry in an age of moral bewilderment. What we have in the novels concerned with social values, such as *The Bertrams*, *Orley Farm*, the Palliser novels, *The Three Clerks* and *The Way We Live Now*, is a society facing the steady decline of traditional patterns of moral and religious certainty, a culture perplexed by new social philosophies. With his contemporaries Trollope dimly recognises some kind of threshold, and a prospect both exhilarating and frightening. Thus his fiction offers an equivocal response, analogous to the restlessness and neurasthenia of much Victorian poetry, sometimes reflecting a wish for escape, sometimes retreating into nostalgia, sometimes looking hopefully to the future. For Trollope is not entirely at ease in the old dispensation; he is too shrewd and honest for that. The ideal of Barsetshire is counterbalanced by the challenge of progress, which, given Trollope's optimism, acquires its full force in his response towards gradual political reform, a liberal attitude to religion, a realistic sense of American influence in the world. Trollope is certainly not the reactionary he is sometimes imagined. Even in the sphere of class divisions, of creating better educational opportunities for the working man, he is, from the standpoint of his time, remarkably liberal. The old Duke embodies something of this moderate progressiveness in *The Duke's Children*: 'As by the spread of education and increase of general well-being every proletaire was brought nearer to a Duke, so by such action would the Duke be brought nearer to a proletaire. Such drawing-nearer of the classes was the object to which all this man's political action tended' (ch. xxii).

The *Last Chronicle of Barset* is not only the triumphant climax of the beloved Barset sequence, but also a forceful statement of man's obligations towards himself and the social organism. Trollope sets before us, with brilliant irony, the values which man must cleave to in his intercourse with the world. Kathleen Tillotson has referred to the novel's 'larger unity [in time] as the "last chronicle" of a long series',[24] and indeed in the perspectives of memory lie its qualities as a masterpiece. No critic has failed to respond to the insight displayed in Josiah Crawley, and the novel is deservedly the most popular of the canon. It has been so since its first appearance; contemporary reviews overleaped one another in urging their readers to take it up, and Trollope himself looked back on it in the *Autobiography* as the best novel he had written. It has 'a true savour of English country life' (ch. xv). He was also proud of what he had achieved in Crawley as a complex revelation of pride, humility, manliness, weakness, conscientious rectitude and bitter prejudice.

For my purpose here, the haunted figure of Mr Crawley is not as important as the social nexus to which old favourites of the series as well as several new characters, are related. My discussion centre rather on the interpretation of this comedy of manners, and Trollope's ideals of conduct in private and professional life. The plot, turning on a clergyman's involvement in forgery and deception, provides Trollope with one of those perplexing moral considerations that delighted him. Although we know Crawley is incapable of lying or having stolen a cheque, the ethical issue remains intriguing: the clergyman, as moral centre of the community, is suspected by large numbers of people as being seriously flawed. In the very first pages of the book we are invited to ponder this point. Why should not a clergyman turn thief as well as anyone else? claims John Walker, the lawyer's son. Men under the cassock are as prone to follies as other men, Trollope often says, but here the matter is posed in circumstances of unusual force and freighted with serious consequences for the moral health of the community. Crawley's position is acutely significant in directing our eyes to various shortcomings of the society around him, and in vindicating principle and honesty amid the general infection of vanity and foolishness. In some curious way, too, Crawley generates the power for the continuing circuit of love, charity and faith which sustains the community in its battle against egotism and greed.

Two versions of doing well in the world are offered for our consideration. Crawley's ascetism, scholarship, and psychological handicaps have confined him to a perpetual curacy at Hogglestock, where he devotes himself to good works among the indigent brickmakers. Archdeacon Grantly, on the other hand, has accumulated wealth, and manages to live as comfortably as an English squire: 'His only daughter had made a splendid marriage. His two sons had hitherto done well in the world, not only as regarded their happiness, but as to marriage also, and as to social standing' (ch. v). When the story opens, his son, Major Henry Grantly, a half-pay officer, is on the verge of proposing to Crawley's daughter, Grace. Thus Trollope deploys a series of ironic comments on the material values of the Grantly world against the spiritual values embodied in Grace Crawley. From the beginning debate turns on the primary values of the archdeacon's world, rank and money. On the latter score Grace is easily disqualified; on the former the Archdeacon has made up his mind in advance, largely through her father's circumstances as a curate and the scandal now hovering over his head. Grantly is so deluded by titles and wealth as to applaud the intelligence of his daughter, Griselda, in having married Lord Dumbello, and it is to her opinions that he defers in the crisis, so far is he removed from good sense and moral perception where self-interest and family name are concerned. The Grantly/Crawley love affair proceeds as an education for the Archdeacon in that conventional axiom of Trollope's that true gentility is a question neither of rank, nor of money, but of pedigree.

'Pedigree' is a matter about which Trollope is disingenuous. Once again the problem lies in the question of what constitutes a gentleman. He tries to convey that being a gentleman is not a matter of birth, that is to say, high rank. As he points out in *The Claverings*, 'High rank and soft manners may not always belong to a true heart' (ch. xxvi), and the implication is always that the gentlemanly code is within reach of the most humble. A man's a man for a' that, Marie Goesler affirms in *Phineas Finn* (ch. liv). To establish the point, Trollope depicts many a high-born person who is mean, tyrannical and perfidious: the Marquis of Trowbridge, Lord Grex, Lord Lovel, Lord de Courcy and Lord Mongrober are obvious cases. Coronet and ermine do not guarantee that the wearer is a gentleman. But Trollope does have great regard for ancestry. *Dr. Thorne* is much concerned with this, and in *Orley Farm* we are told:

> In judging the position which a man should hold in the world, Sir Peregrine was very resolute in ignoring all claims made by wealth alone. Even property in land could not in his eyes create a gentleman. A gentleman, according to his ideas, should at any rate have great-grandfathers capable of being traced in the world's history; and the greater the number of such, and the more easily traceable they might be on the world's surface, the more unquestionable would be the status of the claimant in question. (ch. iii)

This is a limited and superficial view, in keeping with a very conservative landowner, and given with some irony, but it reflects Trollope's own conviction about lineage. For him, country gentry of true yeoman stock are the backbone of English tradition, in whom are instilled love of country and a well-developed sense of duty, honour and chivalry, and from whom come the professional men, politicians and churchmen. Thus in *Dr. Wortle's School* the following distinction is possible: 'And though it is much to be a nobleman, it is more to be a gentleman' (Part V, ch. viii).

The overall tendency of Trollope's fiction is to show that being a gentleman is a state of grace that can be won by effort. But can one be a gentleman bootmender or attorney's clerk? On this question Trollope is reticent, even though his theory suggests that one can. He chooses simply not to confront the issue. Daniel Thwaites is a journeyman tailor and gentleman, but he is shipped off to Australia with Lady Anna. Other citizen gents are hard to find. Generally, characters like Ontario Moggs, or Slide, or, in another context, the Lookalofts and the Greenacres, are conventional would-be gentry whose manners give them away. Even Mr Thomas Toogood, the Gray's Inn lawyer who unravels the mystery of the stolen cheque in *The Last Chronicle*, is, in the words of his fellow-attorney, Mr Walker, 'not quite, you know —'

(ch. xlii). Trollope has his fun with both of them, reminding us of the ubiquitous English preoccupation with social gradations:

> As regards the two attorneys I will not venture to say that either of them was not a 'perfect gentleman.' A perfect gentleman is a thing which I cannot define. (ch. xlii)

He admits again, in *He Knew He Was Right*, that the term is indefinable, and in *The Last Chronicle* also the issue is hard to determine. Adolphus Crosbie is no gentleman, but Johnny Eames is, although he declines to think of himself as one: 'I can't define a gentleman, even in my own mind', he admits (ch. xxiv). But his description of his chief, Sir Raffle Buffle, and of Dobbs Broughton, clearly denies them the title, though it makes Johnny sound rather a snob:

> There is a sort of persons going now, – and one meets them out here and there every day of one's life, – who are downright Brummagem to the ear and to the touch and to the sight, and we recognize them as such at the very first moment. My honoured lord and master, Sir Raffle, is one such. There is no mistaking him. Clap him down upon the counter, and he rings dull and untrue at once. (ch. xxiv)

Fidelity, modesty and honesty are prime qualities of the gentleman. Thus cads, though of the aristocracy or middle class – men such as Burgo Fitzgerald, George Vavasor, Ralph Newton, Lopez, Augustus Scarborough, George Hotspur – are beyond the pale. They are not gentlemen because a gentleman, Trollope notes in *The Prime Minister*, is 'a man who would not for worlds tell a lie' (ch. xxx).

The fact is that gentlemen may be found in any class, but seldom are. In the *Autobiography*, Trollope declares it is most likely that the qualities he admires will be found among those of rank, fortune and pedigree:

> The discerning man will recognize the information and the graces when they are achieved without such assistance, and will honour the owners of them the more because of the difficulties they have overcome; – but the fact remains that the society of the well-born and of the wealthy will as a rule be worth seeking. (ch. ix)

And the practice of the novels, as opposed to the theory, seems to indicate, as Trollope says in *Ralph the Heir*, that 'Nothing on earth can make a gentleman' (ch. xxiv). Mr Monk, though a mechanic's son, might make a very good Prime Minister, but on the whole Trollope's sentiments coincide with those of his odious German in *Ralph the Heir*, Herr Bawwah: 'De peoples should be de peoples, and de nobles should be de nobles' (ch. xxiv). The gentleman, like the poet, is born not made. This is clearly to be seen in *The Prime Minister*, where Emily Wharton finds herself forced into comparisons between her husband, Ferdinand Lopez, and her former lover, Arthur Fletcher. Lopez, a liar and a cheat, is enraged to find himself matched against Fletcher in an election, and when Fletcher writes to Emily explaining that he cannot withdraw and let down his supporters, she is impressed by his integrity; he becomes in her eyes 'so good, so noble, so generous, so true!' (ch. xxx). Lopez construes his action as humbug and treachery, making out that his professed ignorance about the rival candidacy was a lie. Such wicked misjudgement sets Emily thinking about the nature of her husband and Fletcher:

> There was some peculiar gift, or grace, or acquirement belonging without dispute to the one, and which the other lacked. What was it? She had heard her father say when talking of gentlemen, – of that race of gentlemen with whom it had been his lot to live, – that you could not make a silk purse out of a sow's ear . . . She had once ventured to form a doctrine for herself, to preach to herself a sermon of her own, and to tell her father that this gift of gentle blood and of gentle nurture, of which her father thought so much, and to which something of divinity was attributed down in Hertfordshire, was after all but a weak, spiritless quality. It could exist without intellect, without heart, and with very moderate culture. It was compatible with many littlenesses and with many vices. As for that love of honest, courageous truth which her father was wont to attribute to it, she regarded his theory as based upon legends, as in earlier years was the theory of courage, and constancy, and loyalty of the knights of those days. The beau ideal of a man which she then pictured to herself was graced, first with intelligence, then with affection, and lastly with ambition. She knew no reason why such a hero as her fancy created should be born of lords and ladies rather than of working mechanics, should be English rather than Spanish or French. (ch. xxxi)

Emily concedes that it is more likely that one of good family would acquire education and thus be on the high road towards her ideal of conduct, but she still cannot bring herself to think of gentility as a matter of genealogy: 'she did not see why she, or why the world, should go back beyond the man's own self' (ch. xxxi). Lopez, however, is already proving that his gentlemanly manner is mere deportment, and his crude assessment of Fletcher's motives, his own distrust of her, has forced her to an unwelcome change in her convictions. All of this expresses a dubious proposition, for by emphasising the naïveté of Emily's earlier notions, Trollope manages to suggest that the correlation between birth and conduct is vital. Lopez is such an outstanding example of viciousness and vulgarity that it becomes very difficult indeed to believe that the ethical and social standards contained in Trollope's ideal of the gentleman can, in fact, be learned.

A similar point of view is to be found in *Is He Popenjoy?* Dean Lovelace has made his way in the church entirely by his wit and intelligence, without any advantages of birth or riches. The Germains, on the other hand, are hypnotised by their rank, and although Lord George loves Mary, the Dean's beautiful daughter, he is always conscious of being brother to a Marquess, and uncomfortably aware of the Dean's low birth. Much of the interest centres on the Dean's sensitivity about his background, which turns a basically decent man into a snob: 'he had never ceased to be ashamed of the stable yard' (ch. lxiii).

> With great care and cunning workmanship one may almost make a silk purse out of a sow's ear, but not quite. The care which Dean Lovelace had bestowed upon the operation in regard to himself had been very great, and the cunning workmanship was to be seen in every plait and every stitch. But still there was something left of the coarseness of the original material. (ch. ii)

Such a judgement indicates Trollope's strong if sometimes guilty feeling that birth means much. What we regard as a saving grace of vulgarity in Trollope was probably, in the hyper-class-conscious milieu of Victorian England, a source to him of secret and inward pique, which he may well have chosen to work out in his story of the Dean and his daughter, whose vivacity is reproved by the Germains as vulgarity, much to her father's dismay. The Germains are worse snobs than the Dean, joyless, hypocritical and small-minded. A rapprochement is achieved, but it is the Dean's frankness and his daughter's spontaneity and courage which show the superior attitude to life.

The Last Chronicle does not make Trollope's definition of 'gentleman' much clearer, although it splendidly reveals the niceties of English prejudice in the matter. The standard of judgement rests with the old guard of the cathedral close, even though the Archdeacon's materialism has obvious moral shortcomings. Thus the arrivistes with their piety and reforms have brought about a decline. Clergy in the old days took wine, played cards and 'did more of the dancing in Barchester than all the other young men in the city put together'. 'And a good set they were', says the Archdeacon warmly, 'gentlemen every one of them' (ch. xxii). Ambitious clergymen of the new stamp are related to the new men of business, and in this way Trollope links Dobbs Broughton, Musselboro and Mrs Van Siever with his main plot. The new spirit of the age is inimical to the gentlemanly values, which the novel vindicates in the triumph of Grantlys over Proudies and in the reconciliation of the Archdeacon to his son's marriage.

Grantly remains one of the most interesting characters in the novels, proud and dictatorial yet anxious to be loved, vulnerable and generous despite his overbearing manner. He is, of course, a worldly man. We are reminded soon enough that Henry's sister, Griselda, had fully justified the family's ideals by marrying Lord Dumbello. Much is intentionally made of the aristocratic connection, with heavy stress on the coldness and superficiality of the Marchioness, which is meant to strike the reader with ironical force as he is told of the exchange between father and son over Grace.

'By-the-by, how well Griselda is looking.'

'Yes, she is. It's always easy for women to look well when they're rich.' How would Grace Crawley look, then, who was poor as poverty itself, and who should remain poor, if his son was fool enough to marry her? That was the train of thought which ran through the archdeacon's mind. 'I do not think much of riches,' said he, 'but it is always well that a gentleman's wife or a gentleman's daughter should have a sufficiency to maintain her position in life.'

'You may say the same, sir, of everybody's wife and everybody's daughter.'

'You know what I mean, Henry.'

'I am not quite sure that I do, sir.'

'Perhaps I had better speak out at once. A rumour has reached your mother and me, which we don't believe for a moment, but which, nevertheless, makes us unhappy even as a report. They say that there is a young woman living in Silverbridge to whom you are becoming attached.'

'Is there any reason why I should not become attached to a young woman in Silverbridge? – though I hope any young woman to whom I may become attached will be worthy at any rate of being called a young lady.' (ch. iii)

The reproof is just, for the archdeacon's condescension betrays the snobbery which underlies his opposition to the match. It is cleverly overlaid, however, by the suspicion of theft overhanging Mr Crawley, and Trollope conveniently does not have to deal closely with problems of mésalliance or caste. Instead he can focus attention on the archdeacon's worldly wisdom, showing how inadequate such a philosophy is for happy and lasting marriage. At the same time he shows Grantly as victim of his own obduracy and pride, unable to retract from a position he knows in his heart to be unworthy. Yet for all that worldliness is not ridiculed. There is a scene later in the novel in which, with a certain ingenuousness, he tries to impress his son with his future responsibilities as a landowner:

> It is a comfortable feeling to know that you stand on your own ground. Land is about the only thing that can't fly away. And then, you see, land gives so much more than the rent. It gives position and influence and political power, to say nothing about the game. (ch. lviii)

Although there is material for comedy in a prince of the church so disinterested in spiritual values, Trollope esteems a code which insists that it is good to care for the land, to plant oaks and preserve foxes, to hunt and to lay down the best vintages. It represents a continuity and strength that is worth fighting for. Thus it is a real question whether Henry is about to sacrifice himself on a worthy object.

The society around, it seems, is curious about the match, its concern reflecting the importance of appropriate alliances. The emphasis Trollope gives local opinion in such matters is a demonstration of the extent to which a mis-matching might affect the life of the community, as if the crossing of caste lines somehow jeopardises the moral health of the society. Thus, although Henry can justify to his own satisfaction the status of his potential wife, the Reverend Mr Oriel puts serious concerns of the community when he asks tentatively:

> 'Is she, – what you call – ?'
> 'You mean, is she a lady?'
> 'Of course she is by birth, and all that,' said Mr Oriel, apologising for his enquiry. (ch. lv)

Despite Trollope's intention to separate birth from gentility, the question of Grace's social status is still hedged around by the difficulties of her humble situation, quite apart from her father's possible disgrace. It is as if Trollope must relive in the Crawley situation the horrors of his own family's genteel poverty, for he gives a most graphic account:

> None but they who have themselves been poor gentry, – gentry so poor as not to know how to raise a shilling, – can understand the peculiar bitterness of the trials which such poverty produces. The poverty of the normal poor does not approach it; or, rather, the pangs arising from such a poverty are altogether of a different sort . . . But there are pangs to which, at the time, starvation itself would seem to be preferable. The angry eyes of unpaid tradesmen, savage with an anger which one knows to be justifiable; the taunt of the poor servant who wants her wages; the gradual relinquishment of habits which the soft nurture of earlier, kinder years had

made second nature; the wan cheeks of the wife whose malady demands wine; the rags of the husband whose outward occupations
demand decency; the neglected children, who are learning not to
be the children of gentlefolk; and worse than all, the alms and
doles of half-generous friends, the waning pride, the pride that will
not wane, the growing doubt whether it be not better to bow the
head, and acknowledge to all the world that nothing of the pride of
station is left, – that the hand is open to receive and ready to touch
the cap, that the fall from the upper to the lower level has been
accomplished, – these are the pangs of poverty which drive the Craw-
leys of the world to the frequent entertaining of that idea of the
bare bodkin. (ch. ix)

In conscious echoes of the tragic style Trollope explains enough of
Crawley's situation to make his folly over the cheque understandable,
but he also reveals the depths to which his own nature felt the humiliating struggle to keep up appearances. Doubtless such a passage had
many responsive readers in a period so acutely class-conscious. One
notes a curious sense of the stigma felt in loss of station, and it is
this shame and envy, as much as secret pride in his own worth giving
luxury to his woe, that almost drives Crawley insane. Trollope makes
the point that reputation in the eyes of the community is necessary
to man, and moreover that social standing and money are vital to self-
respect.

Yet the class issue is blunted, since Crawley is so obviously well-
bred, quite capable of meeting Barsetshire society on equal terms; despite his poverty, unquestionably a gentleman, as his daughter is a
lady. In fact the Archdeacon's worldly values are cleverly submerged
in the true values of gentility which he comes to recognise in Grace
Crawley. At their meeting he is captivated:

She became suddenly very important in his eyes, and he was to
some extent afraid of her. She was so slight, so meek, so young; and
yet there was about her something so beautifully feminine, – and,
withal, so like a lady, – that he felt instinctively that he could not
attack her with harsh words. (ch. lvii)

As in the case of Mr Harding, there is something in the humility and
meekness of true natures that rebukes and confounds the worldly wise.
Trollope cannot resist an obeisance to the laws of social propriety and
the fitness of things, however, by transforming the little brown girl
into a princess:

No man in England knew better than the archdeacon the difference
between beauty of one kind and beauty of another kind in a woman's
face, – the one beauty, which comes from health and youth and

animal spirits, and which belongs to the miller's daughter, and the other beauty, which shows itself in fine lines and a noble spirit, – the beauty which comes from breeding. (Ibid.)

A similar pledge to the fitness of social distinctions is observed in the reconciliation of the two fathers, related after the event by Mr Crawley:

> 'I would we stood on more equal grounds,' I said. Then as he answered me, he rose from his chair. 'We stand,' said he, 'on the only perfect level on which such men can meet each other. We are both gentlemen,' 'Sir,' I said, rising also, 'from the bottom of my heart I agree with you. I could not have spoken such words; but coming from you who are rich to me who am poor, they are honourable to the one and comfortable to the other.' (ch. lxxxiii)

And with this curious reconciliation of antinomies Trollope draws *The Last Chronicle* to a conclusion.

In forming a *modus vivendi* in which selfhood and principle are respected, Trollope points out the necessity both of compromise and of acquiescence in agreed tenets of behaviour. The Victorians looked, for certainties that science and industrial progress were rapidly denying them, to religion, the family, and a code that demanded form, propriety and convention. Social mobility only led to an obsession with fixed habits of dress, manner and custom, producing widespread anxiety, prudery and snobbery. Trollope's fiction reflects much of this agitation, but it also shows in detail how the individual will fits, or finds itself at odds with, the society around it. Few writers are as adept at estimating what Trollope called the weights and measures of society,[25] and much of the dynamic of his fiction arises from the interplay of the hero's nature with the society where he must function or be excluded. This is one of the interests of *The Warden*. John Bold, acting from the highest principle on behalf of the bedesmen he believes to have been wronged, in some senses transgresses norms of his society and unwittingly allies himself with the aliens and disturbers of the peace. Attention must always be paid, Trollope insists, to the customs and practices of the group. In the case of his love stories, therefore, tension arises not so much from the affair itself as from the ripples it sets off across the waters of society as a whole. 'It's the looks on it, ma'am; it's that I mind,' says a housemaid in *The Three Clerks*, when her fiancé has deserted her to marry another (ch. xvi). Thus while Trollope often shows the dangers of succumbing to popular pressure, and satirises, in such a novel as *The Belton Estate*, the crushing pruderies and offensive prying of the social group, he generally leads his characters to a reconciliation with its conventions:

When any practice has become the fixed rule of the society in which we live it is always wise to adhere to that rule, unless it call upon us to do something that is actually wrong. One should not offend the prejudices of the world, even if one is quite sure that they are prejudices. (ch. xx)

On the other hand Trollope also makes social setting a negative influence, thereby enhancing the courage and honesty of his hero and heroine. What the world says about prudent marriages, for example, is always contrary to the ideal of love. Major Henry Grantly is misled by the opinions of the majority into accepting the likelihood of Mr Crawley's guilt in the matter of the cheque. If, as R. M. Adams has maintained, 'the way of the world is Trollope's touchstone',[26] one must add that his world is multi-faceted, and that he often displays a spirited irony towards the accepted mores. This is noticeable in later novels where the pressures of social opinion have given way to psychological probing, in which the struggle between individual will and society is more marked. I do not think this represents in Trollope a personal problem of identification or disaffection with his public, so much as the gathering perplexity of Victorian society in its final phase. The later novels are not darker to any marked degree than the early ones; it is merely that the survey of what the good man has to contend with is broader and more comprehensive; that the habitual truth of observation Trollope is pledged to takes in growing complications of the moral life. One might claim, for example, that the tone of *The Small House at Allington*, the blackest of his Barsetshire novels, with its rapacious and decadent de Courcys, its cynical playboy, Adolphus Crosbie, and overall mood of disenchantment, differs very little from that of *The Way We Live Now* – only the scale makes the impression vary. As some justification of this view, I would cite the general cast of Trollope's mind when he recalled the writing of this book for his *Autobiography*, which reveals anxiety about the progress of society but not the pessimism some critics have found in it; rather than prophesying doom, he offered a vigorous rejoinder to Carlylism:

If he be right, we are all going straight away to darkness and the dogs. But then we do not put very much faith in Mr. Carlyle, – nor in Mr. Ruskin and his other followers. The loudness and extravagance of their lamentations, the wailing and gnashing of teeth which comes from them, over a world which is supposed to have gone altogether shoddywards, are so contrary to the convictions of men who cannot but see how comfort has been increased, how health has been improved, and education extended, – that the general effect of their teaching is the opposite of what they have intended. (ch. xx)

This optimistic tone is corroborated by an outpouring of novels up to the end of his life, including that effervescent romantic tale *Ayala's Angel*, the exuberant *Mr. Scarborough's Family* and *The Duke's Children*, which expresses cheerful acceptance of misfortune, arguing that man is always liable to error, that idealism must ever be tempered with reasonable commonsense, but that life will continue to be sweet. It is the spirit of his majestic valediction in the *Autobiography* (quoted on pp. 46–7).

Later novels do reflect changes in society, but not to any great extent, and I doubt whether Trollope's views on social organisation underwent much alteration throughout his career. Nobility continued to exert special charm for him, and he continued to show that good and bad existed among the highest in the land. Young aristocrats are invariably comic: in *The Kellys* we have Lord Kilcullen, who is the unwelcome suitor of Fanny Wyndham; in later novels Lord Popplecourt, Lord Hampstead and Lord Fawn with their cheery, vacuous chatter of clubland and the lovelorn Tom Tringle in *Ayala's Angel*. No-one equals Trollope in drawing idiotic members of high society until Waugh and Wodehouse. Dolly Longestaffe in *The Way We Live Now* ('Longstaff' in *The Duke's Children*) is one of the most memorable idiots of Trollopian fiction. Yet the serious implication of an impoverished and effete young aristocracy is quite clearly the extinction of the feudal code and the threat of a commercially based society. Once proud owners of great houses have been driven to seek alliances with entrepreneurs like Melmotte, and are content to be letterhead directors of fake companies. Lord Fawn is debased by his need of money. Lord Mongrober is as greedy for riches as his name implies. The process by which impoverished rank seeks to repair its fortune by a marriage with trade, long a subject of Trollope's satire, is treated in later books with a more disenchanted eye.

The dilution of noble blood by alliances outside its ranks is not seen as altogether undesirable, however, and several of the late novels try to put a theory of assimilation to which Trollope certainly gave intellectual support. Once again, however, there is a good deal of ambiguity which stems from the vexed question of what constitutes a gentleman. In at least two novels, *Lady Anna* and *Marion Fay*, Trollope attempted to bridge the gap between high and low, and in at least two more he dealt with this theme more convincingly by neatly skirting the issue: noble blood allied with a commoner – but the commoner was an American citizen. Trollope, fascinated by egalitarianism free from historical imperatives of the English tradition, depicts his American girls with great vivacity and freshness and they cut through some of the more tedious restrictions of English behaviour. 'In America they carry latch-keys, and walk about with young gentlemen as young gentlemen walk about with each other.'[27] Such approval of the natural freedom of American women was not of late date. He had shown in *He Knew He Was Right* the doubts of Caroline Spalding, niece of the American minister to Italy, about entering English high society by marrying the future Lord Peterborough.

Isabel Boncassen in *The Duke's Children* is an even livelier American heroine who receives the attentions of Dolly Longstaff with a good deal of scorn, but then finds herself in love with Lord Silverbridge, and knowing she must encounter the disapproval of his father, the Duke of Omnium, her pride and independence are challenged. She comes to him with a show of boldness, remarking that her father is descended from a poor dock labourer in New York. The Duke's statement on rank and his private thoughts show a disparity between his political theory and his personal feelings Trollope relishes:

> The peer who sat next to him in the House of Lords, whose grandmother had been a washerwoman and whose father an innkeeper, was to him every whit as good a peer as himself. And he would as soon sit in council with Mr. Monk, whose father had risen from a mechanic to a merchant, as with any nobleman who could count ancestors against himself. But there was an inner feeling in his own bosom as to his own family, his own name, his own children, and his own personal self, which was kept altogether apart from his grand political theories. It was a subject on which he never spoke; but the feeling had come to him as a part of his birthright. (ch. xlviii)

It is this secret pride which makes him prefer his son's alliance with the daughter of the dissolute Lord Grex, and fight his daughter's plan to marry Frank Tregear. In the end he accommodates his prejudices by recognising the essential gentility of both Tregear and Isabel, to whom he says:

> There shall be no feeling but that you are in truth his chosen wife. After all neither can country, nor race, nor rank, nor wealth, make a good woman. Education can do much. But nature must have done much also. (ch. lxxii)

Trollope really tries for an effect in this charmingly observed, cautious and tender reaching-out, epitomising the logical and desirable union of English and American. The chapter is well built, beginning with Isabel's excitement at her future home in Carlton Terrace and her practical eye for the furnishings and fittings, and followed by a consideration of her situation *vis-à-vis* the Duke. Her insistence on being accompanied by her mother irritates Silverbridge, but she has her own way; a small detail which captures both her nervousness and her will. Trollope next shifts attention to the interview, prefacing it with the Duke's reflections on duty to his rank and the consequences for society of alliances such as this. Isabel tries to overcome her nervousness with a deliberately offhand joke, but meeting the Duke she softens her tone, and wins him over by her quiet grace. The friendship is sealed when he presents her with a circlet of diamonds that had once belonged to Glencora. This in itself symbolises a new cycle in the Omnium dynasty.

CHEATERY

Money is the fulcrum on which most Victorian novels turn and it calls out the best in Trollope: the splendidly unified *Orley Farm*, that brilliant comedy of cash and conquest *The Eustace Diamonds*, and a massive onslaught on the commercial world in *The Way We Live Now*. So far I have studied the evils of acquisitiveness and materialism in regard to individual happiness, but the money theme really comes to the fore when Trollope is thinking about a man's public and social roles and how trade and the increasing tempo of Victorian capitalism affects the quality of life. With his usual consistency Trollope ranges widely over such topics as share-swindles, cut-throat competition, false advertising and similar consequences of the cash nexus. This is sounded in *The Bertrams*, which opens to Clough's refrain, 'The devil take the hindmost'. Trollope has most of his characters dance to it, especially the Solicitor-General, Sir Henry Harcourt. Old Bertram, the City's financial wizard, calls the tune and, an unregenerate Chuzzlewit to the last, expires with the words: 'No man is respected without money – no man' (III, ch. xi). Money worship is ingeniously woven into the texture of *Orley Farm* too, where even the upright Mr Furnival is tarnished by the attempt to buy off a witness. As a metaphor of the corruption engendered by money greed in that novel, the salesman, Mr Kantwise, peddles a new line in folding metal furniture about which Mrs Dockwrath rightfully exclaims: 'They're got up for cheatery; – that's what they're got up for' (ch. xlii). Such is progress. As Abraham Mollett reminds Sir Thomas Fitzgerald in *Castle Richmond*, 'Sharp's the word nowadays' (II, ch. i); and Harry Gilmore, putting up at the Bull in *The Vicar of Bullhampton* is left in no doubt as to the way things stand when he meets the travelling salesman, Mr Cockey:

> 'Now, I don't know what you are, sir,' said he.
> 'I'm not much of anything,' said Gilmore.
> 'Perhaps not, sir. Let that be as it may. But a man, sir, that feels that he's one of the supports of the commercial supremacy of this nation ain't got much reason to be ashamed of himself.'

'Not on that account, certainly.'

'Nor yet on no other account, as long as he's true to his employers. Now you talk of country gentlemen.'

'I didn't talk of them,' said Gilmore.

'Well, – no, – you didn't; but they do, you know. What does a country gentleman know, and what does he do? What's the country the better of him? He 'unts, and he shoots, and he goes to bed with his skin full of wine, and then he gets up and he 'unts and he shoots again, and 'as his skin full once more. That's about all . . . I don't see the good of a country gentleman. Buying and selling; – that's what the world has to go by.' (ch. xxix)

Commerce on the grander scale is part of *The Prime Minister* where the honest politician, Arthur Fletcher, is opposed by the adventurer Lopez who is linked with Hartlepod of the San Juan Mining Company. Lopez, in even more dubious association with Sexty Parker, concocts a thoroughly disreputable scheme to promote a health tonic known as 'Bios' by means of billboards up and down the country. Lady Eustace is the ideal choice of a board member for the venture, but she is her usual cautious self when it comes to investing: 'How are you to get people to drink it?' she asks, and receives this very consumer-conscious answer:

By telling them that they ought to drink it. Advertise it. It has become a certainty now that if you will only advertise sufficiently you may make a fortune by selling anything. (ch. liv)

Another of Trollope's imaginative strokes in this novel is in making Lady Glencora an advocate for Lopez when he aims at securing the vacant parliamentary seat of Silverbridge, an act of patronage that staggers her husband and almost brings the Palliser name into disrepute.

These sporadic attacks on commercial practice were Trollope's reflection of growing public concern, not necessarily evidence of personal despair or cynicism. While it is true that money-grubbing looms larger in *The Prime Minister*, *Mr. Scarborough's Family* and *The Way We Live Now*, its treatment is not appreciably more satirical than in earlier novels such as *The Bertrams* or *The Three Clerks*; there is just more of it. It is not a difference in kind but scale. Trollope had always been concerned with the complexity of the moral life and the question his novels posed remained unchanged: how should a man be honest and true, in love, in work, in his comings-in and goings-out? The novels which followed the Barsetshire Chronicles are of more urban character and the tensions of a highly industrialised nation more pronounced. This is why at first sight they appear harsher in tone than the novels of the fifties and sixties, and certainly one reason why they have appeal today. We have a taste for the kind of corruption embodied in Augustus Melmotte or the egotism of a John Scarborough. Trollope's comment in his *Autobiography* elicits a nod of approval from a modern reader:

> Nevertheless a certain class of dishonesty, dishonesty magnificent in its proportions, and climbing into high places, has become at the same time so rampant and so splendid that there seems to be reason for fearing that men and women will be taught to feel that dishonesty, if it can become splendid will cease to be abominable. (ch. xx)

The Way We Live Now unquestionably answers to this conception of the scale of commercial villainy in late Victorian London and, lacking a figure of the moral stature of Mr Harding, it reads a grim warning of the times. Nevertheless it is essentially a continuation of Trollope's concerns with the ethics of public life and individual morality and is best considered in the company of other novels like *The Three Clerks*, in which politics, business and social life are interrelated.

Separated by sixteen years, these two novels are striking evidence of his sustained advocacy of *honestum* in public and private life. In the great watershed of the Reform era, the shape of Victorian business and social life was determined for the next fifty years, altering very little except in accelerated social movement between classes. The significant period for Trollope's development as a social commentator is clearly the last few years of the 1850s, and it is interesting to note that his analysis of British institutions, *The New Zealander*, was produced between 1855 and 1856. The financial whirlwinds of that decade marked the era of big business and high finance and a decisive break with easygoing small house commerce, resulting in joint stock companies handling massive sums in vast share issues. The Crimean War Loan of sixteen million pounds in Consolidated Annuities at three per cent was taken up in 1855 by the de Rothschilds. In the same year Strahan, Paul and Bates were found guilty of fraud and transported for fourteen years. Financial swindles grew in the night like fungus, causing havoc among ordinary investors. The case of John Sadleir, Member of Parliament for Sligo, which was exposed to a horrified public in 1856, is typical of the blight engendered by the unbridled economic race that inspired Trollope to move from cathedral close to market square.

This I take to be the significance of his writing *The Three Clerks* after the successful *Barchester Towers*. Dickens had shown the way with a brilliant analysis of the cash nexus in *Hard Times* (1854), which attacked the citadel of Victorian capitalism, and *Little Dorrit*, published as a monthly serial between 1855 and 1857. It is significant that Trollope submitted an article about it to the *Athenaeum*, and most unfortunate that no copy exists, but we can see its influence on *The Three Clerks*, published in November 1857. Just as the Circumlocution Office was linked with Merdle's empire, so Trollope connected the share-pusher and the politician through the Hon. Undecimus Scott, Alaric Tudor and Mr Manylodes. Rampant commercial dishonesty is the target, as in *Little Dorrit*. 'Buy them cheap and sell them dear; above all things get a good percentage'[28] is Merdle teaching that enmeshes speculators, defaulters and simple victims of the system. Prison looms through the mist of deception and money-grubbing in both novels. Of this period also is *The Bertrams* with its satirical view of the competitive spirit in modern life.

The case of John Sadleir and others like him, and perhaps the unforgettable Merdle, led ultimately to Melmotte, but in *The Three Clerks* there is merely the shadowy figure of the Hon. Undecimus Scott and some of the tub-thumping noticeable in *The New Zealander* arising from a lifelong dread of Caesarism in politics and commercial materialism:

> It has now become the doctrine of a large class of politicians that political honesty is unnecessary, slow, subversive of a man's interests, and incompatible with quick onward movement. Such a doctrine in politics is to be deplored; but alas! who can confine it to politics? It creeps with gradual, but still with sure and quick motion, into all the doings of our daily life. How shall the man who has taught himself that he may be false in the House of Commons, how shall he be true in the Treasury chambers? or if false there, how true on the Exchange? and if false there, how shall he longer have any truth within him? (ch. xxix)

The architect of political expediency was Disraeli, and before him Peel, who had broken faith over the Corn Laws:

> He has taught us as a great lesson, that a man who has before him a mighty object may dispense with those old-fashioned rules of truth to his neighbours and honesty to his own principles, which should guide us in ordinary life. (ch. xxix)

False advertising as the servant of big business led Trollope to write his disastrous *Brown, Jones and Robinson* during this period of burgeoning responsibility towards the institutions and conduct of society.[2']

The cautionary tale of Alaric Tudor's career in public service is a blueprint for all later studies of man poised between the claims of *honestum* and the snares of the world. The equation Trollope offers is between ideals of the past founded upon good moral conduct and a new barbarism bred by the machine. The devil tempts the averagely decent Christian in these terms:

> most men circumstanced as you are have no chance of doing anything good till they are forty or fifty, and then their energies are worn out. You have had tact enough to push yourself up early, and yet it seems you have not pluck enough to take the goods the gods provide you. (ch. ix)

Under the persuasions of Undy Scott and Mr Manylodes, Alaric Tudor writes a glowing official report on a tin mine in Cornwall for which he receives a number of cheap shares, and thus embarks on the downward path by which he is to become 'a robber with an education, a Bill Sykes [sic]' (ch. xxix). The course of Alaric's corruption is dotted with reminders of the contrast betwen gentlemanly practices and those of the modern man of business; the young man had not yet learned 'the full value of the latitude allowed by the genius of the present age to men who deal successfully in money' (ch. xvii). As yet the distinction between the standards of the country gentleman and the man of business is clear cut. Later, when the tentacles of the corporations and subsidiaries spread over the country, there is a blurring of roles. Aristocracy itself allies with trade; as old Maule sardonically remarks in *Phineas Redux*: 'We have earls dealing in butter and marquises sending their peaches to market' (ch. xxx). Strikingly evident in *The Way We Live Now* is the moral decadence of gentlemen who let themselves be tools of the swindler Melmotte. *The Three Clerks* fittingly links London, commercial centre of the world, and base of the capitalist economic structure, with the ambition and egotism which assail the hero:

> Oh, the city, the weary city, where men go daily to look for money, but find none; where every heart is eaten up by an accursed famishing after gold; where dark, gloomy banks come thick on each other, like the black, ugly apertures to the realms below in a mining district, each of them a separate little pit-mouth into hell. (ch. xxxvi)

The bubble of Alaric's great expectations bursts, and he is sent to prison for six months, after which Trollope despatches him to Australia to complete his moral rehabilitation by hard labour, while Undy Scott, as the embodiment of the vicious business world, is treated to excoriating censure over three pages towards the end of the story.

The attack on the commercial spirit in *The Way We Live Now* is based on a similar antagonism between feudal and modern values, but the story is allowed to speak for itself and Trollope engages his targets on many levels with brilliant tactical skill. Again, the circumstances in which the book came to be written have something in common with the anxious fifties. A period of stability and prosperity in the early sixties had given way to unrest: in 1865, the year of Palmerston's death, there had been the Birmingham bank collapse, followed by a rash of company failures, including the sensational crash of Overend, Gurney and Company which caused widespread panic. Cattle disease and crop failure, cholera, Fenian outrages, popular demands for Reform, and a seemingly endless commercial depression had reawakened anxious speculation about the Benthamite view of economic progress. Union actions and strikes threatened the domestic economy, while the growing strengths of women's movements pointed to stresses within the home. Spiritual bafflement, increasing in the early seventies, showed itself in religious controversy and more converts to Roman Catholicism; and all the time scientific materialism was undermining religious faith, redoubling the individual's sense of isolation and paving the way for the great cleavage of science and morality.

In this period of flux Trollope saw the prime threat to the English way of life as the alien and the entrepreneur, the man from nowhere, as Dickens had conceived him in *Our Mutual Friend*, welcomed to his throne by a people worshipping the golden calf and out of touch with their heritage. As he began writing the novel in May 1873, government was lacking inspiration, although Gladstone rallied his party in the course of the year. John Bright categorised the Conservative Party as the Great Sunflower Company, whose affairs were a mystery even to its governing board.[30] This coupling of political activity and corporate business strikes deeply at Trollope's fears and aversions. He had also become familiar with what Sadleir calls the 'sinister tendencies of the time', Jewish and foreign interests in the capital. 'The international financial adventurer had settled on London in his swarms',[31] and through his friend John Delane, of *The Times*, Trollope heard of a swindling Californian huckster who had ruined an English aristocrat with false speculation. Such evidence as this, rather than xenophobia or anti-semitism, accounts for the depiction of men like Lopez or Melmotte.

Augustus Melmotte dominates the novel (although not originally meant to do so), and ranks with the greatest of Trollope's creations, drawing to himself the threads of narrative and symbolising the illusory power for which all the characters will sell their souls. Unlike the giant of capitalism presented in Merdle, who is shadowy and insignificant, Melmotte is grossly, thunderously visible, with his bearish appearance and 'brazen' forehead, a black-browed brutish man with 'a wonderful look of power about his mouth and chin' (ch. iv). Dickens fixes Merdle with a few deft touches: hands clasping each wrist and watchful silence epitomising ruthless financial acumen; Trollope gives every detail of Melmotte's physique, his inner conflicts, his arduous climb to the summit of power and his eventual collapse. He towers over the novel, and by sheer effrontery exercises a spell over the reader. Even his end is not inglorious, as he glares defiantly at the faces around him in the House of Commons; and a certain Roman triumph is apparent in the way he administers the dose of prussic acid. Certainly amid the craven and time-serving figures who surround him Melmotte acquires heroic stature.

Trollope himself grew more fascinated as he built up the character, relishing with sardonic pleasure Melmotte's wizardry in promoting the South Central Pacific and Mexican Railway and buying his way into society. With each success Melmotte swells like the frog in the fable. His presence is overwhelming, his disguises protean, and like the alchemist he seems to have magic powers. 'What is there that money will not do?' (ch. xx). The answer to the question hanging over the lives of all the characters seems to rest in the hands of this conjuror, who practises the art of feeding men's baser instincts for his own purposes. Melmotte's technique in any company of men is skilfully developed. Trollope impresses us with a personality whose changes of mood and manner so conflict as to conceal his true identity. He is eloquent or taciturn; brazenly outspoken or tactfully silent; he bullies, wheedles, coaxes and commands as the occasion suits; he can rattle off financial details or simulate absent-mindedness; and when diplomacy seems of no further use he will disappear down the back staircase. There are even glimpses of the man in isolation which make us abruptly aware that the monster is indeed a human being; this is particularly telling, as one might expect, at the end of the novel, when he is trapped, frightened and ruined. A sombre majesty pervades this prince of Mammon as he remains in his seat in the House until the dinner adjournment, and then in the dining room flaunts his champagne before the hostile eyes of the waiters, 'happy in his own audacity', and yet 'the most utterly wretched man in London' (ch. lxxxiii). In his death scene following the painfully absurd spectacle of his attempt to interrupt the debate, there is a muted pathos which allows the great financier to vanish from the scene with grand contempt for the laws of men and God.

It is easy to see why George Eliot spoke with admiration of this novel, and her own Bulstrode, although he exists in an entirely different sphere, has something in common with Melmotte. Melmotte is the motive force of *The Way We Live Now*, the engine to which the ubiquitous drive for power, money and respectability is harnessed, like the mad elephants of *Hard Times*. The wheels turn and the machine grinds out its quota of petty gains and tasteless triumphs. His advance to the pinnacle of social and political life is the common ambition; his meteoric rise everyone's dream of happiness. Thus a fairy-tale glitter surrounds the great dinner for the Emperor of China, an exotic un- reality that is the perfect analogy for the meretricious nature of events and the fantasy of a happiness based on riches and social advantage. This fusion of reality and illusion is conveyed in various ways: the mansion in Grosvenor Square 'seemed to be endless' (ch. iv), and the many lights on the staircase made it into a 'fairyland'. One thinks of the lights of Jay Gatsby's home used by Scott Fitzgerald to illuminate, metaphorically as well as literally, decadence and illusion. There is also a strong element of fantasy in the description of the Beargarden Club, to which many of the young aristocrats dedicate their leisure. Its owner, Herr Vossner (another alien), is a 'jewel' (ch. iii), but being also a small-scale Melmotte, is a mountebank and conjuror turning night into day. The moral world of the club's habitués is upside-down, just as Melmotte's, in the words of the Grendalls, is 'topsy-turvy' (ch. xliv). The Beargarden Club is new, and aims at cut-price elegance, possess- ing no morning papers, billiards or dining that would attract 'old fogies'. It appeals to idlers and gamblers like Felix Carbury, Lord Nidderdale and Miles Grendall, an adept in the art of cheating. The amiable Vossner helps smooth over the financial embarrassments of his young friends, but in fact operates the club 'with the express view of combining parsimony with profligacy', cheating his members whole- sale (ch. iii). Towards the end of the novel he bolts, and the club is abruptly closed down.

The notion of a world of upside-down values conveyed by the Bear- garden is sustained in other elements of the novel. The link between club and Stock Exchange, noted by Sabine Nathan, aptly emphasises how the young men gamble without real money and sign I.O.U.s which are as airy and insubstantial as Melmotte's railway shares.[32] It is appropriate that Hamilton Fisker, the architect of the non-existent railroad, not only becomes an honorary member of the club but fleeces its members at cards. The scene in which Miles is exposed for cheating is an ironic echo of Melmotte's great fraud.

From Vossner's small-scale operation we pass to the financial web of the maestro, in which all society is enmeshed. 'He could make or mar any company by buying or selling stock, and could make money dear or cheap as he pleased' (ch. iv). His empire extends into high society, embracing an effete aristocracy, the press and government itself. The network of relationships is founded on cynical self-interest; the only criterion is success, and the means to success hypocrisy, lying and fraud. 'It seemed that there was but one virtue in the world, com- mercial enterprise, – and that Melmotte was its prophet' (ch. xliv) Trollope had always contrasted marriage for love and for wealth; here barter in human feelings is put in its most degrading terms. Melmotte is dedicated to selling his daughter, Marie, to a suitably rich and titled family: 'Money expects money' (ch. xxiii). Lord Nidderdale has already offered to 'make her Marchioness in the process of time for half a million down' (ch. iv). Lady Carbury tries to buy her literary reputation with flattery. Lord Alfred Grendall, the aristocratic kept man, is Melmotte's 'head valet' (ch. xxii), another example of the reversal of order postulated in the novel.

Opposed to this anarchy is Roger Carbury, the quaint and rather drab squire of Carbury Hall, who is in love with Henrietta, his cousin. Unfortunately Roger is no match for the vitality of Melmotte, and although 'a more manly man to the eye was never seen' (ch. vi), his tendency to deliver moral homilies whenever he appears robs him of sympathy. He is a lacklustre character, but as a reference point amid the rapaciousness of Melmotte, the vanities of Lady Carbury and the temptations of Paul Montagu, vital to the message of the novel. He is a familiar type in Trollope, doomed to play the long-suffering lover and English country gentleman. His home reflects the dependability and tradition that stand against the ugly materialism of the new rich. His ancestors have been in Suffolk since the Wars of the Roses, and Carbury Manor House is a Tudor building with strong mullioned windows. Other houses round about were superior in material comfort, 'but to none of them belonged that thoroughly established look of old county position which belonged to Carbury' (ch. xiv). Neither rich nor ostentatious, the Carburys 'never had anything but land' (ch. vi), and Roger himself, the last guardian of the family honour, feels at odds with the modern world: 'People live now in a way that I don't comprehend' (ch. xlvi). He is the one fixed point in a vacillating world where most people have adopted expediency as their rule of life. Booker condones puffery because 'circumstanced as he was he could not oppose himself altogether to the usages of the time' (ch. i). People let things drift, as Paul does, when he omits to tell Mrs Hurtle that he does not want to marry her, and acquiesces in unsavoury actions surrounding the railway venture; Lady Carbury has so salved her conscience that 'lying had become her nature' (ch. xxx); Lord Alfred Grendall has ceased to function as a moral being and become Melmotte's creature. Such drifting and evasion of moral responsibility harbour the real danger to society, expressed in Roger's indictment of Melmottism:

> his [Melmotte's] position is a sign of the degeneracy of the age. What are we coming to when such as he is an honoured guest at our tables? . . . You can keep your house free from him, and so can I mine. But we set no example to the nation at large. They who do set the example go to his feasts, and of course he is seen at theirs

in return. And yet these leaders of the fashion know, – at any rate they believe, – that he is what he is because he has been a swindler greater than other swindlers. What follows as a natural conse-quence? Men reconcile themselves to swindling. Though they them-selves mean to be honest, dishonesty of itself is no longer odious to them. Then there comes the jealousy that others should be growing rich with the approval of all the world, – and the natural aptitude to do what all the world approves. It seems to me that the existence of a Melmotte is not compatible with a wholesome state of things in general. (ch. lv).

Roger's own code is in marked contrast with the moral laxity and frivolousness of others in the story. The Longestaffes, for example, are a county family, but insist on maintaining a life-style that demands footmen with powdered hair and makes their allegiance to Melmottism a financial necessity. The victim of moral blindness, Dolly is shown objecting not so much to Miles Grendall's cheating as to Felix Car-bury's bringing it to his notice. On the other hand, he shows his at-tachment to decent values by wishing to preserve the family seat: 'A fellow oughtn't to let his family property to go to pieces' (ch. xxviii). But Dolly is too weak to fight; he needs Squercum, the wily attorney, to wage the battle on his behalf.

The Longestaffes are more important to the novel's strategy than is generally recognised. Through Lady Pomona and her husband, Trollope gives yet another dimension to the central question of true gentility and the good life. They are the wrong type of county family, and although they are not *nouveaux riches*, they have thrown in their hand with the Melmotte tribe. Snobbery and keeping up appearances are apparent in everything they do. Caversham, where they entertain vulgarly, is a miniature of Melmotte's Grosvenor Square mansion and contrasts with the quiet order of Roger Carbury's house. Adolphus Longestaffe Senior covets a place on Melmotte's railway board. But the strongest comment on their misplaced values arises from Georgiana, their daughter, whose desire is to look well in society. It is a blow to her pride when she must in desperation consider marrying Brehgert, Melmotte's Jewish partner, and utterly ignorant of his spiritual worth she loses her opportunity. Brehgert's letters to her are models of dignity and tact which reinforce our sense of her bad taste and folly. At all events Georgiana loses him, and scolds her mother for causing her to end the relationship. Her mother observes 'You couldn't have loved him, Georgiana' (ch. xcv), and the girl's reply underlines the fail-ure of values which the novel has sought to expose. The evolving society, Trollope suggests, faces the extinction of virtue, trust and the happiness of love. Georgiana's desolate cry symbolises the void she faces, and is a masterstroke of compression: 'Loved him! who thinks about love nowadays?' (ch. xcv). Trollope has no greater indictment of the times than to express this perversion of the highest ideal of his fiction.

CATHEDRALS AND PALACES

'Trollope did not write for posterity', said Henry James, 'he wrote for the day, the moment; but these are just the writers whom posterity is apt to put into its pocket.'[33] And so it has proved. Yet even today, as the centenary of his death approaches, there is little agreement about his character and achievement. James' remark underlines the problem Trollope has posed his readers. No English writer trusted inspiration less or scoffed at the word genius more than Anthony Trollope, and it has been my purpose to draw the artist from hiding and show his imaginative range and versatility. This is to confront the paradox: for the Trollopian, facing the great territory of fiction, must resort to summaries and conclusions which Trollope with all his bulk and variety resists. Not only is there a problem of an *oeuvre* so vast, but within it such breadth of viewpoint, moral relativism, fluidity and variation, that all is opposed to neat formulation. Once again the Houdini of fiction threatens to escape the ropes and locks of critical definition.

Yet after long acquaintance with Trollope the critic is led to some tentative conclusions, to correct some lingering false impressions of the man and his motives, and to advance a case for a complete edition of the novels. In making a final assessment I am concerned with three factors. In the first place, apart from Trollope's significance as chronicler, he reveals great wisdom and understanding of the individual psyche. Secondly, it is his unique gift among English novelists to have made out of the orderly, unadventurous circle of life, not only eminently entertaining stories, but a celebration of existence. Without recourse to much in the way of effect or incident he exalts the normal processes of living. Thirdly, his style frequently has grace and eloquence, and even where his narrative technique seems cumbersome it is splendidly attuned to his subject and intention.

Trollope was an ardent observer who trained himself to become a popular writer, with such success that he was rivalled in public affection only by Dickens. His genius lay in the fidelity with which he shaped and moulded his material, not paring or cutting to any great extent, but massing and presenting, resisting any limitations upon his subject matter, the course of his narrative or the imagined lives of his characters. He went with the pull of life instinctively and with the impulses of his own nature. He listened to voices, and the result was an unretouched fiction that not only tells us a great deal about

I

the Victorian way of life, but, far more importantly, has the feel of life in all periods, complex, irregular and illimitable. Frank O'Connor has rightly expressed this genius as 'humility and passivity in the face of life'.[34] Such a gift, said O'Connor, gave Trollope his immense range in exploring character fully, roundly and without superimposed moral judgement.

Henry James praised Trollope's natural aptitude. 'He had, as it were, a good ear. If he was a knowing psychologist he was so by grace; he was just and true without apparatus and without effort.'[35] This is, of course, not altogether unmitigated approval from an artist whose own mode was so utterly dissimilar. Yet it is interesting that a novelist who must surely have been the violator of nearly every Jamesian canon should have so won the affection of the master-stylist himself. For it seems that despite his lack of intellectual reach, his clumsiness, his failures of tact and discrimination Trollope had a precious commodity: the feeling for life, which he illuminated not with a sudden, riveting incandescence, but with the soft, steady play of light over the whole landscape of experience. This is why it is unnecessary to cavil at his want of ideas, or the longwindedness and tedious passages, for invariably his instinct carries him to the mark. If the pith and marrow sometimes eluded him, he had enough of the texture and sinews to matter, for being true to the surfaces of life he did not fail to penetrate the subtler vagaries of human nature. It is wiser to see him as Elizabeth Bowen did: not greatly daring or profound, but not superficial either. More often than happy marriage in Trollope there is Meredithian strife or tyranny. In the city and the House of Commons he finds avarice and ignoble ambition. Young love is too often tarnished by vanity and egotism. Such strains as these are Trollope's third dimension, as sub-texts to romantic stories for Mudie subscribers. Certainly there is more to Trollope's world than rhapsodies of Barsetshire, although the dominant cast of his mind is positive, optimistic and in tune with the progressive side of Victorianism.[36] George Eliot recognised the essentially buoyant nature of the fiction in a memorable letter to the novelist in 1863:

> But there is something else I care yet more about, which has impressed me very happily in all those writings of yours that I know – it is that people are breathing good bracing air in reading them – it is that they are filled with belief in goodness without the slightest tinge of maudlin. They are like pleasant public gardens, where people go for amusement and, whether they think of it or not, get health as well.[37]

Hawthorne's praise is better known, but Eliot's captures the refreshing spirit, the image of a park suggesting exactly the harmony o unsentimental wholesomeness and vigorous entertainment Trollope affords.

Trollope is a writer who needs our time and patience. His style like his output, is generous, and his qualities are not to be savoured by a whirlwind tour, as, indeed, they are not to be fixed critically in a series of snapshot judgements. The long, discursive mode he often employs is an essential part of his total narrative strategy. Usually it is a love problem, a question of choice. Should Harry Clavering return to Julia Ongar or be true to Florence Burton? Shall Mary Lowther accept Harry Gilmore or Walter Marrable of the black eyes and blacker moustache? Can Lucy Robarts oppose Lady Lufton and cleave to her heart's desire? Trollope has a crossword puzzle mind and invents thousands of such problems as the staple of his plots. Is Finn to accept Lord Brentford's patronage? Can Alaric Tudor touch pitch and not be defiled? Should the Wortles protect their school's reputation as a gentlemen's crammer, or defend the good name of their teacher, Mr Peacocke? Can you forgive her? Was he right? Such questions are constantly posed, seldom answered. For in Trollope's world there is respect for the complex mechanism governing decision; that is why he writes absorbing political novels, as Mr Roy Hattersley reminds us;[38] that is why he distrusts absolutes and revels in diversity. Each case has its own peculiar circumstances, its own confounding complications, its quota of mixed or mistaken motives. Therefore Trollope is hard to pin down, almost totally resistant to neat formulation and summary, and, as I have so often complained, to brief illustration.

His plain broadcloth style reinforces the bagginess of his plotting, loose, rambling, verbose. It is a wasteful rhetoric, though not padding to fill up a quota of pages, as has sometimes been accusingly said. Its essential is diffuseness, but a cumulative manner gives it point. He circles round the topic, adding detail upon detail; qualifications pile up one against the other; reflections and asides obtrude themselves on our notice; changes of direction throw up new possibilities; until at last the effect is achieved, not by economical means and certainly not by image, but by fullness of language. Trollope's prose totally lacks the precision and immediacy of metaphor and depends instead on synonym, circumlocution and familiar idiom. With Trollope *le mot juste* is a cliché. Syntactically it is a style of meandering sentences, of lengthy compounding and ponderous subordination, yet sufficiently clear to be read without effort. Indeed, the remarkable thing is that such hasty writing, so shorn of image, is seldom dull, though its unspectacular ease can allow its skilfully placed ironies, its odd felicities of epithet, to be missed.

Appropriately it is the Christian hero, Mr. Harding, who provides a concluding example of the virtues of Trollopian fiction. Trollope's stroll in the purlieus of Salisbury Cathedral in the summer of 1851 was doubly blessed, for not only did it herald the epic of Barset which made his name, but in Harding provided Trollope with a moral centre for all his work. Love, charity and honesty in the individual, the family and larger social contracts, are all to be found in the Reverend Septimus Harding, one time Warden of Hiram's Hospital, Rector of St Cuthbert's, who is, in the beautifully elegiac *Last Chronicle*, living out his remaining years in the cathedral precinct. Harding appears in all the Barsetshire tales, quietly exemplifying the Christian precepts against which society's goals are constantly measured. He represents a metaphor for Trollope resonant in all he writes. The good man exists in a predatory society, caught up in a situation he cannot comprehend, resolve or withstand, yet he persists in forbearance and humility; he makes an assertion about human dignity, conscientious scruple and love. Harding has that saintly innocence that tells the eternal epic of the opposing energies of good and evil; in this respect I think he can be counted among the holy fools of literature, in Shakespeare, or in Melville and Dostoevski. His nature is drawn from the same fount, testifying to realities beyond the illusions and vanities of most men, that simplicity and love will ultimately confound egotism, and leave evil silent and dismayed.

In the plot of *The Warden* Trollope found the perfect vehicle for the Harding virtues. Here is a man more sinned against than sinning, thrust into the power struggles of ambitious men, innocently enjoying luxuries of which he is persuaded to become ashamed, exploited by his son-in-law, exposed to publicity, and forced after years of quiet and inaction to take initiatives. Painfully aware of his shyness and love of ease – he longs to escape from the torments that now trouble his old age – he none the less follows the line of duty as he sees it. The pivotal moment of *The Warden* is his courageous decision to go to London to interview Sir Abraham Haphazard and disclaim all part in the legal proceedings that will clear him. Typically, he is smitten by conscience, seeing his journey as a flight from his dread son-in-law, and he does indeed take sanctuary in Westminster Abbey, where he is fairly certain Dr Grantly will not venture to look for him. Telling his daughter of his plan, he confesses: 'He'll say that I want moral courage and strength of character, and power of endurance, and it's all true; but I'm sure I ought not to remain here, if I have nothing better to put forward than a quibble: so Nelly, we shall have to leave this pretty place' (ch. xiii).

What is being expressed in this maze of contradictory impulses is the grandeur of principle and integrity against the pettiness of worldly wisdom. Noble renunciation and self-sacrifice are more important in the old warden's pilgrimage than his natural fears. Harding's example thus isolates the struggle betwen falsehood, expediency and egotism, and virtue, honesty and the claims of conscience. Henceforth Trollope's fiction never moves from this perennial confrontation, rendered more poignant by the good man's share of the general imperfection. In the case of Crawley there is self-pity and pride; in Palliser love of rank and ambition; in Harding there is the obstinacy of age, stubbornness alongside meekness. The old man is intent on having his own way; he flourishes his obtuseness before his aggravated son-in-law with even a gleam of mischief in his eye. Physically insignificant, he is cubits higher morally than Dr Grantly, and a similar irony resides in his true gentility and breeding alongside his socially superior son-in-law. He is, as Walpole said, Trollope's grandest gentleman.[39]

Where Grantly tries to buy affection, Harding gives love. The old man cannot scheme, but Slope and his kind equivocate and alter course. Harding will always yield where Grantly will fight, and yet it is Grantly who recognises the greatness in his father-in-law, and it is his valediction that gives such force to the beautifully written death scene of *The Last Chronicle*, and illustrates that dimension in time so indispensable in Trollope. The chapter 'Barsetshire Cloisters' (lxxxi) opens with the old man's granddaughter, Posy, sitting on his bed urging him to play with her. Too weak even for cat's-cradle he awaits Dr Filgrave. The doctor's solemn, portentous manner with the archdeacon is tinged with comedy:

'I should say that a day or two would see the end of it. Indeed I will not undertake that twenty-four hours may not see the close of his earthly troubles. He has no suffering, no pain, no disturbing cause. Nature simply retires to rest.' Dr. Filgrave, as he said this, made a slow falling motion with his hands, which alone on various occasions had been thought to be worth all the money paid for his attendance.

Then comes the archdeacon's tribute, for once quietly spoken:

'I seem to have known him all my life,' said the archdeacon. 'I have known him ever since I left college; and I have known him as one man seldom knows another. There is nothing that he has done, – as I believe, nothing that he has thought, – with which I have not been cognisant. I feel sure that he never had an impure fancy in his mind, or a faulty wish in his heart. His tenderness has surpassed the tenderness of woman; and yet, when an occasion came for showing it, he had all the spirit of a hero. I shall never forget his resignation of the hospital, and all that I did and said to make him keep it.'

'But he was right?'

'As Septimus Harding he was, I think, right; but it would have been wrong in any other man. And he was right, too, about the deanery.' For promotion had once come in Mr. Harding's way, and he, too, might have been dean of Barchester. 'The fact is, he never was wrong. He couldn't go wrong. He lacked guile, and he feared God, – and a man who does both will never go far astray. I don't think he ever coveted aught in his life, – except a new case for his violoncello and somebody to listen to him when he played it.' Then the archdeacon got up, and walked about the room in his enthusiasm; and, perhaps as he walked some thoughts as to the sterner ambition of his own life passed through his mind. What things had he coveted? Had he lacked guile? He told himself that he had feared God, but he was not sure that he was telling himself true even in that.

This sums up so much of what is great about Trollope in thought and execution: the scene richly patterned in incident, the texture of physical expression, movement and gesture, the subtleties of reflection, and the haunting reintroduction of motifs in the narration, of which only a glimpse can be had by short quotation. Above all there is that perfect modulation of narrative voice and accurate dialogue which is Trollopian to the core. It shows Trollope as he is, a master builder in prose, laying his bricks, course upon course, standing back, pointing here and there (seldom brushing the mortar off, so much as adding more), building higher until the whole massive structure, so quickly executed, stands wonderfully firm, finished and pleasant to the eye. He has left us cathedrals and palaces of fiction.

Appendix I

A Summary of Events in the Life of Anthony Trollope

24 April 1815	Born in Bloomsbury, London.
1822–34	Educated at Harrow; Winchester.
1834	Joined General Post Office, St Martin's le Grand, London.
1841	Appointed Deputy Postal Surveyor, Banagher, Ireland.
1843	*The Macdermots of Ballycloran* begun.
1844	Married Rose Heseltine.
1846	Birth of son, Henry Merivale.
1847	Birth of second son, Frederick James Anthony.
1852	*The Warden* begun.
1858	First postal mission : Egypt.
1859	Settled at Waltham Cross, Hertfordshire.
	Framley Parsonage commissioned for *Cornhill Magazine*.
1861	Elected to Garrick Club.
	First postal mission to United States (second, 1868).
1863	Death of his mother, Frances Trollope.
1864	First Palliser novel, *Can You Forgive Her?* begun.
1866	*Last Chronicle of Barset* begun.
1867	Resigned from Post Office.
	Edited *St. Paul's Magazine* (until 1870).
1868	Unsuccessfully stood for Parliament.
1871	First visit to Australia (second, 1875).
1872	Settled at Montagu Square, London.
1876	Completed his *Autobiography.*
	Last Palliser novel, *The Duke's Children* begun.
1880	Settled at Harting Grange, Hampshire.
1882	*The Landleaguers* begun.
6 December 1882	Died in London.

Appendix II
Bibliography of Anthony Trollope

(i) MAJOR WORKS

The Macdermots of Ballycloran, 3 vols, London: T. C. Newby, 1847 [abridged in one volume, Chapman & Hall's 'New Edition', 1861].

The Kellys and the O'Kellys: or Landlords and Tenants, 3 vols, London: Henry Colburn, 1848.

La Vendée: An Historical Romance, 3 vols, London: Colburn, 1850.

The Warden, 1 vol, London: Longman, 1855.

Barchester Towers, 3 vols, London: Longman, 1857.

The Three Clerks: A Novel, 3 vols, London: Bentley, 1858. [*The Three Clerks* was not reprinted in its original three-volume form, but abridged in one volume, 1859 and 1860.]

Doctor Thorne: A Novel, 3 vols, London: Chapman & Hall, 1858.

The Bertrams: A Novel, 3 vols, London: Chapman & Hall, 1859.

The West Indies and the Spanish Main, 1 vol., London: Chapman & Hall, 1859.

Castle Richmond: A Novel, 3 vols, London: Chapman & Hall, 1860.

Framley Parsonage [serialised, *Cornhill Magazine*, Jan 1860–Apr 1861] 3 vols, London: Smith, Elder, 1861.

Tales of All Countries, 1 vol, London: Chapman & Hall, 1861.

Orley Farm [monthly numbers, Mar 1861–Oct 1862] 2 vols, London: Chapman & Hall, 1862.

North America, 2 vols, London: Chapman & Hall, 1862.

Tales of All Countries: Second Series, 1 vol., London: Chapman & Hall, 1863.

Rachel Ray: A Novel, 2 vols, London: Chapman & Hall, 1863.

The Small House at Allington [serialised, *Cornhill Magazine*, Sep 1862–Apr 1864] 2 vols, London: Smith, Elder, 1864.

Can You Forgive Her? [monthly numbers, Jan 1864–Aug 1865] London: Chapman & Hall, vol. I, 1864, vol. II, 1865.

Miss Mackenzie, 2 vols, London: Chapman & Hall, 1865.

Hunting Sketches [published in *Pall Mall Gazette*, Feb–Mar 1865] 1 vol., London: Chapman & Hall, 1865.

The Belton Estate [serialised, *Fortnightly Review*, May 1865–Jan 1866] 3 vols, London: Chapman & Hall, 1865.

Travelling Sketches [published in *Pall Mall Gazette*, Aug–Sep 1865] 1 vol., London: Chapman & Hall, 1866.

Clergymen of the Church of England [published in *Pall Mall Gazette*, Nov 1865–Jan 1866] 1 vol., London: Chapman & Hall, 1866.

Nina Balatka, The Story of a Maiden of Prague [serialised, *Blackwood's Magazine*, July 1866–Jan 1867] 2 vols, Edinburgh & London: Blackwood, 1867.

The Last Chronicle of Barset [weekly numbers, Dec 1866–July 1867] 2 vols, London: Smith, Elder, 1867.

The Claverings [serialised, *Cornhill Magazine*, Feb 1866–May 1867] 2 vols London: Smith, Elder, 1867.

Lotta Schmidt: and Other Stories, 1 vol., London: Strahan, 1867.

Linda Tressel [serialised, *Blackwood's Magazine*, Oct 1867–May 1868] 2 vols, Edinburgh & London: Blackwood, 1868.

Phineas Finn: The Irish Member [serialised, *St. Paul's Magazine*, Oct 1867–May 1869] 2 vols, London: Virtue, 1869.

He Knew He Was Right [weekly numbers, Oct 1868–May 1869] 2 vols, London: Strahan, 1869.

Did He Steal It? A Comedy in three acts [dramatisation of *The Last Chronicle of Barset*] London: Virtue, 1869; reissued with an introduction by Robert H. Taylor. Princeton: Princeton Univ. Press, 1952.

The Vicar of Bullhampton [monthly numbers, July 1869–May 1870] 1 vol., London: Bradbury, Evans, 1870.

An Editor's Tales [Stories published during 1868–70 in *St. Paul's Magazine*] 1 vol., London: Strahan, 1870.

The Struggles of Brown, Jones and Robinson: by One of the Firm [serialised, *Cornhill Magazine*, Aug 1861–Mar 1862] 1 vol., London: Smith, Elder, 1870.

The Commentaries of Caesar, 1 vol., Edinburgh & London: Blackwood, 1870.

Sir Harry Hotspur of Humblethwaite [serialised, *Macmillan's Magazine*, May–Dec 1870] 1 vol., London: Hurst & Blackett, 1870.

Ralph the Heir [monthly numbers and simultaneously as Supplement to *St. Paul's Magazine*, Jan 1870–July 1871] 3 vols, London: Strahan, 1871.

The Golden Lion of Granpère [serialised, *Good Words*, Jan–Aug 1872] 1 vol., London: Tinsley, 1872.

The Eustace Diamonds [serialised, *Fortnightly Review*, July 1871–Feb 1873] 3 vols, London: Chapman & Hall, 1873.

Australia and New Zealand, 2 vols, London: Chapman & Hall, 1873.

Phineas Redux [serialised, *Graphic*, July 1873–Jan 1874] 2 vols, London: Chapman & Hall, 1874.

Lady Anna [serialised, *Fortnightly Review*, Apr 1873–Apr 1874] 2 vols, London: Chapman & Hall, 1874.

Harry Heathcote of Gangoil: A Tale of Australian Bush Life [Christmas number of the *Graphic*, 25 Dec 1873] 1 vol., London: Sampson, Low, 1874.

The Way We Live Now [monthly numbers, Feb 1874–Sep 1875] 2 vols, London: Chapman & Hall, 1875.

The Prime Minister [monthly numbers, Nov 1875–June 1876] 4 vols, London: Chapman & Hall, 1876.

The American Senator [serialised, *Temple Bar*, May 1876–July 1877] 3 vols, London: Chapman & Hall, 1877.

South Africa, 2 vols, London: Chapman & Hall, 1878.

Is He Popenjoy?: *A Novel* [serialised, *All the Year Round*, Oct 1877–July 1878] 3 vols, London: Chapman & Hall, 1878.

How the "Mastiffs" Went to Iceland, 1 vol., London: Virtue, 1878.

An Eye for an Eye [serialised, *Whitehall Review*, Aug 1878–Feb 1879] 2 vols, London: Chapman & Hall, 1879.

Thackeray, 1 vol., London: Macmillan, 1879.

John Caldigate [serialised, *Blackwood's Magazine*, Apr 1878–June 1879] 3 vols, London: Chapman & Hall, 1879.

Cousin Henry: A Novel [serialised simultaneously, *Manchester Weekly Times* and *North British Weekly Mail*, Mar–May 1879] 2 vols, London: Chapman & Hall, 1879.

The Duke's Children: A Novel [serialised, *All the Year Round*, Oct 1879–July 1880] 3 vols, London: Chapman & Hall, 1880.

The Life of Cicero, 2 vols, London: Chapman & Hall, 1880.

Doctor Wortle's School: A Novel [serialised, *Blackwood's Magazine*, May–Dec 1880] 2 vols, London: Chapman & Hall, 1881.

Ayala's Angel, 3 vols, London: Chapman & Hall, 1881.

Why Frau Frohmann Raised Her Prices: And Other Stories, 1 vol., London: Isbister, 1882.

Lord Palmerston, 1 vol., London: Isbister, 1882.

The Fixed Period [serialised, *Blackwood's Magazine*, Oct 1881–Mar 1882] 2 vols, Edinburgh & London: Blackwood, 1882.

Marion Fay: A Novel [serialised, *Graphic*, Dec 1881–June 1882] 3 vols, London: Chapman & Hall, 1882.

Kept in the Dark: A Novel [serialised, *Good Words*, May–Dec 1882] 2 vols, London: Chatto & Windus, 1882.

Mr. Scarborough's Family [serialised, *All the Year Round*, May 1882–June 1883] 3 vols, London: Chatto & Windus, 1883.

An Autobiography, 2 vols, Edinburgh & London: Blackwood, 1883.

The Landleaguers [unfinished, but serialised, *Life: a Weekly Journal of Society, Literature, the Fine Arts and Finance*, Nov 1882–Oct 1883] 3 vols, London: Chatto & Windus, 1883.

An Old Man's Love, 2 vols, Edinburgh & London: Blackwood, 1883.

The Letters of Anthony Trollope, ed. Bradford A. Booth, London: O.U.P., 1951.

The New Zealander, intro. by N. John Hall, London: O.U.P., 1972.

(ii) MINOR WRITINGS AND CONTRIBUTIONS TO PERIODICALS

'W. M. Thackeray', *Cornhill Magazine*, IX (Feb 1864).

'The Gentle Euphemia, or Love Shall Still be Lord of All', *Fortnightly Review*, XIX (May 1866).

'Katchen's Caprices', *Harper's Weekly*, 22 Dec 1866–12 Jan 1867 (printed anon.).

'An Essay on Carlylism', *St. Paul's Magazine*, I (Dec 1867).

British Sports and Pastimes [reprinted from *St. Paul's Magazine*] ed. Anthony Trollope, London : Virtue, 1868.

'Mr. Freeman on the Morality of Hunting', *Fortnightly Review*, VI (1 Dec 1869).

'Charles Dickens', *St. Paul's Magazine*, VI (July 1870).

'Christmas Day at Kirkby Cottage', *Routledge's Christmas Annual*, 1870.

'Whist at Our Club', *Blackwood's Magazine*, CXXI (May 1877).

'Catherine Carmichael, or Three Years Running', *Masonic Magazine*, Christmas number, 1878.

'In the Hunting Field', *Good Words*, 1879.

'A Walk in a Wood', *Good Words*, 1879.

'The genius of Nathaniel Hawthorne', *North American Review*, CXXXII (Sep 1879).

'Henry Wadsworth Longfellow', *North American Review*, CXXXII (Apr 1881).

'The Two Heroines of Plumplington', *Good Cheer*, Christmas number of *Good Words*, 1882.

'Not if I Know It', *Life*, Christmas number, 1882.

The Noble Jilt. A Comedy, edited with a preface by Michael Sadleir, 1 vol., London : Constable, 1923.

London Tradesmen, with a foreword by Michael Sadleir, 1 vol., London : Elkin Mathews & Marrot, 1927.

Four Lectures, ed. Morris L. Parrish, London : Constable, 1938.

The Tireless Traveller, ed. Bradford Booth [twenty letters published in the *Liverpool Mercury*, July–Nov 1875] Berkeley and Los Angeles : University of California Press, 1941.

'Trollope's Letters to the *Examiner*', ed. Helen Garlinghouse King, *Princeton University Library Chronicle*, XXVI, 2 (winter 1965).

'Never, Never – Never, Never', *Sheets for the Cradle* 1, 3, 5, Boston, Mass : Susan Hale, 6–11 Dec 1875; privately printed for Lance O. Tingay and Michael J. Tingay, London : Valley Press, 1971.

Appendix III

Selected Bibliography of Studies on Anthony Trollope

(i) BIBLIOGRAPHIES, GUIDES AND MISCELLANIES

Dunn, Esther Cloudman, and Dodd, Marion E., (ed), *The Trollope Reader*, London: O.U.P., 1947.

Gerould, Winifred G., and James T., *A Guide to Trollope*, London: O.U.P. 1948.

Hardwick, Michael, *The Osprey Guide to Trollope*, London: Osprey publishing, 1974.

Helling, Rafael, *A Century of Trollope Criticism* [1956], Port Washington, N.Y.: Kennikat Press, 1967.

Hennedy, Hugh L., 'Trollope Studies, 1963–1973', *British Studies Monitor* VI, 1 (fall 1975) Brunswick, Maine: Bowdoin College.

Irwin, Mary Leslie, *Anthony Trollope: A Bibliography*, New York: H. W. Wilson, 1926.

Lavington, Margaret, in Escott, T. H. S., *Anthony Trollope, His Work, Associates and Literary Originals*, 1913.

Sadleir, Michael, 'Anthony Trollope, 1815–82', *Excursions in Victorian Bibliography*, London: Chaundy & Cox, 1922.

—— *Trollope: A Bibliography*, London: Constable, 1928; supplemented 1934.

—— *Nineteenth Century Fiction, A Bibliographical Record*, 2 vols, London: Constable, 1951.

Smalley, Donald, 'Anthony Trollope', *Victorian Fiction: A Guide to Research*, ed. Lionel Stevenson, Cambridge, Mass.: Harvard University Press, 1964.

—— *Trollope, the Critical Heritage*, London: Routledge & Kegan Paul, 1969.

Tingay, Lance O. (ed.), *The Bedside Barsetshire: A Trollope Anthology*, New York: Scribner's, 1949.

(ii) BIOGRAPHICAL REFERENCES AND REMINISCENCES

William Allingham, A Diary, ed. H. Allingham, and D. Radford, London: Macmillan, 1907.

Ashley, R. P., *Wilkie Collins*, London: Arthur Barker, 1952.

Austin, Alfred, 'Last Reminiscences of Anthony Trollope', *Temple Bar*, LXX (Jan 1884).

Bianconi, M. O'C, and Watson, S. J., *Bianconi, King of the Irish Roads*, Dublin: Allen Figgis, 1962.

Boyd, A. K. H., *Twenty-Five Years of St. Andrews*, 2 vols, London: Longman, 1892.

Bryce, James (Viscount), *Studies in Contemporary Biography*, London: Macmillan, 1903.

Mark Twain in Eruption, ed. Bernard de Voto, New York: Harper, 1941.

Charles Lever, His Life in His Letters, ed. E. Downey, 2 vols, Edinburgh & London: Blackwood, 1906.

Fitzgerald, Percy, *The Garrick Club*, London: Elliot Stock, 1904.

Fitzpatrick, W., *The Life of Charles Lever*, London: Ward Locke, 1884.

Friswell, J. Hain, *Modern Men of Letters Honestly Criticised*, London: Hodder & Stoughton, 1870.

Friswell, Laura Hain, *In the Sixties and Seventies, Impressions of Literary People and Others*, London: Hutchinson, 1905.

Frith, W. P., *My Autobiography and Reminiscences*, 2 vols, London: Bentley, 1887.

Gower, Sir George Leveson, *Years of Content, 1858-1886*, London: Murray, 1940.

Sir William Gregory, An Autobiography, ed. Lady Gregory, London: Murray, 1894.

Haggard, Sir Henry Rider, *The Days of My Life, an Autobiography*, 2 vols, London: Longman, 1926.

A Mid-Victorian Pepys, The Letters and Memoirs of Sir William Hardman, ed. S. M. Ellis, London: Cecil Palmer, 1923.

Hawthorne, Julian, *Confessions and Criticisms*, Boston: Ticknor, 1887.

——*Shapes That Pass, Memories of Old Days*, London: Murray, 1928.

Heywood, J. C., *How They Strike Me, These Authors*, Philadelphia: Lippincott, 1877.

Huxley, Leonard, *The House of Smith, Elder*, London: William Clowes, 1923.

Joline, Adrian H., *Meditations of an Autograph Collector*, New York: Harper, 1902.

Layard, G. S., *A Great "Punch" Editor, Being the Life, Letters and Diaries of Shirley Brooks*, London: Pitman, 1907.

Locker-Lampson, Frederick, *My Confidences, An Autobiographical Sketch Addressed to my Descendants*, ed. Augustine Birrell, London: Smith, Elder, 1896.

McCarthy, Justin, *Reminiscences*, 2 vols, London: Chatto & Windus, 1899.

Newton, A. E., *The Amenities of Book Collecting and Kindred Affections*, London: John Lane, 1920.

Author Unknown, *The Notebooks of a Spinster Lady, 1878-1903*, London: Cassell, 1919.

Payn, James, *Some Literary Recollections*, London: Smith, Elder, 1884.

Pollock, Sir William Frederick, *Personal Remembrances of Sir Frederick Pollock*, 2 vols, London: Macmillan, 1887.

Pollock, Walter Herries, 'Anthony Trollope', *Harper's New Monthly Magazine*, LXVI (May 1883).

Porter, Mrs. G., *Annals of a Publishing House, John Blackwood (William Blackwood and His Sons, Their Magazine and Their Friends, III)* Edinburgh: Blackwood, 1898.

The Letters of Sir Walter Raleigh (1879-1922), ed. Lady Raleigh, 2 vols, London: Methuen, 1926.

Letters of Lady Anne Thackeray Ritchie, ed. Hester Ritchie, London: Murray, 1924.

The Amberley Papers, The Letters and Diaries of Lord and Lady Amberley, ed. Russell, B. and P., 2 vols, London: 1937.

Sala, G. A., *Things I Have Seen and People I Have Known*, 2 vols, London: Cassell, 1894.

Scudder, H. S., *James Russell Lowell, A Biography*, 2 vols, London: Macmillan, 1901.

Sherrard, O. A., *Two Victorian Girls, with Extracts from the Hall Diaries*, ed. A. R. Mills, London: Muller, 1966.

Sichel, Walter, *The Sands of Time, Recollections and Reflections*, London: Hutchinson, 1923.

Smyth, Eleanor C., *Sir Rowland Hill, The Story of a Great Reform, Told by His Daughter*, London: T. Fisher Unwin, 1907.

The Correspondence of Henry Taylor, ed. Edward Dowden, London: Longman, 1888.

Tinsley, William, *Random Reflections of an Old Publisher*, 2 vols, London: Simpkin, Marshall, 1900.

Trollope, F. E., *A Memoir of Frances Trollope*, London: Bentley, 1895.

Trollope, M. N., *A Memoir of the Family of Trollope*, London: Spottiswoode, 1897.

Trollope, Muriel, 'What I Was Told', *Trollopian*, II (Mar 1948).

Trollope, Thomas Adolphus, *What I Remember*, 2 vols, London: Bentley, 1887.

——*The Further Reminiscences of Thomas Adolphus Trollope*, 1 vol., London: Bentley, 1889.

Ward, Mrs. E. M., *Memories of Ninety Years*, London: Hutchinson, 1924.

Ward, Sir Leslie, *Forty Years of "Spy"*, London: Chatto & Windus, 1915.

Waugh, Arthur, *A Hundred Years of Publishing, Being the Story of Chapman and Hall Ltd.*, London: Chapman & Hall, 1930.

West, Sir Algernon, *One City and Many Men*, London: Smith, Elder, 1908.

——*Contemporary Portraits, Men of My Day in Public Life*, London: T. Fisher Unwin, 1920.

Whiting, Lilian, *Kate Field: A Record*, London: Low, 1899.

Wotton, Mabel, *Word Portraits of Famous Writers*, London: Bentley, 1887.

Yates, Edmund, *Edmund Yates: His Recollections and Experiences*, 2 vols, London: Bentley, 1884.

(iii) FULL-LENGTH STUDIES

ap Roberts, Ruth, *Trollope: Artist and Moralist*, London: Chatto & Windus, 1971.

Booth, Bradford A., *Anthony Trollope, Aspects of His Life and Art*, London: Hulton, 1958.

Bowen, Elizabeth, *Anthony Trollope, A New Judgment*, London: O.U.P., 1945.

Brown, Beatrice Curtis, *Anthony Trollope*, London: Arthur Barker, 1950.

Clark, John W., *The Language and Style of Anthony Trollope*, London: Andre Deutsch, 1975.

Cockshut, A. O. J., *Anthony Trollope, A Critical Study*, London: Collins, 1955.

Davies, Hugh Sykes, *Trollope*, London: Longmans, Green, 1960.

Escott, T. H. S., *Anthony Trollope, His Work, Associates and Literary Originals*, London: John Lane, 1913.

Fredman, Alice Green, *Anthony Trollope*, 'Columbia Essays on Modern Writers', New York: Columbia University Press, 1971.

Hennedy, Hugh L., *Unity in Barsetshire*, The Hague & Paris: Mouton, 1971.

Nichols, Spencer Van Bokkelen, *The Significance of Anthony Trollope*, New York: D. C. McMurtrie, 1925.

Pope Hennessy, James, *Anthony Trollope*, London: Cape, 1971.

Polhemus, Robert, *The Changing World of Anthony Trollope*, Berkeley and Los Angeles: University of California Press, 1968.

Pollard, Arthur, *Trollope's Political Novels*, Hull: University of Hull, 1968.

Sadleir, Michael, *Trollope, A Commentary*, London: Constable, 1927.

Snow, C. P., *Trollope*, London: Macmillan, 1975.

Stebbins, L. P., and R. P., *The Trollopes: The Chronicle of a Writing Family*, London: Secker & Warburg, 1946.

Walpole, Hugh, *Anthony Trollope*, London: Macmillan, 1928.

(iv) SHORTER CRITICISMS

Baker, Ernest A., *The History of the English Novel*, 10 vols, London: M. F. & G. Witherby, 1924–1939, vol. VIII, ch. iv.

The Cambridge History of English Literature, ed. Sir A. W. Ward and A. R. Waller, 14 vols, Cambridge: University of Cambridge Press, 1907–16; vol., VIII, article on Trollope by W. T. Young.

Cecil, Lord David, *Early Victorian Novelists, Essays in Revaluation*, London: Constable, 1934.

Chambers's Cyclopaedia of Literature, III, Edinburgh: W. & R. Chambers, 1938.

Darbishire, Helen, *Somerville College Chapel Addresses and other papers*, London: Blackwell Scientific Publications, 1962.

Elton, Oliver, *A Survey of English Literature, 1830–1880*, 2 vols, London: Arnold, 1920.

Essays Critical and Historical dedicated to Lily B. Campbell by Members of the Departments of English, University of California, Berkeley and Los Angeles: University of California Press, 1950.

Garnett, Richard, and Gosse, Sir Edmund, *English Literature, An Illustrated Record*, 4 vols, London: Heinemann, 1903–4.

Gindin, James, *Harvest of a Quiet Eye: the Novel of Compassion*, Bloomington: Indiana University Press, 1971.

Harper, Howard M., Jr., and Edge, Charles, *The Classic British Novel*, Athens: University of Georgia Press, 1972.

Harrison, Frederic, *Studies in Early Victorian Literature*, London: Arnold, 1895.

James, Henry, *Partial Portraits*, London: Macmillan, 1888.
Johnson, Pamela Hansford, 'Trollope's Young Women', *On the Novel*, ed. B. S. Benedikz, London: Dent, 1971.
Lord, W. Frewen, *The Mirror of the Century*, London: Lane, 1906.
MacCarthy, Sir Desmond, *Portraits*, 1, London: Putnam, 1931.
Melville, Lewis, *Victorian Novelists*, London: Archibald Constable, 1906.
Miller, J. Hillis, *The Form of Victorian Fiction*, Indiana: University of Notre Dame, 1968.
Mizener, Arthur, 'The Realistic Novel in the Nineteenth Century: Trollope's Palliser Novels', *The Sense of Life in the Modern Novel*, Boston: Houghton Mifflin, 1964.
More, Paul Elmer, *The Demon of the Absolute*, vol., 1 of *New Shelburne Essays*, Princeton: Princeton University Press, 1928.
Morgan, Charles, *Reflections in a Mirror*, 1st ser. [1944], London: Macmillan, 1953.
O'Connor, Frank, 'Trollope the Realist', *The Mirror in the Roadway, A Study of the Modern Novel*, New York: Knopf, 1956.
Paul, Herbert, *Men and Letters*, London: Lane, 1901.
Peck, Harry T., 'Anthony Trollope', *Bookman* (N.Y.), XIII (Apr 1901).
Praz, Mario, *The Hero in Eclipse in Victorian Fiction*, London: O.U.P., 1956.
Pritchett, V. S., *The Working Novelist*, London: Chatto & Windus, 1965.
Quiller-Couch, Sir Arthur, *Charles Dickens and Other Victorians*, Cambridge: Cambridge University Press, 1925.
Ray, Gordon N., 'Trollope at Full Length', *Huntington Library Quarterly*, XXXI (4 August 1968).
Saintsbury, G., *Corrected Impressions, Essays on Victorian Writers*, London: Heinemann, 1895.
——'Trollope Revisited', in *Essays and Studies by Members of the English Association*, Oxford: Clarendon Press, 1920.
—— *The English Novel*, London: Dent, 1913.
Snow, C. P., 'Trollope: the Psychological Stream', *On the Novel*, ed. B. S. Benedikz, London: Dent, 1971.
Stephen, Sir Leslie, *Studies of a Biographer*, 2nd ser., 4 vols, London: Duckworth, 1898–1902.
Street, G. S., *A Book of Essays*, London: Constable, 1902.
Tillotson, Geoffrey and Kathleen, *Mid-Victorian Studies*, London: Athlone Press, 1965.
Walker, Hugh, *The Literature of the Victorian Era*, Cambridge: Cambridge University Press, 1910.
West, Rebecca, 'Nineteenth Century Bureaucrat', *The Court and the Castle: Some Treatments of a Recurrent Theme*, New Haven: Yale University Press, 1957.

Appendix IV

Selected Bibliography of General Social, Historical and Literary Background

Ausubel, Herman, *In Hard Times, Reformers Among the Late Victorians,* London: O.U.P., 1960.

Baker, Joseph E., *The Novel and the Oxford Movement* [1932] New York: Russell & Russell, 1965.

Butler, Josephine E., ed., *Woman's Work and Woman's Culture,* London: Macmillan, 1869.

Buxton, Charles, *The Ideas of the Day on Policy,* London: Murray, 1866.

Corfe, Tom, *The Phœnix Park Murders; Conflict, Compromise and Tragedy in Ireland, 1870–1882,* London: Hodder & Stoughton, 1968.

de Vere, Aubrey, *Recollections of Aubrey de Vere,* London: Arnold, 1897.

Escott, T. H. S., *England: Its People, Polity and Pursuits,* 2 vols, London: Cassell, 1879.

—— *Masters of English Journalism, A Study of Personal Forces,* London: T. Fisher Unwin, 1911.

Gower, Edward F. Leveson, *Bygone Years, Recollections by the Hon. F. Leveson Gower,* London: Murray, 1905.

Hayward, Abraham, *A Selection from the Correspondence of Abraham Hayward from 1834 to 1884 with an Account of his Early Life,* ed. H. E. Carlisle, 2 vols, London: Murray, 1886.

Hardman, Sir William, *The Letters and Memoirs of Sir William Hardman, 2nd series; 1863–1865,* ed. S. M. Ellis, London: Cecil Palmer, 1925.

Himmelfarb, Gertrude, *Victorian Minds,* London: Weidenfeld & Nicolson, 1968.

Higgins, Matthew [Jacob Omnium], *Essays on Social Subjects. With a Memoir by Sir W. S. Maxwell,* London: 1875.

Houghton, W. E., *The Victorian Frame of Mind, 1830–1870,* New Haven: Yale University Press, 1957.

Linton, Mrs (Elisabeth) Lynn, *My Literary Life, Reminiscences of Dickens, Thackeray, George Eliot etc.,* London: Hodder & Stoughton, 1899.

McCarthy, Justin, *Portraits of the Sixties,* London: T. Fisher Unwin, 1903.

Mackay, Charles, *Forty Years' Recollections of Life, Literature, and Public Affairs from 1830–1870,* 2 vols, London: 1877.

Marchand, Leslie, *The Athenaeum, A Mirror of Victorian Culture,* Chapel Hill: University of North Carolina Press, 1941.

Martin, R. B., *Enter Rumour: Four Early Victorian Scandals*, London : Faber, 1962.

Merivale, Charles, *Autobiography and Letters of Charles Merivale, Dean of Ely*, ed. Judith Merivale, Oxford : privately printed, 1898.

Millais, J. G., *The Life and Letters of Sir John Everett Millais*, 2 vols, New York : F. A. Stokes, 1899.

Payn, James, *Some Private Views*, London : Chatto & Windus, 1881.

—— *The Backwater of Life, or Essays of a Literary Veteran*, London : Smith, Elder, 1899.

Russell, G. W. E., *Collections and Recollections, by one who has kept a Diary*, London : Smith, Elder, 1898.

Ryan, Desmond, *The Fenian Chief, A Biography of James Stephens*, Dublin : Gill, 1967.

Scott, J. W. Robertson, *The Story of the Pall Mall Gazette, of its first editor Frederick Greenwood and of its founder George Murray Smith*, London : O.U.P., 1950.

Sheehy-Skeffington, F., *Michael Davitt, Revolutionary, Agitator and Labour Leader* [1908], London : T. Fisher Unwin, 1967.

Taylor, Sir Henry, *The Statesman, An Ironical Treatise on the Art of Succeeding* [1836], reissue with an introductory essay by Harold J. Laski, Cambridge : W. Heffer, 1927.

—— *Autobiography*, 2 vols, London : Longman, 1885.

Thomas, William B., *The Story of the Spectator, 1828–1928*, London : Methuen, 1928.

Thomson, Patricia, *The Victorian Heroine, A Changing Ideal, 1837–1873*, London : O.U.P., 1956.

Thornley, David, *Isaac Butt and Home Rule*, London : Macgibbon & Kee, 1964.

Vizetelly, Henry, *Glances Back Through Seventy Years, Autobiographical and other Reminiscences*, 2 vols, London : Kegan Paul, 1893.

Nevill, Lady Dorothy, *My Own Times*, edited by her son, London : Methuen, 1912.

—— *The Reminiscences of Lady Dorothy Nevill*, ed. Ralph Nevill, London : Nelson, 1920.

West, Sir Algernon, *Recollections, 1832 to 1886*, 2 vols, London : Smith, Elder, 1899.

White, Terence de Vere, *The Road of Excess*, Dublin : Browne & Nolan, 1946.

Young, G. M., *Early Victorian England, 1830–1865*, 2 vols, London : O.U.P., 1934.

Appendix V

Twenty popular authors stocked by Mudie's Select Library, compiled from catalogues issued between 1857 and 1935

	1857	1858	1865	1869	1871	1875	1888	1900	1910	1920	1934	1935
W. H. Ainsworth	9	8	12	16	16	17	24	32	29	29	17	17
Rhoda Broughton	—	—	—	—	—	5	11	17	20	24	4	4
Miss M. E. Braddon	—	—	7	16	16	25	46	61	71	75	6	6
Wilkie Collins	6	6	9	11	11	15	26	29	29	29	10	10
Mrs G. L. Craik	8	8	14	9	12	17	28	30	30	31	2	2
Disraeli	9	8	8	8	9	9	10	12	12	12	11	11
G. P. R. James	39	30	30	23	12	14	20	25	23	23	1	1
Julia Kavanagh	5	6	8	11	12	13	10	14	—	—	—	—
Charles Lever	13	12	15	20	22	22	26	28	26	26	5	5
E. Bulwer Lytton	20	19	22	21	20	25	26	26	27	27	22	22
Anne Manning	—	—	22	25	27	25	26	28	—	—	—	—
Captain Marryat	21	21	18	17	16	16	20	24	23	23	2	2
Mrs M. Oliphant	8	9	21	22	25	29	53	92	75	73	4	4
Ouida	—	—	—	—	—	—	28	40	43	43	6	6
Charles Reade	4	5	8	9	11	13	18	19	20	20	6	6
Elizabeth Sewell	7	8	10	13	13	14	14	15	8	8	—	—
Anthony Trollope	2	4	14	16	21	30	49	52	45	45	20	20
G. Whyte-Melville	4	4	10	13	15	18	22	23	24	24	5	5
Mrs Henry Wood	—	—	11	11	16	20	33	41	40	40	16	16
Charlotte Yonge	6	6	16	14	20	23	41	71	74	74	1	1

Notes

CHAPTER 1

1 Michael Sadleir, *Trollope, A Commentary* (London: Constable, 1927)
  p. 365; C. P. Snow, 'Trollope: the Psychological Stream', *On the Novel*,
  ed. B. S. Benedikz (London: J. M. Dent, 1971) p. 3.
2 Gordon Ray, 'Trollope at Full Length', *Huntington Library Quarterly*,
  XXXI, 4 (Aug 1968) 313–40.
3 *The Demon of the Absolute, New Shelburne Essays*, I (Princeton:
  Princeton University Press, 1928) 90; Pamela Hansford Johnson, NYTB,
  LXX (25 Apr 1965) 2.
4 *John Caldigate*, ch xiii (London: World's Classics, 1952). Quotations
  from the novels are from World's Classics editions where possible. In
  all other cases quotations are from the earliest available edition, unless
  stated otherwise. Where reference to a novel is unmistakable, a chapter
  reference is included in the text.
5 George Saintsbury, *The English Novel* (London: J. M. Dent, 1913)
  p. 250. See also his varying judgements between *Corrected Impressions,
  Essays on Victorian Writers* (London: W. Heinemann, 1893, and
  'Trollope Revisited' in *Essays and Studies by Members of the English
  Association* (Oxford: Clarendon Press, 1920).
6 *Partial Portraits* (London: Macmillan, 1888) p. 133.
7 *The Letters of Robert Louis Stevenson*, ed. S. Colvin (London: Methuen,
  1911) I, 261–2; George Gissing, *The Private Papers of Henry Ryecroft*
  (London: Everyman, Dent, 1964) p. 166; A. C. Swinburne, *Miscellanies*
  (London: Chatto & Windus, 1886) p. 299.
8 'Anthony Trollope', *Victorian Fiction, A Guide to Research*, ed. Lionel
  Stevenson (Cambridge, Mass.: Harvard University Press, 1964) p. 196.
9 E. L. Skinner, NCF, IV (Dec 1949) 197–207; Benedikz, *On the Novel*,
  pp. 17–33.
10 *Listener*, LXXI (7 May 1964) 754.
11 *Urgent Copy, Literary Studies* (London: Jonathan Cape, 1968) p. 35.
12 *New Statesman*, LXXXII (26 Nov 1971) 756.
13 Raymond Mortimer, 'Books in General', *New Statesman and Nation*,
  XXXIII (19 Apr 1947) 277; Geoffrey and Kathleen Tillotson, *Mid-
  Victorian Studies* (London: Athlone Press, 1965) pp. 56–61; David
  Aitken, ' "A Kind of Felicity"; some Notes about Trollope's Style',
  NCF, XX (Mar 1966) 337–53. See also C. J. Vincent, 'Trollope: A
  Victorian Augustan', *Queen's Quarterly*, LII (1945) 415–28; William
  Cadbury, 'Determinants of Trollope's Forms', PMLA, LXXVIII (1963)

326–32; John W. Clark, *The Language and Style of Anthony Trollope* (The Language Library, London: André Deutsch, 1975).

14 *Orley Farm* (London, World's Classics, 1963) ch. x. Trollope's reference is to Horace, *Odes*, 2, 3.

15 *South Africa* (London: Chapman & Hall, 1878) I, i, 4.

16 T. S. Eliot, *The Cocktail Party*, II (London: Faber, 1949).

17 'Mr. Anthony Trollope', *Spectator*, LV (9 Dec 1882) 1573.

18 *A Mid-Victorian Pepys, The Letters and Memoirs of Sir William Hardman*, ed. S. M. Ellis (London: Cecil Palmer, 1923) p. 159.

19 Mgr R. A. Knox, 'A Ramble in Barsetshire', *London Mercury*, V, 28 (Feb 1922) 385; quoted in Chapter 3, p. 59.

20 James Pope Hennessy, *Anthony Trollope* (London: Cape, 1971).

21 *The Amenities of Book Collecting and Kindred Affections* (London: John Lane, 1920) p. 254. See also G. S. Street, intro., *The Claverings* (London: World's Classics, 1924).

22 *The Court and the Castle* (London: Macmillan, 1958) p. 111.

23 *The Letters and Diaries of John Henry Newman*, ed. C. S. Dessain, XX, July 1861 to Dec 1863 (London: Nelson, 1971) 281.

24 See R. M. Polhemus, 'Cousin Henry: Trollope's Note from Underground', NCF, XX (Mar 1966) 385–9; Pope Hennessy, *Trollope*, p. 129.

25 *Somerville College Chapel Addresses*, intro. K. M. Tillotson (London: Blackwell Scientific Publications, 1962) p. 110.

26 *Studies of a Biographer*, 2nd ser. (London: Duckworth, 1902) IV, 205; see also J. A. Banks, 'The Way They Lived Then: Anthony Trollope and the 1870's' *Victorian Studies*, XII, 2 (Dec 1968) 177–200.

27 *Reflections in a Mirror*, 1st ser. [1944] (London: Macmillan, 1953) p. 72.

28 In original edition, London: Bentley, 1858, II, ch. xii,, excised for the one-volume issue (1859). All further quotations are from World's Classics edition, 1959; *The Landleaguers* (London: Chatto & Windus, 1883) III, ch. xli.

29 T. H. S. Escott, *England, Its People, Polity and Pursuits* (London: Cassell, 1879) II, 402.

30 *Partial Portraits*, p. 107.

CHAPTER 2

1 *An Autobiography* (London: World's Classics, 1961) ch. iv. Beatrice Curtis Brown's valuable study, *Anthony Trollope* (London: Arthur Barker, 1950), speaks of the 'candidly reserved' *Autobiography* (p. 101).

2 Booth, *Trollope*, p. 5.

3 *Letters*, p. xxi. All quotations from letters are from *The Letters of Anthony Trollope*, ed. Bradford Booth (London: O.U.P., 1951). In each case I give the number of the letter followed by a page reference. Where subsequent reference to the letters is clear, these numbers are inserted in the text.

4 A new edition of the letters is in preparation by N. John Hall for Stanford University Press.

5 Sir William Gregory, An Autobiography, ed. Lady Gregory (London: J. Murray, 1894) p. 35.
6 For a paean to club life see his article 'Whist at our club', Blackwood's Magazine, XII (May 1877) 1881.
7 Autobiography, ch. ix.
8 Letters, 678, p. 387.
9 'Anthony Trollope', Macmillan's Magazine, XLVII (Jan 1883) 236–40. Edward Augustus Freeman (1823–92) was Regius Professor of Modern History at Oxford, 1884–92. Trollope knew him as a regular contributor to the Saturday Review, 1855–78, and with him conducted the friendly disputation on blood sports he describes in the Autobiography (ch. x).
10 Ray, 'Trollope at Full Length', p. 317.
11 Julian Hawthorne, 'The Maker of Many Books', Confessions and Criticisms (Boston: Ticknor, 1887) p. 142. See also Charles R. Brown, They Were Giants (New York: Macmillan, 1934) p. 69.
12 See tributes by Walter Herries Pollock, 'Anthony Trollope', Harper's New Monthly Magazine, LXVI (May 1883) 907–12; 'Mr. Anthony Trollope', Saturday Review, LIV (9 Dec 1882) 755–6; Julian Hawthorne, Confessions and Criticisms, pp. 140–62; Frederick Locker-Lampson, My Confidences, An Autobiographical Sketch (London: Smith, Elder, 1896) pp. 331–7; Alfred Austin, 'Last Reminiscences of Anthony Trollope', Temple Bar, LXX (Jan 1884) 129–34.
13 George Smalley, 'Recollections of Anthony Trollope', McClure's Magazine, XX (Jan 1903) 298.
14 Letters, 87, p. 58.
15 Shapes that Pass, Memories of Old Days (London: John Murray, 1928) pp. 226–7.
16 Lilian Whiting, Kate Field, A Record (London: S. Low, 1899) p. 396.
17 Word Portraits of Famous Writers, ed. Mabel Wotton (London: Bentley, 1887) pp. 313–16.
18 Sir Leslie Ward, Forty Years of Spy (London: Chatto & Windus, 1915) p. 105.
19 Sir Rowland Hill, The Story of a Great Reform (London: T. Fisher Unwin, 1907) pp. 277–8. Eleanor Smyth was the daughter of Sir Rowland Hill, the originator of the Penny Post.
20 H. E. Scudder, James Russell Lowell, A Biography (London: Macmillan, 1901) II, 83.
21 The Amberley Papers, The Letters and Diaries of Lord and Lady Amberley, ed. B. and P. Russell (London: L. and V. Woolf, 1937) II, 27.
22 Mark Twain in Eruption, ed. Bernard de Voto (New York: Harper, 1941) pp. 332–3.
23 Macmillan's Magazine, XLIX (Nov 1883) 55.
24 World, XXXVI (24 Feb 1882) 19.
25 Sir Algernon West, Contemporary Portraits (London: T. Fisher Unwin, 1920) p. 140.
26 Things I Have Seen and People I Have Known (London: Cassell, 1894) I, 30.

27 'Anthony Trollope', *Macmillan's Magazine*, XLIX (Nov 1883) 54;
    Studies in Early Victorian Literature (London: E. Arnold, 1895)
    p. 203.

28 *Twenty-Five Years of St. Andrews* (London: Longman, 1898) I, 100.

29 *William Blackwood and His Sons, Annals of a Publishing House*
    (London: W. Blackwood, 1897) III, 197–8.

30 *A Hundred Years of Publishing, Being the Story of Chapman & Hall*
    Ltd. (London: Chapman & Hall, 1930) p. 87.

31 *Edmund Yates: His Recollections and Experiences* (London: Bentley,
    1884) II, 223.

32 Mrs E. M. Ward, *Memories of Ninety Years* (London: Hutchinson,
    1924) p. 147.

33 That Trollope was conscious of this role is evident from his self-parody
    in, for example, Pollock, a 'heavy-weight sporting literary gentleman'
    in *Can You Forgive Her?*, or Bouncer, the novelist interrogated by
    Chaffanbrass in *Phineas Redux* (ch. lxi). For this scene Trollope could
    call on actual experience, having been cross-examined in the witness
    box during his Post Office service in Ireland by the ferocious advocate
    Isaac Butt (1813–79). See Justin McCarthy, *Reminiscences* (London:
    Chatto & Windus, 1899) I, 369–72. A good deal of self-portraiture is
    also to be found in Dr Wortle.

34 *Studies of a Biographer*, 2nd series, IV, 171.

35 Quoted Robert Ashley, *Wilkie Collins* (London: Arthur Barker, 1952)
    p. 105.

36 Scudder, Lowell, II, 82.

37 *The Sands of Time, Recollections and Reflections* (London: Hutchinson,
    1923) p. 217.

38 *Things I Have Seen*, I, 31. See also Percy Fitzgerald, *The Garrick Club*
    (London: Elliot Stock, 1904) p. 78; Sir Henry Rider Haggard, *The*
    Days of My Life (London: Longman, 1926) I, 137.

39 *Some Literary Recollections* (London: Smith, Elder, 1884) pp. 221–2.

40 *My Autobiography and Reminiscences* (London: Bentley, 1887) II,
    335.

41 *My Confidences*, p. 331.

42 *Confessions and Criticisms*, p. 160.

43 Frances Trollope (1780–1863), is best recalled in Sadleir's *Commentary*,
    pp. 29–105, for which he drew on the accounts of her in her sons'
    autobiographies and her daughter-in-law's biography: F. E. Trollope,
    A Memoir of Frances Trollope (London: Bentley, 1895). Indefatigable,
    courageous, strong-willed and good-natured, she virtually saved the
    family from collapse and penury by launching herself on a literary
    career at the age of fifty-one. She wrote over forty books between 1831
    and 1856.

44 *Autobiography*, ch. i.

45 Thomas Adolphus Trollope, *What I Remember* (London: Bentley, 1887)
    I, 4.

46 Quoted C. R. Leslie, *Memoirs of the Life of John Constable*, ed. J.
    Mayne (London: Phaidon Press, 1951) p. 94.

47 *Autobiography and Letters of Charles Merivale*, ed. Judith Merivale (Oxford: printed privately, 1898) p. 11.
48 *The Claverings* (London: World's Classics, 1959) ch. vii.
49 *Lady Anna* (London: World's Classics, 1936) ch. xx.
50 *Autobiography*, ch. i.
51 F. E. Trollope, *A Memoir of Frances Trollope*, I. 131.
52 *What I Remember*, I, 226.
53 *Letters*, 237, p. 154.
54 Cecilia (1816–1849), wife of John Tilley, later Sir John Tilley, General Secretary of the Post Office and Trollope's lifelong friend, also wrote a novel, *Chollerton: A Tale of Our Own Times* (1846); see *Autobiography*, ch. iv.
55 Quoted Sadleir, *Commentary*, p. 70.
56 *Autobiography*, ch. i.
57 F. C. Burnand, *Records and Reminiscences, Personal and General* (London: Methuen, 1904) I, ch. vii; Charles Merivale, *Autobiography*, p. 43.
58 Escott, *Anthony Trollope*, p. 16; R. P. Stebbins, 'Trollope at Harrow School', *Trollopian*, I (summer 1945) 35–44.
59 F. E. Trollope, *Memoir*, I, 95.
60 Ibid., II, 39. C. P. Snow's lively account in *Trollope* (Macmillan: 1975) adds much to our knowledge of the young man's career in the postal service, and makes several suggestions as to how he spent his evenings – reading omnivorously, no doubt – as well as roistering. To this I would add the most likely entertainment for the lonely bachelor seeking romance: the theatre, the opera, the music hall. Letters are relevant here: 'The greatest actors I ever saw were E. Keane [sic], Rachel, Mars, Got, Lemaitres . . . Yates . . . and I would add Robson' (598, p. 344). When did he see all these actors? Another letter records: 'I remember well, when I was quite a young man, being moved to weeping by hearing a solo on the violonchello [sic] by Lindley (506, pp. 300–1). Robert Lindley (1776–1855) was principal cellist at the opera, 1794–1851.
61 *Ayala's Angel* (London: World's Classics, 1968) ch. viii.
62 *Autobiography*, ch. iv.
63 *Letters* I, p. 1. Unfortunately these have not come to light. They were probably bad poems (see letter, quoted p. 34), but note *The Times*, 7 Dec 1882, which says: 'We have Trollope's own authority for saying there were other novels before *The Macdermots*' (p. 6).
64 *Autobiography*, ch. iii.
65 *What I Remember*, I, 257.
66 *Letters*, 265, p. 166.
67 'The Civil Service as a Profession' (1861); 'The Present Condition of the Northern States of the American Union' (1862); 'The Higher Education of Women' (1868); 'On English Prose Fiction as a Rational Amusement' (1870); collected in *Four Lectures*, ed. Morris L. Parrish (London: Constable, 1938).
68 See the list of influential figures and political mentors in the *Auto-*

biography, ch. ix. Club life gave Trollope first-hand study of politicians, and presumably also much behind-the-scenes information. Among his clubland friends were Arthur Russell, nephew of Lord John Russell, and the Honourable Edward Frederick Leveson Gower, the brother of Lord Granville. 'Freddy' Leveson Gower (1819–1907), an incurable gossip, was one of a large class of MPs whose chief business in going up to the House was to collect their mail. In thirty-three years in Parliament, Gower spoke in very few debates. The *DNB* said of him: 'Gifted with agreeable manners, conversational tact, and a good memory, he excelled as a diner-out and giver of dinners', (1901–1911, p. 458). See his charming anecdotal autobiography, *Bygone Years* (London: John Murray, 1905).

69 Emma Caroline, Lady Wood (1820?–79), widow of the Reverend Sir John Page Wood, Vicar of Cressing, was the mother of Trollope's friend Anna C. Steele. See *Letters*, 391, p. 232; 379, pp. 221–2; *Autobiography*, ch. x. A masterly rejoinder to an unknown clergyman taxing him with immorality over the Glencora-Burgo Fitzgerald scenes in *Can You Forgive Her?* is quoted pp. 72–3.

70 *What I Remember*, II, 128–9.

71 *Can You Forgive Her?* (London: World's Classics, 1953) ch. xlv.

72 *Letters*, 398, p. 236. Sir Arthur Helps (1813–1875), historian, novelist, playwright and essayist, was Clerk of the Privy Council from 1860 until his death and a close adviser of Queen Victoria. For her he edited Prince Albert's speeches and prepared the Queen's *Leaves from the Journal of Our Life in the Highlands* (1868) and her *Mountain, Loch and Glen* (1869). He was awarded the Order of the Bath in 1871 and made Knight Commander in 1872. Best known for pious discourses, *Friends in Council* (four series 1847–59) and *Brevia* (1870), he was also acclaimed for his novel *Realmah* (1868).

73 *Autobiography*, ch. x.

74 *Letters*, 162, p. 104; 375, p. 217. His correspondent, Mary Katherine Keemle Field (1838–96) was an American of independent spirit, who dabbled in authorship, journalism, acting, singing and public lecturing. Trollope was devoted to her, and doubtless the vivacity of such heroines as Caroline Spalding and Isabel Boncassen owes something to this friendship.

75 Herman Charles Merivale, *Bar, Stage and Platform, Autobiographical Memories* (London: Chatto & Windus, 1902) p. 96; *Autobiography*, ch. xviii.

76 Frith, *My Autobiography*, III, 386–7.

77 Florence Emily Hardy, *The Life of Thomas Hardy 1840–1928* (London: Macmillan, 1962) p. 113.

78 Trollope, pp. 167–72.

79 Anthony Trollope, *A New Judgement* (London: O.U.P., 1945) p. 20.

80 Yates, *Recollections*, II, 161.

81 Hawthorne, *Shapes that Pass*, p. 227.

82 'What I was told', *Trollopian*, II (Mar 1948) 223–5.

83 *The Letters of Lady Anne Thackeray Ritchie*, ed. Hester Ritchie (London: J. Murray, 1924) p. 125.
84 Sir William Frederick Pollock, *Personal Remembrances of Sir Frederick Pollock* (London: Macmillan, 1887) II, 149–50.
85 *Trollopian*, II (Mar 1948), 225.
86 Quoted Escott, *Trollope*, p. 170.
87 Rev. of *Autobiography*, *Blackwood's Magazine*, CXXXIV (Nov 1883) 594.
88 'Trollope', HLQ (Aug 1968) p. 331.
89 'Anthony Trollope', *Saturday Review*, LVI (20 Oct 1883) 505.
90 *The Letters of Sir Walter Raleigh, 1879–1922*, ed. Lady Raleigh (London: Methuen, 1926) I, 272.

CHAPTER 3

1 *Commentary*, p. 304. For further information on Trollope's reputation see Rafael Helling, *A Century of Trollope Criticism* [1956] (Port Washington, N.Y.: Kennikat Press, 1967); David Skilton, *Anthony Trollope and his Contemporaries, a Study in the Theory and Conventions of mid-Victorian Fiction* (London: Longman, 1972).
2 *Autobiography*, ch. xx.
3 *New Shelburne Essays*, p. 90.
4 *Autobiography*, ch. xx.
5 *Academy*, XXII (16 Dec 1882) 433; 'English Fiction: the Death of Anthony Trollope', *Nation*, XXXVI, 914 (4 Jan 1883) 10; *Month*, XLIX (Sep–Dec 1883) 484.
6 *The Times*, 7 Dec 1882, p. 6.
7 'Mr. Anthony Trollope', *Saturday Review*, LIV (9 Dec 1882) 755; *Spectator*, LVI (20 Oct 1883) 1574; 'The Novels of Anthony Trollope', *Dublin Review*, IX (Apr 1883) 314; *Graphic*, XXVI (16 Dec 1882) 661; 'Anthony Trollope', *Macmillan's Magazine*, XLVII (Jan 1883) 240; *Athenaeum*, 2876 (9 Dec 1882) 773; 'The Literary Life of Anthony Trollope', *Edinburgh Review*, CLIX (Jan 1884) 186; 'Anthony Trollope', *Good Words*, XXIV (1883) 142; 'The Autobiography of Anthony Trollope', *Blackwood's Magazine*, CXXXIV (Nov 1883) 596; 'Anthony Trollope', *Nation*, XXXVII, 958 (8 Nov 1883) 397.
8 *Harper's New Monthly Magazine*, LXVI (May 1883) 907–12; 'Mr. Anthony Trollope', *Spectator*, LV (9 Dec 1882) 1573; *Temple Bar*, LXX (Jan 1884) 129; 'Some Recollections of Mr. Anthony Trollope', *Graphic*, XXVI (23 Dec 1882) 707; *Nation*, XXXVI, 914 (4 Jan 1883) 10; 'Anthony Trollope', *Century*, XXVI (July 1883) 385–95; *Saturday Review*, LIV (9 Dec 1882) 755–6.
9 *Commentary*, p. 362.
10 Heywood, 'A Novelist Who Means Business', *How They Strike Me, These Authors* (Philadelphia: J. B. Lippincott, 1877) pp. 78–96.
11 *Vanity Fair*, IX (5 April 1873) 110–11; Ward, *Forty Years of Spy*, p. 105.
12 For other cartoons, see Frederick Waddy, *Once A Week*, IX (1 June

1872) 499; Linley Sambourne, 'Punch's Fancy Portraits No. 17', *Punch*, LXXX (5 Feb 1881) 58. A parody called 'The Beadle! or The Latest Chronicle of Small-Beerjester by Anthony Dollop', ran in *Punch* between 5 June and 16 Oct 1880.

13   'The Apotheosis of the Novel under Queen Victoria', *Nineteenth Century*, XLI (May 1897) 783. This formed part of his book *Men and Letters* (London: John Lane, 1901).

14   *Random Reflections of an Old Publisher* (London: Simpkin, Marshall, 1900) I, 136.

15   *Victorian Novelists* (London: Archibald Constable, 1906) pp. 168–9.

16   'The Heroines of *The Warden* and *The Small House at Allington*', *Harper's Bazaar*, 34 (13 Apr 1901) 947–53; 'The Heroines of Trollope', (27 Apr 1901) 1075–80; 'Trollope's Mrs. Proudie', 35 (June 1901) 102–9; 'The Art of the Novelist', *Contemporary Review*, LXVI (Aug 1894) 225–42; 'Anthony Trollope', *Bookman* (N.Y.) XIII (Apr 1901) 114–25; Gamaliel Bradford Junior, 'Anthony Trollope', *Atlantic Monthly*, LXXXIX (Mar 1902) 426–32, and XCI (Feb 1903) 272; *Dial*, XXXIV (1 Mar 1903) 141–3. See also *McClure's Magazine*, XX (Jan 1903) 298–9; *Bookman* (N.Y.) XI (June 1900) 311–13; 'The Future of Trollope', XXI (Apr 1905) 137–41; XXIII (Apr 1906) 125–6; XXIX (Mar 1909) 1–2.

17   Margaret Oliphant, 'Success in Fiction', *Forum*, VII (May 1889) 314–22; Frederic Harrison, 'Anthony Trollope's Place in Literature', *Forum*, XIX (May 1895) 324–337; G. S. Street, 'Anthony Trollope', *Cornhill Magazine*, X (Mar 1901) 349–55; G. S. Street, *A Book of Essays* (London: Constable, 1902) pp. 198–212; Sir Leslie Stephen, 'Anthony Trollope', *National Review*, XXXVIII (1902) 68–84; James Bryce, 'Merits and Defects of Trollope', *Studies in Contemporary Biography* (London: Macmillan, 1903) pp. 116–30; 'In Praise of Anthony Trollope's Novels', *Fortnightly Review*, LXXVII (June 1905) 1000–11; 'Anthony Trollope, An Appreciation and Reminiscence', Ibid., LXXX (Dec 1906) 1095–104; Michael MacDonagh, 'In the Throes of Composition', *Cornhill Magazine*, XVII (Nov 1904) 607–27; Stephen Gwynn, 'Anthony Trollope', *Macmillan's Magazine*, LXXXI (Jan 1900) 217–26; Escott, 'The Works of Anthony Trollope', *Quarterly Review*, CCX (Jan 1909) 210–30.

18   J. Hain Friswell, the embodiment of bourgeois taste, noted that Mudie's stock was staple reading matter because it had 'in its conception a noble end', 'Circulating Libraries', *London Society*, XX (Dec 1871) 523. See also Guinevere L. Griest, *Mudie's Circulating Library and the Victorian Novel* (Bloomington: Indiana University Press, 1970).

19   Unpublished dissertation, 'A Critical Study of the Work of Frances Milton Trollope', University of London, 1969. See also Lance Tingay, 'Trollope's Popularity: A Statistical Approach', NCF, XI (Dec 1956) 223–9.

20   *William Allingham, A Diary*, ed. H. Allingham and D. Radford (London: Macmillan, 1907) p. 342; *Contemporary Review*, LXVI (Aug 1894).

21 *Commentary*, p. 362.
22 Edmund Gosse, ed., *English Literature, An Illustrated Record* (London: William Heinemann, 1903) IV, 321.
23 *Miscellanies*, pp. 296, 299.
24 'Anthony Trollope', *Macmillan's Magazine*, XLIX (Nov 1883) 54-5; 'Mr. Trollope's Latest Character', *Atlantic Monthly*, LIII (Feb 1884) 271; 'Anthony Trollope', *Westminster Review*, LXV, new series (Jan 1884) 108; 'The Literary Life of Anthony Trollope', *Edinburgh Review*, CLIX (Jan 1884) 186; 'The Autobiography of Anthony Trollope', *Blackwood's Magazine*, CXXXIV (Nov 1883) 586; *The Times*, 13 Oct 1883, p. 8; 'Autobiography of Anthony Trollope', *Graphic*, XXVI (16 Dec 1882) 661; *Saturday Review*, LVI (20 Oct 1883) 506.
25 Michael MacDonagh, 'In the Throes of Composition', *Cornhill Magazine*, XVII (Nov 1904) 610.
26 Scudder, *Lowell*, II, 82; Bede, *Graphic* (23 Dec 1882) p. 707; 'Anthony Trollope', *Good Words*, XXV (1884) 249.
27 Stephen, *Studies*, IV, 321.
28 'To Anthony Trollope on re-reading his Barsetshire Novels', *Literary Digest*, LI (14 Aug 1915) 310. For an earlier poetic tribute see Mowbray Morris, 'Anthony Trollope', *Graphic*, XXVI (30 Dec 1882) 719.
29 'Books in General', *New Statesman*, XXXII (8 June 1946) 415. Radio adaptations in the forties and fifties testify to this nostalgic appeal. See H. Oldfield Box, 'Trollope on the Radio', *Trollopian*, I (Mar 1946) 23-5. During 1973-4 the BBC broadcast the Barsetshire Novels in a splendid dramatisation by Constance Cox. A 26-part series based on Trollope's novels by Simon Raven and entitled 'The Pallisers' was televised during 1973-4, proving the nostalgic appeal is as strong as ever.
30 R. A. Knox, *London Mercury*, V, 28 (Feb 1922) 385. See also Spencer Van Bokkelen Nichols, *The Significance of Anthony Trollope* (New York: D. C. McMurtrie, 1925).
31 'Novelists', *Blackwood's Magazine*, CXXV (Mar 1879) 338.
32 *Letters*, 375, p. 217.
33 'The Art of the Novelist', *Contemporary Review*, LXVI (Aug 1894) 240.
34 Cecilia Meetkerke, 'Anthony Trollope', *Blackwood's Magazine*, CXXXIII (Feb 1883) 319.
35 *Autobiography*, ch. xii.
36 *Thackeray* (London: Macmillan, 1879) p. 123; see also W. H. Pollock, *Harper's New Monthly Magazine*, LXVI (May 1883) 909.
37 *Fortnightly Review*, LXXX (Dec 1906) 1102.
38 Escott, *Trollope*, p. 170.
39 *The History of the English Novel* (London: H. F. & G. Witherby, 1937) VIII, 122.
40 *Personal Remembrances*, II, 151.
41 See R. W. Chapman, 'The Text of Trollope's *Ayala's Angel*', *Modern Philology*, XXXIX (Feb 1942) 287-94; 'Textual Criticism; a Provisional Bibliography', *Trollopian*, I (summer 1945) 45; 'The Text of Trollope's *Autobiography*', *Review of English Studies*, XVII (Jan 1941) 90-4;

'The Text of Trollope's *Phineas Redux* is Seriously Faulty', XVII (Apr 1941) 184–92 *et seq.*; (July 1941) 322–31; (Jan 1942) 86–92; (Apr 1942) 228. Thus far only meagre analysis has been attempted of a vital part of Trollopian studies.

42 *Letters*, 924, p. 501.

43 *Thackeray*, p. 169.

44 *Macmillan's Magazine*, XLIX (Nov 1883) 55; *Graphic*, XXVI (23 Dec 1882) 707. On occasion, though, he could be brutally frank. See his rejection of E. B. Nicholson (438, p. 254), librarian of the London Institution (1873–82) and subsequently Bodley's librarian, as well as author of many poems, stories and articles.

45 *Dublin Review*, IX (Apr 1883) 331.

46 Bede, *Graphic*, XXVI (23 Dec 1882) 707.

CHAPTER 4

1 *Autobiography*, ch. viii.

2 Booth, *Trollope*, pp. 164–9.

3 Cockshut, *Trollope*, p. 125; Wildman, NCF, I, 1 (Mar 1946) 17–22. Modern criticism is now making far more useful enquiry into Trollope's use of conventional plot materials. See James Gindin, *Harvest of a Quiet Eye: the Novel of Compassion* (Bloomington: Indiana University Press, 1971).

4 J. Hillis Miller, *The Form of Victorian Fiction* (Indiana: University of Notre Dame Press, 1968) p. 125; Cockshut, *Trollope*, p. 112.

5 Cockshut, p. 124.

6 *The Letters of Edward Fitzgerald*, ed. William Aldis Wright (London: Macmillan, 1894) II, 159.

7 *Ayala's Angel*, ch. xxxviii.

8 *The Three Clerks* (London: World's Classics, 1959) ch. xix.

9 That special relationship is well put by William West in 'The Last Chronicle of Barset: Trollope's Comic Techniques' in *The Classic British Novel*, ed. Howard Harper, Jr., and Charles Edge (Athens, Georgia: University of Georgia Press, 1972).

10 'Novel Reading', *Nineteenth Century*, V (Jan 1879) 28.

11 'Novel Reading', pp. 24–43; 'Prose Fiction', p. 98, p. 123; *Thackeray*, p. 188.

12 *The Times*, 14 Nov 1873, p. 10. See also issues of 4 Mar 1876 and 29 Nov 1876.

13 *Letters of George Meredith*, collected and edited by his son (London: Constable, 1912) I, 272–3.

14 'Prose Fiction', pp. 108–9; *Autobiography*, ch. xii.

15 'Novel Reading', p. 33; *Thackeray*, p. 26; *Autobiography*, ch. xii.

16 Hillis Miller, *Victorian Fiction*, pp. 123–39.

17 *Can You Forgive Her?*, ch. xl.

18 *Mr. Scarborough's Family* (London: World's Classics, 1973) ch. xii. Similar frankness has been noted in other novels. See Juliet McMaster, ' "The Meaning of Words and the Nature of Things": Trollope's *Can*

You Forgive Her?' Studies in English Literature 1500–1900, XIV, 4 (autumn 1974) pp. 603–18.

19 A vivid picture of Trollope among the ladies is to be found in Laura Hain Friswell's account of the banquet for Dickens on the eve of his departure for the United States in 1867, *In the Sixties and Seventies, Impressions of Literary People and Others* (London: Hutchinson, 1905) pp. 169–70.

20 *Phineas Finn* (London: World's Classics, 1962) ch. lii.

21 *The Eustace Diamonds* (London: World's Classics, 1960) ch. xli.

22 *Phineas Redux* (London: World's Classics, 1964) ch. xviii.

23 *Framley Parsonage* (London: World's Classics, 1926) ch. xxvi.

24 *Autobiography*, ch. xii.

25 'Mr. Trollope on Novels', *Saturday Review*, XXXVI (22 Nov 1873) 656.

26 *Barchester Towers* (London: World's Classics, 1925) ch. xlix.

27 *The Small House at Allington* (London: World's Classics, 1939) chs ii, xviii.

28 *The Eustace Diamonds*, ch. xiii. The line is from Tennyson's 'Northern Farmer Old Style'.

29 *The Bertrams* (London: Chapman & Hall, 1859) II, ch. ii.

30 *The Duke's Children* (London: World's Classics, 1963) ch. lxxx.

31 *Marion Fay* (London: Chapman & Hall, 1882) ch. xiv.

32 *Is He Popenjoy?* (London: World's Classics, 1965) ch. ii.

33 *Ralph the Heir* (London: World's Classics, 1951) ch. lvi.

34 *He Knew He Was Right* (London: World's Classics, 1963) ch. iv.

35 *Autobiography*, chs vii, xiii.

36 Allingham, *A Diary*, p. 342.

37 W. H. Auden uses the phrase: see 'Poet of the Actual', *New Yorker*, XLVIII (1 Apr 1972) pp. 102–4.

38 *Letters*, 856, p. 468; but see also 443, p. 256, in which he calls Browning 'a very great poet'.

39 'Prose Fiction', p. 123.

40 *Thackeray*, pp. 189–90.

41 'The Genius of Nathaniel Hawthorne', *North American Review*, CXXIX (Sep 1879) 204–22.

42 *Thackeray*, pp. 187–91; 'Prose Fiction', p. 117.

43 Walpole, *Anthony Trollope* (London: Macmillan, 1928) p. 132.

44 'Books in General', *New Statesman*, XXXIII (19 Apr 1947) p. 277.

45 James, *Century*, XXVI (July 1883) 386. Subsequently James modified the phrase to 'a complete appreciation of the usual' (*Partial Portraits*, pp. 100–1).

46 Author unknown, *The Notebooks of a Spinster Lady, 1878–1903* (London: Cassell, 1919) pp. 74–5.

47 *Autobiography*, ch. v.

48 James, *Partial Portraits*, p. 127.

49 See Mario Praz, 'Anthony Trollope', in *The Hero in Eclipse in Victorian Fiction* (London: O.U.P., 1956) pp. 261–318.

50 *Sir Harry Hotspur of Humblethwaite* (London : World's Classics, 1929) ch. xvii.
51 *Dr. Thorne* (London : World's Classics, 1926) ch. xxix.
52 *Barchester Towers*, ch. xlvi. See also N. John Hall, Introduction to *The New Zealander* (London : O.U.P., 1972) pp. 6–7.
53 *Miss Mackenzie* (London : World's Classics, 1924) ch. vii.
54 *Castle Richmond* (London : Chapman & Hall, 1860) I, ch. iii.
55 *Framley Parsonage*, ch. xxvi.
56 Dr. *Wortle's School* (London : World's Classics, 1960) Part II, ch. vi.
57 Dr. *Thorne*, ch. xli.
58 See *Is He Popenjoy?*, ch. ii, and particularly *An Old Man's Love* (London : World's Classics, 1936) ch. iii.
59 *Marion Fay*, I, ch. xii; *Barchester Towers*, ch. xvi; *Dr. Thorne*, ch. ii.
60 *Phineas Finn*, ch. lxviii.
61 'Trollope's Young Women', *On the Novel*, pp. 17–33.

CHAPTER 5
1 *The American Senator* (London : World's Classics, 1962) ch. xl.
2 *The Three Clerks*, ch. xlvii; *Ayala's Angel*, ch. lxiv.
3 *The Victorian Heroine, A Changing Ideal, 1837–1873* (London : O.U.P., 1956) p. 111.
4 J. S. Mill's *The Subjection of Women* (1869) was written in 1861, and its issues much debated in the decade.
5 *He Knew He Was Right*, ch. xxix.
6 *Marion Fay*, I, vii, II, iii.
7 *Phineas Finn*, ch. lxxi; *The Small House at Allington*, ch. xvii; *Marion Fay*, I, ch. iv; *The Duke's Children*, ch. xx.
8 *Phineas Redux*, ch. iii.
9 *Can You Forgive Her?*, ch. xxv.
10 *The Prime Minister* (London : World's Classics, 1961) ch. vi.
11 *The Duke's Children*, ch. i.
12 *Spectator*, XXXVII (9 Apr 1864) 422.
13 *The Duke's Children*, ch. i.
14 *Kept in the Dark* (London : Chatto & Windus, 1882) ch. iv.
15 James, *Partial Portraits*, p. 109.
16 *National Review*, XVI (Jan 1863) 27.
17 *Saturday Review*, XIV (11 October 1862) 444.
18 Walpole, *Trollope*, pp. 126, 127.

CHAPTER 6
1 *Miss Mackenzie*, ch. xi.
2 *The George Eliot Letters*, ed. Gordon S. Haight, IV (London : O.U.P., 1955) 110.
3 *Rachel Ray* (London : World's Classics, 1924) ch. i.
4 *The Vicar of Bullhampton* (London : World's Classics, 1963) ch. ix.
5 Frances Power Cobbe (1822–1904). Born of comfortably-off Irish parents,

she devoted herself to social work, assisting Mary Carpenter at the Red Lodge Reformatory, Bristol, in the late fifties, and writing on religion, education and morals. Among her large miscellaneous output the best known work is *Broken Lights: an Inquiry into the present condition and future prospects of religious faith* (1864). She was a founder of the Anti-Vivisection Society and an ardent feminist. To Sadleir's link with Miss Todd (*Commentary*, p. 384) one may add the figures of several feminists in the novels.

6 *The Way We Live Now* (London: World's Classics, 1962) ch. xcv.

7 *Saturday Review*, XXV (14 Mar 1868) 339–40. Mrs Elisabeth Lynn Linton (1822–98), novelist and essayist, worked for the *Morning Chronicle* (1848–51) and the *Saturday Review* after 1866. Although a dedicated anti-feminist Mrs Linton was herself a prime example of the modern emancipated woman. Separated from her husband, William James Linton, the engraver, soon after their marriage, she enjoyed a vigorously independent career. Perhaps she repaid Trollope for his frankness by leaving in her autobiography only one catty reference – and that about his mother: 'just a vulgar, brisk, and good-natured kind of well-bred hen-wife, fond of a joke and not troubled with squeamishness', *My Literary Life, Reminiscences of Dickens, Thackeray, George Eliot etc.* (London: Hodder & Stoughton, 1899) p. 89.

8 'Higher Education of Women' (1868) in Parrish, *Four Lectures*, p. 73.

9 *St. Paul's Magazine*, I (Feb 1868) 735.

10 The 'unfeminine' nature of the feminists dogged the movement from its 'Bloomer' days, and Trollope simply followed in the wake of this unseemly prejudice. Even attractive heroines with aggressive leanings towards independence, such as Violet Effingham, he portrayed with mixed feelings. The little-known short story 'Miss Ophelia Gledd' is a case in point, turning on the question as to whether the energetic, self-willed young Bostonian girl can really be called a lady, and her own doubts as to marrying into English middle class. (*Lotta Schmidt: and Other Stories*, London: Strahan, 1867).

11 Although seeking identities for Trollope's characters is idle occupation for the most part, the possibility of a link between Glencora and an actual person is intriguing. The Countess Lady Waldegrave, a charming and beautiful hostess with a flair for witty conversation did much to help the political career of her retiring husband, Chichester Fortescue, later Lord Carlingford. This is particularly interesting in the light of Escott's association of Fortescue and Palliser (*Fortnightly Review*, LXXX (Dec 1906) 1097). On the other hand, Fortescue has also been suggested as a source for Phineas Finn, and certainly there are similarities between Fortescue's difficulties in addressing the House and the circumstances of Finn's maiden speech (*Phineas Finn*, ch. xxvi). All my example suggests is the kind of data of his society that Trollope wove into his situations and characters. See O. W. Hewett, *Strawberry Fair: A Biography of Frances, Countess Waldegrave, 1821–1879* (London: Murray, 1956) p. 236; . . . *and Mr. Fortescue, A Selection from the Diaries of Chichester Fortescue, Lord Carlingford, K.P.* (London: Murray, 1958) pp. 10–11, 31.

K

12 *The Belton Estate* (London: World's Classics, 1964) ch. vii.
13 *An Eye for An Eye* (London: Chapman & Hall, 1879) II, vii.
14 Sadleir, *Commentary*, p. 212.
15 It is tempting to speculate on possible links between the character of Lizzie Eustace and some of the demi-mondaines of Trollope's London scene. Catherine Walters, affectionately known as 'Skittles', was a leading member of her profession, in 1862 causing traffic jams in Hyde Park when she appeared (*A Mid Victorian Pepys*, ed. S. M. Ellis, p. 214). He also knew the lady described by Julian Hawthorne as Eustacia, a woman of northern English or Scottish blood, 'and of patrician lineage, but poor in purse' whose marriage to a rich manufacturer enabled her to entertain in state at Prince's Gate. Here this Venus with pagan vitality and pink gums was resplendent, 'dressed and jewelled exceedingly', an insolent diamond at her throat. Her guests on one occasion (doubtless in the mid-seventies) included Trollope, Milnes, Henry James, Dilke and Frederick Leighton (*Shapes That Pass*, pp. 134–5).
16 *Autobiography*, ch. xix.

CHAPTER 7
1 *North America* (London: Chapman & Hall, 1862) II, ch. xvi.
2 R. Donovan, *Modern Philology*, LII (Feb 1956) 180–6. See also 'Mr. Trollope's last Irish novel', *Dublin Review*, XIII (Oct 1869) 361–77; 'The Novels of Anthony Trollope', XIX (Oct 1872) 393–430; 'The Novels of Anthony Trollope', IX (Apr 1883) 314–32; Stephen Gwynn, 'Trollope and Ireland', *Contemporary Review*, CXXIX (Jan–June 1926) 72–9; Constantia Maxwell, 'Anthony Trollope and Ireland', *Dublin Magazine*, XXI (1955) 6–16; Doris Asmundsson, 'Trollope's first novel: a re-examination', *Eire-Ireland*, 6 (fall 1971) 83–91.
3 Sadleir, *Commentary*, p. 144. Sadleir's earlier comments on them in *Excursions in Victorian Bibliography* (London: Chaundy & Cox, 1922) p. 27, were more favourable.
4 *Dublin Review* (Oct 1872) p. 414; 'Mr. Anthony Trollope', *Athenaeum*, 2876 (9 Dec 1882) 773; *Academy*, XXII (16 Dec 1882) 433; XXIV (27 Oct 1883) 274; 'Mr. Anthony Trollope's Novels', *Edinburgh Review*, CXLVI (Oct 1877) 457.
5 Gwynn, *Contemporary Review* (Jan–Jun 1926) pp. 72–9; Brown, *A Reader's Guide to Irish Fiction* (London: Longman, 1910) pp. 60–79; *Douglas Jerrold's Weekly Newspaper*, 29 May 1847, p. 661.
6 See Lance Tingay, 'The Reception of Trollope's First Novel', *NCF*, VI (Dec 1951) 195–200; *Trollope, the Critical Heritage*, ed. Donald Smalley (London: Routledge & Kegan Paul, 1969) Appendix, pp. 546–52.
7 Escott, *Trollope*, p. 61.
8 Saintsbury, *Essays and Studies by Members of the English Association*, VI, p. 45.
9 *Spectator*, LII (19 July 1879) 916.
10 *Autobiography*, ch. viii.

11 *Castle Richmond* (London: Chapman & Hall, 1860) I, ch. i.
12 Sir William Henry Gregory (1817–92) was an important figure in
   Trollope's life, not simply because of their Harrow school connection
   (see Chapter 2), but because of his social and political influence upon
   Trollope's thinking about Irish affairs, especially in later years, as I
   indicate in commenting upon *The Landleaguers*. Gregory was elected
   MP for Dublin in 1842. Defeated in 1847, he became High Sheriff of
   Galway in 1849. In 1857 he was returned for Co. Galway as a liberal-
   conservative supporter of Palmerston. He supported Gladstone in Irish
   disestablishment and the Land Act of 1870. In 1871 he was appointed
   Governor of Ceylon, holding the office between 1872 and 1877.
13 *North America*, II, ch. xvi.
14 Lord Dunsany, *My Ireland* (London: Jarrolds, 1937) pp. 184–5.
15 Escott, *Trollope*, p. 44.
16 Dunsany, *My Ireland*, p. 189.
17 Elizabeth Bowen, *Collected Impressions* (London: Longmans, Green,
   1950) p. 172.
18 *Autobiography*, ch. iv.
19 *Blackwood's Magazine*, CXXXIV (Nov 1883) 586.
20 Escott, *Trollope*, p. 52.
21 *Autobiography*, ch. iii.
22 *Autobiography*, ch. iv.
23 Ruth ap Roberts, *Trollope, Artist and Moralist*, p. 16.
24 *Autobiography*, ch. ix; Gwynn, 'Trollope and Ireland', *Contemporary
   Review* (Jan–June 1926) p. 79.
25 *Correspondence of Henry Taylor*, ed. Edward Dowden, p. 297.
26 V. S. Pritchett, *Midnight Oil* (London: Chatto & Windus, 1971) p. 115.
27 I follow Sadleir's classification (*Commentary*, Appendix II). *An Eye For
   An Eye*, though set in County Clare, fails to make the Irish scene
   more than window-dressing for an extravagantly sensational plot, while
   its chief character is an English cavalry officer.
28 *Athenæum*, 1020 (15 May 1847) 517.
29 See my article 'Three Lost Chapters of Anthony Trollope's First Novel',
   NCF, XXVII (June 1972) 71–80; also *Notes and Queries*, CLXX, 20
   (3 Mar 1973) 90–1.
30 Mrs S. C. Hall's *The Whiteboy* appeared in Chapman & Hall's Monthly
   Series in 1845; William Carleton's *Rody the Rover, or the Ribbonmen*
   and *Valentine M'Clutchy, the Irish Agent*, 1845; *Tales of the O'Hara
   Family*, I, by John and Michael Banim, reappeared in the Parlour series,
   1846; *The Collegians* came out in the Parlour Library in 1847.
31 The seven letters appeared in the *Examiner* on 25 Aug 1849, and
   between 30 Mar and 15 June 1850. See Helen Garlinghouse King,
   'Trollope's Letters to the *Examiner*', *Princeton University Library
   Chronicle*, XXVI, 2 (winter 1965) 71–101. In later years Trollope
   treated other Irish topics: 'The Irish Church' (*Fortnightly Review*, 15
   April 1865); 'The Irish Church Debate' (*St. Paul's Magazine*, May
   1868); and probably 'Irish Prison Fare' (*Pall Mall Gazette*, 16 May
   1867).

32 *The Macdermots of Ballycloran,* I, ch. iv.
33 Morton D. Zabel, introduction to *Bleak House* (Boston: Houghton Mifflin, 1956) p. xxi.
34 Escott, *Trollope,* p. 66.
35 *Athenæum,* 1081 (15 July 1848), 701.
36 *The Landleaguers,* III, ch. xxxix.
37 Sadleir, *Commentary,* p. 138.
38 The sufferings of the League's founder, Michael Davitt, in English prisons from 1870 to 1878, must equal many instances of the League's atrocities. See F. Sheehy-Skeffington, *Michael Davitt, Revolutionary, Agitator and Labour Leader* [1908] (London: T. Fisher Unwin, 1967).
39 See H. Ausubel, *In Hard Times, Reformers Among the Late Victorians* (London: O.U.P., 1960) pp. 284–5.
40 Among Trollope's friends at the Cosmopolitan in Berkeley Square were several of the 'hawks' of the Irish problem: Davenport, Knatchbull Hugessen, Vernon Harcourt and W. E. – 'Buckshot' – Forster, so nicknamed for his coercion policies. For accounts of the land troubles at this time see J. C. Beckett, *The Making of Modern Ireland 1603–1923* (London: Faber, 1966) pp. 389–404; Tom Corfe, *The Phoenix Park Murders, Conflict, Compromise and Tragedy in Ireland 1879–1882* (London: Hodder & Stoughton, 1968).
41 Corfe, *Phoenix Park Murders,* p. 109.
42 Quoted Corfe, *Phoenix Park Murders,* p. 159. With hindsight we can appreciate how courageous Gladstone's policy was, given the pressures upon him. His first Land Act (1870) avowed that landlord power should be broken. The Land Act (1881) carried this principle further, probably because of response to the Act of Disestablishment (1869), which proved that tenants would buy land if they could. By 1880, over 6000 of 8400 tenants had taken the option of buying their holdings on former church lands (Beckett, *The Making of Modern Ireland,* p. 369).
43 II, ch. xvii. This character may have been modelled on Henry George, a member of the League, who advocated land nationalisation and extreme measures for dealing with the landowners. A John O'Mahony was also active in conducting fund-raising activities for the League in New York. See Desmond Ryan, *The Fenian Chief, A Biography of James Stephens* (Dublin: Gill, 1967) p. 362.
44 Another novel, *Ayala's Angel,* suggests the comparison. Gilbert and Sullivan's *Patience,* a caricature of aestheticism and militarism, opened in April 1881. *Ayala's Angel,* written three years earlier, therefore made a timely appearance in June 1881. It too had a super-virile soldier-hero and an artist who is clearly 'an ultra-poetical super-aesthetical/Out-of-the-way young man'.

CHAPTER 8

1 Trollope's translation, *The Life of Cicero* (London: Chapman & Hall, 1880) I, ch. i.
2 Sadleir tentatively attributes to Trollope, *Bibliography,* p. 240.

3 Autobiography, ch. x.
4 The Last Chronicle of Barset (London: World's Classics, 1948) ch.
   lxxxiv.
5 Lord Palmerston, English Political Leaders (London: Isbister, 1882).
   John Halperin has developed this idea in 'Politics, Palmerston, and
   Trollope's Prime Minister', Clio, III (2 Feb 1974) 187–218.
6 Cicero, I, ch. i.
7 'Cicero as a Politician', Fortnightly Review, XXI, 124 (1 Sep 1877) 417.
8 Ibid., p. 504.
9 'Cicero as a Man of Letters', Fortnightly Review, XXII, 129 (1 Sep
   1877) 417.
10 'The Divided Mind of Anthony Trollope', NCF, XIV, 1 (June 1959)
   1–26.
11 Phineas Finn, ch. xxxi.
12 Henry Taylor (1800–86), much admired by Trollope, combined
   eminence in the Civil Service and in letters. He devoted about forty-
   eight years to the Colonial Office, and his highly successful poetic
   drama, Philip Van Artevelde (1834), established his literary fame. In
   1869 he was made K.C.M.G. See Correspondence of Henry Taylor, p.
   296. Trollope was doubtless also familiar with Sir William Vernon
   Harcourt's The Morality of Public Men, A Letter to the Rt. Hon. the
   Early of Derby, Signed by an Englishman (London: James Ridgway,
   1852).
13 The Statesman [1836] (Cambridge: W. Heffer, 1927) p. 80.
14 Sadleir, 'Trollope and Bacon's Essays', Trollopian, I (summer 1945)
   21–34.
15 Phineas Finn, ch. xlvii.
16 The Prime Minister, ch. xli.
17 Cockshut, Trollope, pp. 96, 99.
18 Can You Forgive Her?, ch. xvii.
19 The Prime Minister, ch. lxii.
20 ch. vii. See R. B. Martin, Enter Rumour; Four Early Victorian Scandals
   (London: Faber, 1962).
21 'Mr. Anthony Trollope's Novels', CXLVI (Oct 1877) 455–88.
22 Phineas Finn, ch. xxvi.
23 Captain Edward Sterling (1773–1847) began writing for The Times
   in 1811 as 'Vetus', later 'Magus', and between 1830 and 1840 the
   paper was much identified with his views. He retired soon after 1840
   (DNB, LIV, 193). See The Story of the Pall Mall Gazette, p. 149.
24 Intro., Everyman ed., (1966) pp. v–xi.
25 The Belton Estate, ch. xxv.
26 'Orley Farm and Real Fiction', NCF, VIII (June 1953) 27–41.
27 Mr. Scarborough's Family, ch. xlvii.
28 The Three Clerks, ch. ix.
29 The Struggles of Brown, Jones and Robinson was serialised in the
   Cornhill Magazine, Aug 1861–Mar 1862.
30 Annual Register, 1873, ch. iii, p. 86.
31 Sadleir, Commentary, p. 397.

32 'Anthony Trollope's Perception of the Way We Live Now', [sic] *Zeitschrift für Anglistik und Amerikanistik*, X, 3 (1962) 261–78.

33 *Partial Portraits*, p. 132.

34 Frank O'Connor, 'Trollope the Realist', *The Mirror in the Roadway* (New York: Knopf, 1956) pp. 165–83.

35 *Partial Portraits*, p. 105.

36 I have in mind the currently unfashionable sides of Tennyson and Browning; in terms of social thinking the cautious but progressive liberal idealism of Bagehot and James Fitzjames Stephen and the ideas embodied in the work of F. D. Maurice and Kingsley.

37 *George Eliot Letters*, IV, 110.

38 'How the essential Trollope was lost', *Listener*, 25 July 1974, pp. 105–7.

39 *Trollope*, p. 46.

Index

Hardy, Thomas, 36
Harrison, Frederic, 19–20, 53, 56, 58, 63
Hattersley, Roy, 245
Hawthorne, Julian, 17, 21, 39
Hawthorne, Nathaniel, 32, 89, 244; on Trollope's realism, 88
He Knew He Was Right, 34, 87, 106, 111, 116, 132, 136–40, 148–9, 167, 213–14, 232
Helps, Sir Arthur, 33, 268n
Heywood, J. C., 52
Higgins, Matthew (Jacob Omnium), 202
Hill, Sir Rowland, 20
Hillis Miller, J., 67, 74
Holmes, Oliver Wendell, 18
Howells, William Dean, 53
Hugessen, Edward Knatchbull (later Baron Brabourne), 18
Hughes, Thomas, 27
Hutton, R. H., 6, 51, 129, 176
Huxley, T. E., 18

Is He Popenjoy?, 86, 103, 113–17, 132, 150, 158–9, 165, 218, 225

James, Henry, 2–3, 8, 12, 38, 51, 69, 94, 97, 137, 243, 244, 273n
James, Sir Henry (afterwards Lord James of Hereford), 32
John Caldigate, 2, 14, 45, 49, 77, 82, 92, 103, 147, 161, 164, 218
Joline, Adrian, 157
Journey to Panama, The, 151

Kellys and the O'Kellys, The, 164, 175–6, 179, 181–2, 189–90, 231
Kent, Charles, 64
Kept in the Dark, 8, 101, 132, 135–6, 137, 138, 160, 165, 206
Kingsley, Charles, 2, 187, 191
Knoepflmacher, Ulrich, 7
Knox, Father Ronald, 7, 59

Lady Anna, 16, 23, 85, 132, 147, 222, 231
Lady of Launay, The, 147

Landleaguers, The, 8, 11, 23, 35–6, 39–40, 49, 175–6, 179, 181, 192–200
Last Chronicle of Barset, The, 34, 45, 65, 79, 90, 98, 126, 131, 149–50, 204–5, 220–1, 225–9, 247–8
Laurence, Samuel, 32
Lerner, Lawrence, 3, 4
Lever, Charles, 55, 176, 177, 189
Leveson-Gower, The Hon. Frederick, 18, 33, 196, 268n
Lewes, G. H., 41
Life of Cicero, The, 34, 48, 201, 205–7, 212
Linda Tressel, 37
Linton, Mrs. Lynn, 156, 275n
Locker-Lampson, Frederick, 19, 21
Lotta Schmidt: and Other Stories, 179, 275n
Lowell, James Russell, 18, 21, 34, 58
Lytton, Sir Edward Bulwer, 20, 55, 57, 89, 111, 184

Macdermots of Ballycloran, The, 8, 31, 175–6, 178–80, 182–9, 192, 195
Macleod, The Reverend Douglas, 58
Mansfield Park, 141
Marion Fay, 29, 85–6, 106, 111, 148, 192, 231
Martineau, Harriet, 26
Meetkerke, Adolphus, 22, 23, 24
Melmotte, Augustus, 10, 217, 235, 236, 238–42
Melville, Lewis [pseud. of Lewis S. Benjamin], 52, 53
Mère Bauche, La, 147
Meredith, George, 6, 72, 109, 244
Merivale, Charles, 23, 27, 35, 205
Merivale, Herman, 23, 35
Merivale, John, 272
Mill, John Stuart, 18–19, 110, 155, 160
Millais, John Everett, 33, 43, 146
Miller, Joaquin, 18
Miss Mackenzie, 66, 144, 148–50, 155, 219